D1613970

An Expanding World
Volume 29

Families in the Expansion
of Europe, 1500–1800

AN EXPANDING WORLD
The European Impact on World History, 1450–1800

General Editor: A.J.R. Russell-Wood

Please note titles may change prior to publication

An Expanding World
The European Impact on World History 1450–1800

Volume 29

Families in the Expansion of Europe, 1500–1800

edited by
Maria Beatriz Nizza da Silva

Ashgate
VARIORUM

Aldershot • Brookfield USA • Singapore • Sydney

This edition copyright © 1998 by Ashgate Publishing Limited, and Introduction by Maria Beatriz Nizza da Silva. For copyright of individual articles refer to the Acknowledgements.

Published in the **Varioum Expanding World Series** by

Ashgate Publishing Limited
Gower House, Croft Road
Aldershot, Hampshire GU11 3HR
Great Britain

Ashgate Publishing Company
Old Post Road
Brookfield, Vermont 05036–9704
USA

ISBN 0–86078–520–3

British Library CIP data
>Families in the Expansion of Europe, 1500–1800.
>(An Expanding World: The European Impact on World History,
>1450–1800: Vol. 29).
>1. Family–History. 2. Social History 3. Europe–History–
>1492–
>I. Silva, Maria Beatriz Nizza da.
>306.8'5'09

US Library of Congress CIP data
>Families in the Expanison of Europe, 1500–1800 / edited by
>Maria Beatriz Nizza da Silva..
>p. cm. – (An Expanding World: The European Impact on World
>History, 1450–1800: Vol. 29). Includes bibliographical references.
>1. Acculturation. 2. Civilization, Modern–European influences.
>3. First contact of aboriginal peoples with Westerners. 4. Family–
>History.
>I. Silva, Maria Beatriz Nizza da. II. Series: Expanding World: Vol.
>29.
>GN366. F36   1998   98–26155
>303.48'2–dc21   CIP

This book is printed on acid free paper.

Printed and bound by Athenaeum Press, Ltd.,
Gateshead, Tyne & Wear.

AN EXPANDING WORLD 29

Contents

Acknowledgements

The chapters in this volume are taken from the sources listed below, for which the editor and publishers wish to thank their authors, original publishers or other copyright holders for permission to use their material as follows:

Chapter 1: Muriel Nazzari, 'Parents and Daughters: Change in the Practice of Dowry in São Paulo (1600–1770)', *Hispanic American Historical Review* LXX, no. 4 (Durham, NC, 1990), pp. 639–665. Copyright © 1990 by Duke University Press. Reprinted with permission.

Chapter 2: Patricia Seed, 'The Church and the Patriarchal Family: Marriage Conflicts in Sixteenth- and Seventeenth-Century New Spain', *Journal of Family History* X (Thousand Oaks, CA, 1985), pp. 284–293. Copyright © 1985 by Sage Publications, Inc.

Chapter 3: Donald Ramos, 'Marriage and the Family in Colonial Vila Rica', *Hispanic American Historical Review* LV (Durham, NC, 1975), pp. 200–225. Copyright © 1975 by Duke University Press. Reprinted with permission.

Chapter 4: Nancy F. Cott, 'Divorce and the Changing Status of Women in Eighteenth-Century Massachusetts', *William and Mary Quarterly* (3rd series) XXX (Williamsburg, VA, 1976), pp. 586–614. Copyright © 1976 by The Omohundro Institute of Early American History and Culture. Reprinted by permission of the author and The Omohundro Institute of Early American History and Culture.

Chapter 5: Ann Twinam, 'Honor, Sexuality, and Illegitimacy in Colonial Spanish America', in ed. Asunción Lavrin, *Sexuality and Illegitimacy in Colonial Latin America* (Lincoln, NE, 1989), pp. 118–155. Copyright © 1989 by the University of Nebraska Press.

Chapter 6: Lynne Paquette and Réal Bates, 'Les naissances illégitimes sur les rives du Saint-Laurent avant 1730', *Revue d'Histoire de l'Amérique Française* XL, no. 2 (Montreal, 1986), pp. 239–252. Copyright © 1986 by Institut d'Histoire de l'Amérique Française.

Chapter 7: Edith Couturier, 'Women and the Family in Eighteenth-Century Mexico: Law and Practice', *Journal of Family History* X (Thousand Oaks, CA, 1985), pp. 294–304. Copyright © 1985 by Sage Publications, Inc.

Chapter 8: Alida C. Metcalf, 'Women and Means: Women and Family Property in Colonial Brazil', *Journal of Social History* XXIV (Pittsburgh, PA, 1990), pp. 277–298. Copyright © 1990 by Carnegie Mellon University Press.

Chapter 9: Toby L. Ditz, 'Ownership and Obligation: Inheritance and Patriarchal Households in Connecticut, 1750–1820', *William and Mary Quarterly* (3rd series) XLVII (Williamsburg, VA, 1990), pp. 235–265. Copyright © 1990 by The Omohundro Institute of Early American History and Culture. Reprinted by permission of the author and The Omohundro Institute of Early American History and Culture.

Chapter 10: Sarah Cline, 'The Spiritual Conquest Re-examined: Baptism and Christian Marriage in Early Sixteenth-Century Mexico', *Hispanic American Historical Review* LXXIII, no. 3 (Durham, NC, 1993), pp. 453–480. Copyright © 1993 by Duke University Press. Reprinted with permission.

Chapter 11: A.J.R. Russell-Wood, 'The Black Family in the Americas', *Societas: A Review of Social History* VIII, no. 1 (1978), pp. 1–38.

Chapter 12: Edgar F. Love, 'Marriage Patterns of Persons of African Descent in a Colonial Mexico City Parish', *Hispanic American Historical Review* LI (Durham, NC, 1971), pp. 79–91. Copyright © 1971 by Duke University Press. Reprinted with permission.

Chapter 13: Leonard Guelke, 'The Anatomy of a Colonial Settler Population: Cape Colony, 1657–1750', *International Journal of African Historical Studies*, XXI, no. 3 (Boston, MA, 1988), pp. 453–473. Copyright © 1988 by the African Studies Center, Boston University.

Every effort has been made to trace all the copyright holders, but if any have been inadvertently overlooked the publishers will be pleased to make the necessary arrangement at the first opportunity.

General Editor's Preface

A.J.R. Russell-Wood

An Expanding World: The European Impact on World History, 1450–1800 is designed to meet two objectives: first, each volume covers a specific aspect of the European initiative and reaction across time and space; second, the series represents a superb overview and compendium of knowledge and is an invaluable reference source on the European presence beyond Europe in the early modern period, interaction with non-Europeans, and experiences of peoples of other continents, religions, and races in relation to Europe and Europeans. The series reflects revisionist interpretations and new approaches to what has been called 'the expansion of Europe' and whose historiography traditionally bore the hallmarks of a narrowly Eurocentric perspective, focus on the achievements of individual nations, and characterization of the European presence as one of dominance, conquest, and control. Fragmentation characterized much of this literature: fragmentation by national groups, by geography, and by chronology.

The volumes of *An Expanding World* seek to transcend nationalist histories and to examine on the global stage rather than in discrete regions important selected facets of the European presence overseas. One result has been to bring to the fore the multicontinental, multi-oceanic and multinational dimension of the European activities. A further outcome is compensatory in the emphasis placed on the cross-cultural context of European activities and on how collaboration and cooperation between peoples transcended real or perceived boundaries of religion, nationality, race, and language and were no less important aspects of the European experience in Africa, Asia, the Americas, and Australia than the highly publicized confrontational, bellicose, and exploitative dimensions. Recent scholarship has not only led to greater understanding of peoples, cultures, and institutions of Africa, Asia, the Americas, and Australasia with whom Europeans interacted and the complexity of such interactions and transactions, but also of relations between Europeans of different nationalities and religious persuasions.

The initial five volumes reflect the changing historiography and set the stage for volumes encompassing the broad themes of technology and science, trade and commerce, exploitation as reflected in agriculture and the extractive industries and through systems of forced and coerced labour, government of empire, and society and culture in European colonies and settlements overseas. Final volumes examine the image of Europe and Europeans as 'the other' and the impact of the wider world on European *mentalités* and mores.

An international team of editors was selected to reflect a diversity of educational backgrounds, nationalities, and scholars at different stages of their professional careers. Few would claim to be 'world historians', but each is a recognized authority in his or her field and has the demonstrated capacity to ask the significant questions and provide a conceptual framework for the selection of articles which combine analysis with interpretation. Editors were exhorted to place their specific subjects within a global context and over the *longue durée*. I have been delighted by the enthusiasm with which they took up this intellectual challenge, their courage in venturing beyond their immediate research fields to look over the fences into the gardens of their academic neighbours, and the collegiality which has led to a generous informal exchange of information. Editors were posed the daunting task of surveying a rich historical literature and selecting those essays which they regarded as significant contributions to an understanding of the specific field or representative of the historiography. They were asked to give priority to articles in scholarly journals; essays from conference volumes and *Festschriften* were acceptable; excluded (with some few exceptions) were excerpts from recent monographs or paperback volumes. After much discussion and agonizing, the decision was taken to incorporate essays only in English, French, and Spanish. This has led to the exclusion of the extensive scholarly literature in Danish, Dutch, German and Portuguese. The ramifications of these decisions and how these have had an impact on the representative quality of selections of articles have varied, depending on the theme, and have been addressed by editors in their introductions.

The introduction to each volume enables readers to assess the importance of the topic *per se* and place this in the broader context of European activities overseas. It acquaints readers with broad trends in the historiography and alerts them to controversies and conflicting interpretations. Editors clarify the conceptual framework for each volume and explain the rationale for the selection of articles and how they relate to each other. Introductions permit volume editors to assess the impact on their treatments of discrete topics of constraints of language, format, and chronology, assess the completeness of the journal literature, and address *lacunae*. A further charge to editors was to describe and evaluate the importance of change over time, explain differences attributable to differing geographical, cultural, institutional, and economic circumstances and suggest the potential for cross-cultural, comparative, and interdisciplinary approaches. The addition of notes and bibliographies enhances the scholarly value of the introductions and suggests avenues for further enquiry.

I should like to express my thanks to the volume editors for their willing participation, enthusiasm, sage counsel, invaluable suggestions, and good judgment. Evidence of the timeliness and importance of the series was illustrated by the decision, based on extensive consultation with the scholarly community, to expand a series, which had originally been projected not to exceed eight volumes, to more than thirty volumes. It was John Smedley's initiative which gave rise to discussions as to the viability and need for such a series and he has overseen the publishing, publicity, and marketing of *An Expanding World*. As

General Editor, my task was greatly facilitated by the assistance of Dr Mark Steele who was initially responsible for the 'operations' component of the series as it got under way; latterly this assistance has been provided by staff at Variorum.

The Department of History,
The Johns Hopkins University

Introduction

Maria Beatriz Nizza da Silva

When Europeans settled in the Americas, Africa, Asia and Australasia, they tended to preserve those patterns of family life which had prevailed in their places of origin. Though they sometimes occupied uninhabited territories, as was the case in Madeira and the Azores, in most of these new regions they found populations whose familial organizations differed from their own. The encounter of cultures had a broad range of outcomes, from full displacement of indigenous mores to compromises integrating aspects of both original patterns.

Historians of the Americas took inspiration from the development of European family history. As early as the 1950s, French historical demography began influencing demographers of Quebec. The richness of Quebec's population records enabled historians to refine methodologies initiated in France. The subsequent advent of computer technology opened new avenues in the reconstruction of the population of New France. Yet the primary source for this project, namely parish registers, provided only a skeleton for family history. Today, historians of French Canada combine demographic materials with non-quantitative sources to provide a more complete picture of families in New France.

The demographic approach predominant in Spanish and Portuguese colonial family history in the 1970s concentrated on rates of nuptiality, fertility and illegitimate births. In the 1980s a new approach displaced the earlier emphasis on demography: household analyses, inspired by the Cambridge school, emphasized those kin who lived together under the same roof. A household, in these studies, included dependents, servants and slaves. This approach highlighted among other things female-headed households and group economics. Population censuses have been used not only to recreate the structure and composition of families, but also to reveal the diversity of economic activities of individual family members. Women's work is not generally acknowledged in this literature, except when the women were heads of households. Young children and adolescents who contributed to the household economy are similarly neglected.

These two approaches, the demographic and the household analyses, use mostly quantitative methods. A third approach, institutional in focus, is mainly qualitative, using case studies to analyze family relationships, marriage, divorce, inheritance, and illegitimacy. In addition to parish registers and population censuses, historians employing this institutional approach use other sources: notarial deeds, wills and inventories, court suits and, especially in Catholic colonies, marriage, separation and annulment materials, as well as petitions to local authorities and the Crown. Because it is the most recent and comprehensive approach to family history, I have opted for greater representation of materials of this institutional focus in the articles selected for this volume.[1]

This book brings together thirteen essays that help us to see the diversity of families in European overseas colonies prior to the end of the eighteenth century. Colonial American family history predominates in this volume because historians of colonial Africa and Asia have largely disregarded this field of historical research, excepting only the European settlement in South Africa for which the same source materials exist as for Colonial America. The relatively late settlement by Europeans of Australia makes family history in Australia before the nineteenth century a non-viable field of study. The combination of source materials, different historiographical traditions, and differing patterns of European overseas settlement prior to 1800 has resulted in the imbalance in the geographical coverage of this volume.

The articles included here deal with dowry and marriage, divorce, illegitimacy, inheritance and, thanks to the growing contribution of women's history to the history of the family, women's roles in colonial families. Less prominent are the topics of courtship, sexuality within and outside marriage, bigamy, relations between husbands and wives, child rearing and education, old age, widowhood and spinsterhood, women secluded in convents and other current themes in family history.

There has been little research on life cycles in the study of families in European overseas colonies since John Demos in the 1970s pointed out the importance of the whole process of individual growth and change.[2] Even if our concepts of childhood and youth are different from those in the past, it is incumbent on historians to make the effort to reconstitute the lives of younger members of the family household. Most colonial societies had a rite of passage wherein parents placed young boys into other families when they reached the age of seven. These sons were generally sent to a craftsman's or a merchant's house in order to learn a job. They received a small amount of money during the period of apprenticeship. The differences from familiar, modern relationships that this pattern would engender in family relations constitute a good example of an under explored topic. While it is true that colonial sources rarely give

---

[1] See Louise A. Tilly, 'Women's History and Family History: Fruitful Collaboration or Missed Connection', *Journal of Family History* XII, nos. 1–3 (1987), pp. 303–315. Tilly refers to Michael Anderson's taxonomy of approaches (demographic, household economics, and sentiments and attitudes) adding a fourth approach, the political/institutional, 'which emphasizes connections between family and other processes and institutions'. As early as the 1970s John Demos considered another approach, the psychological one, in his article 'Demography and Psychology in the Historical Study of Family Life: A Personal Approach', in eds., Peter Laslett and Richard Wall, *Household and Family in Past Time* (Cambridge, 1972).

[2] John Demos, ibid., p. 564.

the ages of individuals, fruitful research can still be done within broad age categories.[3]

The nature of the relationship between parents and their children of both sexes until they married or otherwise achieved adulthood should certainly receive further attention by historians of the family in the European colonies. Other important topics include the lives of older people living with a married son or daughter, or surviving in their own houses with the help of a servant or a slave. While these topics have been addressed by certain historians, most notably by Patricia Seed in her book on marriage choice in colonial Mexico, they have not received the sustained attention necessary for incorporating these facets of family relations into our general understanding. Family history must focus on every stage of the life cycle, and on the experience of the stage rather than only the transition to married adulthood or widowhood.

The issue of the influence of migration on the size and location of kin groups has received much attention; historians have studied both migration from Europe to other continents, and migration from a coastal point of disembarkation to the hinterland. Geographical mobility, especially male mobility, led to family dispersion. These features of colonization, along with the compensating female migration in the first centuries of European settlement, have become central topics in colonial family history,[4] but there still remains much work to do on these topics.

Historians of the colonial family have pursued other issues more fully. First, the influence of indigenous families on European familial patterns has received sustained attention. A second concern is whether certain behaviours, such as concubinage and illegitimacy, were aggravated in a colonial environment. A third popular topic is the role of white women in colonial societies, particularly whether they had more or less economic independence and privileges than in Europe. Finally, there is also the concern to investigate the impact both on Amerindian and European families of the African slave trade and the existence of a black population.

In the period of initial cultural encounter, especially in the first century of colonization when white women were scarce, some male Europeans married according to the 'custom of the country', choosing native Indian American and, later, mixed-blood women as wives. This happened in colonial Latin America in the sixteenth century and in the Hudson Bay among fur traders in the seventeenth

---

[3] See Roger Thompson, 'Adolescent Culture in Colonial Massachusetts', *Journal of Family History* IX, no. 2 (1984), pp. 127–144; N. Ray Hiner, 'Adolescence in Eighteenth-Century America', *The History of Childhood Quarterly* III (1975), pp. 253–280.

[4] Alida C. Metcalf, *Family and Frontier in Colonial Brazil. Santana de Parnaiba, 1580–1822* (Berkeley, Los Angeles, 1992), and John W. Adams and Alice Bee Kasakoff, 'Migration and the Family in Colonial New England: The View from the Genealogies', *Journal of Family History* IX, no. 1 (1984), pp. 24–43.

and eighteenth centuries.[5] Even when marriage was solemnized in a ceremony according to Catholic rites, some historians see the new marriage forms as significantly different from both Amerindian and European patterns.[6]

Concubinage and illegitimacy rates were in fact higher in Portuguese and Spanish America than in Europe; this was not, however, the case in French Canada or in the British colonies. Illegitimacy rates can be calculated for Catholic colonies through baptismal records. For urban areas, data are often extant on foundlings, who fall in the category of illegitimate children. However, quantitative analysis using these sources fails to reveal the complexity of this social phenomenon, because some illegitimate children were legitimized later in life and inherited their father's or mother's property. Children who had been illegitimate at birth could later, by petitioning the Crown or through testamentary provision, achieve the status of legitimacy. Illegitimacy cannot thus be collapsed into an indicator of sexual and marital latitude in colonial society; it had complex lineal and patrimonial implications in these societies as well.

Laws on women's rights in the family were substantially the same in Europe and in the colonies. Colonial women nonetheless had more frequent opportunities to administer the family property, due in part to male geographical mobility in some regions, as well as heightened death rates in some British colonies, with the consequent frequent naming of wives as administrators in the absence of surviving adult offspring. Wives also often had, if intermittently, control over the family affairs when husbands were away fighting in the Indian wars or boundary conflicts, or trading on and exploring the frontier. Sometimes male relatives were given this responsibility during a husband's absence; nonetheless colonial wives were often expected to be, as Laurel Ulrich has shown for early New England, 'deputy husband'.[7]

When colonists began the slave trade, their emphasis on importing male Africans as a labour force resulted in an early sexual imbalance in the black population. The resulting lack of slaves born in the colonies led some slave owners to promote sexual alliances between Africans and Indian women. This pattern is especially apparent in seventeenth-century Brazil, when the potential for reproduction of the slave labour force was limited by the small population of African women. Indians could not legally be enslaved, but the offspring of miscegenation constituted a labour force which was often unpaid even if the Amerindian mother was legally free.

---

[5] Sylvia van Kirk, '"The Custom of the Country": An Examination of Fur Trade Marriage Practices', in ed., Bettina Bradbury, *Canadian Family History: Selected Readings* (Toronto, 1992).

[6] Robert McCaa, 'Marriageways in Mexico and Spain, 1500–1900', *Continuity and Change* IX, no. 1 (1994), pp. 11–43.

[7] Laurel Thatcher Ulrich, *Good Wives: Image and Reality in the Lives of Women in Northern New England, 1650–1750* (New York, 1982).

Comparative family history of European overseas colonies is a difficult task. Often a comparison is not possible: themes are not generally dealt with in comparable depth or coverage by historians of different regions and periods. It is easier to compare Catholic Spanish with Portuguese America and even New France than any of these colonies with the Protestant British American colonies. The religious and legal characteristics of these two groups of colonies – leaving aside the avowedly commercial and religious Dutch settlements in America – will be seen in these selected readings.

The marriage dowry customarily given to daughters of propertied families both in Spanish and Portuguese America was in fact an advance made on the inheritance they would receive when each parent died.[8] Yet other members of the family in addition to the parents could also contribute to the dowry in order to give a young woman better marital prospects. In Brazil, the dowry was sometimes only promised verbally; in the Spanish colonies, however, a marriage contract was often drawn up by a notary. This notarized document would be presented when one of the parents died, and half the dowry value would be subtracted from the daughter's share of the parental estate. When the second parent died the same process occurred. Where the dowry was greater than the sum she would inherit, the daughter could choose to keep the dowry instead of receiving her inheritance (see chapter 1).

In societies in which parents customarily had little control over how their estate would be distributed to their heirs, the marriage contract specifying the amount of dowry was an important device allowing parents to prefer certain children over others in order to enhance the overall family standing. Testamentary laws in the Spanish colonies determined that all legitimate children, both sons and daughters, would inherit equally – although the eldest son might receive a double portion. The ability to provide a dowry as an advance on the inheritance both reflected the social and financial status of a family and could serve to enhance such a family's status – if an inflated portion for a particularly promising daughter might gain an influential son-in-law. Of course, poor couples without property could not afford a dowry. Wealthy families in societies such as the British colonies, where parents enjoyed great discretion in the distribution of their estates among their various heirs, often did not produce such formal dowry agreements because the dowry had no later influence on inheritance.

A dowry could include cash, slaves, jewels, a trousseau, and sometimes horses and cattle. Real estate might also be included, depending on the financial means of the parents. If the parents had several houses, or plantations, they could

---

[8] Although the word 'dote' (dowry) could be used for loans to sons, in Iberian colonial society it had a different meaning. Sons who left the paternal house to establish themselves as merchants or explorers in the hinterland sometimes received horses or mules, saddles, and guns, but rarely slaves to help them in their new independent life.

give one to each daughter according to the principle of equality which applied to the distribution of dowries among sisters. Even daughters who did not marry received their portions: the young women who became novices and later took their final vows as nuns in Catholic convents received dowries in cash to pay for food, clothes and medicine during illness. These religious dowries for the 'brides of Christ' were of about the same value as marriage dowries. In Portuguese, the phrase 'tomar estado' applied equally to entering holy matrimony and entering a conventual life.

In the Iberian colonies, parents were allowed to dispose freely of one third of each partner's property – that is, only two-thirds of a parent's estate would be subject to the testamentary laws requiring equal inheritance. Whereas some parents preferred to allocate their thirds to a spinster daughter, others chose to give this share to enhance the dowry of one daughter without breaking the principle of equality. The marriage dowry was so important in Spanish and Portuguese America that even poor orphans and foundlings received a small amount of money as pious legacies in wealthy people's wills to enable them to find husbands. Some charitable institutions, such as the Misericórdias in colonial Brazil, took charge of dowry distribution among destitute young women.

In Spanish colonies, many grooms presented their brides with a special wedding gift known as *arras*, limited to one tenth of the groom's estate.[9] In Brazil, marriages with *arras* were rare; a marriage contract including the *arras* and drawn up before a notary would, at the husband's death, limit the widow to a portion, also called *arras*, which was not to exceed one-third of her dowry. This device thus voided the usual widow's inheritance of half the couple's property. In British America, a similar process was achieved by the use of jointures; women signing jointures at their weddings were entitled to inherit the amount of the jointure, whether it exceeded or was less than the usual one-third of the estate to which colonial British widows were entitled. In both the Iberian and British colonies, these devices were characteristically used only by the élite.

Marriage in colonial America followed the norms established by the Council of Trent in the sixteenth century (see chapters 2 and 3 below) – the Anglican church did not substantially alter marriage practice from the Catholic traditions, so there was no significant statutory difference between British, Spanish, Portuguese, and French forms of marriage. Canon law permitted males to marry at the age of fourteen and females at twelve, or even earlier if they were thought to be mature enough. In practice, marriage at this young age is rarely noted in documentation of ecclesiastical archives. Males had to be economically independent before they could marry, although a good dowry might enable an earlier marriage. The evidence at our disposal suggests that women married much

---

[9] Eugene H. Korth and Della M. Flusche, 'Dowry and Inheritance in Colonial Spanish America: Peninsular Law and Chilean Practice', *The Americas* XL, no. 4 (1987), pp. 395–410.

younger than did men; the average age of first marriage in seventeenth-century Virginia and Maryland was sixteen for native-born white women, and around thirty for white men.

The Catholic church had the institution of premarital promises; the Anglican church similarly upheld marriage 'pre-contract'. These Church-blessed engagements bound together a prospective bride and groom, preventing them from marrying any other, and only the Church could dissolve the agreement. That is not to say there were no breaches of these promises. Quite often the young woman was abandoned by the husband-to-be after having consented to a pre-marital sexual relationship; sometimes it was the man who was left brideless when the woman to whom he thought himself engaged married another. A woman thus abandoned had recourse in ecclesiastical courts; men were on the whole less likely to bring breach-of-promise suits, and also less likely to win such a suit.

Perhaps the high rates of concubinage and illegitimacy in Catholic America were attributable to the difficulties in meeting all the demands imposed by the Church. First, a baptismal certificate was needed: sometimes this was difficult to obtain, especially when the groom had been baptized in Europe, or when he was a slave baptized in another region. The solution to this problem was for witnesses to testify before a priest that baptism had occurred, but this process cost money and was inconvenient, and poor people could not afford such expense. Secondly, there were many impediments to marriage, including consanguinity and affinity. The couple had to pay the Church for dispensation from such impediments. To preclude bigamy, the marriage banns had to be read in the parish church on three successive holy days. It could happen that someone would stand up and announce that the groom was married in another region of the colony or even in Europe, and to refute such allegations was extremely costly. The marriage process cost time and money and most poor and coloured people, as well as some whites, decided not to have a Church-sanctioned marriage. The rich could receive a dispensation from public banns and be married privately with the bishop's consent. Such near-secret marriages preserved the name and honour of the female partner and of her family, and prevented community gossip about a pre-marital sexual relationship or even a secret pregnancy.

Matrimonial rules in the British colonies diverged markedly from Anglican doctrine. In the northern, Puritan colonies, marriage was declared to be a civil contract, and only civil magistrates, not ministers of the Church, were permitted to solemnize marriages. Most of the New England colonies began virtually exclusively with civil marriages and forbade the clergy from performing marriage services. Marriage entailed fewer administrative tasks and hence was less costly, more available to even the poor. The high rate of marriage in the north, and exceptionally low rate of pre-nuptial pregnancy in the first century of settlement, can in part be attributed to the ease with which people could marry. Even in the southern Anglican colonies, the lack of sufficient churches and ministers made it rare for couples to be able to marry according to normal Anglican modes. While the wealthiest families still sought Church-sanctioned marriages, it was perfectly legal and respectable to be married by a magistrate. Colonists who were poor, geographically isolated, or members of non-Anglican churches might marry without even the presence of a magistrate: in such cases, the testimony of their friends and neighbours that they presented themselves as and lived as a married couple could suffice to prove the marriage. In these Anglican colonies, illegitimacy and pre-marital pregnancy rates were high not because the Church imposed so many burdens on couples wishing to marry, but because the definition of what constituted marriage was so fluid.

Marriage was a family affair in most colonies. Minors could not marry without their fathers' or their widowed mothers' permission. For a woman, achieving the age of majority did not mean much when she was still living under the parental roof and was economically dependent, without legacies or inheritances that would allow her independently to choose a husband. Parental opposition might be reinforced with the threat of disinheritance both for daughters and sons. In practice, young couples had some legal recourse; they could contact a local judge or a crown judge and prove with witnesses that they were of the same social status and that their parents could not find better partners for them.

The main issue in colonial marriages was that there be social parity between prospective partners, even when there was an inequality in the assets each possessed. Race constituted one major aspect denoting disparity. If a white man sought to marry a coloured woman, his parents or relatives would usually ask the civil authorities to intervene. The authorities generally exiled the coloured woman to another town, forbidding her to return to the place of residence of the prospective groom. Another possibility open to governors and military authorities was to enlist the young man in the army and post him to a distant garrison.

Within social and racial limits, how did colonists choose their partners? Was there a preference for close-kin marriages? The religious norms certainly differed. In the American colonies there were Catholics, Quakers, Presbyterians, Anglicans, Puritans, and others. The Catholic Church forbade marriage to close-kin and even affined persons, but at the same time granted dispensations on payment of sufficient money. Religious diversity in English America created different patterns for each colony, but consanguinity and affinity remained barriers to marriage. The English generally discouraged marriage across religious lines, with Quakers casting out those members of the faith who married non-Quakers. Prohibitions on marriage to near kin remained strong even when their pool of potential mates was small. Unlike in the Catholic colonies, no dispensation with payment seems to have been granted.[10]

---

[10] Robert J. Gough, 'Close-kin Marriage and Upper-class Formation in Late Eighteenth-Century Philadelphia', *Journal of Family History* XIV, no. 2 (1989), pp. 119–136.

For Catholics, there were so many impediments that, without dispensation, the marriage choice would have been too restrictive, especially in small townships far away from urban centers. Besides consanguinity and affinity, illicit sexual intercourse with some kin of the bride or groom also required a dispensation. For instance, if a young man had sexual intercourse with a girl's sister or mother, he could not marry the girl without a dispensation; ecclesiastical records reveal that this happened quite often in small communities.

If marriage within the family circle was common in isolated towns, in urban centers there was sometimes a preference for partners belonging not only to the same social group but also to the same profession. Merchants in Buenos Aires and other commercial towns throughout colonial America tended to be an endogamous group.[11] Members of other professional groups had to submit their choice of brides either to the local authorities, in the case of regular army offices of a lower rank, or to the Crown, if the men were magistrates, higher nobility, or senior army officers.[12]

The indissolubility of marriage was sustained both by the Catholic and the Anglican Churches but, whereas in the Catholic colonies this principle was accepted, in the British colonies full divorce, allowing partners to remarry, was sometimes granted despite English laws and the Anglican Church doctrine opposing this practice. In the Puritan colonies, the belief that marriage was a civil undertaking rather than a religious sacrament made the dissolution of highly disorderly marriages – unions typified by fighting, child endangerment, or abandonment – quite acceptable. Adultery and desertion were usually grounds for divorce in Puritan and non-Puritan British colonies, but there was no legal uniformity. Sometimes a 'divorce' consisted of an agreement for separate living and financial support for the wife, without any permission for the re-marriage of either partner. Different divorce laws and policies separated the northern and the more conservative southern colonies (see chapter 4). After the War of Independence, many state legislatures in the United States did pass divorce laws.[13]

In Catholic colonies, canon law regarding irrevocably broken marriages warranted only separation from bed and board, although the word divorce was employed. Taking colonial Brazil as an example, most petitions to begin a divorce

---

[11] Susan Migden Socolow, 'Marriage, Birth, and Inheritance: The Merchants of Eighteenth-Century Buenos Aires', *Hispanic American Historical Review* LX, no. 3 (1980), pp. 387–406. See especially p. 391 on a high degree of group endogamy: 'The vast majority of Buenos Aires merchants chose to marry the daughters of older, more established merchants, thus using marriage to strengthen previous commercial ties'.

[12] Gary M. Miller, 'Bourbon Social Engineering: Women and Conditions of Marriage in Eighteenth-Century Venezuela', *The Americas* XLVI, no. 3 (1989), pp. 261–290.

[13] See Roderick Phillips, *Untying the Knot: A Short History of Divorce* (Cambridge, 1991), chapter 2.

suit were presented by women in the ecclesiastical courts, whereas in English America it was often men who filed divorce petitions although evidence from the Chesapeake may suggest otherwise.[14] When seeking separation, Brazilian wives preferred to allege mistreatment rather than adultery in their petitions because mistreatment was easier to prove before the ecclesiastical judges. They could say that their lives were in danger and thus they could immediately be physically separated from their husbands. Men did not begin legal action based on female adultery because Portuguese law favoured punishment of an errant wife without resort to divorce. An unfaithful wife could be sent to a convent for life, and when formally accused of adultery before a civil court the woman's property, in the absence of children, would pass to the husband. As the partners could not re-marry, these so-called divorces in practice meant only physical separation and the possibility for husband and wife each to have independent administration of his or her share of the couple's property. If the partners already had children, the husband's access to the adulterous wife's property was unlikely; and if they did not, the man's chance to father legitimate heirs would be compromised by such a separation. Such 'divorce' thus threatened both the patrimony and the lineage, making men's recourse to such a drastic step unlikely.

In Brazil, by the end of the eighteenth century a new type of uncontested divorce appeared, involving separation by 'mutual consent', or even on 'amicable' terms. Contested separations based on accusations of mistreatment (sevicias) or adultery, or both, continued to take place, but many married couples increasingly chose instead to work out a mutual agreement about the division of property or the custody of children. All evidence indicates that divorces by consent, in addition to being cheaper, were simpler to process and easier to obtain from the ecclesiastical courts.

Concubinage took different forms in colonial America according to the races of the participants. Both religious and civil law recognized multiple possibilities for colonists to commit this sin and sexual crime (see chapters 5 and 6). According to the Catholic Church, every couple regardless of race – white, Indian, black, or mixed blood – should marry because there was no salvation outside of holy matrimony for the sexually active. Catholic priests were exhorted to convince those in their parishes who lived in concubinage to marry. If their admonitions were not obeyed, the priests had the right to deny Communion during Easter and even, if the couple were obdurate, to excommunicate the disobedient. The priests should also insist that slave-owners took care of their slaves' souls by allowing them to marry in church. In British America, only Quakers were similarly interested in slaves' souls; concerns that Christian doctrine would impel slaves

---

[14] Maria Beatriz Nizza da Silva, 'Divorce in Colonial Brazil: The Case of São Paulo', in ed., Asunción Lavrin, *Sexuality and Marriage in Colonial Latin America* (Lincoln, 1989).

to yearn for freedom limited the amount of work Anglican and other priests did among the slave populations. Efforts to convert Indians were similarly infrequent. For the British, concubinage became the normal condition of slave and even Indian relationships. However, civil society throughout colonial America had double standards toward concubinage. For the white population, an illicit sexual relationship might be overlooked provided it was not conducted so openly as to cause public scandal in the community; that is to say, this sexual crime should only be committed in strict privacy. These were not openly consensual unions with both partners living in the same house with or without children. The concubines visited each other at night, clandestinely, but they did not dare live together. Only blacks and mixed bloods could openly have consensual non-marital unions.

Illicit sexual relationships often led to illegitimate children. Studying the Saint Laurence Valley, French Canadian historians find only 1.25 per cent of births were illegitimate during the years between 1700 and 1729. Most mothers of illegitimate children were single; one-third then married the children's fathers and so the children became legitimate.[15] Marie-Aimée Cliche, a historian of New France, examined 126 cases of court proceedings derived from the jurisdictions of Québec, Montréal and Trois Rivières. That there were no cases of pre-marital pregnancy was attributable to such cases being resolved by unanticipatedly early marriages. In short, marriage resolved what might otherwise have appeared as pre-marital pregnancy. But her research does provide a great variety of information on illicit relationships, similar to what historians have found for Iberian colonies.[16]

White widows and separated women also had illegitimate children. Sexual relationships that culminated in extramarital pregnancies were clearly quite diverse in character, ranging from rape to consensual affairs pursued by adult women. All of these sexual activities were prohibited by the Catholic Church, but colonial societies allocated the blame differently depending on the circumstances.

We do not yet know much about abortion or infanticide in colonial societies, but there is substantial documentation on child abandonment.[17] Many white women were anxious to preserve their reputations and, after giving birth secretly, left the newborn in a public place where the infant would soon be found. Some of these children were not *bona fide* foundlings; they were sometimes baptized

---

[15] Lyne Paquette and Réal Bates, 'Les naissances illégitimes sur les rives du Saint-Laurent avant 1730', *Revue d'histoire de l'Amérique française* XL, no. 2 (1986), pp. 234–252.

[16] Marie-Aimée Cliche, 'Unwed Mothers, Families, and Society during the French Regime', in ed., Bettina Bradbury, *Canadian Family History: Selected Readings* (Toronto, 1992).

[17] Infanticide was routinely legislated against in colonial New England and prosecutions for this crime appear regularly, if infrequently, in court proceedings. For an excellent article on abortion, see Cornelia Hughes Dayton, 'Taking the Trade: Abortion and Gender Relations in an Eighteenth-Century New England Village', *William and Mary Quarterly* (3rd series) XLVIII, no. 3 (1991), pp. 19–49.

infants for whom the parish register would record 'unknown mother'. But mothers might put such offspring on the threshold of a relative or friend. Once her social or financial situation improved, the mother sometimes reclaimed her child, legitimized him or her and made the child her heir.

When a white woman could not marry her lover because he was already married or because he was of a superior social status, monetary compensation was often offered in cases of loss of virginity or pregnancy. This cash settlement allowed the girl to find a husband or at least to raise her child. Even non-consensual relationships, if proven in court, would usually result in compensation for the woman rather than substantive punishment for the man. Some girls in colonial societies were abducted from their parents' homes. Civil law distinguished between abduction by violence (against the girl's wishes) and abduction by seduction (against her parents' wishes). In Europe, both cases were considered capital crimes, but in the colonies the punishment was less severe. In early Puritan New England, rape was a capital crime, but elsewhere the punishment was variable. Throughout the American colonies, most courts preferred to address seduction by forcing the seducer to marry the girl or otherwise atone for his offense, even when there was no pregnancy. A pregnant girl who refused to marry her abductor when the courts and the man involved agreed to this solution would herself be punished: one Virginia servant woman who refused to marry an abusive man who had made her pregnant was whipped for her stand, and the man relieved of any burden of child support.

In Catholic colonies there was a typology of illegitimacy. The children of Catholic priests were called sacrilegious and often born of white women. Adulterine children were fathered by white men and born of either coloured women or of separated white women. Natural children were the offspring of two unmarried individuals: a white single or widowed man and a white or coloured single or widowed woman. Even limiting ourselves to those cases where one of the partners was white, there are a great number of possible variations. The development of a public language delimiting the various kinds of illegitimacy suggests the degree to which such births became commonplace in the colonies.

If the Catholic colonies have richer documentation for the study of concubinage and illegitimacy, Protestant America can claim resources equal to those of Catholic America for the study of inheritance. Scholars of almost all of the regions of colonial America have devoted considerable attention to this issue. (the exception is French Canada, for which the emphasis on demographic studies appears to have eclipsed other kinds of analyses of colonial society). The most outstanding difference between Iberian and English inheritance law lies in the testator's freedom. In Portuguese and Spanish law, all children had an equal right to their parents' property, always excepting entailed property. Also, according to Iberian civil codes, the surviving spouse had a right to half the couple's property, except when there was an *arras* contract. In English America, the testator's freedom to prefer some heirs over others was a well accepted principle (see chapter 9). Thus we have equality among heirs on the Iberian side, inequality on the English side, independent widows in Portuguese and Spanish America, and dependent ones in English America. While daughters in Iberian colonies received dowries that were advances on their inheritances, in the English colonies many sons received portions of land before their fathers' death, usually at the time of their marriages.

Three issues dominate the study of inheritance in the different colonies. First is the right of primogeniture and entailed property. Second, historians examine differences in sons' and daughters' shares. Third, they also focus on preference for a favoured son among the male heirs. These studies reveal more differences in Catholic and Protestant colonial practice, as well as some interesting similarities. Entail is a practice connected with noble families and was more frequent in Spanish and Portuguese colonies than in Anglo America, even before the American revolutionaries abolished the practice. Entailed property is in a sense never fully owned by an individual; instead, it is held in trust by an individual in the name of the lineage, and no one man ever gains the ability legally to influence who will be heir to such property. The landed aristocracy was not equally represented in colonial territories, and in some regions entailed property never existed. Even in those regions in which only land comprised true wealth, for example in the British southern mainland colonies, élite planters often avoided creating entail.[18] Dying patriarchs in fact employed a number of strategies in order to enact their preferences rather than necessarily following the testamentary law of the colony in which they held property. Strategies could be found in order to establish inequality where equality was the norm, and also the reverse. Nonetheless testamentary law and societal expectations influenced family life during the patriarch's lifetime: where the testator had more freedom of decision about the shares to be given to each heir, he also had greater authority and power in the family. A man whose property would be divided equally among his heirs, sons and daughters alike, had substantially less power over his family.

A comparative study of women's roles in European expansion is long overdue. Different marriage systems and testamentary laws led to a diversity in the social position of women in North and South American colonies. Though much work has been done on this subject, there still more research needed before we have an adequate understanding of women and property in the colonial world (see chapters 7 and 8). Certain questions in particular must be addressed. At what point in their life cycle – and the cycle of colonial settlement and expansion – did women take into their own hands the administration of their property? Were

---

[18] See Holly Brewer, 'Entailing Aristocracy in Colonial Virginia: 'Ancient Feudal Restraints' and Revolutionary Reform', *William and Mary Quarterly* (3rd series) LIV (1997).

they protected against prodigal husbands? When separated or divorced, did a female partner receive an equal share of the couple's property and did she assume full responsibility for the administration of her assets? Did single women come into possession of their inheritances when they came of age or did they always remain under the tutelage of a male relative? When daughters took their vows to enter the Church did they receive a smaller share of their parents' property or were the shares equivalent? Anecdotal and regional studies that examine some of these issues must be considered in relation to one another, and broader and more systematic studies undertaken, before we can develop a more sophisticated general understanding of colonial women as property owners.

According to European codes, women held clearly defined rights to family property as heirs and as wives, but in the colonies women also exercised powers of administration at certain times in their lives. In widowhood they certainly decided what to do with their share of the couple's property. Unless they were wealthy widows with sugarmills and slaves or some other kind of income-generating estate, however, old age might well find them without adequate means to support themselves. Many widows had to live with married sons or daughters, losing their economic independence and becoming dependents in another household.

In Iberian colonies there was no counterpart to the dower in the British colonies. The dower was a minimum one-third share of the couple's estate, not an equal share, and the widow could lose the property altogether when she remarried. Property thus set aside for a widow's 'maintenance' was often resented by the other heirs; her inability to influence who would inherit her dower made her an obstruction to inheritance rather than an influential property-owner. The goal in these English colonies was less to protect a woman's property rights than to prevent such women from becoming burdens on the community. There is no doubt that women were better protected in the Iberian world; but this protection was not translated into power in the community, although wealthy widows contributed financially to the needs of local governments and were liable for payment of taxes as would be males.

The study of women's roles in the family and in the community must take into account not only propertied women but also those who were poor, including whites, Indians and persons of African descent. Poor women worked to support themselves and their families; many of them were unwed mothers. Such women were peddlars, seamstresses, laundresses, cotton weavers, bakers, cooks, wetnurses, midwives, and healers. They lived in the world outside their homes and they had to struggle for survival.

Indian families have been studied more thoroughly for Spanish, French and English America than for Brazil. This Portuguese colony's Indian population has been depicted by historians primarily as a labour force to be compared with African slaves (see chapter 10) The information we have on Indian families in

Catholic colonies is mostly obtained from documents produced by members of religious orders. Jesuits in Brazil and New France, and members of other orders in the Spanish colonies, were quick to criticize indigenous domestic arrangements and sexual mores, especially perceived polygamy and open homosexuality, and comment on indigenous adoption of Catholic practices such as holy matrimony – a monogamous, permanent, procreative union blessed by God. Baptism preceded marriage, but mass baptism of native populations did not automatically translate into an eagerness to adopt the Catholic concept of marriage. Many friars confessed their failure to acculturate, and thus save, the Indians.

Acculturation depended on the intensity and duration of contacts between Indians and representatives of the religious orders. Those Indians who lived far away from friars and priests could maintain their traditional forms of marriage and their traditional domestic, sexual, and family mores. Those who had settled among the whites or near them had to change their own ways to comply with the standard white family pattern. How effective and deep this change was cannot be evaluated solely by reference to either ecclesiastical or civil sources.

Compared to Catholic missionary activity in the Iberian and French colonies, the British efforts to control and shape Indian life appear less intense. What Catholic missionaries did not accomplish, however, English law sometimes did, by confronting the accultured Indians with punishment for practices which to the English were sexually deviant. Those best able to resist English mores lived far away from the English settlements, or were members of several still-strong tribes such as the Iroquois Confederation or the Powhatan, and were able to maintain their traditional ways. Only converted Indians were directly subject to colonial authority, and tensions arising from such submission are a new theme for historians.[19]

Catholic colonies used godparenthood ('compadrazgo' in Spanish, 'compadrio' in Portuguese) as ritual ties which bound together godparents and godchildren. These religious ties could impede marriage. Studying the late sixteenth-century plantations in Bahia, Brazil, Stuart Schwartz found a high percentage of whites as godfathers among the Indian baptisms he examined. White men served as godfathers for more than eighty per cent of the baptisms of the children of Indian mothers.[20] On the Spanish side, Paul Charney studied how godparent ties functioned between Indians and Spaniards of the Lima valley, and the consequences these ties had for native society in the early 1600s; but here

[19] Ann Marie Plane, "'The Examination of Sarah Ahhaton": The Politics of "Adultery" in an Indian Town of Seventeenth-Century Massachusetts', in ed., Peter Benes, *Algonkians of New England, Past and Present: Proceedings of the Dublin Seminar for New England Folklife* (Boston, 1994).

[20] Stuart B. Schwartz, *Sugar Plantations in the Formation of Brazilian Society; Bahia, 1550–1835* (Cambridge, 1985), p. 63.

he found that the percentage of Indian godparents was much higher than that of Spanish ones.[21]

More studied than Indian families, black families throughout colonial America are the subject of recent analyses both from a demographic perspective and from a social point of view (see chapters 11 and 12). A new approach in the study of slave families is the analysis of mixed marriages between a slave and a freed partner, a strategy that served as one marital solution to the difficulty of marriage between two slaves. In late colonial Brazil, the free partner often agreed to follow the slave partner in the case of the latter's sale to another owner. Sometimes, the free spouse was able to pay for his or her partner's freedom by offering the owner the market price or another slave as a substitute. The success of this strategy depended on whether a slave-owner was willing to sell or not, because only the king had the power to force the owner to part with his property.

In Catholic colonies, parish priests pressured slave-owners to encourage their slaves to marry, but marriage was more frequent on plantations and sugarmills where one owner sometimes possessed more than a hundred slaves. Planters and small owners provided less encouragement for their slaves to marry, and the rural isolation of many of these settings further prevented such marriages. While the principle of slave marriage was upheld by the Catholic Church, the ecclesiastical bureaucracy made things difficult for those who planned to marry even with an owner's approval. Even for slaves, a baptismal certificate was required, as well as proof of celibacy or widowhood. The penalties were the same as for free persons, and most slaves or owners were either unable or unwilling to pay for the dispensation. As was the case for poor white couples, a church marriage meant heavy expenses that many persons of African descent, and particularly slaves, could not afford. Masters would occasionally pay these expenses, but in general owners were indifferent to slave marriages, believing that concubinage was a slave's lot. This is the reason why Catholic parish registers contain only a small percentage of slave marriages.

Although we have some demographic information on marriages between persons of African descent, both slave and free, we still know very little about their married life and the way they raised their children.[22] Difficulties keeping families together in a slave society lead to a large number of female-headed households among African-descended Americans. When a household consisted of a single African-American woman and her children, the children might well be

---

[21] Paul Charney, 'The Implications of Godparental Ties between Indian and Spaniards in Colonial Lima', *The Americas* XLVII, no. 3 (1991), pp. 325–341.

[22] See Allan Kulikoff, *Tobacco and Slaves: The Development of Southern Cultures in the Chesapeake, 1680–1800* (Chapel Hill, 1986); Herbert Gutman, *The Black Family in Slavery and Freedom, 1750–1925* (New York, 1976); and Eugene Genovese, *Roll Jordan, Roll: The World the Slaves Made* (New York, 1974).

mulattos. Whether these children received support from their white fathers can be studied through wills, in which legacies were sometimes made to protect these illegitimate mulatto offspring. The dramatic transformation from an illegitimate mulatto child into an heir, while possible, rarely appears in notarial documentation.

Leaving the Americas and turning to family history for Africa, we find only a small bibliography. The family life of white colonists in Africa has not received scholarly attention except for settlements in Southern Africa, notably the Cape Colony (see chapter 13). European administrators, slave traders, and convicts generally left their families in Europe. White women were scarce in Africa. Blacks in the whites' service have not been adequately studied. Historians of Africa, influenced by anthropologists, are interested in African societies and their patterns of family life independent of the impact of European colonization and their involvement in enslaving Africans for labour in the Americas. Strangely enough, there is nothing comparable to the family history in the Americas for the period we are concerned with, although some articles have been written on nineteenth-century Africa.

The annual census of all free people of the Cape Colony, along with such other sources as property records, land revenue books, and inventories, has provided good information on the South African settlers. The source materials are sufficiently rich that relationships within the household, and women's roles within the family, have been studied productively.[23] As in Catholic America, women benefitted from the Cape inheritance system: a widow received half of a husbands' estate, the other half being divided among the children. This form of inheritance enhanced the social position of Cape widows. The demographic scarcity of women brought changes in the application of Dutch law in the Cape, and at the same time it led to marriages between white settlers and coloured women – the women, often ex-slaves, who were manumitted before the marriages took place. In those regions of the colony where European women were more numerous, the incidence of miscegenation and inter-racial marriages declined proportionally.

We sincerely hope, that in the next decade, the family history of Europeans not only in Africa but also in Asia will become a major subject for historians whose interests have focused on administrative, military, and economic history. Likewise, the impact of colonization and the slave trade on family organization and dynamics within black African societies should also receive further attention. Family history has yet to fulfill its promise as a rich field for comparative and cross-cultural approaches.

---

[23] Robert Shell, 'Tender Ties: Women and the Slave Household, 1652–1834', in *Collected Seminar Papers*, number 42, *The Societies of Southern Africa in the 19th and 20th Centuries*, vol. 17 (London, 1992).

Articles in this Volume

The articles selected for republication in this volume present the major issues in the study of the family in European expansion. Muriel Nazzari's study of dowry in colonial São Paulo, Brazil, is a classic on the subject, describing significant changes in the practice of dowry. Patricia Seed and Donald Ramos deal with marriage in different approaches and places. The article by Nancy Cott was one of the first to use divorce proceedings to analyse a woman's situation when separation occurred. Ann Twinam and the New France historians Lynne Paquette and Réal Bates write of illegitimacy in a different way, more as institutional family history in one case, and more as demographic family history in the other. Property and inheritance are the subjects of Edith Couturier, Alida Metcalf, and Toby Ditz, all of whom use the same source material, notarial documents – wills, inventories, and deeds. Sarah Cline's article focuses on acculturation of the Indians through the Catholic practices of baptism and marriage. A.J.R. Russell-Wood in a comprehensive way and Edgar Love with a more detailed case study both put in perspective the black family in the Americas. Finally, Leonard Guelke takes us to South Africa and the Cape Colony. He analyses population censuses to demonstrate the sex-ratio imbalance, and then studies the consequences of this demographic fact for marriage and household formation in this colony. Together, these articles should provide insight both into the impact of European colonization on family structures and dynamics, and the variety of ways historians have succeeded in answering our questions about this sometimes elusive topic.

Selected Bibliography

Books

Allen, David Grayson, *In English Ways: The Movement of Societies and the Transferral of English Local Law and Custom to Massachusetts Bay in the Seventeenth Century* (Chapel Hill, 1981).

Anderson, Karen, *Chain Her by One Foot: The Subjugation of Women in Seventeenth-Century New France* (London and New York, 1991).

Charbonneau, Claudette, et al., *The First French Canadians: Pioneers in the St. Lawrence Valley* (Newark, 1993).

Cott, Nancy F., *The Bonds of Womanhood: 'Woman's Sphere' in New England, 1780–1835* (New Haven, 1977).

Demos, John, *A Little Commonwealth: Family Life in Plymouth Colony* (Oxford, 1971).

Ditz, Toby, *Property and Kinship: Inheritance in Early Connecticut, 1750–1820* (Princeton, 1986).

Greven, Philip J., Jr., *Four Generations: Population, Land, and Family in Colonial Andover, Massachusetts* (Ithaca, N.Y., 1972).

Jeddrey, Christopher M., *The World of John Cleaveland: Family and Community in Eighteenth-Century New England* (New York, 1979).

Lavrin, Asunción, ed., *Sexuality and Marriage in Colonial Latin America* (Lincoln, 1989).

Metcalf, Alida C., *Family and Frontier in Colonial Brazil: Santana de Parnaiba, 1580–1822* (Berkeley, 1992).

Morgan, Edmund, *The Puritan Family: Religion and Domestic Relations in Seventeenth-Century New England* (rev. edn, New York, 1966).

Nazzari, Muriel, *The Disappearance of the Dowry: Women, Families, and Social Change in São Paulo, Brazil, 1600–1900* (Stanford, California, 1991).

Salmon, Marylynn, *Women and the Law of Property in Early America* (Chapel Hill, 1986).

Seed, Patricia, *To Love, Honor and Obey in Colonial Mexico: Conflicts over Marriage Choice, 1574–1821* (Stanford, 1988).

Smith, Daniel Blake, *Inside the Great House: Planter Family Life in Eighteenth-Century Chesapeake Society* (Ithaca, N.Y., 1980).

Socolow, Susan M., *The Merchants of Buenos Aires, 1778–1810: Family and Commerce* (Cambridge, 1978).

Thompson, Roger, *Women in Stuart England and America: A Comparative Study* (London, 1974).

Articles

Adams, John W., and Alice Bee Kasakoff, 'Migration and the Family in Colonial New England: The View from Genealogies', *Journal of Family History* IX (1984), pp. 24–43.

Auwers, Linda, 'Fathers, Sons, and Wealth in Colonial Windsor, Connecticut', *Journal of Family History* III (1978), pp. 136–49.

Bates, Réal, 'Les conceptions pré-nuptiales dans la vallée du Saint-Laurent avant 1725', *Revue d'histoire de l'Amérique française* IV (1986), pp. 136–49.

Burnard, Trevor, 'Family Continuity and Female Independence in Jamaica, 1665–1734', *Continuity and Change* VII (1992), pp. 181–98.

Carr, Lois Green and Lorena S. Walsh, 'The Planter's Wife: The Experience of White Women in Seventeenth-Century Maryland', *William and Mary Quarterly* (3rd series) XXXIV (1977), pp. 542–71.

Chandler, D.S., 'The Montepios and Regulation of Marriage in the Mexican Bureaucracy, 1770–1821', *The Americas* XLIII (1986), pp. 47–68.

Charney, Paul, 'The Implications of Godparental Ties between Indians and Spaniards in Colonial Lima', *The Americas* XLVII (1988), pp. 325–41.

Cliche, Marie-Aimée, 'Unwed Mothers, Families, and Society during the French Regime', in ed., Bettina Bradbury, *Canadian Family History: Selected Readings* (Toronto, 1992).

Desjardins, Bertrand, Pierre Beauchamp, and Jacques Legaré, 'Automatic Family Reconstitution: The French-Canadian Seventeenth-Century Experience', *Journal of Family History* II (1977), pp. 56–76.

Gough, Robert J., 'Close-kin Marriage and Upperclass Formation in Late Eighteenth-Century Philadelphia', *Journal of Family History* XIV (1989), pp. 119–36.

Greven, Philip J., Jr., 'The Average Size of Families and Households in the Province of Massachusetts in 1764 and in the United States in 1790: An Overview', in eds., Peter Laslett and Richard Wall, *Household and Family in Past Time* (Cambridge, 1972).

Gudemen, Stephen, and Stuart Schwartz, 'Cleansing Original Sin: Godparentage and the Baptism of Slaves in Eighteenth-Century Bahia', in ed., Raymond T. Smith, *Kinship Ideology and Practice in Latin America* (Chapel Hill, 1984).

Keim, C. Ray, 'Primogeniture and Entail in Colonial Virginia', *William and Mary Quarterly* (3rd series) XXV (1968), pp. 545–86.

Kellog, Susan, 'Households in Late Prehispanic and Early Colonial Mexico City: Their Structure and its Implications for the Study of Historical Demography', *The Americas* XLIV (1988), pp. 483–94.

Kicza, John E., 'The Great Families of Mexico: Elite Maintenance and Business Practice in Late Colonial Mexico City', *Hispanic American Historical Review* LXVI (1982), pp. 429–57.

Kirk, Sylvia van '"The Custom of the Country": An Examination of Fur Trade Marriage Practices', in ed., Bettina Bradbury, *Canadian Family History: Selected Readings* (Toronto, 1992).

Korth, Eugene H., and Delia M. Flusche, 'Dowry and Inheritance in Colonial Spanish America: Peninsular Law and Chilean Practice', *The Americas* XLIII (1987), pp. 395–410.

Kuznesof, Elizabeth A., 'Clans, the Militia and Territorial Government: The Articulation of Kinship with Polity in Eighteenth-Century São Paulo', in ed., David J. Robinson, *Social Fabric and Spatial Structure in Colonial Latin America*. Published for the Department of Geography, Syracuse University, by University Microfilms International, 1979.

Lavrin, Asunción and Edith Couturier, 'Dowries and Wills: A View of Women's Socioeconomic Role in Colonial Guadalajara and Pueblo, 1640–1740', *Hispanic American Historical Review* LIX (1979), pp. 280–304.

Levy, Barry, '"Tender Plants": Quaker Farmers and Children in the Delaware Valley, 1681–1735', *Journal of Family History* III (1978), pp. 116–35.

Love, Edgar F., 'Legal Restrictions on Afro-Indian Relations in Colonial Mexico', *Journal of Negro History* LV (1970), pp. 131–39.

McCaa, Robert, 'Calidad, Class and Marriage in Colonial Mexico: The Case of Parral, 1788–1790', *Hispanic American Historical Review* LXIV (1984), pp. 477–501.

Metcalf, Alida C., 'Fathers and Sons: The Politics of Inheritance in a Colonial Brazilian Township', *Hispanic American Historical Review* LXIII (1986), pp. 455–84.

—, 'Searching for the Slave Family in Colonial Brazil: A Reconstruction from São Paulo', *Journal of Family History* XVI (1991), pp. 283–98.

Miller, Gary M., 'Bourbon Social Engineering: Woman and Conditions of Marriage in Eighteenth-Century Venezuela', *The Americas* XLVI (1989), pp. 261–90.

Myers, Kathleen A., 'A Glimpse of Family Life in Colonial Mexico: A Nun's Account', *Latin American Research Review* XXVIII (1993), pp. 63–87.

Norton, Mary Beth, 'The Evolution of White Women's Experience in Early America', *American Historical Review* LXXXIX (1984), pp. 593–619.

Plane, Ann Marie, '"The Examination of Sarah Ahhton": The Politics of "Adultery" in an Indian Town of Seventeenth-Century Massachusetts', in ed., Peter Benes, *Algonkians of New England, Past and Present*, Proceedings of the Dublin Seminar for New England Folklife (Boston, 1994).

Russell-Wood, A.J.R., 'Women and Society in Colonial Brazil', *Journal of Latin American Studies* IX (1977), pp. 1–34.

Shell, Robert, 'Tender Ties: Women and the Slave Household, 1652–1834', in *Collected Seminar Papers*, number 42, *The Societies of Southern Africa in the 19th and 20th Centuries*, vol. 17 (London, 1992).

Silva, Maria Beatriz Nizza da, 'Divorce in Colonial Brazil: The Case of São Paulo', in ed., Asunción Lavrin, *Sexuality and Marriage in Colonial Latin America* (Lincoln, 1989).

Smith, Daniel Blake, 'The Study of the Family in Early America: Trends, Problems, and Prospects', *William and Mary Quarterly* (3rd series) XXXIX (1982), pp. 3–28.

Smith, Daniel Scott, 'Parental Power and Marriage Patterns: An Analysis of Historical Trends in Hingham, Massachusetts', *Journal of Marriage and the Family* XXV (1973), pp. 419–28.

Socolow, Susan M., 'Marriage, Birth, and Inheritance: The Merchants of Eighteenth-Century Buenos Aires', *Hispanic American Historical Review* LX (1980), pp. 387–406.

Thompson, Roger, 'Adolescent Culture in Colonial Massachusetts', *Journal of Family History* IX (1984), pp. 127–44.

Tutino, John, 'Power, Class, and Family: Men and Women in the Mexican Elite, 1750–1810', *The Americas* XXXIX (1983), pp. 359–81.

Wells, Robert V., 'Quaker Marriage Patterns in a Colonial Perspective', *William and Mary Quarterly* (3rd series), XXIX (1972), pp. 415–42.

Withey, Lynne E., 'Household Structure in Urban and Rural Areas: The Case of Rhode Island, 1774–1800', *Journal of Family History* III (1978), 37–50.

1

Parents and Daughters: Change in the Practice of Dowry in São Paulo (1600–1770)

Muriel Nazzari

IT is generally accepted that there were few changes in the structure of the Brazilian colonial family, and that only in the nineteenth century did the power of the patriarch decline.[1] This essay challenges the view of an immutable colonial family by describing significant changes in the practice of dowry between the midseventeenth and mideighteenth centuries that reflect a shift in patriarchal/parental power.[2] I have used the term "parental" interchangeably

*Research for this project was partially supported by a Tinker Foundation Summer Grant and by a Woodrow Wilson Women's Studies Fellowship.

1. For this change in Brazil, see Antônio Cândido, "The Brazilian Family," in *Brazil: Portrait of Half a Continent*, T. Lynn Smith and Alexander Marchant, eds. (New York, 1951) and Linda Lewin, *Politics and Parentela in Paraíba: A Case Study of Family-Based Oligarchy in Brazil* (Princeton, 1987), esp. 188–200. For the importance of the larger kin group in Brazil, see Charles Wagley, *An Introduction to Brazil* (New York, 1963), 184–204 and Lewin, "Some Historical Implications of Kinship Organization for Family-Based Politics in the Brazilian Northeast," *Comparative Studies in Society and History*, 21:2 (Apr. 1979). For an "ideal" conceptualization of the elite patriarchal extended Brazilian family, see Gilberto Freyre, *The Masters and the Slaves* (New York, 1956) and "The Patriarchal Basis of Brazilian Society," in *Politics of Change in Latin America*, Joseph Maier and Richard Weatherhead, eds. (New York, 1964).

Mariza Corrêa criticizes both Freyre and Cândido for assuming that their descriptions of the structure and behavior of elite families of very specific regions could be applied to the families of different classes, regions, and periods. See "Repensando a família patriarchal brasileira," in *Colcha de retalhos: Estudos sobre a família no Brasil*, Maria Suely Kofes de Almeida et al., eds. (São Paulo, 1982).

2. See Muriel Nazzari, "Women, the Family, and Property: The Decline of the Dowry in São Paulo, Brazil (1600–1870)" (Ph.D. diss., Yale University, 1986). Other studies of dowry for Brazil include: Maria Beatriz Nizza da Silva, "Sistema de casamento no Brasil colonial," in *Ciência e Cultura*, 28:11 (Nov. 1976) and *Sistema de casamento no Brasil colonial* (São Paulo, 1984), 97–110; Eni de Mesquita Samara, "O dote na sociedade paulista do século XIX: Legislação e evidências," *Anais do Museu Paulista*, 30 (1980–81). For other parts of Latin America, see Asunción Lavrin and Edith Couturier, "Dowries and Wills: A View of Women's Socioeconomic Role in Colonial Guadalajara and Puebla, 1640–1790," *HAHR*, 59:2 (May 1979); Silvia Marina Arrom, *The Women of Mexico City, 1790–1857* (Stanford, 1985), chap. 3; Couturier, "Women and the Family in Eighteenth-Century Mexico: Law and Practice," in *Journal of Family History*, 10:3 (Fall, 1985); Susan Socolow, *The Mer-*

with "patriarchal" because my study of seventeenth-century Paulista society indicates that widows exercised the same patriarchal power over sons and daughters as had their husbands, and that wives, though subordinate to their husbands, shared some of those powers, especially when they acted as their husbands' representatives during the men's absence on bandeiras.

In the first half of the seventeenth century, Paulista patriarchs and their wives felt free to endow their daughters so magnificently that their sons' inheritance was diminished, yet sons not only accepted this situation willingly but also worked to increase their sisters' dowries. By giving their daughters such large dowries, parents controlled not only the marriage choice of their daughters, but that of their sons-in-law, undoubtedly influenced by the size of the dowry of the intended brides. One century later, in contrast, most Paulistas no longer offered such large dowries, losing the leverage a magnificent dowry gave over their daughters' marriages. In those cases in which parents did give very large dowries, sons increasingly litigated, curtailing their parents' right to favor their sisters. I will argue that these changes in dowry practices were due to a transformation in the marriage bargain that came about with the rise of a strong merchant class that changed the pool of suitors.

The changes in question occurred simultaneously with great socioeconomic transformations in the São Paulo region. Because it did not have the export crops of the Northeast, sixteenth- and seventeenth-century São Paulo was neglected by the crown, and it thus developed a society that was unique in Brazil. As in other regions of the world where state power was weak or nonexistent, seventeenth-century Paulista society was organized through the extended family or clan, which controlled all economic, political, and military activities.[3]

São Paulo's economy was based in large part on exploratory and slaving expeditions called bandeiras that replenished the Indian labor force for Paulistas, or as an alternative, provided the Indian captives to be sold to other parts of Brazil, especially during the Dutch occupation of Recife and Angola in the second quarter of the seventeenth century, which slowed down the slave trade and increased the demand for Indians. In São Paulo enslaved Indians produced, among other things, wheat, flour, rum, and

---

chants of Buenos Aires, 1778–1810 (Cambridge, 1978), chap. 2; Laurel Bossen, "Toward a Theory of Marriage: The Economic Anthropology of Marriage Transactions, Ethnology, 28:2 (Apr. 1988).

3. See Luiz de Aguiar Costa Pinto, Lutas de famílias no Brasil (São Paulo, 1980) for a study of this family-based society in São Paulo. For the clan as organizing principle of other societies with weak governments, see Jack Goody, The Development of the Family and Marriage in Europe (Cambridge, 1983), 15.

sailcloth, which Paulistas sold to other regions of Brazil, and even Angola.[4] These commodities were transported by countless Indian porters over the rugged Serra do Mar that separated São Paulo from the port of Santos.

The first half of the eighteenth century was a period of rapid economic, military, and political changes in São Paulo that entailed both losses and gains for propertied families. After the discovery of gold in Minas Gerais in the early 1690s, many of the old families' most enterprising members moved to the mining regions, but wealth trickled back and countless Portuguese newcomers took their place in the city. Though the extended family did not disappear, by the middle of the eighteenth century São Paulo's clans had lost the absolute power they and their ancestors had enjoyed previously.[5] After the discovery of gold, the crown aggressively sought to gain control of the region, thereby curbing the clans' autonomy and diminishing their authority.[6] Instead of being the

4. For the history of the bandeirantes, see Richard M. Morse, ed., *The Bandeirantes: The Historical Role of the Brazilian Pathfinders* (New York, 1965) and *From Community to Metropolis: A Biography of São Paulo, Brazil* (Gainesville, 1958); Affonso d'E. Taunay, *História geral das bandeiras paulistas*, 11 vols. (São Paulo, 1951). For commerce in seventeenth-century São Paulo, see Roberto Simonsen, *História econômica do Brasil (1500–1820)* (São Paulo, 1978), 215–219; John French, "Riqueza, poder e mão-de-obra numa economia de subsistência: São Paulo, 1596–1625," *Revista do Arquivo Municipal*, 45:195 (1982).

5. Perhaps the ultimate example of São Paulo's previous independence was the unilateral measures taken by the municipal council in 1690 regarding the value of coins, which were always in short supply since merchants who brought goods from Portugal wanted payment only in specie. Despite colonial requests for the creation of a colonial coin that could not be used in Portugal, in 1688 the crown decreed that coins would have uniform value in the entire empire, increasing the shortage throughout Brazil. But it was only in São Paulo that countermeasures were taken when in 1690 the municipal council decreed that coins in São Paulo would be worth more than in the rest of the empire and set exchange rates for trade with other towns (Simonsen, *História econômica*, 222–227; d'E. Taunay, *História da cidade de São Paulo* [São Paulo, 1953], 52–56). Three years later, the value of specie was reflated even further in São Paulo, leading the exasperated governor-general to write that the crown's monetary reform was enforced without opposition in the whole colony, "save only in São Paulo, where they know neither God, nor Law, nor Justice, nor do they obey any order whatsoever" (as quoted in Charles R. Boxer, *The Golden Age of Brazil, 1695–1750* [Berkeley, 1962], 34). Interestingly enough, by 1694 the crown had decided to create a colonial coin with greater value than the Portuguese.

6. Raymundo Faoro, *Os donos do poder: Formação do patronato político brasileiro*, 2 vols. (Pôrto Alegre, 1979), I, 162, argues that the biggest push toward state control took place in the eighteenth century.

Until then the *vila* of São Paulo had belonged to the donatary captaincy of São Paulo and São Vicente. In 1709, a wealthy Paulista, José de Góis Morais, offered to buy the captaincy from the donatary captain for 40,000 cruzados, but instead the crown bought it at the same price with the income from the tax on gold (Simonsen, *História Econômica*, 229). Though the crown was to elevate São Paulo to the status of a city in 1711, it progressively dismembered the captaincy, creating the separate captaincies of Rio Grande do Sul, Minas Gerais, Mato Grosso, and Goiás, and, finally, in 1748 further diminished São Paulo's independence by making it a part of the captaincy of Rio de Janeiro until 1765 (see Sérgio Buarque de Holanda, *História geral da civilização brasileira* [São Paulo, 1981], I, part 2, 34–36).

main source of power, clans now had to manipulate the sources of power.[7] At the same time, the virtual slavery of Indians permitted during the seventeenth century under the guise of their "administration" was finally abolished in 1758.[8]

The loss to the mines and to freedom of their plentiful Indian labor force weakened the great Paulista families that now had to compete in the growing eighteenth-century market economy in order to accumulate the capital to buy African slaves. The seventeenth-century expeditions had provided an infusion of labor to the São Paulo economy that led to increasing production and gradual development. The eighteenth-century Paulista expeditions for gold, in contrast, caused an exodus of both people and assets.

Agricultural production in São Paulo was stagnant by the middle of the eighteenth century. Immediately after the discovery of gold in Minas Gerais, São Paulo became the source of imports and local agricultural products for the mines. But when a new road joining Rio de Janeiro directly to Minas Gerais was inaugurated in 1733, trade to Minas bypassed São Paulo.[9] Paulistas, however, continued to sell mules and oxen transported from the south to Minas Gerais, and after the discovery of gold in Cuiabá and Goiás, Paulistas supplied them on river fleets of canoes, called monções.[10] The cargo of the monções only initially included agricultural products, since the high cost of transportation raised the final price of food sufficiently to stimulate agricultural production near the mines. The trade from São Paulo thereafter consisted mostly of imported tools, other necessary supplies, such as salt, and African slaves.

Not only did São Paulo's agricultural sales to the gold mines disappear, but the various markets for exports through the port of Santos had also disappeared by the middle of the eighteenth century, undoubtedly helped along by the disappearance of slave Indian porters.[11] Agricultural production in São Paulo during the first half of the eighteenth century was therefore mostly subsistence farming, with the sale of surplus to local markets. Portuguese crown officials, interested in the development of ex-

7. See Taunay, História da cidade, 118; Elizabeth A. Kuznesof, "The Role of the Merchants in the Economic Development of São Paulo, 1765–1850," HAHR, 60:4 (Nov. 1980).

8. Alvará of May 8, 1758. See Caio Prado, Jr., The Colonial Background of Modern Brazil, Suzette Macedo, trans. (Berkeley and Los Angeles, 1971), 102.

9. See Mafalda P. Zemella, O abastecimento da capitania das Minas Gerais no século XVIII (São Paulo, 1951).

10. See Sergio Buarque de Holanda, Monções (São Paulo, 1976).

11. The market for agricultural commodities exported through Santos, mainly sugar and rum, was only to rise after São Paulo renovated the road over the Serra do Mar in the 1770s. See Kusnesof, "The Role of the Merchants" and Maria Thereza Schorer Petrone, A lavoura canavieira em São Paulo: Expansão e declínio (1765–1851) (São Paulo, 1968).

port crops, spoke in 1767 and 1775 of the "decadence" of São Paulo.[12] To be sure, Maria Luiza Marcílio argues that eighteenth-century São Paulo could not have been decadent because it had never been ascendant.[13] Seventeenth-century *inventários*, the Brazilian judicial processes for the settlement of estates, certainly show that there was no great monetary wealth then in São Paulo.[14] Yet those same *inventários* show that the main resources of the seventeenth-century Paulista elite—land, labor, and military might—though not given a monetary value were enormous compared to the resources of their mideighteenth-century descendants. Eighteenth-century genealogist Pedro Taques was therefore probably right when he described seventeenth-century Paulistas in glowing terms as potentates, thereby implicitly acknowledging São Paulo's later decline.[15]

Whatever may be the proper characterization of the period, the discovery of gold and the decline of agriculture led to a change in the principal sources of wealth in the city of São Paulo. By the middle of the eighteenth century, the wealthiest Paulistas were no longer planters but large-scale merchants, especially those who supplied the gold mines with slaves, tools, and other provisions, or those who transported mules from the South to the mines.[16] Since trade was still frowned on, however, most merchants were Portuguese newcomers to São Paulo who married into Paulista families, and whose daughters would wed merchants while their sons would become planters, army officers, lawyers, judges, or priests.[17]

12. Morgado de Mateus, 1767, quoted in Alice P. Canabrava, "Uma economia de decadência: Os níveis de riqueza na capitania de São Paulo, 1765/67," *Revista Brasileira de Economia*, 26:4 (Oct.–Dec. 1972), 115–116. Also Governor Martim Lopes, 1775, quoted in Paulo Prado, *Paulística, história de São Paulo* (Rio de Janeiro, 1934), 147. Canabrava, in "Uma economia de decadência," 117–118, believes decadence came about with the decline of gold mining activities in all mining areas after 1765; also see the opinion of Simonsen in *História econômica*, 231. Buarque de Holanda, in "Movimentos da população en São Paulo no século XVIII," *Revista de Estudos Brasileiros*, 1 (1966), 110, maintains, however, that the greatest decadence was during the period when São Paulo was under the captaincy of Rio de Janeiro, 1748–65. This is a more reasonable periodization, since agriculture and the provincial economy improved in the last third of the century with the growing production and commercialization of sugar.

13. Maria Luiza Marcílio, "Crescimento demográfico e evolução agrária paulista, 1700–1836" (Livre-Docência thesis, University of São Paulo, 1974), 293.

14. This is the central thesis of Alcântara Machado's *Vida e morte do bandeirante* (Belo Horizonte, 1980).

15. Pedro Taques de Almeida Paes Leme, *Nobiliarquia paulistana histórica e genealógica* 5th ed. (São Paulo, 1980).

16. See Canabrava, "Uma economia de decadência," 115–116 and Kuznesof, "The Role of the Merchants," 100. The four wealthiest estates in my eighteenth-century sample were of merchants.

17. For the low status of merchants, see Holanda, *Monções*, 117; for the marriage of merchants into Paulista families, see Kuznesof, "The Role of the Merchants," 576, 583; for evidence of merchants marrying their daughters to merchants but having their sons follow other careers, see Nazzari, "Women, the Family and Property," 156–160.

Paulista property owners continued to have a rural base, for practically everyone in the sample, including the wealthy merchants, owned one or more farms or *sítios*. The structural transformations were accompanied, on the other hand, by considerable change in the practice of dowry, even though there was no change in the laws regarding dowry.[18]

The analysis made in this article is part of a larger study on the disappearance of the dowry, which compares its practice in São Paulo in approximately the first half of the seventeenth century with that in the first half of the eighteenth and the first half of the nineteenth centuries.[19] The documents used were *inventários*, which include not only the inventory of an estate but also the will of the deceased (if there was one), all litigation among heirs, lists of debts owed the estate, the demands of creditors, receipts of payment, the accounts of guardians of minor heirs, and the final apportionment of the estate among the heirs. *Inventários* are useful in the study of dowry practices because, according to Portuguese and Brazilian family law, dowry was an advance on a daughter's inheritance.[20] Since all legitimate children were necessary heirs—that is, they could not be disinherited—an *inventário* that had married daughters or their children as heirs to the estate usually included references to daughters' dowries, unless they had received none, which the *inventário* would also document.

To make the longitudinal study manageable, I limited the geographic area to the city of São Paulo and its surroundings, and mainly studied *inventários* from the middle years of each century. To eliminate subjectivity in the choice of *inventários*, I created a sample for statistical purposes. The sample for the seventeenth century consists of all 48 published *inventários* that have married daughters or their heirs for the period 1640–51 in *Inventários e testamentos* (44 volumes, São Paulo, 1921–75); for the eighteenth century, all 68 manuscript *inventários* with married daughters or their heirs for 1750–69 in "Inventários não publicados" at the Arquivo do Estado de São Paulo.[21] Since the date of an *inventário* does not correspond

18. Family law during the seventeenth and eighteenth centuries was contained in the code promulgated by Philip III. See Candido Mendes de Almeida, ed., *Codigo philippino ou ordenações do Reino de Portugal*, 14th ed. (Rio de Janeiro, 1870). All references are to this 14th edition, hereafter called *Ordenações*.

19. Nazzari, "Women, the Family, and Property."

20. See *Ordenações*, livro 4, tit. 96, para. 12 and tit. 97.

21. The only criterion used for choosing *inventários* for the samples of each time period was the presence of married daughters of the deceased (or their children). The seventeenth-century sample is 32.8% (48 out of 147) of the published *inventários* for 1640–1651 (which are *all* the extant *inventários* in São Paulo for the period). The eighteenth-century sample is 28.5% (71 of 249) of the *inventários* for the period 1750–69 in "Inventários Não Publicados" (I excluded from the sample three *inventários* that had been damaged by water and were unreadable). The collection "Inventários Não Publicados" contains approximately half the

CHANGES IN DOWRY IN SÃO PAULO (1600–1770)   645

to the date when the deceased parents gave a dowry to their daughter, an *inventário* dated in the middle of the century could describe dowry as practiced up to 50 years before.

The Early Seventeenth-Century Practice of Dowry

A wife's dowry was of much consequence in seventeenth-century São Paulo. Unless he had already inherited, there were mainly two ways a single man could acquire assets: he could go on a bandeira with an arrangement to receive some of the captives, or he could marry and receive in his wife's dowry the property needed to set up a separate productive unit. Marriage was also the best way for a man to become independent of his father's or widowed mother's legal control. Though age of majority was 25 throughout colonial times, single men (or women) did not become automatically emancipated at that age, but had to ask for a judicial emancipation, so that most men and all women remained under their parents' control until they married.[22]

The offspring of property owners in seventeenth-century São Paulo needed property to marry and establish themselves, yet parents typically channeled the necessary property through their daughters and not through their sons. Only 3 out of 35 families with adult sons had given gifts of property to those sons during their parents' lifetime. In contrast, daughters never went into marriage empty-handed. Most of them had received a dowry: parents endowed their daughters in 43 out of 48 families with married daughters, 91.5 percent of the seventeenth-century sample.[23] And every one of the married daughters in those 43 families had received a dowry. The four families that did not give explicit dowries were of widows or widowers whose daughters still took property to their marriage, their paternal or maternal inheritance.[24]

extant *inventários* for the period. The low percentage of *inventários* with married daughters is explained by the fact that both samples were taken from collections of *inventários* with minor heirs, by definition skewed against the existence of adults as heirs to the estate. The extant *inventários* appear to be quite representative of property owners, considering the relatively small size of São Paulo during the period—an estimated 400 European or mestizo households in the midseventeenth century (Buarque de Holanda, "Movimentos da população") and 14,760 free inhabitants in 1765 (Marcílio, *A Cidade de São Paulo, povoamento e população* [São Paulo, 1974], 98).

22. See Clovis Bevilaqua, *Direito de família* (Rio de Janeiro, 1933), 392.

23. The sample was 48 families with married daughters between 1640 and 1651. Four of these had not been given dowries, and to a fifth, who came from a bankrupt estate, it is unclear whether a dowry was given.

24. Estates with married daughters where there were no dowries were Anna Cabral, 1643, in *Inventários e testamentos* (hereafter *IT*), 44 volumes (São Paulo, 1921–1975) XXIX; Domingos Simões, 1649, *IT*, XXXIX; Gaspar Barreiros, 1646, *IT*, XXXIII; and Manoel de Massedo, 1650, *IT*, XLI.

Such a large portion of a family's property was spent on dowries that when Martim Rodrigues Tenório promised a dowry to his third daughter and her husband, he listed several of the items as fractions of his possessions. He promised a third of the fields he had planted, a third of the pigs he owned, a portion of his land, half his stock of tin, the house where he lived on the farm, plus his house in town, and he stated that if the houses were not acceptable he was prepared to build other ones or provide the money and land for others to be built.[25] Clearly, Martim Rodrigues was willing to go to great lengths for his daughter's marriage.

Most other parents also went out of their way to endow their daughters, so that many dowries consisted of much more property than what sons later inherited. For example, when Maria Gonçalves married in 1623, her father gave her, among other things, at least 16 Indians.[26] When her father died 18 years later, her brother inherited only 5 Indians.[27] The livestock in Maria's dowry also compares favorably with his inheritance, for she received ten head of cattle and a horse and saddle, whereas he inherited only three pigs (see Table I).

The dowry or gift given to a daughter or son was legally an advance on that heir's inheritance. The Portuguese code of law in effect during colonial times decreed that the estate of a deceased was to be divided only among those children who had not received a dowry or other gift, unless those heirs wanted to bring their dowries or gifts back into the estate, the process known as colação. Since all endowed daughters and heirs who had received other gifts from their parents were given this option of colação, a vital part of the judicial process was the formal question posed officially to each heir: do you want to inherit or not? If the heir refused, it meant he or she inherited nothing more than the dowry or gift received during the lifetime of the parent.

The process of colação was meant to ensure equality among heirs. When the dowry came in à colação, it was added to the net estate, then the total was divided equally among all children, and the dowry counted as part of the married daughter's equal share of the inheritance, her legítima. If the dowry was found to be larger than the daughter's legítima, she and her husband were expected to give back the difference to her siblings.[28] We can therefore safely assume that most heirs who refused to

25. Martim Rodrigues, 1603–1612, IT, II, 30. The dowry also contained six Indians, twelve cows, one bull, one colt, a tablecloth, six napkins, towels, a table, and a dress.

26. Maria Gonçalves, 1599, IT, I.

27. Clemente Alveres, 1641, IT, XIV.

28. Since the dowry was given by both parents, who owned their property jointly as community property, only half the value of the dowry came in à colação at the time of each parent's death (the surviving spouse retained one-half the estate). The exception was when a widow or widower endowed a daughter; then the whole dowry came in à colação.

See Ordenações, liv. 4, tit. 96, para. 17. Also Eni de Mesquita Samara, "O dote na

CHANGES IN DOWRY IN SÃO PAULO (1600–1770)   647

TABLE I: A Dowry Compared to a Brother's Inheritance

Dowry of Maria Gonçalves, 1623. (Her maternal *legítima** plus)	Inheritance (paternal *legítima*) of Alvaro Rodrigues, her brother, 1641. (He probably received his maternal *legítima* when he married.)
1 chest	1 chest
1 tablecloth, 6 napkins	1 buffet
6 silver spoons	2 chairs
6 plates	1 mattress
2 towels	1 book
8 scythes	3 pigs
8 hoes	Debt owed the estate, 2$000
8 wedges	5 Indians
10 head of cattle	
1 horse and saddle	
At least 16 Indians	
(List is incomplete)	

*Legítima: the inheritance to which a son or daughter was entitled by law, arrived at by dividing the net estate of the deceased parent equally among all children. Thus, the *legítima* of a brother and sister were equal.
Note: The monetary unit in the seventeenth century was the real (plural, réis). One thousand réis were written 1$000, called milréis, which became the monetary unit by the end of the eighteenth century. One thousand milréis were one conto, written 1:000$000. Prices found in *inventários* that help to understand the value of the 2$000 credit Alvaro Rodrigues received: a mare, 2$000; 2 silver tumblers and 6 silver spoons, 6$000; 1 small house, 3$200 (no value for the land it was on); 2 *covados* (measurement equal to 66 centimeters) of imported serge, 1$000.

inherit did so because they feared their dowries or gifts would be larger than their *legítima*.[29]

Declining to inherit was the most common practice for seventeenth-century endowed daughters, indicating that most daughters had received dowries that were larger than what their siblings would later inherit. Fewer than 10 percent of families in the sample had daughters who brought their dowry back *à colação,* and many times it was just one or two of a family's married daughters who did so (see Table II). An example of the practice is in the *inventário* of Catharina do Prado. Though she had eleven children, when she died there were only three heirs because her eight married daughters refused to inherit.[30] Since most endowed daughters in the seventeenth century refused to inherit, dowry in such cases can

———————

sociedade paulista do século XIX: Legislação e evidências," *Anais do Museu Paulista*, 30 (1980–81) and Maria Beatriz Nizza da Silva, *Sistema de casamento no Brasil colonial* (São Paulo, 1984), 101–102.

29. Refusing the inheritance also absolved the heir from the responsibility for a deceased parent's debts.

30. Catharina do Prado, 1649, *IT*, XV.

TABLE II: Families with Endowed Daughters Who Refused to Inherit or Brought Their Dowries à *Colação*

Families	17th century		18th century	
Where all married daughters refused to inherit	37	(90.2%)	11	(22.4%)
Where some married daughters refused and some brought dowry à *colação*	3	(7.3%)	8	(16.3%)
Where all married daughters brought dowry à *colação*	1	(2.4%)	30	(61.2%)
	41	(99.9%)	49	(99.9%)
Missing variables	2		6	
Total number of families who gave dowries	43		55	

Source: sample.

be viewed as given in lieu of an inheritance. Suzanna Dias's will is quite explicit on this point. She declared that she was leaving nothing to her four daughters because in the dowries she gave them she had included everything that they could have inherited from her husband or herself.[31]

Endowing daughters often depleted the family's property to the detriment of sons or single daughters, even if the dowry had not yet been paid when one of the parents died, for the promised dowry was considered a debt, and all debts were subtracted from assets before dividing the estate among the heirs. For example, when Pedro de Oliveira was presumed dead after seven years on a bandeira, his estate was worth 143$163, but since his debts mounted to 118$770, his wife's half share of the estate was only 12$201, and each of his minor children inherited only 2$440.[32] However, his married daughter, Antonia de Paiva, who refused to inherit, had received a dowry, 12$850 of which was still unpaid and included in the debts. This debt was therefore worth more than the entire estate left to the other children, and it was only a part of her dowry, the total of which was not recorded.[33] Antonia was therefore much wealthier than her brothers or sisters, or even her mother.

31. Suzanna Dias, 1628, *IT*, XXXIII, 13.
32. When a married woman or man died, the community property was first divided in half, with the surviving spouse keeping his or her half. The other half was considered the estate of the deceased. The law required that two-thirds of the estate of the deceased be divided equally among the necessary heirs of the deceased, his or her children (or grandchildren, per stirpes, in the case of children's having predeceased the parent), or, in the absence of children, to the parents of the deceased. Spouses did not inherit from each other, they just kept their half of the property, though they could receive bequests. See *Ordenações*, liv. 4, tit. 46, para. 1 and tit. 96.
33. Pedro de Oliveira, 1643, *IT*, XIV. When her husband died five years later, Antonia's half of the estate was worth 61$310. (Affonso Dias, 1648, *IT*, XV.)

Maria Leite's case is another example of depletion of an estate for a promised dowry. She had recently married when her father, Pedro Dias Paes Leme, died in 1633. His net estate was only worth 33$530. Dividing it in half gave his widow 16$765, and each of his eight other children received an inheritance of only 2$098. But Maria Leite was highly favored, for out of the sum reserved for payment of debts, she received her promised dowry of 80$000.[34]

Giving property to a son who was not a priest, on the other hand, was not common. Not only were there few families who gave gifts to these sons, neither were gifts to sons as large as dowries. The largest gift Messia Rodrigues gave a son was worth less than a tenth of the value of the largest dowry she gave.[35] Manoel João Branco had also given his son, Francisco João Leme, a gift, but it was worth slightly over a third the value of the *smallest* of his two daughters' dowries.[36]

Sons who were priests were the exception; they were the only sons to receive premortem gifts from their parents that were as substantial as their sisters' dowries.[37] This fact, in itself, illuminates the importance of dowry for young men in seventeenth-century São Paulo. All sons of property owners needed property for themselves in land and Indians to establish an independent life, but priests were the only sons who could not marry and receive that property in a wife's dowry.

Though it was brothers who bore the brunt of the extreme favoring of sisters, they were encouraged to think that that was as it should be.[38] Wills constantly exhorted sons to provide for their sisters' marriages, and providing for sisters was one of the reasons most frequently given for joining a bandeira, as in the case of Estevão Furquim's son who went "to look for a remedy for himself and for his sisters."[39] Since at least half the Indians brought back by single sons remained their parents' property, sons did in fact contribute to their sisters' dowries.

Only rarely did a male heir object to the favoring of his female relatives. One example is that of Ursulo Colaço, who complained in his will

34. Pedro Dias, 1633, *IT*, IX, 56, 65–67.

35. His gift was worth 59$200, the largest dowry, 718$000. Messia Rodrigues, 1665, *IT*, XVII.

36. His gift, 60$000; her dowry, 170$500. We know the total value of only the smallest dowry, for it was the one to come back into the estate. Manoel João Branco, 1641, *IT*, XIII.

37. There were no priests in my seventeenth-century sample itself. Priests had to own property to maintain themselves, for the crown received tithes but did not redistribute them so that all parish priests received support. See Dom Oscar de Oliveira, *Os dízimos eclesiásticos do Brasil nos períodos da colônia e do império* (Belo Horizonte, 1964).

38. Stanley Chojnachi, "Dowries and Kinsmen in Early Renaissance Venice," *Journal of Interdisciplinary History*, 5:4 (Spring 1975), 593, shows that in Venice brothers also bore the brunt of the custom of giving ever-larger dowries.

that his widowed grandmother gave such large dowries to her granddaughters that there was nothing left for him to inherit when she died.[40] Yet his grandmother's action is consonant with the prevalent practice among property owners in seventeenth-century São Paulo.

The favoring of daughters started early in their lives. Bequests or outright presents were bestowed on girls explicitly for their dowry long before they married, even in childhood or before they were born. For example, while Izabel de Proença was still a little girl, her uncle gave her a herd of cattle for her dowry.[41] A clear instance of the explicit favoring of daughters over sons that was characteristic of seventeenth-century São Paulo is found in Pedro de Araujo's will.[42] When he lay dying in 1638, knowing that his wife was pregnant with their first child, he took into account the sex of the unborn child in his will. He declared that if the child was a girl, she was to receive not only her *legítima* (that is, her legal share of the inheritance) but also the *remanescente da terça*—what was left of his *terça*, the third of his estate that he could legally bestow after his funeral, masses, and other small legacies had been deducted.[43] As his daughter would customarily only take possession of her inheritance when she married, he was obviously thinking of the property she would take into marriage, her dowry. However, if the child was a boy, Pedro did not want the *remanescente* to go to his son, but instead to his wife.[44]

When a single daughter received the *remanescente,* it meant she took to marriage much more property than her brothers inherited. Thus, in 1643, after being absent seven years in the sertão, Domingos Cordeiro was presumed dead and his estate was settled according to the will in which he left his *remanescente* to his single daughter Antonia. Each of Antonia's two surviving brothers received *legítimas* of 33$763, but she received that amount plus the *remanescente,* a total of 84$410, more than twice her brothers' inheritance.[45]

The manner in which wives contributed greatly to their marriages is well exemplified by the case of Maria de Proença, daughter of Baltazar Fernandes and his wife Izabel de Proença. On May 6, 1641, the parents went to the home and office of the Parnaíba notary to register a dowry contract for their daughter and her future husband, João Borralho Dalmada.

39. Estevão Furquim, *IT*, XVI, 301. Also *IT*, XVII, 55.
40. Ursulo Colaço, 1641, *IT*, XXXIX, 21–22.
41. Izabel de Proença, *IT*, XXXVII, 113.
42. A. J. R. Russell-Wood, "Women and Society in Colonial Brazil," *Journal of Latin American Studies*, 9:1 (May 1977), 15.
43. Testators were allowed to freely dispose of only one-third of their estate (in the case of married testators, one-sixth of the community property). See *Ordenações*, Liv. 4, tit. 96.
44. Pedro de Araujo, 1638, *IT*, XXIX.
45. Domingos Cordeiro, 1643, *IT*, VIII.

Before the notary and other witnesses, they jointly promised to give the following in dowry to their daughter and her husband:

> First, their daughter dressed in black satin, with two other fine dresses and gold earrings and a gold necklace.[46]
> A bed with its curtains and linens, a table and six chairs, a buffet, tablecloths and towels, 30 china dishes, two chests with their locks, a large and a small copper pot.
> A farm in São Sebastião with a tiled house, a field of *mandioca*, and a field of cotton.
> A house in town.
> Twenty agricultural tools.
> Two African slaves.
> Thirty Indians.
> One boat or canoe with oars.
> Five hundred *alqueires* of flour placed in Santos.[47]

Maria de Proença's dowry illustrates the principal characteristic of seventeenth-century Paulista dowries: large or small, they all contained the means of production and Indians or African slaves necessary to start a new enterprise. Large dowries included other objects such as clothes for the bride, jewels, bed and table linens, and other housekeeping objects which smaller dowries lacked. Antonia Dias received a dowry consisting of a dress and four Indians, while Beatriz Rodrigues only received nine Indians.[48] Maria Vidal received one dress, a cow, two sheets of silver, and two Indians.[49] A wife's contribution of Indians was particularly vital to the support of her new family, for the labor of those Indians provided their own and the family's subsistence plus commodities to sell.

Though Indians were the most frequent component of dowries, the larger dowries included other important means of production, such as land and houses and maybe one or two African slaves. Many women received cattle, pigs, or horses. Others received planted fields of cotton, wheat, or manioc, ready for harvest. Because of the lack of specie, few women received cash; instead they got commodities ready for sale, such as loads of flour or wheat, which would be sold to supply the capital for buying cattle, tools, and supplies.

---

46. It would appear that the daughter herself is listed as a part of the dowry, but since she is one of its recipients, I would argue that the emphasis is on the extremely expensive clothes, the idea being that the bride went to marriage dressed as befitted her station. Alcântara Machado first documented examples of this wording in seventeenth-century dowries in *Vida e morte*, 156–158.

47. Arquivo do Estado de São Paulo (hereafter *AESP*), Livro de Notas 1640–1642, Ord. 6074, #26. I thank John Monteiro for bringing this dowry to my attention.

48. Izabel Fernandes, 1641, *IT*, XXVIII; Pedro de Moraes Dantas, 1644, *IT*, XIV, 289.

49. Mecia de Siqueira, 1648, *IT*, XXXVII.

The most obvious advantage to parents of giving large dowries to daughters and little to sons was the leverage they obtained in the arrangement of marriages. This is quite clearly suggested by the case of Raphael de Oliveira, who had his stepdaughter, the daughter of his second wife by her first husband, marry his son by his first wife. He gave his stepdaughter a dowry that included her maternal inheritance, yet, when he died 20 years later, he had still not paid his son, her husband, his maternal inheritance.[50] Certainly, if Raphael de Oliveira's son had received his maternal inheritance and thereby become independent from his father, he might not have married the girl his father wanted him to marry. Indeed, he might not have married at all, contenting himself with an Indian concubine instead.

Though most patriarchs and their wives did not control both bride and groom as Raphael de Oliveira did, his example illuminates how dowry allowed parents to control the way in which their family and class were reproduced. When parents gave dowries to their daughters, but not equivalent gifts to their sons (which might make them independent to marry the woman of their choice), they were both retaining control of whom their daughters married and ensuring that their sons married women of their class, the only women who could provide dowries such as those their sisters received.

Besides helping to dictate who married whom, large dowries also influenced where the new couple lived. Captain João Mendes Giraldo of the village of Parnaíba was quite explicit about endowing his daughter with a house in order to have her live near her parents. In the document he made listing his daughter's dowry, he said that he would give his son-in-law a house with a tiled roof in Parnaíba, if the newlyweds lived in Parnaíba. If they did not, he did not consider himself under any obligation to give them a house.[51] This was a forceful condition, considering that his future son-in-law lived in São Paulo, not Parnaíba. Indeed, whenever dowries included land and houses, they had the potential to determine the residence of the couple. Of 33 seventeenth-century Paulista dowries, 17 contained land, 9 of which also included an urban house, while 8 other dowries had just an urban house.[52] Those 25 couples who received land or houses in their dowries would naturally tend to live near the wife's family.

How did men's economic contribution to the marriage compare with

50. Raphael de Oliveira, 1648, IT, III, 309–310. Another example of this kind of marriage is that of Catharina Conçalves's daughter by her first husband, who married her second husband's son by his first wife. See Luis Gonzaga da Silva Leme, Genealogia paulistana, 9 vols. (São Paulo, 1903–1905), IV, 429, n. 1.

51. Pedro de Araujo, 1638, IT, XXIX, 254.

52. It is possible that some of the dowries that did not list land, nevertheless still contained it, just as many seventeenth-century inventários did not list the land belonging to the estate, though it appeared in later documents.

CHANGES IN DOWRY IN SÃO PAULO (1600–1770)   653

that made by their wives with their dowries? The marriage system used in Portugal and Brazil was of complete community property, in which the dowry and any other property brought by husband or wife to the marriage disappeared into the couple's pool of goods; it was therefore not listed separately when either of the spouses died, making it difficult to learn how much a husband had contributed to marriage. However, in some midseventeenth-century cases we know the wife's dowry and the estate of at least one of the parents of the groom, so we can arrive at an approximate idea of what each brought to the marriage. We find that in the several cases examined the wife contributed much more property than her husband: this was true of Thomazia Pires and her husband Francisco de Godoy, and of Anna Pires and her husband João da Cunha. Thomazia and Francisco both contributed approximately the same number of Indians to their marriage, but Francisco inherited from both parents only one-ninth the other assets Thomazia brought in dowry.[53] In the case of Anna Pires, her dowry contained twice the number of Indians and twice the quantity of other assets that her husband inherited from his parents.[54]

Pedro d'Araujo also contributed much less than his wife to the marriage. The information we have about him is more clear-cut than the preceding cases because he died shortly after he married Izabel Mendes.[55] His wife's dowry is listed in his *inventário* and can therefore be subtracted from the total assets owned by the couple to reveal that both husband and wife contributed approximately the same amount of moveable goods, but that Izabel's dowry included five hundred *braças* of land. Though Pedro had several fields planted with different crops, he did not have title to any land.[56] The Indians that Izabel contributed were likewise more numerous than those her husband owned. Pedro had brought 4 Indians back from an expedition to the sertão, which, added to the Indians he had received when his father died, made a total of 18 adult Indians with some children.[57] His wife's dowry included 30 adult Indians: 20 to do agricul-

53. Messia Rodrigues, 1665, *IT*, XVII, 119–120, 143; Belchior de Godoy, 1649, *IT*, XXXIX.

54. Catharina do Prado, 1649, *IT*, XV; João Gago da Cunha, 1639, *IT*, X. Anna Pires's husband and his father were famous bandeirantes (see Francisco de Assis Carvalho Franco, *Dicionário de bandeirantes e sertanistas do Brasil* [São Paulo, 1954], 133).

55. Pedro d'Araujo, 1638, *IT*, XXVIII. He was married in November 1637, at the age of 23, and he had been to the sertão at least once (p. 251). His age was calculated from the fact that Pedro was 3 years old in 1617 in the inventário made after his father, also Pedro d'Araujo, died in the sertão (*IT*, V, 171). See another reference to his father in Carvalho Franco, *Dicionário*, 35. His father and his mother, Anna de Alvarenga, are mentioned in Taques, *Nobiliarquia paulistana*, III, 280, but Taques confuses Pedro's wife and heirs.

56. Unless land had been received in sesmaria, seventeenth-century Paulistas did not have title to the land they worked, and *inventários* just appraise the value of crops.

57. When Pedro's mother died in 1644, Pedro's son received six Indians who would have been his father's had he lived long enough (Anna de Alvarenga, 1644, *IT*, XXIX.).

tural work (10 men and 10 women and their children), equipped with the requisite tools, plus 10 women for service in the house.[58] Izabel therefore provided almost two-thirds of the couple's labor force.

Precisely because a bride's dowry in seventeenth-century São Paulo was usually larger than the property the groom took to marriage, the marriage bargain was weighted in favor of the wife and her family, giving the latter leverage in choosing a husband for their daughter, in determining where the couple would live, and in overseeing how the property was administered. Even though brides thus married down economically, the bargain was likely to be evened out through the grooms' white blood, membership in an important clan, claim to nobility, technological expertise, or just hard work. The fact that a daughter's marriage thus expanded the family's alliances, while incorporating another male into its military, political, or economic projects, was sufficient reason for her dowry to take precedence among the family's expenditures.

Though in matters of inheritance brothers bore the brunt of the favoring of their sisters, the practice I have described of wives taking more property to marriage than their husbands naturally gave the brothers the opportunity of marrying women with large dowries. The final outcome was therefore approximate equality between married brothers and sisters. By the middle of the eighteenth century, however, this equality no longer existed.

The Early Eighteenth-Century Practice of Dowry

By the first half of the eighteenth century, though dowry was still important, its practice had altered. Daughters still received substantial dowries, but the inequality between dowries and sons' inheritance was not as pronounced as in the preceding century. When favoritism on the earlier scale was attempted, this expression of patriarchal will was likely to be curtailed by a strict interpretation of the law brought about through the intervention of the state and the efforts of other heirs.

Most families of property owners in the first half of the eighteenth century still gave their daughters dowries, even if the proportion was slightly smaller than in the preceding century. Eighty-one percent of the families in the eighteenth-century sample endowed their daughters, as against 91.5 percent in the seventeenth century.[59] Five of the 13 families (out of 68) which did not endow their daughters were those of widows or wid-

58. Pedro de Araujo, 1638, IT, XXIX, 253.
59. Fifty-five of the 68 families in the eighteenth-century sample gave dowries; 43 of the 48 families in the seventeenth-century sample gave dowries (in one *inventário* information is missing).

owers who allowed them to marry only with their inheritance, and two were families that had not endowed the husband's illegitimate daughters.

There were, however, six families that let their daughters marry empty-handed. It is probable that they could not easily afford to give dowries, for they had relatively small estates, lying within the less wealthy half of the sample. The largest property owner of the six families was João Fernandes da Costa, who owned a farm in the *bairro* of Santana, cattle, and ten slaves, yet his estate was worth less than 2 percent of the largest estate in the sample.[60] Besides one married daughter who had not received a dowry, he also had a single daughter over 25 who was emancipated. We can speculate that a dowry might have facilitated her marriage or, looked at from another angle, curtailed her independence. The other five families with small estates that did not give dowries had much less property than João, and the scarcity of their assets undoubtedly determined their decision.

The existence of a small number of property-owning families that allowed their daughters to marry empty-handed was itself a change from the practice a hundred years before. No daughter of proprietors in seventeenth-century São Paulo married without property, for, as we saw above, *all* families in the sample either endowed their daughters or had them marry with their inheritance.[61]

Most eighteenth-century Paulista property owners continued to give dowries, even if they were not quite as large as those of the preceding century. In the seventeenth century, the dowry of every married daughter in a family was usually much larger than the *legítima*. Though many dowries are listed in *inventários*, most married daughters refused to inherit, so that we do not know the monetary value of both the dowry and the *legítima* except in five cases, which were not necessarily of the largest dowry given in the family. In those five cases, the average dowry was 250 percent of the *legítima*. In the eighteenth century, on the other hand, while dowries were still sizable, in each family usually only one or at the most two married daughters received dowries of greater value than their *legítima*. Using the value of the largest dowry given by each family in the sample, I found that their average size was one and one half the daughter's subsequent *legítima*. However, the richer the estate, as mea-

60. João Fernandes da Costa, 1750, *AESP*, INP #ord. 523 c. 46. His net estate, minus the half belonging to his widow, was worth 255$600, while the net estate of the widower José Rodrigues Pereira was worth 14:632$500, the largest in the sample.

61. Of course, people could acquire property more easily in the seventeenth century than in the following one. A man could acquire Indians by going on a bandeira with an arrangement to receive a percentage of the captives. There was plenty of unoccupied land to settle on, and after a man had acquired a few Indians and married, he could apply for a grant of land from the crown, a *sesmaria*.

sured by the number of slaves owned, the smaller the proportion of the *legítima* represented by the largest dowry.[62] And in none of the *inventários* of my eighteenth-century sample were there disparities such as that between Maria Leite's dowry worth 80$000 in 1633 and her siblings' inheritance of only 2$098 each.

Because eighteenth-century dowries were relatively not as large as in the seventeenth century, most married daughters did not refuse to inherit but instead brought their dowries back into the estate, *à colação*. In over 60 percent of the families of the sample all married daughters brought their dowries *à colação*, while another 16 percent had some daughters coming in *à colação*. This meant that in only 22 percent of eighteenth-century families did all endowed daughters refuse to inherit, compared to 90 percent in the preceding century[63] (see Table II).

This change was one of practice, for the law had not been altered. Despite allowing heirs to decline the inheritance, the code limited the right of parents to favor one child over others with a dowry or gift. Heirs who refused to inherit could be obliged to repay their siblings if the dowry or gift had been larger than the *legítima* plus the *terça* (the third of the estate the parent was allowed to dispose of freely).[64] The underlying assumption was that a parent had the right to dispose only of his or her *terça* to favor a child and should not favor any one child to the detriment of all others.

Seventeenth-century Paulistas did not usually put this part of the law into practice, though they were well aware of it.[65] In this regard, they put the patriarchal privilege of arranging marriages before the equality among heirs. In the seventeenth century, daughters were favored excessively and then permitted to refuse to inherit so that they need not return

---

62. The average dowry was 147 percent of the *legítima* in the whole sample (47 estates in which their value and the number of slaves are known), 97 percent in families with more than ten slaves, 131 percent in families owning four to nine slaves, and 163 percent in families with fewer than four slaves.

63. Moreover, the eighteenth-century practice established a trend, for by the nineteenth century there were no cases in my sample of daughters refusing to inherit; the practice had completely disappeared. A nineteenth-century jurist, T. de Freitas, confirms the trend, declaring in a note to *Ordenações*, liv. 4, tit. 97, article 119 that people no longer were using the right given by the law to refuse to inherit; everyone brought dowries or gifts back *à colação*.

Spanish law must have had a procedure similar to *colação*, because it also required that a dowry be subtracted from the *legítima* (Law XXVI of Toro). See Lavrin and Couturier, "Dowries and Wills," 286, n. 19.

64. This third is in fact one-sixth of the community property owned jointly by both spouses. *Ordenações*, livro 4, tit. 97, para. 3. A nineteenth-century jurist, Coelho da Rocha, explains that the purpose of *colação* was to preserve equality between children in relation to their parents' estate, only allowing parents the free disposition of one-third of their estate. See *Ordenações*, liv. 4, tit. 97, para. 1, p. 968, n. 4.

65. See Messia Rodrigues, 1665, *IT*, XVII.

anything to their siblings. And even if the dowry had not been fully paid, daughters and their husbands retained the advantage because the debt was discounted from the gross estate before the *legítima* of their brothers and sisters was even calculated.

Eighteenth-century Paulistas, in contrast, frequently litigated to see that the law was followed scrupulously, suggesting that the equal rights of all heirs were becoming more important than the right of parents to arrange marriages.[66] The case of Maria de Lima de Siqueira illustrates the system used in the eighteenth century when a married daughter refused to inherit.[67] Maria was a widow with six married daughters. The two eldest had married during their father's lifetime, and when he died they had refused to inherit, doing the same thing when their mother died. Each of these dowries was worth over two contos (2:000$000) and exceeded the sum of the paternal and maternal *legítimas* by 462$346 and 300$364 respectively. We get an idea of the worth of these amounts when we consider that the average price of a slave in the sample was 68$000, and the average price of a house in town was 168$000. Because they refused to inherit, the *terça* was brought into the picture. Starting with the first dowry given, the *legítima* was subtracted from the dowry and the resulting difference was deducted from the *terça*. Both dowries of Maria's eldest daughters fit into their *legítimas* plus the *terça*. When the dowry was so large that the *terça* did not cover the difference, however, the daughter and her husband—or even their heirs, if the daughter and son-in-law predeceased their parents—were expected to make up the difference to her siblings.

Increasingly strict adherence to the *Ordenações* in eighteenth-century São Paulo limited the rights of parents to dispose of their property as they wished. In effect, they could no longer give lavish dowries but had to consider the size of their *terça* and whether it would be enough to hold the excess between the dowry and *legítima*. And if they gave large dowries, they also knew that their *terça* would be diminished and would not hold as many bequests as they might want to make.

People well understood the consequences of bringing a large dowry back into the estate. When Manoel Pacheco Gato died in 1715, his heirs

66. *Inventários* with litigation: Captain Antonio Rodrigues de Medeiros, 1764, *AESP*, INP #ord. 542 c. 65; Manoel João de Oliveira, 1760, *AESP*, INP #ord. 537 c. 60; Suzanna Rodrigues de Arzão, 1754, *AESP*, INP #ord. 542 c. 55; Maria Leite de Barros, 1773, *AESP*, INP #ord. 550 c. 73; João do Prado de Asevedo, 1790, *AESP*, Inv. 1° Of. #ord. 693 c. 81; João Machado da Silva, 1756, *AESP*, INP #ord. 533 c. 56; Ignacio Correa de Lemos, 1787, *AESP*, Inv. 1° Of. #14.768; and Anna Pires de Barros, 1750, *AESP*, INP #ord. 523 c. 46.

67. Maria de Lima de Siqueira, 1769, *AESP*, INP #ord. 545 c. 68. Because of the accounting process involved, both kinds of dowries had to be appraised. Contrary to the situation in the seventeenth century, therefore, we know the value of all eighteenth-century dowries in the sample.

included a married daughter, two single daughters, and five single sons, one of them a Franciscan friar. The heirs agreed among themselves that it was best if the married daughter did not come in *à colação*. One of their main arguments, which convinced the judge, was that not having her bring the dowry back into the estate would protect the two single daughters who had received a bequest of the *remanescente*. If the dowry did not come back into the estate, it would not be deducted from the *remanescente* and the sisters would receive it entire.[68] All heirs, however, would receive a smaller *legítima*, because the amount of the dowry was not added to the net estate before the equal division among heirs. Here, as in the early seventeenth century, brothers were sacrificing themselves for their sisters (both the married and the single ones), and preference was being given to the intentions of the patriarch.

Even in the seventeenth century, however, some sons had tried to rebel at such seeming inequity. For example, Manoel João Branco's eldest daughter, Anna Leme, received half a ship for the trade to Angola in dowry. When Manoel João died, his only son, Francisco João Leme, tried to have the ship appraised in a vain effort to equalize his inheritance with his sister's dowry. If he could have made her come in *à colação*, she would have owed him money.[69] Instead, his sister's rights were given priority. She was paid, at least on paper, the amount that was still owed her on her dowry even before the estate was divided to give their mother her half. Besides receiving the part of her dowry that was still unpaid, Anna received the *remanescente* when her mother died. All along, Francisco João had been slighted in favor of his sister and brother-in-law. His frustration is evident in his continuous litigation against his mother and, after her death, his sister; he even went so far as to steal and kill their cattle. It is significant, however, that Francisco João did not do these things while his father, the patriarch, was still alive, though it had been his father's decision to give such a large dowry to Anna and her husband.

The decline in respect for a patriarch's wishes led to more frequent court battles over inheritance. When parents favored their daughters with excessively large dowries, siblings, with the aid of lawyers and judges, litigated so that the law was followed strictly, discounting from the *terça* the difference between the dowry and the *legítima*. Considering that in the seventeenth century daughters were privileged vis-à-vis sons, and the tendency continued, though to a lesser degree, in the eighteenth century, we can see the legal battle for equality as a battle of brothers against their sisters. And since the privilege of daughters was based on the parents'

68. Manoel Pacheco Gato, 1715, *IT*, XXVI, 469.
69. Manoel João Branco, 1645, *IT*, XIII; Maria Leme, 1663, *IT*, XIII.

view of what was best for the family, the eighteenth-century battles for sibling equality can also be seen as a claim for the rights of individuals—sons—over the right of the patriarch and his wife or widow to decide what was best for the family.

Even in the seventeenth century, parents had been conscious of the possibility that after their death their sons would attempt to right the injustice they felt had been done, which may be why Constantino Coelho Leite enlisted his sons' agreement to the large dowries he gave his daughters and included that information within his will, a legal and religious document that had to be respected. Pero Nunes in his 1623 will called down his curse on any son who dared to contest his only daughter's possession of the things he had given her during his lifetime.[70] Eighteenth-century parents no longer had such power over their sons.

Since parents were constrained from giving excessively large dowries to their daughters in marriage, it was no longer as much a buyer's market for the bride as in the preceding century. The marriage bargain was changing. This development is corroborated by the eighteenth-century genealogist, Frei Gaspar da Madre de Deus, who maintained that Paulistas could no longer afford to give such large dowries as they had in the preceding century. He attributed the change to the enforcement of laws prohibiting the captivity and administration of Indians, commenting that the wealth of seventeenth-century families had allowed them to be more interested in a prospective son-in-law's birth than in his fortune, whereas his contemporaries had to first consider a son-in-law's fortune.[71]

Frei Gaspar thus bemoaned the passing of the grand old age when it was a buyer's market for propertied families with marriageable daughters, which could pick the suitors and impose the terms of marriage. Their options were more limited than in the preceding century, because they could no longer afford to provide all the means of production and labor necessary for the support of the couple; hence they tried to marry their daughters to wealthy men.

A study of the rate of remarriage of widows and widowers confirms this change in the marriage market. A. J. R. Russell-Wood's study of 165 published seventeenth-century São Paulo wills demonstrates the tendency of women to remarry more than men: 16 percent of the female testators had married more than once, while only 11 percent of the males had done so.[72] The percentage of women in my seventeenth-century sample who had married more than once was much higher, 39 percent versus 17 per-

---

70. Pero Nunes, 1623, *IT*, VI, 59.
71. Frei Gaspar da Madre de Deus, *Memórias para a história de São Vicente, hoje llamada de São Paulo* (São Paulo, 1953) 83–84.
72. Russell-Wood, "Women and Society," 19.

66o | HAHR | NOVEMBER | MURIEL NAZZARI

TABLE III: Men and Women in Sample Who Married More Than Once

Century	Deceased women	Married more than once	Deceased men	Married more than once
17th	18	7 (39%)	30	5 (17%)
18th	32	5 (16%)	36	9 (25%)

Source: sample.

cent for men (see Table III). The higher percentage of remarriage for both sexes in my sample is probably due to its being by definition composed of the parents of married daughters, mostly middle-aged and therefore with a greater chance of having remarried. The marriage market had changed by the middle of the eighteenth century, for widows no longer remarried more frequently than widowers. The proportion of men who married more than once in my sample rose from 17 percent to 25 percent, while the proportion of women marrying more than once declined precipitously, from 39 percent in the seventeenth century to 16 percent in the eighteenth.[73]

Since all the widows of the sample were by definition property owners, I would argue that their declining rate of remarriage is due to a change in the male's need to have property to marry, that is, a change in the marriage bargain. Propertied widows remarried in such large numbers in the seventeenth century precisely because men at the time needed to receive property from their wives to be able to establish themselves, creating a buyer's market for women with assets.[74] Since fewer widows remarried in the first half of the eighteenth century, we can assume that a widow's property was no longer sufficient inducement for a man to marry her.

Besides giving their daughters relatively smaller dowries, eighteenth-century Paulistas appear to have been helping all their children to a

73. A study by Marcílio shows the same tendency. She examined marriage registers in the Sé parish of São Paulo for the period 1728 to 1770, and found that 9.6 percent of the men were remarrying versus only 8 percent of the women; 887 marriages were studied. See Marcílio, *A cidade de São Paulo*, 166. The trend for fewer and fewer widows to remarry intensified in the nineteenth century, for only 10 percent of the female deceased in my sample had married more than once.

74. The seventeenth-century São Paulo pattern of more women than men remarrying appears to be very unusual. Studies of certain communities in France and Bavaria in Europe in the seventeenth and eighteenth centuries and in the United States in the early nineteenth century show that there is an inverse relationship between age at widowhood and the proportion of widows who remarry, and a much lower remarriage rate for women than for men except among the very young. At the same time, there appeared to be no direct or inverse correlation between remarriage and wealth. See Susan Grigg, "Toward a Theory of Remarriage: A Case Study of Newburyport at the Beginning of the Nineteenth Century," in *Marriage and Fertility: Studies in Interdisciplinary History*, Robert I. Rotberg and Theodore K. Rabb, eds. (Princeton, 1980).

greater extent than in the seventeenth century. The percentage of families that had given gifts to sons other than priests almost doubled, going from 9 percent in the seventeenth century to 17 percent in the eighteenth. The percentage of families who loaned money to sons doubled, and that of families who loaned to married daughters and their husbands also increased. And parents continued to allow their adult offspring, especially their sons, to use their slaves and land.

The fact that children generally, but especially sons, were receiving more help from their parents than a hundred years before inevitably diminished the particular advantage daughters had had. In this pattern it is probable that families were reacting to the difficult situation in São Paulo's agriculture in the early eighteenth century. Money was only being made in the gold mines of Minas Gerais, Goiás, or Cuiabá, or else by merchants supplying those mines. Sons needed help to emigrate to the mines, and parents increasingly outfitted them with a horse and saddle, a rifle, and, if possible, a slave or two.[75] In fact, as dowries became smaller, many sons received gifts of property equivalent to their sisters' dowries, such as the sons of Mariana Machado who all received approximately what their sisters did, except for the somewhat larger dowry of their eldest sister.[76]

The economic contribution of the marriage partners also changed by the middle of the eighteenth century. The daughters of seventeenth-century Paulista property owners had married either penniless Portuguese newcomers or family friends or relatives who contributed less property to the marriage than their wives. In the eighteenth century, in contrast, the new opportunities to accumulate capital through commerce strengthened the position of merchants as future bridegrooms, thereby changing the pool of suitors, which led to a pattern in which husbands contributed more than their wives to the couple's property.

Alida Metcalf concluded that eighteenth-century families chose one or several daughters to be favored, and that these daughters and their husbands took the place of their parents in the community, while their siblings either emigrated or suffered downward mobility. She studied the number of slaves owned by the children of several families of Parnaíba, first in the records of dowries and inheritance received and then in several succeeding censuses, finding that daughters who had received large dowries consistently showed up in later censuses with more slaves than

75. Some *inventários* in which parents outfitted sons were Domingos Lopes de Oliveira, 1766, *AESP*, INP #ord. 544 c. 67; Catharina Ribeiro, 1757, *AESP*, INP #ord. 533 c. 56; Maria de Araujo, 1755, *AESP*, INP #ord. 535 c. 58; Salvador Lopes de Medeiro, 1760, *AESP*, INP #ord. 537 c. 60; Bartholomeu de Quadros, 1722, *IT*, XXVI, 271.

76. Mariana Machado, 1759, *AESP*, INP #ord. 537 c. 59. Also see Bras Leme do Prado e Maria Domingues de Mattos, 1751, *AESP*, INP #ord. 525 c. 48; and Joanna da Cunha, 1766, *AESP*, INP #ord. 544 c. 67.

their brothers.[77] This result could only have come about, however, because the sons in those families had not been able to find wives with dowries as large as their sisters'. The situation was therefore opposite to that of the seventeenth century. As shown above, seventeenth-century men married women who initially brought more to the marriage than they did. Even if daughters were favored, their brothers could make up their disadvantage by marrying women with equivalent dowries. In the eighteenth century, this was no longer the case, for though many dowries were sizable and daughters still tended to be favored over sons, parents now expected a son-in-law to contribute more to the marriage than their daughter contributed. This meant that parents' initial favoring of daughters resulted in permanent advantage for them, since sons encountered similar expectations which prevented them from marrying women with dowries as large as their sisters'. The situation brought about an imbalance between siblings that probably contributed to the increased litigation visible in eighteenth-century *inventários*.

The case of three of Maria de Lima de Siqueira's children demonstrates the new marriage bargain in which men contributed more property to the couple's fortune than did their wives (see Table IV). Her two married daughters and their husbands had fortunes two and a half and five and a half times as large as their brother's. Though the daughters contributed more to their marriages than the eldest son, the disparity is too small to account for the difference in their fortunes. The difference must lie in the daughter-in-law's smaller dowry and in the men's methods of accumulation.

Both sons-in-law engaged in trade, though Captain Ignacio Soares de Barros, the husband of Maria's fourth daughter, Martha de Camargo Lima, was also an important planter. He owned 81 slaves and had a partnership for the transportation of horses from Curitiba. In her dowry she only brought 1:982$194 to their community property which was worth 6:617$194 in 1759. The rest was therefore property her husband contributed, whether he had inherited it or acquired it through business.

The fortune of Maria's eldest daughter, Maria de Lima de Camargo, is an even clearer illustration of the tendency for husbands to take more property to marriage than their wives, especially if they were merchants. She married a merchant and pharmacist who died only six years after their marriage, leaving a fortune seven times her dowry and more than twice the size of her sister and brother-in-law's fortune. Since their dowries were approximately the same size, the simplest explanation for the dif-

77. Alida Metcalf, "Fathers and Sons: The Politics of Inheritance in a Colonial Brazilian Township," *HAHR*, 66:3 (Aug. 1986), 476–78.

CHANGES IN DOWRY IN SÃO PAULO (1600–1770)   663

TABLE IV: Comparison Among the Estates of Three Heirs of Maria de Lima de Siqueira

	Amount received from parents	Net estate with spouse
Joseph Ortiz de Camargo Lima (d. 1785), eldest son		
Paternal *legítima* (1742)	884$254	
Maternal *legítima* (1769)	872$092	
His mother's bequest to his wife	45$000	
Total:	1:801$346	2:656$933
Licenciado Manoel José da Cunha (d. 1746), husband of Maria de Lima de Camargo, eldest daughter		
Her dowry, received 1740	2:218$640	14:829$388
Captain Ignacio Soares de Barros (d. 1759), husband of Martha de Camargo Lima, 4th daughter		
Her paternal *legítima* (1742)	884$254	
Her share of the *remanescente* left by her father to his four single daughters	605$581	
Her dowry (given by mother alone)	492$340	
Total:	1:982$175	6:617$194

Sources: Maria de Lima de Siqueira, 1769, *AESP*, INP #ord. 545 c. 68; Joseph Ortiz de Camargo, 1785, *AESP*, INP #ord. 689, c. 77; Licenciado Manoel José da Cunha, 1746, *AESP*, Inv. 1° Of. #14.123; Ignacio Soares de Barros, 1759, *AESP*, Inv. 1° Of. #14.328.

ference between the sisters' fortunes is the amount contributed by their husbands, whether initially or as they plied their business.

Their brother, Joseph Ortiz de Camargo Lima, left an estate roughly one-fourth the size of Maria's fortune and half the size of Martha's. Since the amount of the inheritance he took to his marriage was almost the same amount as what his sisters took to theirs, it is likely that the difference in their property was due not only to the fact that as full-time or part-time merchants his brothers-in-law made much larger contributions to their marriages, but also that his wife must have brought a smaller dowry or no dowry. To be sure, another factor may have been that he was a farmer at a time when farming was not very profitable (his principal property appears to have been his parents' farm in which he cultivated cane to distill rum).

Thus, though siblings inherited or received in dowry approximately equal amounts of property, it was now common for sisters to marry up economically and brothers to marry down.[78] The fortune of a daughter

78. The children of the merchant Thomé Alves de Crasto are also a good example of the continuing inequality brought about by the changing marriage bargain. Thomé died at 85 in 1772. Through his *inventário*, we know the value of his daughters' dowries and the gifts he made in his lifetime to his sons; we can make a good estimate of what their maternal *legítima*

who received a dowry was therefore no longer, as in the seventeenth century, a function of her dowry. Not only did her husband usually contribute much more property than her dowry contained, but his entrepreneurial ability also made a difference. This was especially true when women married merchants, for they appear to have consistently experienced great upward mobility in the eighteenth century. The best example is that of Anna de Oliveira, who married Lieutenant José Rodrigues Pereira. Her dowry had consisted of one male slave in his prime and some jewels, two gold chains, and a ring, for a total of 198$400.[79] Yet, many years later, Pereira reported an estate worth 28:000$000 to the census.[80] Their large property had obviously not been created on the basis of her dowry.[81]

The favoring of daughters with large dowries or bequests had functioned well to reproduce the propertied class according to the patriarch's design—as long as sons were able to marry women with dowries as large as their sisters'. But the marriage market changed with the addition of a growing number of Portuguese merchants to the pool of would-be sons-in-law. Merchants could accumulate capital mainly through their own entrepreneurial skills, giving them leverage in the marriage bargain, not only because of their wealth but because they did not *need*, as planters did, to receive property in dowry to establish a productive enterprise. When in the seventeenth century the parents of the bride had offered in dowry everything a couple required to start a productive unit, theirs was the greater strength in the marriage negotiations. In the eighteenth century, merchants were able to marry women with comparatively small dowries and choose their brides for other considerations than a dowry, thereby altering the bargain in their favor. Parents therefore lost some of the control they had previously enjoyed over their daughters' marriages.

The introduction of merchants into the pool of suitors for the daughters of property owners naturally changed the expectations of parents.

---

had been, and through the censuses of 1765 and 1767 we know the declared capital of two sons and two daughters. Thomé's two daughters had undergone upward mobility, for the fortunes they declared to the census takers were, for the second daughter, twice as large as her dowry, and, for the third, four times as large. His sons had remained at his level at best, for one declared property one-tenth the size of his maternal inheritance (underdeclaring to the census taker was common), while the second declared approximately the same amount as his inheritance.

79. Escolastica Vellozo, 1753, *AESP*, INP #ord. 530 c. 53.

80. 1767 Census in *Documentos interessantes para a história e costumes de São Paulo* (São Paulo, 1895–), LXII, 268.

81. She had, however, contributed something else to the marriage that was more important to a merchant than a dowry, for both her stepfather and her maternal grandfather were merchants, providing him with a network of merchant relatives and an entry into one of the founding families. See Manoel Vellozo, 1752, *AESP*, INP #ord. 528 c. 51. Also see the Maciel family in Silva Leme, *Genealogia*, VIII, 167 ff.

CHANGES IN DOWRY IN SÃO PAULO (1600–1770)   665

With the possibility of marrying daughters to wealthy merchants, parents now expected a son-in-law to make a contribution to marriage that was significantly greater than the dowry his wife would receive. It therefore became difficult for men who were not merchants to continue, as in the seventeenth century, marrying women with dowries larger than their own property. To put the matter differently, men married down economically while their sisters married up. The resulting lifetime inequality between married brothers and sisters not only led heirs to litigate against their parents' right to favor daughters excessively, but undoubtedly modified what parents themselves thought was right, so that they decreased the size of dowries and aided their sons during their lifetime more frequently than in the preceding century. The rise of commerce as a way to wealth based less on the ownership of capital than on entrepreneurial skills—that is, human capital—thus changed the marriage bargain and the practice of dowry.

2

The Church and the Patriarchal Family: Marriage Conflicts in Sixteenth- and Seventeenth-Century New Spain

Patricia Seed

Abstract: Traditional European families have long been presumed to be characterized by parental control over their children's choices of a marriage partner; a control aided by the support of the Catholic church. This essay focuses on the role of the Catholic church in family conflicts over marriage in the Spanish New World colony of Mexico. It demonstrates that the Spanish Catholic church not only failed to support parental authority over their offspring's marriages but that it intervened decisively to prevent families from interfering in the young couple's decision to marry. The Spanish Catholic church's actions stemmed from a strong commitment to traditional Catholic orthodox views on matrimonial freedom as well as from a cultural heritage opposing marriages for social or economic gain.

Marriage in traditional society usually has been seen as a course of action motivated by economic or political considerations and controlled by parents. While recent historical scholarship has chipped away at the first generalization by insisting upon including love as well as money as a basis for marriage, our basic vision of the role of parents in marriage choices has been supported by historical research. Parents selected or vetoed marriage partners throughout France, England, and many of the German principalities during the sixteenth and seventeenth centuries, the era of the traditional family (Shorter, 1975; Stone, 1977; Flandrin, 1979; Gottlieb, 1980; Ozment, 1983). An influential role has also been attributed to fathers in the Anglo-American colonies during this same period (Morgan, 1966; Smith, 1978). Because of evidence from these three fundamentally European cultures, historians have assumed that other European countries had similar traditions supporting the role of parents in "traditional" families.[1]

One institution thought to have reinforced the authority of parents over marriage is the Roman Catholic church. From studies of the Catholic areas of Western Europe, notably France, the support of the church for parental control of marriage has come to be regarded as the accepted wisdom. There are grounds, however, to question this assumption. The Council of Trent reaffirmed the orthodox Catholic definition of marriage as the consent of the couple. These decrees, however, were not promulgated initially in France because the council had refused to require parental consent to marry despite intensive lobbying by the French

Research for this essay was supported by Fulbright and Social Science Research Council fellowships and the National Endowment for the Humanities.

[1]A tentative and incomplete exception is Donahue (1983).

Fall, 1985   JOURNAL OF FAMILY HISTORY   285

delegation (Esmein, II, 1929:157–95). As a result, the king of France not only refused outright to allow the decrees of Trent to be issued, but instead issued laws mandating parental consent for marriage. When French bishops complained, King Henry III in theory allowed marriages without parental consent in 1579, in accord with the decrees of Trent. But, he added, such marriages would be defined as rape and the penalty for them was death (Esmein, II, 1929:194, 283–84; Traer, 1980:33–34). Not only was the spirit of Trent rejected, but the official Catholic decrees on marriage were nullified. Hence the French position was far from representative of orthodox Catholic policy.

Spanish Catholic officials, on the other hand, accepted the decrees of Trent as the true Catholic doctrine of marriage. As the head of the Counter Reformation Spain was dedicated to fighting the Protestant threat; including any doctrine that contained elements of Protestantism. Parental consent for marriage was not required by Catholic tradition, and was rejected by Trent. On the other hand, parental consent was adopted by Protestants, and embraced by Protestant leaders (Joyce, 1948: 178–81). The lines were clearly drawn.

In later decades, Spanish officials, for their part, accused French Catholics of heresy for their failure to adhere to the orthodox norm of free individual consent as set forth by the Council of Trent (Camargo, 1636). In the late sixteenth and early seventeenth centuries Spanish Catholics pointed with pride to their orthodox beliefs regarding the freedom to marry, and the primacy of individual consent. As one of the most popular religious manuals of seventeenth-century Spain observed, "Parents cannot force their children to marry, nor impede (veto) their marriages, because in this matter they are *sui juris*" (Villalobos, 1682:trat. 13 dif. 38

n. 3; Ripodas Ardanaz, 1977:223–34, 259–62; Gil Delgado, 1961:345–78). A clearly different environment therefore existed in the Hispanic world with respect to both parental authority and the role of the Catholic church.

This article will examine the limits of parental authority over marriage in the traditional New World colony of New Spain. In examining existing evidence, traditional sixteenth- and seventeenth-century Hispanic society contrasts sharply with those of France, England, and the German principalities; these societies endorsed parental control over offsprings' marriages. Furthermore, unlike the French Catholic church, the Spanish Catholic church in the New World not only failed to support parental attempts at exercising control but frequently intervened outright to prevent parental interference. The difference between the role of the church in France and its role in New Spain, one of Spain's most important colonies in the New World, stemmed not only from a greater adherence to Catholic orthodoxy in Spain but also from a fundamental disparity in social and cultural values.

In sixteenth- and seventeenth-century Hispanic society, honor, if not *the* supreme social value, was of paramount importance for social respect and consideration. For women, honor signified premarital chastity and postnuptial fidelity. Any such transgression as premarital sex and pregnancy would then result in a loss of honor and social disgrace. Because of its cultural significance, honor took precedence even over the wishes of parents. Sexual relations were thus an effective means to pressure families into accepting a marriage.

The area for which the practices and attitudes of the Spanish Catholic church have been examined was the New World colony of New Spain. The archdiocese of

286   JOURNAL OF FAMILY HISTORY   Fall, 1985

Mexico, centered in Mexico City, was chosen for study by virtue of its centrality and importance. The archbishops of this diocese were often influential Spanish prelates who later headed dioceses in the old country (Cuevas, 1946–47, III:139–40; IV:113, 120). The archdiocesan court in Mexico City was also the court of appeals for cases from other dioceses in the territory. As a geographic unit, the archdiocese included not only the city of Mexico and its immediate vicinity, but portions of present-day surrounding states of Hidalgo, Guerrero, Tlaxcala, Queretaro, and Veracruz, the heart of the viceroyalty's most prosperous agricultural and mining regions (Shiels, 1961; Vasquez de Espinosa, 1969:lib. 3 cap. 23 no. 464; Lopez de Velasco, 1971:96–106).

To study the role of the Catholic church in limiting parents' control over marriage choices, two large bodies of evidence were examined: all the records of the archdiocesan court relating to marriage questions for the archdiocese of Mexico from 1560 until 1690, and all initial applications for a marriage made in the Spanish and racially mixed parishes of Mexico City between 1575 and 1690 (AGN, Matrimonios; Clero Regular y Secular; Bienes Nacionales; Archivo del Provisorato). Every couple seeking to marry was required to make an initial declaration to the parish priest concerning their eligibility to marry, and also had to provide witnesses who could to attest to this eligibility. Approximately 8,000 such applications survive.[2] *All* these petitions were ex-

amined in order to find out which cases contained evidence of a family conflict. These cases did not constitute a separate or special category of marriage petitions but are randomly distributed throughout the records, thus making it necessary actually to read every application. These petitions contain the first evidence of conflict, since in the course of taking information the young couple had been asked or had volunteered information that members of their family were trying to prevent their union. Few of these incidences ever became formal lawsuits or even civil or criminal cases during the sixteenth and seventeenth centuries, and so provide a much broader picture of the range and complexity of family conflicts over potential marriage partners.

Of all the marriage petitions in this period, 379 (about 5 percent of the total) contained evidence of opposition by family members to the match. Relatively few marriages, therefore, produced insoluable disagreement within families. What such conflicts do illustrate, however, are the limits of the authority of both sides, and perhaps more important, the reaction of both community and religious officials to such dissension.

Most of the conflicts uncovered in the marriage petitions and church court records came from what might be called the upper half of colonial society: Spanish families in conflict with other Spanish families. A few were racially mixed, and a small number of conflicts—less than 6 percent—involved interracial marriages. About two-thirds of this group were moderately to very wealthy and included titled families as well as prosperous farmers and merchants. The remaining third of the group consisted of much

---

[2]While not used in this present paper, I also studied all the extant marriage applications from two of the city's Indian parishes as well as applications from the Spanish and racially mixed parishes of Mexico City from 1690 until 1820, the close of the colonial period. The records of all civil and criminal suits in ecclesiastical court were also examined for the same time period. The material selected thus covers nearly all the surviving records of marriage petitions for the Spanish and racially mixed popula-

tion of Mexico City from the sixteenth and seventeenth centuries, as well as all the surviving civil and criminal suits in archdiocesan courts from the same period.

Fall, 1985   JOURNAL OF FAMILY HISTORY   287

humbler people: artisans, muleteers, shoemakers, domestic servants, and even a small proportion of slaves.[3]

It is not surprising to learn that conflicts over marriage would more greatly concern the upper half of colonial society than the lower half. Marriage itself in colonial Mexico was far more frequent at the top and at the bottom of society than in between. The Indians at the bottom of the social hierarchy were more closely supervised by priests and hence married frequently. The racially mixed individuals who occupied an intermediate social position, between blacks and Indians on the one hand and Spaniards on the other, were less closely monitored by friars or secular clergy. For them, concubinage (or what today would be called "living together") became the solution to familial opposition. The number of illegitimate births occurring (one very rough measure of the extent of nonmarital unions among the racially mixed group) was extremely high for this group—about 50 percent during most of the seventeenth century.

Marriage was also more frequent among the wealthy, who needed the legitimacy provided by marriage in order to receive income from the family or to inherit property. Any expectation of support from parents or relatives would be lost if a couple chose to live together without benefit of matrimony, and the couple might have difficulty in making ends meet. Furthermore, any children born of such a union would be ineligible for the substantial inheritances that went to legitimate children of a marriage. Conflict with one's parents or relatives within the top half of colonial society was thus more

likely to pit two sides against each other, since the children of the wealthy were more determined to marry. That is not to say that the poorer members of colonial society did not equally want to marry. Many of them did, but the wealthier individuals had greater numbers of options in seeking support for their matrimonial aims.

Reasons for the conflicts within families over marriage partners were wide and varied. Testimony on the exact source of the conflict was provided by the witnesses (friends, relatives, or reputable members of the community) who accompanied the couple to ecclesiastical court or to the offices of the parish priest. These witnesses denounced the parents, other relatives, or even employers for what they often saw as "unjust interference" in the marriage plans of a young couple. In other words, young people seeking to marry were frequently able to obtain the support of their friends, relatives, and even influential leaders in the community against the wishes of their parents.

What these witnesses saw as "unjust interference" fell into three major categories. Fully one-third of all the conflicts within families over marriages were rooted in economic differences. As might be expected, wealthy families vigorously objected to their sons marrying women of lesser wealth. Witnesses for a couple in such cases found status-oriented ambitions on the part of parents uniformly objectionable. So, too, did witnesses find the greed of parents or relatives to retain control of an inheritance.

In one case, Don Gerónimo Vargas was heir to an entailed estate left him by his father. Before his death, the father remarried and left the entail to his widow until Gerónimo married or came of age. At 22, Don Gerónimo decided to marry an 18-year-old Spanish girl named Doña Catalina Villalobos. Realizing that the in-

---

[3]The comparison was made between the occupational distribution (insofar as it was available) for the marriage petitioners and the only census of colonial Mexico City to show the occupational distribution for the city. The census exists only in summary form in AGN, Historia, vol. 523.

come from the entail would·be lost to her should Gerónimo marry Catalina, the stepmother tried to force Gerónimo into marrying her own sister's daughter and thus keep the entail in the family. Gerónimo resisted, and with the assistance of friends who testified as to the stepmother's greed and the ecclesiastical court, Gerónimo overcame the resistance of his stepmother to marry Catalina (AGN, Archivo del Provisorato, caja 20).

Parents who wanted their son or daughter to marry for money were also considered objectionable. Lope de Vega (1918:59) most poetically criticized this common parental attitude in "Amigo hasta la muerte," that to have one's daughter marry for money was "to sell her, . . . and not at a fair price."

Juana Moreno came from a comfortable Spanish family in Mexico City. Her father wanted her to marry a wealthy man, preferably someone twice her age and with an established fortune. Juana, who was only age 15, wished to marry someone closer to her own age and she did not wish to marry for money. She wished to marry Juan de Monguiar. Her father would not be swayed, so Juana and Juan eloped. Despite the unmistakable opposition of her father, church officials allowed the pair secretly to marry, and did not notify her father (AGN, Matrimonios, vol. 88, fols. 339ff.). The church's assistance reinforced social values on two levels. It reasserted the authority of individual choice over parental issues, and second, it protected the honor of the young woman. The code of honor thus indirectly forced parents to accept less wealthy sons and daughters-in-law than they might have wanted.

Social and personal reasons were sources of another third of all familial conflicts over marriage partners. Parents tried to prevent marriages when they wanted their offspring to enter the priesthood or a nunnery. Others were merely domineering or tyrannical personalities who viewed their offspring as extensions of themselves and thus saw their children's individual personalities, interests, or aims as of little consequence. Such parents came in for equally harsh judgment by their contemporaries who saw such behavior as malicious interference in the selection of a marriage partner. Such attitudes differ widely from those found in France or England at this time, in which tyrannical and domineering parents found not only the society but the law itself on their side.[4]

In the remaining cases no source of conflict—social, personal, or economic—could be found. Instead the witnesses objected to the extreme measures families used to attempt to force their offspring to desist or to marry someone else. Viewed as unwarranted and unreasonable interference were such actions as beatings, threats, locking the young person up at home or in a convent, or jailing. In over half the cases (including those for which there were other motives as well) witnesses attested to the use of unreasonable force. Spanish Catholic canonists, in the wake of the Council of Trent, laid down clear guidelines for the extent of parental authority over their offsprings' marriages. Parents might counsel, advise, and even warn children about making a marriage, but they were not to exercise force (beating, jailing) or to induce fear (threats). When parents resorted to force, they then had exceeded the limits of their authority (Azpilcueta, 1570; Rodríguez Lusitano, 1597:cap. 224 no. 3; Sanchez, 1636:"metus" nos. 8, 9, 13, 15; Noonan, 1973; Chatham, 1950; Sangmeister, 1932; Sheehan, 1978; Gil Delgado, 1961). Anti-

---

[4]In France, the law was on the side of the parents (Esmein, II, 1929:194, 283-84; Traer, 1980) and in England there was little public support for such attitudes (Stone, 1977; Joyce, 1948:82).

Fall, 1985   JOURNAL OF FAMILY HISTORY   289

pathy to the use of force was clearly and frequently expressed in testimony of hundreds of witnesses in colonial New Spain.

One afternoon in 1628 in Mexico City, six armed men on horseback appeared at the residence of 21-year-old Ana Maria Vargas, banged on the door, and shouted that she would die before her fiance, Alonso Delgado, could enjoy her. (Why they were so antagonistic to this match was never clear.) Then, galloping toward the nearby church of San Pablo, the six men, all Ana Maria's male relatives, spied Alonso Delgado walking down the street. They charged, but soon a large group of the young couple's friends and neighbors swarmed around the horsemen and forced them to retreat. Alonso in the meantime managed to slip through a nearby patio and escape. The next morning, Alonso, accompanied by a parade of witnesses—neighbors, friends, and even passers-by who had witnessed the threats against Alonso and Ana Maria—testified in the local church court. The willingness of friends, family, and neighbors to intervene, and to testify against the unreasonable exercise of force being used against this young couple, illustrates the degree to which antipathy to the use of force was a public, community matter, a violation of commonly held norms and values (AGN, Matrimonios, vol. 48, exp. 122).

Most striking, however, were the results of these conflicts and the role played by the Catholic church in resolving them. The outcomes of family conflicts over the selection of marriage partners yielded some surprising results, especially for those convinced that the traditional Catholic church supported parental control over marriage decisions. Between 1574, the date of the first recorded conflict, and 1689, there were 379 marriage applications involving conflicts over marriages between parents (or other relatives)

and a couple. Of these cases, the outcome could not be determined for 12 percent. Of the remainder, however, 93 percent of the marriages took place *over familial objections*. In other words, conflict within families over marriage choices resulted in the marriage of the couple in question more than 90 percent of the time. While this does not show the extent of informal pressure by parents for the veto of a partner, it does show that once the Catholic church had knowledge of marital opposition, parents were largely unable to force their wishes upon their offspring.

What may be even more surprising is that in 82 percent of these cases, it was actions by officials of the Catholic church that prevented parents from halting a marriage. Catholic church officials in seventeenth-century New Spain took young people out of parental custody (by force if necessary), placed them in temporary protective custody, and hid them from parental wrath when their families threatened to interfere with their desire to marry. Clergymen, with the full blessing of the highest church authority in New Spain, married these couples in secret. In fact, such secret marriages (made without the knowledge or consent of the family and most frequently in direct opposition to familial wishes) were granted by the highest ranking clergymen in New Spain in over two-thirds of all instances of familial interference.

In 1584 in Mexico City a poor Spanish orphan named Luisa de Ávila became engaged to a wealthy muleteer named Pedro Hernández. The banns (or prenuptial publicity) for the couple's impending nuptials were first announced on the last Sunday of August. Upon hearing this public statement of the marriage, three of Pedro's married sisters attempted to stop it. Their opposition stemmed from the economic inequality between the pair; their brother was wealthy while Luisa was impoverished. The sisters felt helpless to prevent the marriage themselves but believed their father would know how to prevent it. They told several acquaintances of their intention to notify their father (who was in Acapulco on business) of his son's impending wedding. Church officials, however, did not wait for Pedro's father to be notified of the match. Upon learning of his sisters' threat to write their father, church officials allowed the remainder of the prenuptial publicity to be eliminated, and issued permission for the couple immediately to be married. This action permitted a secret marriage between Pedro and Luisa *before* news could reach the groom's father in Acapulco. In effect, church officials allowed the marriage to take place without even formally notifying the young man's father of his son's intentions. In fact, the church's effort was meant to prevent any formal effort at notification (AGN, Matrimonios, vol. 10, fols. 343–45). The contrast to this type of situation is greatest with sixteenth-century France, where parental notification was not only required but parental *consent* mandated as well.[5] In New Spain parental consent was not necessary nor in this case was notification even desirable.

Secret marriage was not the only option used by the church in Mexico to prevent parents or other relatives from impeding a

marriage. The archbishop's representative personally ordered the removal of young people from homes when their parents held them at home against their will, in order to prevent them from marrying. Ana de Rua, for example, wanted to keep her stepdaughter, Sebastiana Rodríguez, at home in order to help her with the housework. When she learned that Sebastiana planned to marry, the stepmother refused to allow her out of the house. The archbishop's representative called upon the royal police to accompany a church court notary to Sebastiana's home. There the church official presented Sebastiana's stepmother with a decree from the church that ordered her to release Sebastiana to the church. The royal policeman accompanied the church official to ensure that Ana de Rua complied with the church's orders (AGN, Matrimonios, vol. 90, fols. 120–23v).

Nor was parental custody of a child viewed as an inalienable right, especially when the parents put excessive pressure upon their offspring to marry. Twenty-two-year-old Antonia Castañon, a member of a comfortable Spanish family in the town of Cuernavaca, became engaged in October 1646 to Juan Crespo, a Spanish employee of the Royal Mint. Antonia's father, however, opposed her marrying Juan because he wanted her to marry someone else. He threatened Antonia, and so the archbishop's representative ordered her removed from her father's home and placed in temporary custody in Mexico City (AGN, Archivo del Provisorato, caja 17). Parents who used threats or unreasonable pressure on their offspring were subject to the potential loss of custody of their children to church authorities.

The actions of the Catholic church in granting secret marriages or removing young people from the custody of abusive parents were seen by the denizens of New

[5]Thomas Barlow, bishop of Lincoln, wrote in 1691, "'Tis certain that a father hath a just authority by the law of God and of nature to consider and judge what is good for his children, and not only to command their obedience, but to use threats and meances: yea castigations and whippings too, to make them do their duty and obey his just commands" (Joyce, 1948:82; see also Stone, 1977: 166–78, 182–83). Martin Luther's criticism of excessive parental force is weak and unconvincing. His preference is for parental authority; he mandates parental consent and lacks checks on unreasonable and malicious behavior by parents (Joyce, 1948:82, note 2; also Marvick, 1974; Hunt, 1970:83–158; Ozment, 1983).

Fall, 1985   JOURNAL OF FAMILY HISTORY   291

Spain as proper and reasonable. The reason was that in so acting, the Catholic church was conserving and defending the central social values of colonial Hispanic society: distaste for the use of force against one's offspring, respect for matrimonial freedom, and antipathy to forcing young people to marry for money or parental convenience. In other cases, such as that of Juana Moreno, church officials defended another Spanish concern, protection of the sexual honor of young women. In fact honor was mentioned openly as a factor in nearly half of all the marriage oppositions of the seventeenth century.

The Spanish Catholic church's position on marriage also stemmed from a firm commitment to religious orthodoxy. As the spearhead of the Counter Reformation in Western Europe, Spain not only accepted, but openly embraced the decrees of the Council of Trent and even modified civil law in order to accommodate its decrees. Medieval Spanish law, for example, had allowed parents to disinherit daughters for marrying without parental consent, or against parental wishes. In the first half of the sixteenth century, prior to the Tridentine doctrine on marriage, this penalty was reaffirmed. After Trent, however, legal and canonical commentators debated whether this action conflicted with Catholic doctrine; the consensus was that in fact it had. Parents could only disinherit a daughter who had married beneath her station and secretly; they could not disinherit for failure to adhere to parental wishes. Furthermore, no disinheritance was permitted if parents had either treated her badly or had tried to use economic coercion against her (Rodríguez Lusitano, 1597:cap. 24, nos. 2, 3; chap. 14, no. 4). The eminent sixteenth-century canonist Alonso de la Vera Cruz even chastised parents by saying that attempting to disinherit children

for marrying against their wishes was a sin.[6] Civil laws allowing disinheritance for marriage against parental wishes were not revived until the final decades of the eighteenth century. In the meantime Spanish families were mostly forced either to reconcile themselves to the sons- and daughters-in-law they had initially opposed, or grudgingly hand them the minimum due under law. From remarks made by contemporaries, it appears that most families eventually reconciled themselves to the marriage.

In allowing secret marriages and in preventing parents and family members from interfering in the choice of a marriage partner, the Catholic church in colonial New Spain adopted a position radically different from that of the church in France, but one wholly in accord with the dominant cultural and religious values of the area. This is not to say that the parents of New Spain were less greedy in trying to hold onto inheritances or less desirous of attempting to marry their children for money. New Spain parents, like parents elsewhere, also attempted to use force—beatings, threats of disgrace, or jail—to make their offspring to give up a loved one or to marry someone they had chosen for monetary or political gain. Simply put, however, the dominant cultural beliefs of the Hispanic community regarded such conduct as malicious and unreasonable. The critical difference between New Spain and much of the rest of Western Europe society was that in New Spain such actions were unanimously condemned.[7] Not only was there clear con-

---

[6]Ripodas Ardanaz, 1977:264–65. Ripodas cites evidence that in seventeenth-century Ecuador the question of disinheritance for marriage against parental wishes was a controversial one among ecclesiastics, but that in practice most young people married as they wished.

---

[7]It should also be noted that French civil law outlawed marriages without prenuptial publicity

demnation of such actions, but the full backing of the Catholic church helped to enforce these cultural beliefs.

While a patriarchal church fits symmetrically with a patriarchal family, it would be a mistake to assume that analogy or symmetry is identical to reality. In its internal organization, the Roman Catholic church was and is highly structured, patriarchal, and some would argue even authoritarian. But to assume this internal structure corresponded to a motivation to support patriarchal domination throughout all institutions of sixteenth- and seventeenth-century society would be a mistake. Regarding marriage, traditional Catholic Spanish prelates in New Spain supported the independence of children from their parents' control during the sixteenth and seventeenth centuries. Catholic religious tradition and Hispanic cultural belief favored matrimonial freedom and the safeguarding of sexual honor, and exhibited powerful antipathy to the use of force or economic coercion by parents, especially in the

---

even though such marriages had been specifically permitted by the Council of Trent. The Ordinance of Blois (1579) states; "Ordonnos que nos sujets, de quelque qualité et condition qu'ils soient, ne pourrent valablement contracter mariage sans proclamation précédente de bans faits par trois divers jours festes avec intervalle compétente, *dont on ne pourra obtenir dispense* sinon après la premiere proclamation faite, et seulement pour quelque cause urgente et légitime *et a la réquisition des principaux et les plus proches parents communs des parties contractantes:*" (emphasis added). The Council of Trent had specifically allowed bishops to dispense of all the banns for "just cause." The most eminent theologian of the period, Tomas Sanchez, described what was meant by just cause, the fear of malicious interference by parents or near relatives (Esmein, II, 1929:196–200). The Ordinance of Blois thus effectively nullified the decrees of the Council of Trent which were intended to protect marrying couples from malicious parents or relatives. This is simply another example of French heterodoxy, or as the Spanish would call it, heresy, regarding Catholic doctrine on marriage.

selection of a marriage partner. Cultural values in different types of social conflicts do not always yield predictable or consistent results when compared with other institutions in the same society. Social reality is more complex than mere symmetry, and each area of cultural behavior must be examined on its own terms.

BIBLIOGRAPHY

Archivo General de la Nación, Mexicana. Cited as AGN.
    Bienes Nacionales
    Clero Regular y Secular
    Historia
    Matrimonios
    Archivo del Provisorato
Azpilcueta, Martín de Navarro
    1570   Manuel de confesores y penitentes. Valldalolid.
Camargo, Gerónimo
    1636   Respuesta a la resolución de la junta de los eclesiasticos de Francia en razón de los matrimonios de los principe de sangre hechos sin el consentimiento del rey. Madrid: Imprenta Francisco Martínez.
Chatham, Joseph
    1950   Force and Fear as Precluding Matrimonial Consent: The Element of Injustice. Washington, D.C.: Catholic University of America.
Cuevas, Mariano
    1946–   Historia de la Iglesia Mexicana, 5th ed.
    47   Mexico City: Editorial Patria.
Donahue: Charles, Jr.
    1983   "The Canon Law on the Formation of Marriage and Social Practice in the Later Middle Ages." Journal of Family History 8:144–58.
Esmein, Adhemar
    1929   Le Mariage dans le Droit Canonique, 2d ed., rev. and enl. by Robert Genestal. 2 vols. Paris: Recueil Sirey.
Flandrin, Jean-Louis
    1979   Families in Former Times: Kinship, Household and Sexuality. Translated by Richard Southern. Cambridge: Cambridge University Press.
Gil Delgado, Francisco
    1961   "El matrimonio de los hijos de familia." Revista Espanola de Derecho Canonico 16: 345–78.

Fall, 1985   JOURNAL OF FAMILY HISTORY   293

Gottlieb, Beatrice
  1980 "The Meaning of Clandestine Marriage."
         In Robert Wheaton and Tamara Hareven,
         eds., Family and Sexuality in French His-
         tory, pp. 49–83. Philadelphia: University
         of Pennsylvania Press.
Hunt, David
  1970 Parents and Children in History: The Psy-
         chology of Family Life in Early Modern
         France. New York: Basic Books.
Joyce, George
  1948 Christian Marriage: An Historical and
         Doctrinal Study, 2d ed. London: Sheed
         and Ward.
Lope de Vega
  1918 Comedias, vol. 4. Madrid: Biblioteca de
         Autores Espanoles.
Lopez de Velasco, Juan
  1971 Geografía y Descripción Universal de las
         Indias. Madrid: Ediciones Atlas.
Marvick, Elizabeth Wirth
  1974 "Nature versus Nurture: Patterns in Seven-
         teenth Century French Child-Rearing." In
         Lloyd de Mause, ed., Childhood in His-
         tory. New York: Psychohistory Press.
Morgan, Edmund S.
  1966 The Puritan Family, rev. ed. New York:
         Harper and Row.
Noonan, John T., Jr.
  1973 "Power to Choose." Viator 4:419–34.
Ozment, Stephen
  1983 When Fathers Ruled: Family Life in Refor-
         mation Europe. Cambridge, Mass.: Har-
         vard University Press.
Ripodas Ardanaz, Daisy
  1977 El Matrimonio en Indias: Realidad social
         regulación jurídica. Buenos Aires: Funda-
         ción para la Educación, la Ciencia, y la
         Cultura.
Rodriquez Lusitano, Manuel
  1597 Suma de los casos de conciencia. Sala-
         manca: Juan Fernandez.

Sanchez, Tómas
  1626 In totus tractum matrimonii. Lyons.
Sangmeister, Joseph
  1932 Force and Fear as Precluding Matrimonial
         Consent: An Historical Synopsis and Com-
         mentary. Washington, D.C.: Catholic Uni-
         versity of America Press.
Sheehan, Martin
  1978 "Choice of Marriage Partner in the Middle
         Ages: Development and Mode of Applica-
         tion of a Theory of Marriage." Studies in
         Medieval and Renaissance History 1 (new
         ser.): 3–33.
Shiels, William Eugene
  1961 King and Church: The Rise and Fall of the
         Patronato Real. Chicago: Loyola Univer-
         sity Press.
Shorter, Edward
  1975 The Making of the Modern Family. New
         York: Basic Books.
Smith, Daniel Scott
  1978 "Parental Power and Marriage Patterns:
         An Analysis of Historical Trends in Hing-
         ham, Massachusetts." In Michael Gordon,
         ed., The American Family in Social His-
         torical Perspective, 2d ed. New York: St.
         Martin's Press.
Stone, Lawrence
  1977 The Family, Sex and Marriage in England
         1500-1800. New York: Harper and Row.
Traer, James F.
  1980 Marriage and Family in Eighteenth Cen-
         tury France. Ithaca: Cornell University
         Press.
Vásquez de Espínosa, Antonio
  1969 Compendio y descripción de las Indias
         Occidentales. Madrid: Ediciones Atlas.
Villalobos, Enrique de
  1682 Suma de la teología moral y canonica, 13th
         ed. Madrid: Imprenta Bernardo Villa
         Diego.

3

Marriage and the Family in Colonial Vila Rica

Donald Ramos

TRADITIONALLY the family has been viewed as the nexus of a constellation of social institutions which together comprised Luso-Brazilian society. While a number of studies have appeared describing contemporary Brazilian social organization, not until very recently has more than scant attention been paid to the colonial antecedents of present-day social phenomena. This essay is an effort to fill in that background, using Vila Rica, the capital of colonial Brazil's goldmining region, as a case study. Three major contentions will be advanced. First, the patriarchal, extended family, so often viewed as the predominant colonial family type, existed for only a handful of people. Second, in preindustrial Vila Rica a wide range of family types existed, with nuclear and matrifocal families predominating. Third, marriage was not a means of integrating the society but served instead to differentiate segments of the population.

Foremost among earlier efforts to describe colonial social organization is the pioneering work of Gilberto Freyre, exemplified by his major works, *Casa-grande & senzala* and *Sobrados e mucambos*.[1] In these studies, Freyre traced the development of the upper-class patriarchal family, then its displacement from the plantation "big house" to the city. In both settings, the patriarchal extended family was considered the central institution for transmitting culture.

Freyre's observations had a great impact on other students of social organization. But, whereas he precisely identified the patriarchal,

1. Gilberto Freyre, *Casa-grande & senzala: formação brasileira sob o regime de economia patriarchal*, 14th ed. (Rio de Janeiro, 1969) 2 vols. Gilberto Freyre, *Sobrados e mucambos: decadência do patriarcado rural e desenvolvimento do urbano*, 4th ed. (Rio de Janeiro, 1968) 2 vols.

extended family as only one of a range of family types and limited to specified socioeconomic environments,[2] others carelessly generalized from his conclusions. This is particularly evident in the works of Fernando de Azevedo, João Camillo de Oliveira Torres, and L. A. Costa Pinto.[3] These authors focused their attention exclusively on the patriarchal, extended family, and ignored alternative forms of social organization. The same basic position is found in T. Lynn Smith's influential *Brazil, People and Institutions*, wherein the traditional family is defined as the patriarchal family, which "early obtained almost unlimited sway in Brazil."[4]

Other social scientists commented in passing on the existence of alternate family types but generally ignored these in their analyses, or allowed their personal social values to interfere with their objective examination of these alternative forms. Of these Antônio Cândido and Thales de Azevedo are typical. Antônio Cândido, in one of his early works, described colonial society as divided into two groups: the familial (or patriarchal family) and the nonfamilial. The latter was composed, he said, "of a nameless mass of the socially degraded, those cast off by family groups or brought up outside of them . . . [and who] reproduced themselves haphazardly and lived without regular norms of conduct."[5] Antônio Cândido, whose primary concern was the contemporary family, presented the modern conjugal family as having developed from its patriarchal predecessor.[6] Azevedo presented a similar analysis, contending that although alternative family types, such as the "partial family" headed by a woman, had existed during the colonial period, the patriarchal extended variety had been the most significant.[7] He partially ascribed the development of the nuclear family in the twentieth century to the disintegration of the patriarchal family.[8] These studies' reliance on subjective impressions, rather than

2. Freyre, *Sobrados e mucambos*, I, xlvii.
3. Fernando de Azevedo, *A cultura brasileira*, 4th ed. (São Paulo, 1964), p. 513; João Camillo de Oliveira Torres, *Estratificação social no Brasil* (São Paulo, 1965), p. 35; João Camillo de Oliveira Torres, *História de Minas Gerais* (Belo Horizonte, n.d.), II, pp. 487, 519; L. A. Costa Pinto, *Lutas de famílias no Brasil: introdução ao seu estudo* (São Paulo, 1949), pp. 46–50.
4. T. Lynn Smith, *Brazil, People and Institutions*, rev. ed. (Baton Rouge, 1963), p. 459.
5. Antônio Cândido, "The Brazilian Family," in *Brazil: Portrait of Half of a Continent*, ed. T. Lynn Smith and Alexander Marchant (1951; rpt. Westport, Conn., 1972), pp. 303–304.
6. Ibid., p. 292.
7. Thales de Azevedo, *Social Change in Brazil* (Gainesville, Fla., 1963), pp. 17–18.
8. Ibid., p. 17.

on analytical data, for the colonial era is not surprising since they focus primarily on the contemporary period, using a description of the colonial system only to provide general background.

But not all social scientists have accepted this view of colonial society. Emílio Willems, for example, was able to escape the all-pervading impact of Freyre's analysis. Willems's study of rural society led him to suggest a differentiation of family types along class lines, with the patriarchal, extended family seldom being a feature of lower-class society.[9] While concerned with contemporary social phenomena, Willems's analysis reopened the examination of colonial familial organization, which the general acceptance of Freyre's conclusions had precluded. Foremost among those who have sought to redefine the nature of the colonial family are Maria Luiza Marcílio and Luis Lisanti. In a number of recent publications dealing with São Paulo they have begun to look beyond Freyre to challenge existing theories on family size and composition.[10] The present article will contribute to the same effort.

The urban center used for this study, Vila Rica, was one of the leading centers of eighteenth-century Brazil. Founded after major gold deposits were discovered in the interior province of Minas Gerais in 1695, it rapidly evolved into the major economic center of the mining district, and, after 1720, became its political capital. The peak of the town's growth was reached in the 1740s, when more than 1,000 houses were registered for the densely packed urban core alone and the town's total population probably numbered about 15,000 people. The period after 1752 witnessed a decline in the economic fortunes of the region, a decline that became precipitous after 1760. By the end of the century the situation had stabilized.[11] The remaining population,

9. Emílio Willems, "Structure of the Brazilian Family," *Social Forces*, 31 (1953), 339–346.

10. Luis Lisanti and Maria Luiza Marcílio, "Estrutura demográfica, social, e econômica da vila de Lajes, 1798–1808," *Estudos Historicos*, 8 (1969), 9–52. Maria Luiza Marcílio, "Tendances et structures des ménages dans la capitainerie de São Paulo (1765–1868) selon les listes nominatives d'habitants," in *L'Histoire quantitative du Brésil de 1800 a 1930*, ed. Frédéric Mauro, Colloques Internationaux du Centre Nacional de La Recherche Scientifique (Paris, 1973), pp. 157–165; Maria Luiza Marcílio *La ville de São Paulo: peuplement et population, 1750–1850* (Rouen, 1968).

11. While the economic recession that struck the mining district probably resulted in major demographic movements within the captaincy as a whole, these do not appear to have resulted in a substantial change in the population of Vila Rica. The population reports for the parish of Ouro Prêto during the period 1796–1799, for example, show the population remaining constant (5639, 5635, 5635) and the free male population actually increasing slightly (1569, 1577, and 1586),

hovering around the 7,000 mark, was supported by residual gold deposits, the advantageous position of the town as a trade center, and its administrative prominence as the capital of Minas Gerais. During this phase of its history Vila Rica also became a major cultural center.

It was also during this period of genteel decadence that census taking was initiated. One of these censuses—that of 1804—provides much of the data for this study.[12] Because of the critical importance of this material some mention need be made of its nature. The *termo*, or county, of Vila Rica was divided into parishes. The urban parishes of Antônio Dias and Ouro Prêto (the name by which Vila Rica is known today) were then divided into smaller districts: Antônio Dias into Morro, Alto da Cruz, Padre Faria and Taquaral, and Antônio Dias itself, and Ouro Prêto into Cabeças and Ouro Prêto. The enumeration of the residents of each district was carried out by militia officers.

The census tracts for these six districts are consistent, each district's being divided into residential units. Each residential unit is then divided into its major component parts: the primary family encompassing the head of the household, his spouse, and their children; secondary families composed of married children or single children who were heads of families;[13] agregados, dependents or retainers, including relatives; boarders; and slaves. The census provides the

---

Mappa da população, Ouro Prêto, 1796–1799, Arquivo Público Mineiro (cited hereinafter as APM), Belo Horizonte, Planilhas 20364 and 20357. It appears that the primary effect of the later coffee boom was to drain slave labor away from Vila Rica; the free population increased significantly during the first quarter of the nineteenth century, from 6385 in 1804, 6637 in 1815, 6867 in 1818, to 7762 in 1823, Mappas da população, Termo de Vila Rica, 1815 and 1818, in APM, Maço da População; Mappa Estadistico do Termo da Imperial Cidade do Ouro Prêto, 1823, Arquivo Nacional, Rio de Janeiro (cited hereinafter as ANRJ), Cód. 808.

12. This census has been transcribed and published by Herculano Gomes Mathias, *Um recenseamento na capitania de Minas Gerais: Vila Rica—1804* (Rio de Janeiro, 1969). This article is based on an analysis of all those enumerated by the census takers.

13. Discussions of household typologies often focus on the importance of the "conjugal link" in defining the family. The use of this link may be relevant for European societies where the majority of the heads of households were or had been married. Peter Laslett, "Mean Household Size in England since the Sixteenth Century," in *Household and Family in Past Time*, ed. Peter Laslett (Cambridge, Eng., 1972), p. 147. It is not, however, as relevant to a study of Vila Rica, where only about one-third of household heads were married. Because of this low marriage rate, I have included within the definition of the family, groupings of a single parent and children. Marriage and/or paternity are the basis of my working definition of the basic family unit.

TABLE I. Mean Houseful Size (MHFS) in Vila Rica: 1804 (N = 1705).

Simple MHFS	5.11
MHFS, excluding slaves	2.95
MHFS, excluding single-member housefuls	5.53
MHFS, excluding slaves and single-member housefuls	3.57

following information for each person: name, marital status, race, title, occupation,[14] age, and relationship to the head of the residence.

A central problem in the analysis of the census data is the formulation of an operational definition of the family as opposed to the household. Portuguese attitudes evidence extensive confusion between the two. An eighteenth-century Portuguese dictionary defined the family as "the people who make up a house, parents, children, and servants."[15] According to one student of eighteenth-century Portuguese society, this dictionary definition was applied generally.[16] It would appear that the family, as a descriptive term, is synonymous with the "houseful," and thus is similar to the definition used in other parts of Europe.[17] In this study, however, "houseful" refers to all those individuals who live on the premises, which includes such structures as slave quarters that are physically separated (but connected by authority) to the nearby main house. The "houseful" may contain individuals who do not constitute a family because they are not biologically or juridically related. The "household" refers to those people sharing the same dwelling. Thus, a houseful contains one or more households.[18]

In Brazil this definition is applied to a socioeconomic environment that included large numbers of agregados and slaves. Although often

14. Only in the district of Ouro Prêto were records of occupations consistently provided for slaves.

15. Raphael Bluteau, *Vocabulário portuguez e latino*, 8 vols., (Coimbra, 1712–1721) IV, 28. João António Andreoni (Andre João Antonil), *Cultura e opulência do Brasil* (São Paulo, 1967) p. 142. Antonil, in lumping together "family, sons, and slaves," suggests that this definition was used in Brazil.

16. Suzanne Chantal, *A vida quotidiana em Portugal ao tempo do terramoto*, trans. Àlvaro Simões (Lisbon, n.d.), p. 105. Chantal defines the family as "all those belonging to the house, whatever their status. The very term used to designate servants was significant. They were called *criados*, meaning people raised in the family and comprising a part of it."

17. Phelippe Ariès, in his study of the family and childhood in France, defined the family as including the conjugal unit, servants, friends, and protégés: Phelippe Ariès, *Centuries of Childhood: A Social History of Family Life*, trans. Robert Baldick (New York, 1962), p. 393.

18. Peter Laslett, "Introduction," in *Household and Family*, pp. 23–41.

mentioned, the agregado has escaped the detailed study he deserves, unlike the slave who has been subjected to intensive examination. Some dependents and slaves were related to the head of the house and can be considered as members of the household—the primary means of differentiation being personal relationship to the head of the houseful and place of dwelling.[19] Most, however, were not related to the houseful head. The image of the Brazilian houseful that emerges from the census data is one of concentric circles, with the head and his immediate family at the center surrounded, first by dependents who are related to the head; then in the next circle, by the nonrelated dependents and some of the slaves; and finally, by the majority of the slaves in the circle furthest removed from the center.

Closely related to the structure of the houseful is its size. Perhaps surprisingly, in place of the large houseful usually depicted as prevailing in colonial Brazil, we discover a houseful which, in terms of size, was not unlike that found in early modern Europe. Furthermore, in this characteristic Vila Rica does not appear to differ from other areas of colonial Brazil.[20] The average size of the houseful in Vila Rica was only 5.11.

19. The English traveler James Wells noted that a fazendeiro dined surrounded by his family and countryfolk, undoubtedly agregados, who "according to their position, sit above or below the salt, as in old feudal days." James Wells, *Exploring and Travelling Three Thousand Miles through Brazil from Rio de Janeiro to Maranhão* (London, 1886), I, 202–203.

20. Laslett's data for 100 English communities from 1574 to 1821 show a simple mean household size (hereafter MHS) of 4.841, with a range of 3.63 to 7.22; when the Vila Rica data are recomputed using the household rather than the houseful, the simple MHS are almost identical—4.841 for England and 4.888 for Vila Rica, Laslett, *Household and Family*, p. 133. While there are some variations reflecting the rural-urban dichotomy, the houseful size in Vila Rica was not unusually low for Minas Gerais. An examination of 45 different localities within Minas Gerais during the first one-third of the nineteenth century reveals a range of houseful size of 3.30 to 9.84, with the median being 6.15. Termo de Marianna, 1831; Mappas da População, Termos de Sabará, 1815, Queluz, 1831, and Itaverava, 1831, APM, Maço da População; Mappa Estadístico do Termo de . . . Sabará, 1823; and Mappa Estadístico do Termo de . . . São Carlos de Jacuí, 1823, ANRJ, Cód. 808. Neither this range nor the mean houseful size (hereafter MHFS) of Vila Rica itself appears unusual in comparison with other areas of Brazil. The MHFS in the province of Santa Catharina in 1830, for example, varied from 6.26 for the capital to 3.94 for the other districts; the average for the entire province was 5.14, Mappa da População da Provincia da Santa Catharina, 1830, ANRJ, Cód. 808. The 15 districts comprising the capital of Brazil and the province of Rio de Janeiro exhibited an average houseful size of 8.63, with a range of 6.94 to 10.32. Mappa. . . da Cidade e Provincia do Rio de Janeiro, 1821, ANRJ, Cód. 808. Houseful size in the province of São Paulo was very similar to that of Minas Gerais, fluctuating from 5.9 to 6.6 during the years 1798–1836. Marcílio, "Tendances et structures des ménages," p. 159.

TABLE II. Structure of Housefuls.

Type	No.	% of Total
Houseful with Nuclear Core		
Husband-Wife	126	7.4
Husband-Wife-Children	277	16.2
Father-Children	67	3.9
Mother-Children	408	23.9
Subtotal	878	(51.4)
Solitary Houseful		
Male	165	9.7
Female	136	8.0
Subtotal	301	(17.7)
Solitary Houseful with Retainers and/or Relatives and/or Slaves		
Male	301	17.7
Female	225	13.2
Subtotal	526	(30.9)
TOTAL	1705	100.0

As suggested in Table I, slaves and dependents comprised significant proportions of the population of Vila Rica. Of all housefuls
44.9 percent contained dependents and 41.4 percent slaves. Retainers
represented 18.4 percent and slaves 30.0 percent of the total population. It is significant that 602 households, comprising 35.3 percent
of the total, were simple or nuclear housefuls without dependents or
slaves.

It is also clear that the concept of a patriarchal head of an extended
family is not applicable to the vast majority of the households of Vila
Rica. Based on the 1804 census returns, 13.5 percent of all housefuls
contained relatives other than children, or three or more generations
including the head; and, of the 230 housefuls, 91 were headed by
men. Thus only 5.3 percent of all housefuls can be described as being
composed of patriarchal, extended families. The identifiable racial
composition of the heads of extended housefuls was 16.7 percent white,
44.2 percent mulatto, 5.1 percent *cabra*, and 37.0 percent black.[21]
The fact that so many of the extended or multiple housefuls were
headed by nonwhites suggests that family members may well have
served as economic contributors rather than as proof of status—they
fulfilled an economic role rather than reflecting conspicuous consumption.

21. Of the 230 heads of housefuls, race was given for 138. It is important to
note that the census identifies only resident relatives and provides no information
on relatives residing in nearby but separate housefuls. Nor can the census data
identify those families that had passed through an extended family experience.
The data provide only a static view of a dynamic situation.

TABLE III.   Marital Status of Houseful Heads.

Sex	Single	Married	Widowed	Total
Male	512	403	22	937
Female	638	21	109	768
TOTAL	1150	424	131	1705

It is usually assumed that the bonds linking the family together rest upon the institution of marriage. Like the concept of the extended family itself, this is not supported by the evidence from Vila Rica. (See Table II.) Less than one-third of the heads of extended family housefuls were recorded by the census taker as legally married. The low marriage rate of heads of all housefuls is even more significant (Table III). Two-thirds of these men and women had apparently never been married and of these the majority were single women. The appearance of so many women as heads of housefuls, 45.0 percent, is startling and will be examined in greater detail below. It is probable that most of the women still single would not marry: 39.4 percent were 50 years old or older, 60.0 percent were 40 or older, 81.6 percent were 30 or over, and 94.1 percent were over the median age of first marriage—22 years.

While it may appear that 32.6 percent is a low marriage ratio, it is clear that this was still higher than the rate for the population at large (see Table IV). Over 83 percent of the population of Vila Rica over the legal age of marriage was single, a figure which seemingly supports August de Saint-Hilaire's remark that Brazil was "a country where there existed extensive repugnance to legitimate unions."[22] Clearly marriage was not the bond that held together the family.

The low incidence of marriage existed despite the efforts of church and state to encourage people to marry. The Portuguese government was interested in marriage as a means of imposing law and order on the turbulent miners of Minas Gerais. As early as 1721, King João V ordered the governor of Minas Gerais to urge "the important residents [pessoas principais] and even others" to marry. Furthermore, he sought the advice of the governor on the advisability of restricting public service to married men.[23] The Portuguese authorities hoped that once

22. August de Saint-Hilaire, Viagem pelas provincias de Rio de Janeiro e Minas Gerais, trans. Clado Ribeiro de Lessa (São Paulo, 1938), I, 160.
23. Royal Letter to Count of Assumar, Mar. 22, 1721, in Elmar G. Quiroga, "O valor sociológico de um documento," Revista do Instituto Histórico e Geográfico de Minas Gerais 2(1946), 144, and APM, Cód. 23(SG), fol. 6.

TABLE IV.   Distribution of Eligible Population by Structural Segment and Marital Status.[a]

	Number	Percentage			
		Single	Married	Widowed	Total
Heads of Housefuls	1705	67.4	24.9	7.7	100
Children	1100	96.4	3.2	0.4	100
Relatives	349	95.7	3.2	1.1	100
Agregados	1008	93.4	5.2	1.4	100
Boarders	14	85.7	14.3		100
Subtotal	4176	83.7	12.6	3.7	100
Wives	441		100.0		100
Subtotal	4617	75.7	20.9	3.3	100
Slaves	2281	98.9	1.0	0.1	100
TOTAL	6898	83.4	14.3	2.3	100

[a] Eligibility based on legal age of marriage—14 years of age for men and 12 for women.

the miners established roots they would be less inclined to threaten royal control—rebellions against royal authority having occurred in 1708–1709 and 1720. In addition, it was assumed that children raised in a married family household "would be even more obedient."[24] The suggestion was opposed by the governor on the grounds that there was an insufficient number of women in the mining district.[25] The primary thrust of royal policy was to tie down the elite with family burdens; should "even others" be convinced to marry, that would be a bonus.

It is probable that the local elite did not need royal pressure to marry, but rather a sufficient number of suitable women. Marriage had become a symbol of status—an indication of social differentiation. A suggestion of this can be found in the accounts of foreign travelers during the nineteenth century; for example, James Wells described a well-to-do black man who made it a point to introduce his wife and informed Wells "proudly" that they "were married in all due form by the priest."[26] The fact that he had been married legally was used as a mark of status. The same conclusion is also implied by the census data. As is indicated by the 1815 report of population summarized in Table V, there was a greater propensity for whites to marry than there was for either mulattoes or blacks.[27] Whites represented a greater

24. Ibid.
25. Assumar's response appears in Feu de Carvalho, "Primeiras aulas e escolas de Minas Gerais," Revista do Arquivo Público Mineiro, 24(1933), 350–351.
26. Wells, Exploring, I, 84–85.
27. The 1815 population summary is used, rather than the 1804 census, because it racially defined the entire population.

TABLE V. Free Population of Vila Rica by Sex, Race, and Marital Status: 1815.

| Sex | Race | Marital Status | | % Married, by Sex and Race | % of Total Married, by Sex | % of Pop. by Race |
		Single	Married			
Male						
	White	565	171	23.2	43.8	35.0
	Mulatto	813	141	14.8	36.2	45.4
	Black	335	78	18.9	20.0	19.6
					100.0	100.0
Female						
	White	647	158	19.6	36.2	29.9
	Mulatto	1086	196	15.3	45.0	47.6
	Black	524	82	13.5	18.8	22.5
					100.0	100.0
Subtotal	White	1212	329	21.3	39.8	32.1
	Mulatto	1899	337	15.1	40.8	46.6
	Black	859	160	15.7	19.4	21.3
TOTAL		3970	826	17.2	100.0	100.0

Source: Mappa da População do Termo de Vila Rica do anno 1815, APM, Maço da População.

proportion of the married than of the population as a whole. While the differences are greater for males than for females, those for the latter are still significant.

This conclusion is supported by an examination of people identifiable as being of high social status. Whereas in 1804 only 16.6 percent of the general population over the legal age was married, 37.1 percent of all women listed as *donas*, or ladies, and 31.5 percent of all titled males were married.[28] Thus two indicators of status—race and title—show some degree of correlation with marriage.

This generally low marriage rate must be viewed against a background of an ecclesiastical policy that allowed people to marry at a comparatively young age. Canon law permitted males to marry at the age of 14 and females at 12 or even earlier, if "possessed of discretion and sufficient disposition."[29] This encouragement of early marriage was probably a response to the necessity for maintaining and expanding the population in the face of a high mortality rate,

28. Forty women were listed as "donas" and, of these, fifteen were married. There were 214 titled males and, of these, 85 were or had been married. Priests were excluded from the data.

29. *Constituições primeiras do arcebispado da Bahia* (Lisbon, 1765), Livro 1, Titulo 64, 117.

TABLE VI. Age of Mother at Birth of Eldest Residing Child.[a]

Age	Number	Percentage
19 or younger	266	32.1
20–29	342	41.3
30–39	153	18.5
40 and over	67	8.1
TOTAL	828	100.0
Mean age: 24.1	Median age: 23	

[a] This Table includes all mother-child combinations on which there was information on ages.

especially that of infants. Probably for economic reasons, men seldom married at the legal age. Women, however, were more likely to do so.[30]

This suggestion is supported by an analysis of the census data to ascertain the age of the mother when she gave birth to the eldest child still residing in the household and, thereby, to provide an approximate age at marriage (Table VI). The results should be viewed as maximum figures, because there is no way of ascertaining elapsed time between marriage and the birth of that child, nor of determining whether the eldest child listed was the firstborn (the firstborn could have died in infancy or, conversely, could have survived to set up a separate household).[31] The overall average age was 24.1 and the median 23. When a minimum period of nine months (for pregnancy) is assumed, the median age is lowered to approximately 22 years. Even this maximum figure is significantly lower than that reported for most parts of Western Europe during this period.[32]

30. This is supported by the initial results of a long-range family reconstruction the author presently has underway. Of a small sample from the third quarter of the eighteenth century, 21 cases yielded precise information on the age of one or both spouses. The age of first marriage was calculated for 16 women, who ranged in age from 12 to 27. The mean age at marriage was 17.4, and the median was 17. The age at marriage for 6 husbands ranged from 19 to 30, with the mean being 23.3 and the median, 22. While this is too small a sample upon which to draw conclusions, it is indicative of the youthfulness of women at the time of marriage. The sources used for the family reconstruction include the registers of baptisms and marriages of the parish of Antonio Dias.

31. On the other hand, there is no way to account for those cases in which a woman married a widower, and no notation was made differentiating natural from stepchildren.

32. Pierre Goubert has shown that in eighteenth century France the average age of mothers was 26–27 at the time of giving birth to a first child. Laslett has described English women in the seventeenth and eighteenth centuries as marrying at an average age of 24. Vilaricano women, therefore, married at least 2–5 years before their European counterparts. Of special significance is Goubert's view that people under 25 could exist with security only within the family. In Vila Rica, 8.1 percent of all heads of housefuls and 20.1 percent of wives were 25 or under.

TABLE VII. Age Differential between Spouses by Race of Husband.

	White	Mulatto	Black	Race Unknown	Total
Number of Cases	62	99	83	130	374
Age Differential	7.3	6.8	8.1	6.8	7.1

Conversely, the age differential of spouses was larger than that reported for Western Europe.[33] On the average, husbands were 7.1 years older than their wives, and for blacks the differential was 8.1 years. Some of the disparities were extreme, as in the case of Francisco de Crasto, who was 43 years older than his wife.[34] In 28 cases, or 7.5 percent, the variation in age was 20 years or more. On the other hand, in only 52 cases, representing 13.9 percent of the total, was the wife older than her husband, and in 26 others (7.0 percent) she was the same age as he.

If women could and did marry while relatively young, it is not surprising that marriage engagements could legally be made when the participants were as youthful as seven years of age. Engagements were called *desposorios de futuro*, or promises of future marriage.[35] The ecclesiastical records of the Archdiocese of Mariana, in whose district Vila Rica was located, attest to the use and abuse of this provision. A bizarre example involves the successful efforts of Fernando Dias Leite to have the Bishop of Mariana dissolve his promise of marriage to a very young girl so that Leite would be free to marry the girl's recently widowed mother. Leite freely acknowledged that his sudden shift in affection was due to the widow's sizeable inheritance.[36] Abuses of engagement contracts were legion. Often they were used to entice a young woman to engage in premarital sexual

---

Pierre Goubert, "Legitimate Fecundity and Infant Mortality in France during the Eighteenth Century: A Comparison," *Daedalus*, 98 (Spring, 1968), 593–603; and Peter Laslett, *The World We Have Lost* (New York, 1965), pp. 82–83. In Laslett's study the median age of women at marriage was 22 years, 9 months.

33. Goubert contends that in France men married at an age that averaged 2–4 years older than women, Goubert, "Legitimate Fecundity," p. 594. The age differential in seventeenth-century England was 3 years, Laslett, *The World We Have Lost*, pp. 82–83.

34. Mathias, *Um recenseamento*, p. 191.

35. *Constituições primeiras*, Livro 1, Titulo 63, 115.

36. Petition of Fernando Dias Leite, 1765, Arquivo da Curia de Mariana, Mariana, Minas Gerais (cited hereinafter as ACM), Casamentos, No. 495. The petition was approved.

activities, with the prospective groom disappearing after learning of the girl's pregnancy, or shortly before the wedding day.[37]

While the church authorized early engagements and encouraged marriages, it also created certain barriers to matrimony that made marriage an ideal attainable only by some. Among these obstacles were such traditional impediments to marriage as affinity within the fourth degree, impotency, consanguinity, and the use of force or false pretenses.[38] In order to ascertain whether these or other restrictions existed, engaged couples were required to have their marriage bans read in their parish churches on three successive holy days, so that anyone having derogatory information could report it secretly. If problems were uncovered, as they often were, the couple could then petition the bishop for a waiver of the troublesome provision. The petition process, however, cost money and time, and this probably served to prevent some couples from formalizing their relationships.

Far more important as a barrier to marriage than the church's traditional restrictions was the great inconvenience resulting from the church's insistence that positive evidence be presented that the engaged couples were single. For those born and residing in and around Vila Rica the problems which this entailed were minimal. But, for those born elsewhere, the perplexities escalated in proportion to the red tape involved. Thus, for example, the wedding of Domingos Ferreira and Anna Rodrigues da Fonseca was delayed by the insistence of the church that the bans be read in Oporto where the prospective groom was born. Affidavits were required of the parish priest in Oporto stating that the bans had been read and that no negative evidence was presented.[39]

On other occasions, pending receipt of positive proof of marital status, the wedding ceremony was performed with the proviso that the marriage not be consummated until the evidence was received. An illustration is the case of Manuel da Rocha Perreira and Anna Maria de Jesus. They were married on January 26, 1764, with the stipulation that "under pain of excommunication . . . they are not to cohabit until they present certification of the bans from the district of Sabará where the groom had resided, [this requirement] having been waived prior to the wedding ceremony by the Illustrious and Most Reverend Canon,

---

37. The petition of Isabel Antónia Maciel, July 16, 1748, ACM, Casamento Avulso, is a good example of the abuses that frequently accompanied engagements.
38. *Constituições primeiras*, Livro 1, Titulo 67, 124–126.
39. Marriage Petition of Domingos Ferreira, Mar. 18, 1795, Arquivo da Paroquia de Ouro Prêto, Ouro Prêto, Minas Gerais (cited hereinafter as APOP), Avulso No. 95.

Capitular of this Diocese."[40] The restrictions were lifted in such situations, and the couples were allowed to live together only after certification had been received that the bans had been read.[41] When there was substantial evidence supporting the contention of an individual that he was single, provision was made for the couple to post a bond with the ecclesiastical authorities, to ensure the satisfactory fulfillment of the provisions of canon law.[42] These ecclesiastical restrictions not only functioned to delay many weddings but, because of the costs involved, probably dissuaded others from seeking the sacrament of marriage.

Such provisions were not applied exclusively to the free population. There is substantial evidence that the same requirements for evidence of singleness were applied to slaves also. This was an impossible demand for those slaves born in Africa—a problem resolved by the ecclesiastical authorities by requiring proof of marital status only for the period after Catholic baptism. Thus slaves, either crioulo or African-born blacks, were required to have their marriage bans read in the areas where they had resided. João Batista and Maria, both African-born slaves, were required to have their marriage bans read in Rio de Janeiro and also in Salvador, where they formerly had resided.[43] Clearly this requirement was a complication to slaves and ex-slaves in their efforts to marry, and its existence helps to explain the especially low marriage rate among slaves.

While the church hierarchy often insisted upon the fulfillment of all the provisions of church law, local church authorities not infrequently made exceptions for influential residents. Consequently, the requirement that the bans be read publicly prior to the wedding ceremony was waived occasionally. In this regard the church was inclined to exercise a wide range of powers, even to the point of disregarding the wishes of the parents. An example of this exercise of power was the suspension of the public reading of the bans of Dr. Manuel Rodrigues Pacheco de Morais and Clara Maria do Pilar until after the wedding. This ruling was made out of deference to Dr.

40. Marriage Registration of Manuel da Rocha Perreira and Anna Maria de Jesus, Jan. 26, 1764, Arquivo da Paroquia de António Dias, Ouro Prêto, Minas Gerais (cited hereafter as APAD), Livro de Casamentos, fol. 218.
41. Marriage Registration of João Ferreira da Silva and Teresa Jacinta de Jesus, June 22 and July 9, 1759, APAD, Livro de Casamentos, fols. 189 and 190.
42. Petition of Manuel Carlos de Abreu Lima, Apr. 20, 1773, APOP, Avulso No. 97.
43. Petition of João Batista and Maria Obu, Jan. 8, 1728, ACM, Casamentos, No. 42.

Morais's fear that the family of the bride would react violently to the news, perhaps even preventing the wedding from taking place.[44] On still another occasion bans were not read publicly because the husband, a Portuguese-born militia officer, wished to marry his slave without notoriety.[45] Thus if the petitioners were sufficiently influential, the church was willing to allow exceptions.

The activity of the church authorities in waiving impediments to matrimony was not limited to dispensing with the public reading of the bans. The church often exercised its power to legitimize situations caused by such illegal activities as kidnapping and seduction. Both of these actions were means of presenting the authorities—parental, civil, and ecclesiastical—with a fait accompli. This also was a way around many of the difficulties inherent in the process of getting married and probably absolved the father from paying a dowry. The church had no alternative but to authorize the marriage, if petitioned, since to do otherwise would have been to punish the female victim of these acts. A clear statement on the ramifications of the act of seduction was made by Antônia Martins Cerqueira: "The petitioner finds herself dishonored by her co-petitioner, for which reason if she does not marry him, she will be villified, with neither anyone wishing to marry her and thus being without redemption [*desempenhada*], nor being able to support herself because she is abjectly poor."[46] Kidnapping had the same impact, since the news soon became "public and notorious gossip," thereby preventing the victim from finding a husband "of her station in life."[47] These examples demonstrate how crucial was the "purity" of the woman; once having been "dishonored," the woman was forced to marry her abductor or suffer loss of status and the opportunity to marry a social peer. Furthermore, it points to the strength of the traditional norm that a bride had to be a virgin at the time of marriage: the woman either married her abductor or lived a single life. No such restrictions, of course, were placed on the male. The same ethical considerations often forced the church to waive impediments arising from blood relationships within the fourth degree

44. Petition of Dr. Manuel Rodrigues Pacheco de Morais, 1763, ACM, Casamentos, No. 466.

45. See Marriage Registration of Captain Manuel Correa de Paiva and Jacinta de Barros, Aug. 4, 1737, in Geraldo Dutra de Morais, *História de Conceição do Mato Dentro* (Belo Horizonte, 1942), p. 215.

46. Petition of Manuel Ferreira Marques and Antônia Martins Cerqueira, Sept. 20, 1749, ACM, Casamentos, No. 337.

47. Dispensation granted Manuel Francisco Dias and Josefa Maria de Jesus, Mar. 15, 1749, ACM, Cód. 12, fols. 136v–137.

or spiritual relationships emanating from godparentage (it was assumed that godparents of the same child held a bond as strong as that imposed by blood relationships). Marriages between relatives, familial or spiritual, were common, and many of the petitions made to the bishop of Mariana fell into this category.

Beyond the aspects of ecclesiastical policy that served to restrict marriage, the traditional importance of the dowry played a similar, albeit harder to define, role. The custom of providing a dowry was common in eighteenth-century Minas Gerais, the amount depending on the social position of the family and the status of the child—legitimate or illegitimate.[48] Many individuals included in their wills provisions for giving money to orphans to be used as dowries.[49] Furthermore, this pressure was so great that some of Vila Rica's poorer residents found themselves compelled to solicit the municipal council for assistance. For example, one "abjectly poor" father asked the council for a small sum to be used as a dowry for his daughter who was "so poor and miserable [that she] did not have clothes in which to appear [in public] or other necessities for her personal use."[50] The efforts that were made to obtain governmental assistance imply that marriage was still a norm of the society. It was, however, a standard attainable only by some, due to the limitations imposed both by ecclesiastical restrictions and social customs.

The impact of these social and ecclesiastical requirements was to make marriage difficult for many people. But by themselves they probably would not account for the low marriage rate, for the demographic situation was favorable for marriage. There was a major sex imbalance with 79 males for every 100 females. Thus eligible females were available for marriage. It seems very probable that the economic recession, which was into its second half-century made the responsibilities of marriage too onerous for many men. This probably served to restrict marriage only to those who could afford it. Perhaps because of these difficulties, marriage formed the bonds holding together only about one-third of the housefuls of Vila Rica.

Housefuls varied significantly in size. The greatest range is found among female-headed housefuls. Widows headed housefuls that

48. See will of Salvador Fernandes Furtado, May 24, 1725, in Felix Guisard Filho, "Bandeirantismo Taubateano: testamentos e inventarios," *Revista do Arquivo Municipal de São Paulo*, 17(1935), 41–46.

49. E.g., will of Antônio Fernandes Braziella, 1742, Arquivo do Patrimonio Histórico e Artístico Nacional—Ouro Prêto (cited hereinafter as APHAN), Cód. 93, No. 1198.

50. Petition of Hieronimo da Cunha, July 2, 1749, APM, Documento Avulso.

TABLE VIII. Structural Components of the Houseful by Sex and Marital Status of Head.

Houseful Heads Category	No.	Children		Agregados		Slaves		Total[a]	
		No.	Mean per House-ful	No.	Mean per House-ful	No.	Mean per House-ful	No.	Mean per House-ful
Single Male	512	187	0.37	515	1.01	1025	2.00	2239	4.37
Married Male	403	911	2.26	315	0.78	742	1.84	2757	6.84
Widowed Male	22	35	1.59	22	1.00	37	1.68	116	5.27
Subtotal	937	1133	1.21	852	0.91	1804	1.92	5112	5.46
Single Female	638	745	1.17	687	1.08	565	0.89	2635	4.13
Married Female	21	35	1.67	29	1.38	60	2.86	145	6.90
Widowed Female	109	239	2.19	206	1.89	270	2.48	824	7.56
Subtotal	768	1019	1.33	922	1.20	895	1.17	3604	4.69
TOTAL	1705	2152	1.26	1774	1.04	2699	1.58	8716	5.11

[a] Total includes spouses where appropriate.

averaged 7.56 persons, while those headed by single women averaged only 4.13—reflecting generally higher economic status. While the typical houseful headed by a male was larger than that headed by a female, women who were or had been married headed larger housefuls than males who were or had been married—7.45, as compared to 6.75. (See Table VIII.) The difference is due, in part, to the large number of slaves owned by married houseful heads—reflecting generally higher economic status—and the number of children still residing in the household. The average size of the married male's houseful was 6.84, while that of the female's houseful was only 4.69.

TABLE IX. Marital Status by Employment Category of Male Houseful Heads.

Category	No.*	% Single	% Married, Widowed
Haulers/Carriers	18	11.1	88.9
Farmers	15	40.0	60.0
Soldiers	56	44.6	55.4
Public Employees	76	47.4	52.6
Artisans	283	47.7	52.3
Miners	106	50.0	50.0
Salaried	18	61.1	38.9
Businessmen	119	65.5	34.5
Services	42	66.7	33.3
Miscellaneous	10	70.0	30.0
Unlisted/Beggars	162	61.1	38.9
Total	905	53.0	47.0

* Does not include 32 priests.

TABLE X. Marital Status by Age: Male Houseful Heads.

Age Category	Single			Married			Widowed		
	No.	%	Cum. %	No.	%	Cum. %	No.	%	Cum. %
19 and under	5	1.1	1.1	1	0.3	0.3	0	—	—
20–29	53	11.1	12.2	35	9.0	9.3	1	4.5	4.5
30–39	107	22.4	34.6	108	27.6	36.9	2	9.1	13.6
40–49	87	18.2	52.8	117	29.9	66.8	2	9.1	22.7
50–59	96	20.1	72.9	65	16.6	83.4	8	36.4	59.1
60–69	74	15.5	88.4	44	11.2	94.6	4	18.2	77.3
70–79	35	7.3	95.9	19	4.9	99.5	3	13.6	90.9
80 and over	20	4.2	99.9	2	0.5	100.0	2	9.1	100.0
Subtotal	477			391			22		
Unknown	35			12			0		
TOTAL	512			403			22		

The occupational characteristics and age of single and married male heads are set out in Tables IX and X. There was a greater tendency for miners, farmers, soldiers, and haulers to be married than for other men, although only in the last category was the difference appreciable. The employment rate among married men was slightly higher than for single men, 85 percent versus 81 percent, again emphasizing the correlation between economic factors and marriage. In terms of age, the two groups are roughly similar, except that single heads are evenly distributed from 30 to 69 years of age, whereas the ages of married males evidences a bell curve, with the peak coming between 40 and 49 years. The rapid decline of the number of married males 50 years or older is a reflection of high mortality rates, as suggested by the dramatic increase of the number of widowers aged 50 or older.

The traditional view of the patriarchal family obviously applies to these housefuls headed by males. Custom and law gave the male head extensive powers over all the members of the household. By law he could punish "his servant, or apprentice [discipulo], or his wife, or his child, or his slave."[51] More importantly, however, the dominance of the male head was rooted in custom. It is reflected in the contemporary literature, such as Antonil's comparison of the father to a herdsman who must keep his cattle and horses penned to prevent straying.[52] It also is reflected in many facets of everday life. A married

51. Ordenações Filipinas, Livro 5, Titulo 35, Para. 1 in Pinto, Lutas de família, p. 186.
52. Antonil, Cultura e opulência, p. 166.

woman could not join the status-conveying brotherhood of Saint Francis of Assisi without her husband's approval and signature, the same restriction applying to dependent children.[53] Time after time a husband who named his wife as executor of his estate or tutor of his minor children felt compelled to justify his decision in terms of her special competency.[54]

But this discussion of the institution of marriage and of households dominated by married males should not obscure the fact that ecclesiastical bonds of matrimony were a reality for only 16.6 percent of the population over the legal age and for only 32.6 percent of the heads of housefuls. Marriage, while existing as the norm of the society, was not relevant to the lives of the great majority of people.[55] The internal dynamics of a society whose economic infrastructure, in the course of one century, had undergone tremendous fluctuations had created a different pattern of social organization.

Numerically the most significant of the family units was the matrifocal family; women headed 45.0 percent of all housefuls.[56] Of these housefuls, 83.1 percent were headed by women who, as far as the census taker recorded, had never been married. Should this phe-

53. Institutos da Irmandade de São Francisco, Livro 26, Capitulo 26. Arquivo da Irmandade de São Francisco, Ouro Prêto.

54. E.g., Will of Amaro de Araújo, Nov. 5, 1752, APHAN, Cód. 300, No. 6481.

55. It is possible that some part of the society recognized alternative forms of marriage beyond the church ceremony. However, this would not appear to be very general for male-headed housefuls. There were 534 cases in which the head was a single or widowed male. Of these, only 64—12.0 percent—had residing children; and 183—34.3 percent—resided completely alone, or only with resident children. Clearly in these cases no consort was present. In 124 cases—23.2 percent—the male resided with slaves and/or resident children. Given the nature of the society, it is unlikely that long-term, socially accepted relationships existed between master and slave. In fact, wills and testaments suggest that the more common practice was to free the female slave and provide her with clothing, jewels, a house, slaves, etc. More likely was the establishment of non-jural ties with persons listed as agregados. This was possible in 102 cases where one or more eligible women were present. This is a maximum figure as it includes a number of instances where there is a low probability of the existence of an accepted conjugal unit. Even so, non-jural conjugal units were possible for only 18.7 percent of all eligible male houseful heads and 6.0 percent of all housefuls.

56. Matrifocal is used to refer to a "women-centered" houseful; that is, a houseful whose head was recognized by the census taker to be a woman. This definition does not preclude the presence of a male serving in the role of "husband" and/or father, but it assumes that the census taker was reflecting the community's view of the role of the female head. Obviously, had the enumerator assumed that only a male could head a houseful then the female would have been listed as an agregado, and the houseful characterized at patrifocal. That the census taker listed so many women as houseful heads precludes coincidence as a general explanation.

nomenon be found to apply generally for colonial Brazil, a reevaluation of the basic nature of colonial society will be in order.[57]

In terms of size, the matrifocal houseful is comparable to that headed by males, except for the number of slaves. Whereas only 34.8 percent of all slaves resided in matrifocal housefuls, 47.4 percent of all dependent children and 52.0 percent of all agregados did so. Looked at in another way, the matrifocal houseful averaged 1.33 children, while the patrifocal averaged 1.21; for agregados the figures are 1.20 and 0.91. However, there were only 1.17 slaves per matrifocal houseful, as opposed to 1.92 per patrifocal houseful. This difference, plus the presence of the spouses of the married males, results in a mean houseful size that is significantly larger for patrifocal than for matrifocal housefuls—5.46 compared with 4.69.

It is not surprising that this structure evolved. The barriers to marriage were great enough to turn this sacrament into a symbol of status differentiation, despite a sex ratio, as noted earlier, of 79 males to every 100 females. Long gone were the days when, as in the early eighteenth century, the low ratio of married couples could be attributed to a shortage of women.[58] The ensuing surplus of women probably encouraged promiscuity and created the conditions leading to the evolution of numerous matrifocal households. The process was apparently encouraged by the relative lack of jobs for men, while domestic employment for women was more readily available. Furthermore, as the economy entered a period of recession, it is probable that spatial mobility increased, with men moving on to other gold fields or to the cattle and coffee areas of southern Minas Gerais. Women remained as the stable elements of the population.

The racial structure of the female heads of housefuls is significant. Of those whose race is known, only 10.5 percent were white, with mulattoes and blacks accounting for the remainder. Even when all those whose race is unknown are considered as white, the total of whites is still only slightly over one-third. Thus, there is no question that

57. Significantly, parishes as diverse as rural Casa Branca in Minas Gerais and urban São Pedro in Salvador, Bahia, show similar patterns: The proportion of women heading housefuls was 37.3 percent and 41.5 percent, respectively, Relasam dos Moradores da Freguezia de Santo António de Casa Branca do Termo de Vila Rica da Capitania de Minas Gerais, Aug. 12, 1804, AN, Lata 130, Pasta 2. Avelino de Jesus da Costa, "População da cidade de Baía em 1775," in V Coloquio Internacional de Estudos Luso-Brasileiros, Actas (Coimbra, 1963), Vol. I, pp. 191–286.

58. Feu de Carvalho, Ementário da história de Minas; Felipe dos Santos Freire na sedição de Vila Rica—1720 (Belo Horizonte, 1930?), p. 21; and especially see Lourenço de Almeida to João V, undated, in Feu de Carvalho, "Primeiras aulas," 351.

220   HAHR | MAY | DONALD RAMOS

TABLE XI. Racial and Marital Status of Matrifocal Housefuls.

Race	Single		Married/Widowed		Total no.	% of Total
	No.	% single	No.	%		
White	42	72.4	16	27.6	58	7.5
Mulatto	164	79.2	43	20.8	207	26.9
Crioula	172	93.5	12	6.5	184	24.0
Preta	84	97.7	2	2.3	86	11.2
Cabra	14	93.3	1	6.7	15	2.0
Unknown	162	74.3	56	25.7	218	28.4
TOTAL	638	83.1	130	16.9	768	100.0

the vast majority of the women who headed housefuls were nonwhite. In support of the hypothesis that marriage served as a means of status differentiation, it is also important to note the disproportionate share of whites who were, or had been, married.

The implication that the large number of female heads generally represented a social grouping characterized by lower-class standing is supported by the very low number of female houseful heads identified as ladies or donas. Only 40 of these women were so labeled, comprising only 5.2 percent of the total. Fifteen of these were, or had been, married. Thus, only 25 women who were titled and single were acting as heads of housefuls.

The housefuls headed by women show significant variations in size. These variations follow the racial identity of the heads, with the largest housefuls headed by whites and the lowest by African-born blacks. To a large degree this was obviously a reflection of the differences in economic status demonstrated by the ownership of slaves.

TABLE XII. Female Headed Housefuls: Component Size by Race of Head.

Race	Total	Children		Agregados		Slaves		Total Mean[a]	Total Mean Minus Slaves[a]
		No.	Mean	No.	Mean	No.	Mean		
White	58	63	1.09	77	1.33	145	2.50	4.92	2.42
Mulatto	207	313	1.51	245	1.18	225	1.09	3.78	2.69
Crioulo	186	267	1.44	189	1.02	70	0.38	2.84	2.46
Preto	86	48	0.56	43	0.50	56	0.65	1.71	1.06
Cabra	15	14	0.93	16	1.07	4	0.27	2.27	2.00
Unknown	216	314	1.45	352	1.63	395	1.83	4.91	3.09
TOTAL	768	1019	1.33	922	1.20	895	1.17	3.70	2.53

[a] Does not include head of houseful.

When the slaves are removed from the data, housefuls headed by whites are surpassed in size by those headed by mulattoes and crioulos, Brazilian-born blacks.

The large number of households headed by women also suggest the need to reevaluate the role and status of women in traditional Brazilian society. The traditional view was fostered by many of the travelers who crisscrossed Minas Gerais in the nineteenth century. Time after time they depicted the women of the house scurrying away in embarrassment, or spying and giggling at the strange customs of the traveler.[59] Occasions when these travelers were able to meet, dine, or talk with women were exceptional.[60] But these travelers generally visited representatives of the local aristocracy; seldom were they forced to reside with members of the lower strata, and even more rarely did they seek to describe the social configuration of these households. Clearly their view of *mineiro* society was one-sided. The stereotype of women as mere shadows of their husbands, involved only with children, cooking, church, and the supervision of domestic slaves is only partially true.

Customs that had governed the behavior of women in Portugal were modified in Brazil. This modification is illustrated by a confrontation between the Portuguese Overseas Council and a bishop of Rio de Janeiro who, in the early eighteenth century, prohibited women from going outdoors after dark. The bishop was chastized by the Council as well-meaning but badly informed about the situation in Brazil. The Council contended that it was necessary for poor women to do their shopping and water-carrying after dark. More importantly, the bishop was urged not to equate immorality and sinfulness with going out after dark.[61] Women in Brazil could not be forced to remain in the seclusion to which their Portuguese sisters were accustomed.

Many women in Vila Rica worked to help sustain their households. Much of their work was domestic, such as weaving, sewing, and washing clothes, but a significant number of women were shopkeepers and gold prospectors. Women owned about 40 percent of all the shops

59. E.g., Saint-Hilaire, *Viagem*, I, 14, 142; Wells, *Exploring*, I, 302, and II, 2–4, 14, 27, 66, and 254; Richard F. Burton, *Explorations of the Highlands of the Brazil with a Full Account of the Gold and Diamond Mines* (London, 1869), I, 248.

60. Wells, *Exploring*, II, 20; Saint-Hilaire, *Viagem*, I, 248; John Mawe, "Viagens ao interior do Brasil particularmente aos districtos do ouro e do diamante, em 1809–1810," in *Collectanea de scientistas extrangeiros*, ed. and trans. Rudolfo Jacob, (Belo Horizonte, 1930), I, p. 20.

61. See Consulta of the Overseas Council, Sept. 4, 1703, in *Documentos históricos*, pp. 93, 158–159.

222   HAHR | MAY | DONALD RAMOS

TABLE XIII.   Occupations of Female Heads of Housefuls.

Occupation	No.	Percentage	Occupation	No.	Percentage
Sewing	58	18.6	Selling	18	5.8
Shopkeeping	56	17.9	Washing	14	4.5
Prospecting	46	14.7	From Alms	20	6.4
Textiles	20	6.4	Other	13	4.2
Farming	19	6.1	As Best as		
Cooking	6	1.9	Possible*	42	13.5
			TOTAL	312	100.0
			Unlisted	456	

* Listed as "das suas agencias."

in Vila Rica and comprised at least one quarter of the prospectors and more substantial miners. But the majority of women who headed housefuls either had no occupation listed or had marginal jobs, implying that resident children and agregados were important economic supports of the household.

The implications of the widespread existence of the matrifocal household are far reaching. What was the impact this structure had upon the identity formation patterns of children? Many were raised without the presence of a father (34.6 percent of the total children) while fathers of others were not present because of abandonment or death (12.7 percent).[62] One possible implication is suggested by the work of Roger Burton and John Whiting into the process of identity formation in matriarchal societies. They suggest that in societies where the child sleeps with or near the mother, the mother becomes the identity model since, by controlling the resources wanted by the infant, she becomes the subject of envy and then of emulation. Girls raised in this environment, Burton and Whiting contend, follow the lifestyle of their mothers. Boys become overly dependent, infantile, and adopt characteristics socially defined as feminine, until they come under the influence of older boys and men, at which time they seek to obliterate the primary female identity by rejecting all feminine influence and behaving in an exaggerated masculine manner.[63] This hypothesis is highly suggestive for an understanding of the dynamics of identity formation in colonial Vila Rica. In a society where a sig-

62. It is possible that for some of these matrifocal housefuls, the father was listed as an agregado. It would appear, however, that the existence of many such situations is improbable since the structure of the census was based on authority rather than on economic status.
63. Roger V. Burton and John W. M. Whiting, "The Absent Father and Cross-Sex Identity," Merrill-Palmer Quarterly of Behavior and Development, 7 (April, 1961), 85–95.

nificant number of all children were raised in matrifocal homes, presumably with little opportunity to identify with males until old enough to participate in the male-dominated world beyond the home, the pyschological impact of the absence of the father must have been important. The conflict between a primary female identity and the patriarchal environment might help explain the exaggerated masculinity known as machismo.

Another effect that the large number of these households had on the social system was to create a class of people who were technically illegitimate. About 43 percent of the total number of dependent children resided in households where the parent of record had never been married. The existence of so many illegitimate children necessitated the evolution of a system flexible enough to blur the differences between the legitimate and the illegitimate and to integrate the latter into the society without creating major dysfunctions. Accommodations were, in fact, made on both local and imperial levels. Charters legitimatizing children were available for a price. These were probably of greater importance to the elite, since through them the children were allowed to inherit the title and entailed estate of the parent.[64] Certainly the charters were of little importance to the majority of the population. For the majority of the illegitimate children questions of inheritance were resolved by the wills of their parents. Many wills contained provisions for "natural" children.[65] In other wills parents recognized the paternity of children living in matrifocal households.[66] But the society confronted by so many illegitimate children had been forced to modify other rules. Even the priesthood was not closed to illegitimate children, since this restriction could be waived by the proper authorities.[67]

In addition to those children whose parents were not married, however, there were a number of children whose parents were unknown. Called *enjeitados*, these were children who had been abandoned by their parents. Responsibility for them rested with the municipal council, which often paid foster parents to raise the waifs. Because of the

64. Royal Carta de Legitimação, May 31, 1740, APM, Colonial Section, Documento Avulso.
65. E.g., will of António Gonçalves de Araújo, Jan. 28, 1756, APAD, Livro de Obitos, No. 3, fols. 262v–263.
66. Will of João Barbosa de Amorim, Dec. 3, 1771, APHAN, Cód. 335, No. 7041.
67. For example, António Leite Esquerdo petitioned the bishop of Mariana in 1779 to have two obstacles to his ordination waived. The impediments were "mulatismo e ilegitimidade." The petition was approved. Petition of A. L. Esquerdo, Aug. 21, 1779, ACM, Habilitações, No. 199.

large number of *enjeitados*, this had become a considerable expense for the council.[68] The 1804 census listed 146 *enjeitados*. Enumerated among the agregados, they comprised 8.7 percent of all agregados and 6.1 percent of dependent children.

The council had, on occasion, reacted to this situation, going so far as to call the mothers of the *enjeitados* prostitutes.[69] Presumably included among these so-called prostitutes were the mistresses maintained by the well-to-do; some mothers were forced to abandon newly born children by the exigencies of their status.[70] It seems probable that the word "prostitute" was used by the town fathers to deal with a social structure—the matrifocal family—which they perceived as immoral. To limit the practice of abandoning children, the council appointed sworn inspectors who were responsible for ensuring that pregnant women in their districts did not desert their children. The inspectors were enjoined to be especially watchful of mulatto and black women, since they were viewed as more likely to abandon their children.[71] The abandonment of children was viewed as being connected with a specific social class—the poor and nonwhite.

The church also was active in trying to curb this practice by curtailing concubinage. The most effective tool in its arsenal was the ecclesiastical visitation, from which judicial action (including exile) could arise.[72] The visitation was an effort to impose on the parish priest the values of the church hierarchy. Some visitations were meticulous and forceful, especially during the first half of the eighteenth-century. For example, one of these ordered that mistresses,

---

68. During the 1758 *correição* conducted by a royal judge, the council complained of "the excessive number of *enjeitados*, whites as well as mulattoes and Negroes. . . ." Correição, Dec. 31, 1758, APM, Cód. 22 (Câmara Municipal do Ouro Prêto, cited herein after as CMOP), fol. 139.

69. The council asked all citizens to report cases where known "public prostitutes . . . resorted to the abominable practice of abandoning their children." Council Ordinance, Mar. 2, 1763, APM, Cód. 77 (CMOP), fols. 240v–241.

70. An example of this is the accusation made against a priest charging that he had lived with a woman for years and had "children by her, sending her out of the hamlet when it was time to give birth, and [then] abandoning the children in different parts." The priest was found innocent, but the charges were not viewed as outlandish and were investigated. Sentence of Padre António Vieira de Matos, Apr. 15, 1750, ACM, Livro que ha de servir para registrar todos os mandados sentenças e ordens pertencentes ao foro contenciozo, fol. 10.

71. Correição, Oct. 24, 1761, APM, Cód. 22 (CMOP), fols. 142v–143.

72. A mulatto freedwoman was exiled for one year after being accused of being a "public and scandalous prostitute" who took part in "lascivious dances and diabolical batuques," and of having become the mistress of a resident. Registration of the Condemnation and Exile of the Defendant Rita de Oliveira, Dec. 1, 1751, ACM, Cód. 10, fols. 50v–51.

"even if useful for running the household," were to be ejected from the home and all relationships with mistresses outside of the home were to cease. To enforce these orders, priests were instructed not to confess those men supporting mistresses nor accept as parishioners couples who could not prove that they were married.[73] The policies of the church paralleled those of the state: the church tried to root out extra-marital relationships (while not really changing the prerequisites for marriage), and the state, attempted to avoid the expenses resulting from these relationships (without attacking the institution of concubinage itself).

The family structure in the region of Vila Rica during the late colonial period is more complex and diverse than that usually portrayed for Brazil. The traditional patriarchal, extended family, based on co-residential patterns, is found in relatively few housefuls. Far commoner were nuclear and matrifocal families, with the large number of the latter emphasizing the status-differentiating function of marriage. The role of women emerges from this analysis as having been very significant, both in numerical and social terms. If the conclusions reached for Vila Rica are, in fact, generalizable, then the hypothesis that the extended Brazilian family subsequently disintegrated under the twin onslaughts of industrialization and urbanization is not valid. The extended family as a common residential unit has not disappeared—it never existed. It may be more correct to state that modernization has led to the increase in the number of nuclear families and a decrease in mono-focal families.

73. Visitation, Apr. 26, 1727 in Morais, *História de Conceição*, pp. 92–93.

4

Divorce and the Changing Status of Women in Eighteenth-Century Massachusetts

Nancy F. Cott

WHEN a neighbor asked John Backus, silversmith of Great Barrington, Massachusetts, in 1784, why he kicked and struck his wife, John replied that "it was Partly owing to his Education for his father often treated his mother in the same manner."[1] John's mother may have tolerated that abuse but his wife did not: she complained of his cruelty, desertion, and adultery, and obtained a divorce.

This epitome of two generations' marital strife, one item in early Massachusetts divorce records, suggests how valuable such records may be to the interpretation of marriage and family life in the past. Divorce proceedings not only elucidate customs and ideals of marriage; they also disclose the marital behavior of the litigants. The history of divorce practice documents sex-role expectations, permits comparison between the obligations and freedoms of husbands and of wives, and provides a test of the double standard of sexual morality. Divorce records from provincial Massachusetts are especially interesting because the years they cover are those least explored in studies of marriage and family in New England. Historians have yet to explain the transition from "Puritan" to "Victorian" standards, but current research has begun to suggest that unrest and change in patterns of sexual and familial behavior were conspicuous during the eighteenth century.[2] Records of divorce in provincial Massachusetts illuminate these little-known aspects of individuals' lives.[3]

---

[1] Deposition of William Whiting, Jr., Suffolk Court Files #129846, Suffolk County Court House, Boston, 106.

[2] Robert V. Wells, "Quaker Marriage Patterns in a Colonial Perspective," *William and Mary Quarterly*, 3d Ser., XXIX (1972), 415-442; Daniel Scott Smith, "Parental Power and Marriage Patterns: An Analysis of Historical Trends in Hingham, Massachusetts," *Journal of Marriage and the Family*, XXXV (1973), 419-439; Daniel Scott Smith and Michael Hindus, "Premarital Pregnancy in America, 1640-1966," *Journal of Interdisciplinary History*, VI (1975), 537-570.

[3] See Nancy F. Cott, "Eighteenth-Century Family and Social Life Revealed in

Massachusetts divorce proceedings between 1692 and 1786 can be fairly readily traced because they took place (with a few notable exceptions) before one body, a "court" composed of the governor and his Council.[4] One hundred twenty-two wives and 101 husbands filed 229 petitions in all (six wives petitioned twice).[5] So far as their occupational and residential characteristics are known, the petitioners included the whole range of types in the population. Slightly more than a quarter of them lived in Boston, the others in all varieties of towns, from the smallest to the largest, the most remote to the most advantageously located.[6] Almost 63 percent of the petitioners

---

Massachusetts Divorce Records," *Journal of Social History*, X (1976), where these documents are used to investigate questions about privacy and community, relations among conjugal-family and extended-family members, and romantic love and sex.

[4] In June 1692 the General Court declared that "all controversies concerning marriage and divorce shall be heard and determined by the governor and council." *Acts and Resolves, Public and Private, of the Province of Massachusetts Bay* ... (Boston, 1869-1922), I, chap. 25, sec. 4, 61. The state constitution of 1780 confirmed this practice, until "An Act for Regulating Marriage and Divorce" of Mar. 16, 1786, located jurisdiction over divorce suits in the Supreme Judicial Court held for each county. *Acts and Resolves of Massachusetts, 1784-1785* (Boston, ca. [1892]), 564-567.

[5] The most informative records are the original petitions and depositions preserved for most of the cases between 1739 and 1786 in volumes 793-796 of the Suffolk Court Files. Similar documents from some earlier cases appear in volume IX of the Massachusetts Archives, at the Archives Dept., State House, Boston. A single bound manuscript volume labeled "Divorces, 1760-1786," hereafter cited as "Divorces," located with the Suffolk Files, summarizes most of the divorce petitions and decrees between those dates. Mass. Archives, CXL, contains a fairly complete record of divorces between 1780 and 1786. Additional cases before 1780 have been recovered from the executive records of the Council, also at the Archives Dept., hereafter cited as Council Recs. Surprisingly, the Council Records do not contain the most inclusive recording of petitions and decrees; their completeness varies considerably through the years. The legislative records of the Council, a separate series in the Archives Dept. called Court Records, have been used in those cases that involved legislation.

[6] The overrepresentation of Bostonians—for the city held only 6% of the province's population in 1765—was at least partially owing to the requirement that petitioners appear before the governor and Council at their sessions in Boston. The legislation of 1786 shifted jurisdiction over divorce to the superior courts held in each county because of remote petitioners' difficulty in getting to Boston. I have estimated the geographical distribution of petitioners by using the population figures in the 1764-1765 provincial census, obviously not an exact means since the divorce cases span almost a century, but the only one available. Place of residence was disclosed in almost 90% of the suits. On the basis of 1764-1765 population figures, 24.6% of petitioners resided in towns of less than 1,000 pop.; 22.6% in towns of 1,000 to 1,999; 15.9% in towns of 2,000 to 2,999; 8.2% in towns of 3,000 to 5,000; and 28.7% in Boston. More than two-fifths of the petitioners lived in the populous counties of Suffolk and Essex; a slightly smaller proportion in the eastern counties of Middlesex, Worcester, Bristol, Plymouth, Barnstable, and Dukes; and the remainder (slightly under a fifth) in the remote and lightly populated counties of Hampshire, Berkshire,

disclosed the occupation of the man of the family. Thirty-two percent of these cases involved families of artisans or traders; 22 percent, husbandmen or yeomen; and another 22 percent, mariners or fishermen. About 17 percent originated in families in which the husbands had the more prestigious status of gentlemen, merchants, professionals, ship captains, or militia officers; and the remaining 7 percent involved families at the lower end of the occupational scale—laborers, truckmen, and servants. Although one would need to know the petitioners' wealth to ascertain their economic standing or to judge how accurately they typified the Massachusetts population, it is likely that the great majority—perhaps three-fourths—occupied the "middling ranks."[7] Whether or not they were a representative sample, the group included all varieties of the Massachusetts population, urban and rural dwellers, rich and poor.

The petitioners had an easier time gaining divorce in provincial Massachusetts than they would have had in the mother country.[8] In England marital controversies were judged by the ecclesiastical courts, and these courts applied canon law, under which a valid marriage was regarded as indissoluble. True divorce (*divortium a vinculo matrimonii*), allowing the partners to remarry, was never granted unless a marriage was judged null to begin with, on grounds such as consanguinity, bigamy, or sexual incapacity. Such causes as adultery, desertion, or cruelty warranted only separation from bed and board (*divortium a mensa et thoro*), which sustained the legal obligations of marriage, excepting cohabitation, and did not allow either partner to remarry. At the end of the seventeenth century, in order to relieve the stringency of ecclesiastical rule for noblemen whose wives were adulterous, the House of Lords began to dissolve marriages by private act. Only a select group could take advantage of this avenue to divorce. The cost often

---

Cumberland, Lincoln, and York. See J. H. Benton, *Early Census Making in Massachusetts* (Boston, 1905).

[7] There are some interesting differences between the occupational levels of male petitioners and female—the latter judged by their *husbands'* occupations, however. Among the 122 wives, 73 disclosed the occupations of their husbands. Fifteen percent were esquires, gentlemen, or merchants; 4% doctors or officers; 19% husbandmen or yeomen; 16% mariners or fishermen; 37% craftsmen or traders; and 8% laborers, servants, or truckmen. Among the 101 husbands, 67 disclosed their occupations. Only 4.5% were esquires, gentlemen, or merchants; 9% professionals or officers; 25% husbandmen or yeomen; 28% mariners (reflecting the high incidence of adultery on the part of wives whose husbands were at sea for long periods); 27% craftsmen or traders; and 6% the lower occupations.

[8] They may have had an even easier time in Connecticut, which had the most liberal divorce policy of all the colonies; both judicial and legislative divorces were granted there. Between 1740 and 1789, 174 superior court divorces were recorded in Hartford County alone. Henry S. Cohn, "Connecticut's Divorce Mechanism: 1636-1969," *American Journal of Legal History*, XIV (1970), 43, n. 39.

amounted to several thousand pounds, because a petitioner was expected to have first obtained a decree of divorce *a mensa* and a civil judgment against the adulterers. The Lords passed only about ninety private acts of divorce between 1697 and 1785, all resting on adultery charges and all awarded to husbands.[9] Divorce *a vinculo* from a valid marriage was more frequent in Massachusetts during the same period. Between 1692 and 1786, 110 divorces were granted in the province on grounds other than those considered legitimate by the English ecclesiastical courts—63 to men, 47 to women— and England and Wales had a population of almost seven million in 1765, when the Massachusetts population was under 250,000.[10]

The authority of the governor and Council over divorce originated in provincial statute. No causes for divorce were codified, however, and their divorce policy combined elements of English practice, Puritan divorce theory, seventeenth-century Massachusetts precedents, and innovation. Opposing canon law, Puritan divorce theory held that marriage was a civil contract which could and should be dissolved for such breaches as adultery, long absence, or irremediable cruelty.[11] In the seventeenth century the civil courts of Massachusetts tried to effect this theoretical position, so far as is shown by the results of forty known petitions between 1639 and 1692. The county courts and the General Court, as well as the Court of Assistants (predecessor to the Council) judged petitions for divorce, even after the Code of 1660 gave jurisdiction to the assistants. They annulled marriages on grounds of consanguinity, bigamy, and sexual incapacity, and dissolved them for long absence and for adultery alone or in combination with desertion, neglect, or cruelty. No clear decrees of separate bed and board have been discovered, but

[9] This discussion of English divorce practice relies on George Elliott Howard, *A History of Matrimonial Institutions, Chiefly in the United States and England* . . . (Chicago, 1904), II, 52-57, 77-85, 92-93, 102-107; Reginald Haw, *The State of Matrimony* (London, 1952), 74-89; Oliver McGregor, *Divorce in England* (London, 1957), 1-12; Joseph W. Madden, *Handbook of the Law of Persons and Domestic Relations* (St. Paul, Minn., 1931), 256-260; and L. Kinvin Wroth and Hiller B. Zobel, eds., *The Legal Papers of John Adams*, I (Cambridge, Mass., 1965), 280-285. The several accounts of divorce in England differ slightly in their estimates of numbers of parliamentary divorces before 1800.

[10] The population figure for England and Wales is estimated from a table in J. D. Chambers, *Population, Economy, and Society in Pre-Industrial England* (London, 1972), 108.

[11] The document best illustrating Puritan divorce reform theory in England is the *Reformatio Legum Ecclesiasticarum*, authorized by Parliament and drafted by eminent divines in 1552. The *Reformatio* regarded marriage as a civil contract rather than an indissoluble sacred bond, omitted mention of separate bed and board, allowed dissolution of marriage for adultery, desertion, continued absence without news, or unmitigable enmity or cruelty by either spouse—and was never put into effect. Howard, *Matrimonial Institutions*, II, 78-79.

our knowledge of seventeenth-century divorce proceedings is probably incomplete.[12]

When the governor and Council assumed more uniform jurisdiction over divorce after 1692, they granted annulments, divorces (literally, dissolutions of marriage bonds) allowing the innocent party to remarry, and decrees of separate bed and board.[13] The years 1754 to 1757 formed a curious exception. During that period, for reasons not apparent in the historical record, the governor and Council declined to dissolve valid marriages and decreed separate bed and board for petitioners who formerly and subsequently would have been granted divorce.[14] In 1755, 1756, and 1757, six petitioners whose spouses were adulterous sought relief from the General Court and obtained legislative divorces instead of divorce decrees. These legislative divorces were the only ones enacted under the provincial charter of 1691.[15] In passing them the General Court assumed the role of Parliament in England; and in two of the six, the governor and Council filled the role of the English ecclesiastical courts by granting prior decrees of separate bed and board. Since they were legislative acts, these divorces were subject to review by the imperial Board of Trade, as was all colonial legislation. Reporting on the first three in 1758, the board called them "extraordinary" and "liable to great objections." The specific points of disapproval highlighted some of the differences between English and Massachusetts divorce policy. All three suits—two of them brought by women—rested on adultery charges. The divorces granted to the two women were called unprecedented, "the first of their kind . . . in the colonies or elsewhere." Moreover, the proofs of adultery were not clear enough; criminal conviction of the adulterers had not preceded the three divorce bills; and only one was supported by a prior decree of separate bed and board. Beyond these objections, which seemed sufficient grounds for

[12] Ibid., 331-338; Edmund S. Morgan, The Puritan Family: Religion and Domestic Relations in Seventeenth-Century New England (New York, 1966), 35-37; John Demos, A Little Commonwealth: Family Life in Plymouth Colony (New York, 1970), 92-97; D. Kelly Weisberg, "Under Greet Temptations Heer: Women and Divorce in Puritan Massachusetts," Feminist Studies, II (1975), 183-194. Since Howard's list of divorce suits for the period 1692-1786 is incomplete (he lists only 107 suits), it is likely that his list of 40 for the period 1639-1692 is similarly fragmentary.

[13] Wroth and Zobel, eds., Legal Papers of Adams, I, 282, erroneously states that jurisdiction to grant divorce a vinculo was ambiguous after 1692 and that the governor and Council did not grant divorces between 1692 and 1760.

[14] They did so despite a law enacted by the General Court in 1755, empowering them to enforce their decrees in divorce suits by ordering imprisonment for disobedience. Acts and Resolves, Mass. Bay, III, chap. 15, 782.

[15] The acts are in ibid., VI, 165, 169, 170, 173, 174, 177, and can be corroborated in Court Recs., XX, 337-338, 346, 351-352, 373, 379, 460, 461, 468, XXI, 97, 157, 161, 329, 497, 500, 517, 540, XXII, 40. Howard, Matrimonial Institutions, II, 340, errs in saying that "after 1692 the legislature does not seem to have interfered in divorce suits either on appeal or in the first instance."

disallowance, doubt existed whether any colonial legislature had the right to assume the parliamentary prerogative of granting divorces. The board referred the matter to the attorney-general and the solicitor-general for a decision whether to disallow the acts or declare them null; but no hearing took place, and these divorce bills and the subsequent three in Massachusetts were apparently allowed to stand.[16]

The interlude of legislative divorce in Massachusetts clarified the advantage the province gained through its usual practice of divorce by decree. If Massachusetts had taken the legislative route, the history of divorce there would probably have been quite different. Legislative divorces might well have been disallowed for lack of conformity to English practice, or declared null for invading the authority of Parliament. In fact, between 1769 and 1773 several colonial acts of legislative divorce, passed in Pennsylvania, New Jersey, and New Hampshire, met this fate. The crown's resentment of them resulted in a directive of 1773 to all royal governors to withhold consent from any divorce act passed by a colonial legislature.[17] This order halted divorce in the colonies other than Massachusetts until the Revolution, but in that province both petitions for and grants of divorce continued to multiply. Petitioners no longer resorted to the General Court, for in 1760, after investigating their own precedents for dissolving marriages before 1755, the governor and Council returned to the policy of decreeing divorces *a vinculo.*[18]

---

[16] Report of the Lords of Trade, June 6, 1758, Mass. Arch., XXII, 9-10. See also *Acts and Resolves, Mass. Bay,* VI, vi-vii, and Joseph Henry Smith, *Appeals to the Privy Council from the American Plantations* (New York, 1950), 582-585. Smith points out that in 1741 the Lords disallowed a Jamaica act of legislative divorce passed in 1739.

[17] See William Renwick Riddell, "Legislative Divorce in Colonial Pennsylvania," *Pennsylvania Magazine of History and Biography,* LVII (1933), 175-180; Thomas R. Meehan, " 'Not Made Out of Levity': Evolution of Divorce in Early Pennsylvania," *ibid.,* XCII (1968), 441-464; Leonard Woods Labaree, ed., *Royal Instructions to British Colonial Governors, 1670-1776,* I (New York, 1935), 154-155.

[18] A bill "for enabling the Governor and Council to grant Divorces from the Bands of Matrimony," passed by the House of Representatives in Aug. 1757, never became law because the Council neglected or declined to concur. Mass. Arch., IX, 419; *Journals of the House of Representatives of Massachusetts, 1757,* XXXIV (Meriden, Conn., 1961), 105. On July 30, 1759, the Council appointed four of its members to investigate the precedents of divorce actions before 1756. Why the Council had so short a collective memory—when several members had been on the Council in the early 1750s—is puzzling. The committee reported (accurately) on Nov. 10, 1759, that the Council had decreed seven divorces and one separation between 1747 and 1754. See Mass. Arch. IX, 432-434, and Council Recs., XIV, 122, 134. Another influence leading to the Council's resumption of divorce by decree may have been Gov. Thomas Pownall's message of Feb. 2, 1760, which touched on the Council's power as a divorce court. Josiah Quincy, Jr., *Reports of Cases Argued and Adjudged in the Superior Court of Judicature of the Province of Massachusetts Bay between 1761 and 1772* (Boston, 1865), 573-579.

TABLE I

NUMBER OF PETITIONS/NUMBER OF FAVORABLE DECREES, BY DECADE

Peti-tioners	1692-1704	1705-1714	1715-1724	1725-1734	1735-1744	1745-1754	1755-1764	1765-1774	1775-1786	Total
all	7/5	6/5	5/2	9/4	23/15	21/11	26/16	46/24	86/61	229/143
female	4/3	3/2	4/1	4/1	8/4	12/6	12/7	29/13	53/37	128/74
male	3/2	3/3	1/1	5/3	15/11	9/5	14/9	18/11	33/24	101/69

Note: Favorable decrees include divorce, annulment, and separate bed and board.

Divorce petitions and decrees showed a general pattern of increase during the eighteenth century in Massachusetts. As Table I indicates, more than half of the petitions and decrees between 1692 and 1786 occurred after 1764, and more than a third of them after 1774. This striking concentration took place without any change in the laws regarding divorce. What caused it? The population grew, but not nearly as rapidly as did the number of petitions. The incidence of petitions per decade increased by 77 percent from 1755-1764 to 1765-1774, and by 61 percent from 1765-1774 to 1775-1784, while the white population grew by approximately 5.7 percent from 1760 to 1770, and by approximately 14 percent from 1770 to 1780.[19]

Perhaps the governor and Council became more willing to consider and grant divorces after 1765, thus encouraging larger numbers of petitioners. In these pre-Revolutionary years the Council may have been more assertive in its divorce practice, which opposed England's, just as it became more independent of the royal prerogative in political matters, and more sympathetic to the whig leaders in the legislature.[20] Two decrees of the early 1770s in particular indicated that the Council would proceed on its own initiative in divorce actions whether or not the governor agreed. The Council alone declared Abigail Bradstreet separated from her husband in 1771, and James Richardson divorced from his wife in 1772, although Gov. Thomas Hutchinson did not judge these decrees warranted by the evidence and would not sign them.[21]

The chronological coincidence of the concentration of divorce petitions with the War for Independence suggests a causal link. We might suppose

[19] The white population of Massachusetts in 1780 was about five-and-a-half times as large as it had been in 1690, but there were twelve times as many petitions and decrees in the years 1775-1786 as in 1692-1704. Population data are from U.S. Bureau of the Census, *Historical Statistics of the United States: Colonial Times to 1957* (Washington, D.C., 1960).

[20] See Francis G. Walett, "The Massachusetts Council, 1766-1774: The Transformation of a Conservative Institution," *WMQ*, 3d Ser., VI (1949), 605-627.

[21] Abigail Bradstreet v. Joseph Bradstreet, Suffolk Files #129762, "Divorces," 68-70; James Richardson v. Hannah Richardson, Suffolk Files #129769, "Divorces," 70-72.

that wartime disruption of families led to an increase of petitions, but there is little direct evidence of this. Very few petitions originated from war-related grievances, such as a married man's adultery with a campfollower or a woman's pregnancy while her husband was absent in military service.[22] Gauged by the evidence of prenuptial pregnancy, premarital sexual relations increased dramatically during the mid- to late eighteenth century—suggesting the possibility of a similar rise in adultery—but that phenomenon antedated the war.[23]

Most likely, divorce petitions increased not because spouses more often had legitimate marital grievances but because they were more often motivated to respond to marital wrongs by seeking divorce. Perhaps, then, the rise in divorce related in a general way to the War for Independence in the sense that a certain personal outlook—one that implied self-assertion and regard for the future, one that we might label more "modern" than "traditional"—may have led a person to seek divorce and also to support American independence.[24] The evidence that aggrieved spouses desired to have their marriages ended officially, rather than taking more traditional measures such as "self-divorce" through desertion, or resigning themselves to the ties of unsatisfactory marriages, suggests a modernization of attitudes.[25] Communication about the granting of divorces may also have had a cumulative effect: the more divorces were allowed, the more likely it became for a discontented spouse to consider the possibility. Especially in small towns, news of divorces being obtained must have encouraged more men and women to petition. The growth in petitions seems to indicate that more individuals were asserting control over the direction of their lives and were refusing to be ruled by unhappy fates—characteristics which are also considered "modern." In the Revolutionary period this kind of self-assertion may have gone along with an

[22] For example, Chloe Welch v. Luke Welch, Suffolk Files #129790, "Divorces," 122-125, and Andrew Gage v. Elizabeth Gage, Suffolk Files #129829, "Divorces," 192-193; see also Ann Lovell v. John Lovell, Jr., Suffolk Files #129778.

[23] See Smith and Hindus, "Premarital Pregnancy," *Jour. Interdisciplinary Hist.,* VI (1975), 537-570.

[24] See Kenneth A. Lockridge, "Social Change and the Meaning of the American Revolution," *Jour. Soc. Hist.,* VI (1973), 403-439, for several hypothetical models of "preparedness" for the War for Independence.

[25] On modernization in New England see *ibid.,* and two articles by Richard D. Brown: "Modernization and the Modern Personality in Early America, 1600-1865: A Sketch of a Synthesis," *Jour. Interdisciplinary Hist.,* II (1972), 201-228, and "The Emergence of Urban Society in Rural Massachusetts, 1760-1820," *Journal of American History,* LXI (1974), 29-51. For a typology of the "modern" personality see Alex Inkeles, "Making Men Modern: On the Causes and Consequences of Individual Change in Six Developing Countries," *American Journal of Sociology,* LXXV (1969), 208-225, and "The Modernization of Man," in Myron Weiner, ed., *Modernization: The Dynamics of Growth* (New York, 1966), 138-150.

enhanced sense of citizenship and legal rights. Not only men claimed the
rights of citizens. At least one Boston woman in 1784 and another in 1785
petitioned "as a citizen of this Commonwealth" for a hearing of her case.[26]

More wives than husbands sued for divorce during the period 1692-1786,
and the concentration of women's petitions during the Revolutionary years
was more marked than that of men's. One can only speculate whether these
figures mean that women generally had more marital grievances or that their
grievances were growing faster or being more readily voiced. Several variables hindered or encouraged men and women to seek divorce. A man might
hesitate because he was shy of the authorities, hated to arouse adverse
publicity about his marriage, or could not afford the expense, whatever it
was; or because the worth of his wife's domestic service seemed to outweigh
her transgressions. Male domination of colonial public life suggests, however,
that men were less shy of the authorities than were women, better able to
stand adverse publicity about their marriages without risking their entire
reputation, significantly more independent economically, and better equipped
than women to pay legal expenses. A man could also take the initiative in
acquiring a second spouse.

All the feelings that might have kept men from suing for divorce
probably affected women even more intensely. Consider the doubts and
anguish of Abigail Bailey as she pondered whether to seek divorce from her
husband, who had committed incest with their daughter and had also had
sexual liaisons with several other women. "Whether it would be consisted
[*sic*] with faithfulness to suffer him to flee, and not be made a monument of
civil justice, was my query. The latter looked to me inexpressibly painful.
And I persuaded myself, that if he would do what was right, relative to our
property, and would go to some distant place, where we should be afflicted
with him no more, it might be sufficient; and I might be spared the dreadful
scene of prosecuting my husband."[27]

Women apparently expected less success with their petitions than did
men. While men always asked for divorce (dissolution of the bonds of
marriage), women frequently equivocated; they requested divorce or, if that
were not possible, whatever separation the governor and Council were willing
to grant.[28] Perhaps other wives who had cause did not even petition because

[26] See Sarah Vernon v. William Vernon, Suffolk Files #129840, petition, 78, and
Rebecca Simpson v. Ebenezer Simpson, *ibid.* #129854, petition, 140.

[27] *Memoirs of Mrs. Abigail Bailey . . . written by herself . . .* , ed. Ethan Smith
(Boston, 1815), 58-59. Mrs. Bailey eventually did petition and obtain a divorce in
1792.

[28] For example, Mary Fairservice v. John Fairservice (1767), petition in "Divorces," 40-42; Sarah Gould v. William Gould (1773), Suffolk Files #129772,
petition, 56; Sarah Kingsley v. Enoch Kingsley (1771), Suffolk Files #129773,
petition, 58; Martha Air v. Adam Air (1773), Suffolk Files #129779, petition, 85.

they did not expect to win. According to the most recent study, illiteracy handicapped half or more of the female population in initiating civil actions, compared to 10 or 20 percent of the male population. The female petitioners were distinguished by their literacy: almost three-quarters of them (two-thirds of the non-Boston residents) could sign their names.[29] The high rate of literacy among female petitioners suggests that they may have been a group self-selected by stronger-than-average initiative or education, who did not fully represent the frequency of wives' dissatisfaction in marriage.

Whatever the inhibitions, powerful reasons urged unhappy wives to sue for divorce—reasons that did not so affect husbands. Self-preservation compelled wives whose husbands were physically abusive. A woman whose husband deserted or failed to provide for her gained little advantage from marriage, and the marriage contract hindered her from supporting herself because her property and earnings legally belonged to her husband. Many women pointed this out. In her petition of 1759, for example, Henrietta East Caine of Boston lamented that while her marriage contract lasted, "her Friends will not supply her with Goods to carry on her business as before." Another Boston woman warned that she and her three children would become public charges if she remained subject to her husband, whereas if divorced "she apprehends she shall be able to find Friends that will place her in some business to maintain herself and children." Sarah Backus claimed in 1783 that she "would be content by the most penurious industry to gain a support for herself and Child, but every Idea of comfort is banished from her Breast when she reflects, that by Law her Person is subjected to be con-

[29] Kenneth A. Lockridge, *Literacy in Colonial New England: An Enquiry into the Social Context of Literacy in the Early Modern West* (New York, 1974), esp. tables on pp. 24 and 41, indicates that Boston women's ability to sign moved from about 40% in 1700 to a peak of 68% in 1758-1762, and then fell to 60% by 1787, while rural women's ability remained below 40% for the whole period; and that Boston men's ability to sign moved from about 75% in 1700 to 80% in 1758-1762, while rural men's ability moved from 65% to 75%. Literacy data (signature or mark) appeared for 96 female divorce petitioners and 56 male petitioners. Sixty-one percent of these female petitioners before 1765 could sign—all of the 9 Boston women, and 8 of the 19 non-Boston women. Seventy-eight percent of the female petitioners between 1765 and 1786 could sign, including 16 of the 20 Boston women and 37 (77%) of the 48 non-Boston women. Among 17 male petitioners before 1765, 94% could sign—that is, all except one black man of Boston, a servant. Of 39 male petitioners between 1765 and 1786, 95% could sign—all of the 8 Boston men and all but two of the 31 non-Boston men. If Lockridge's figures are correct for the general population, both male and female divorce petitioners, as judged by ability to sign, had literacy above the norm. For a control group independent of Lockridge's study, there are the scores of deponents who testified in the divorce cases. They suggest a different norm. The ability to sign of 495 male deponents was 98.4%; it was 100% among the 64 deponents before 1765, and 98.1% among the 431 deponents between 1765 and 1786.

596   WILLIAM AND MARY QUARTERLY

TABLE II

PETITION RESULTS

	Male Petitions	Female Petitions	All
Divorce	64	51	115
Annulment	4	7	11
Separate bed and board	1	16	17
Dismissed or not granted	11	19	30
Unresolved	21	35	56
Total	101	128	229

trouled by a man possessing no one tender sentiment, but on the contrary under the entire dominion of every criminal and foul pollution."[30]

Sixty-eight percent of the husbands and 58 percent of the wives succeeded in gaining favorable action on their petitions, but 67 percent of the husbands gained freedom to remarry, in contrast to only 45 percent of the wives. Sixteen of the seventeen separations from bed and board granted during the period went to wives. When petitioners failed to obtain favorable action, it was more often because their suits remained unresolved than because they were dismissed. Fewer than 15 percent of the women's and 11 percent of the men's petitions were actually dismissed, but more than 27 percent of the women's and 20 percent of the men's never resulted in decrees. (See Table II.) It is unclear if the lack of resolution of these cases reflected some aim of the court or the petitioner, or whether the records are faulty or missing. No significant pattern of economic or geographic discrimination, or unusual lack of clarity in the cases, appears to account for the fate of these petitions; but the percentages reveal that women's petitions were slightly more likely than men's to suffer this end.[31]

The ability to sign of 224 female deponents was 58%; it was 68% among 50 deponents before 1765 and fell to 55.1% among the 174 deponents between 1765 and 1786. Both male and female deponents included large proportions of low-status persons, such as hired laborers and domestic servants, but the male deponents also included many of high status.

[30] Henrietta Maria East Caine v. Hugh Caine, Suffolk Files #129736, "Divorces," 2-3; Mary Hunt v. Richard Hunt (1761), "Divorces," 8-9; Sarah Backus v. John Backus, Suffolk Files #129846, 100. See also Sarah Bloget v. John Bloget, Mass. Arch., IX, 211.

[31] Ten of the unresolved petitions—seven from women and three from men—show no sign of ever having been read by the Council. If these petitions are removed from the comparison, the difference between the number of men's and the number of women's petitions left unresolved (after at least a first reading) diminishes.

Analysis of the suits by cause clarifies the comparison of men's and women's experiences and of the results of their petitions. All suits involved invalidity or breach of the marriage contract. The causes (and the numbers of petitions) can be categorized as follows:[32]

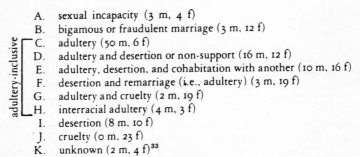

A. sexual incapacity (3 m, 4 f)
B. bigamous or fraudulent marriage (3 m, 12 f)
C. adultery (50 m, 6 f)
D. adultery and desertion or non-support (16 m, 12 f)
E. adultery, desertion, and cohabitation with another (10 m, 16 f)
F. desertion and remarriage (i.e., adultery) (3 m, 19 f)
G. adultery and cruelty (2 m, 19 f)
H. interracial adultery (4 m, 3 f)
I. desertion (8 m, 10 f)
J. cruelty (0 m, 23 f)
K. unknown (2 m, 4 f)[33]

The first two causes, sexual incapacity and invalid marriage, warranted annulment, but the governor and Council were not always consistent in wording when they granted petitions on these grounds. Two of the three men's petitions charging their wives with incapacity for coitus were granted after court-appointed "discreet Matrons" confirmed the charges, one by annulment (1739) and the other by dissolution of marriage bonds (1781). This is unremarkable, except that the one husband waited five years after marrying, and the other, eight, before petitioning for divorce.[34] Men fared better than women in this category of suits. None of the three women's

[32] In a few cases it is debatable whether the suit should be placed in one category or another: I and J in particular tend to overlap. Any of the adultery causes, C through H, might have included the charge of illegitimate offspring; as a divorce charge, this was included rather as a means of proving adultery than as a separate grievance.

[33] The records are so sparse in this category that the charges are not apparent. Rachel Draper won her divorce in 1709, and Joseph Hale's suit was dismissed in 1779; the results of the four others remain as mysterious as the charges. Rachel Draper v. John Draper, Council Recs., V, 124; Mary Parce v. John Parce, *ibid.*, XVIII, 100; Experience Simpson v. husband, *ibid.*, XXIV, 392; Elizabeth Laud v. David Laud, Mass. Arch., CXL, 194; Joseph Hale (or Hail) v. Isabella Hale, Council Recs., XXIII, 64, 76, 414; Thomas Patter v. wife, *ibid.*, XXIII, 64.

[34] Jesse Turner v. Grace Turner, Suffolk Files #129727, Council Recs., X, 331, 378; George Sherman v. Phebe Sherman, Suffolk Files #129796, Council Recs., XXIII, 92, XXIV, 206, 301, XXVI, 104, "Divorces," 137-140. Jeremiah Ingraham petitioned for divorce from Mercy Ingraham for this cause in 1733, after 15 years of marriage, but his charge was not substantiated and his petition was dismissed. Council Recs., IX, 464, 533.

petitions to the governor and Council was granted: one was dismissed and the others were left unresolved, although in one of these cases the husband acknowledged his debility. In a unique instance, however, the General Court in 1780 enacted a legislative annulment of a marriage upon proof of the wife's complaint that her husband was impotent.[35]

Twelve female and three male petitioners pursued divorce for the second cause that warranted annulment—bigamous or fraudulent marriage. Two men, in 1762 and 1770, proved their wives to be bigamists, and their marriages were declared null. Another argued that his recent marriage was invalid because he had been tricked into it, while drunk, by kinfolk of a young woman who was pregnant with his child. The governor and Council believed him and ruled the marriage null.[36] Women also had considerable success in ending bigamous marriages. Nine of the twelve wives' petitions were granted, six by annulment and three by dissolution, while three others remained unresolved.[37] Women's petitions against bigamous husbands revealed some of the vagaries of marriage in eighteenth-century Massachusetts. In only two instances had the husband's prior marriage taken place long before and in another country.[38] In five, the husband's prior marriage occurred in another New England town between two and eight years earlier (and in one other case, fifteen years earlier).[39] Six of the bigamous husbands

[35] Sarah Maggin v. William Maggin (dismissed, 1736), Council Recs., X, 47; Elizabeth Bredeen v. Joseph Bredeen (1744), Suffolk Files #129728, Council Recs., XI, 151, 156, 174-175, 184; Judith Walker v. Simeon Walker (1773), Suffolk Files #129777; "An Act for dissolving the Marriage of Philip Turner and Mercy Turner," Acts and Resolves, Mass. Bay, VI, 229.

[36] William Davidson v. Hannah Davidson (1762), "Divorces," 16-17; Samuel Lefebvre v. Sarah Lefebvre (1770), Suffolk Files #129758, "Divorces," 57-59; Gill Belcher v. Mary Finney alias Belcher (1739), Suffolk Files #129726, Mass. Arch., IX, 228-229, Council Recs., X, 254-315.

[37] Annulled: Susanna T. Kennet v. Edward Kennet (1694), Council Recs., II, 290; Reliance Drew v. John Drew (1737), ibid., X, 79, 122; Elizabeth Eldredge v. Ezekiel Eldredge (1751), Suffolk Files #129730, Mass. Arch., IX, 354-356, Council Recs., XII, 219; Rachel Wormley v. John Wormley (1765), Suffolk Files #129744, "Divorces," 33-34; Mary Bates v. Henry Bates (1771), Suffolk Files #129759, "Divorces," 59-62; Mehetabel Nicholson v. Joshua Nicholson (or Nickerson) (1771), Suffolk Files #129761, "Divorces," 62-64. Marriage dissolved: Rebecca Wansford v. Nicholas Wansford (1698), Council Recs., II, 562; Mary Hamilton alias Arthur v. George Arthur (1756), Mass. Arch., IX, 399-402, Council Recs., XIII, 140; Sibble Babcock v. George Babcock (1784), Suffolk Files #129835, "Divorces," 202-203. Not resolved: Abigail Hamen v. John Hamen (1748), Mass. Arch., IX, 321-323, Council Recs., XII, 46; Henrietta Maria East Caine v. Hugh Caine, Suffolk Files #129736, "Divorces," 2-3; Mary Drinkwater v. William Drinkwater (1771), Suffolk Files #129765

[38] Mary Arthur and Henrietta Maria East Caine.

[39] Abigail Hamen, Elizabeth Eldredge, Mary Bates, Mehetabel Nicholson, Mary Drinkwater, and Sibble Babcock.

TABLE III

PROPORTION OF PETITIONS RECEIVING FAVORABLE DECREES, 1692-1786

	All Causes	Adultery-Inclusive Only	Adultery-Exclusive Only
male petitioners	68%	72%	50%
female petitioners	58%	65%	47%

Note: Favorable decrees include divorce, annulment, separate bed and board.

had also deserted, either to return to their first wives or to marry third wives.[40] These cases, especially when considered together with cases involving desertion, suggest the ease and perhaps the appeal of running away from one partner and finding another—the traditional "self-divorce." Husbands more frequently made such escapes and new starts than did wives. Twelve wives but only three husbands charged bigamy (category B); sixteen wives but only ten husbands complained of their spouses' desertion and adulterous cohabitation with another (E); nineteen wives but only three husbands charged their partners with desertion and remarriage (F); ten wives but eight husbands petitioned on grounds of desertion alone (I). Men moved more easily from place to place, it seems; certainly, according to custom, they, and not women, took the initiative in deciding to marry or remarry.

The bulk of the petitions—84 percent of the husbands', 59 percent of the wives'—included the grievance of adultery. Men had more success than women in adultery-inclusive causes, but both sexes fared better in these causes than in others. (See Table III.) The comparison between men's and women's experiences in suing on grounds of adultery is especially interesting because it can inform us of the presence of a double standard of sexual morality. Were men's and women's infidelities considered equally cause for divorce? The cultural heritage of Massachusetts contained equivocal answers to this question. Despite the seventh commandment, English tradition enshrined the double standard, forgiving a husband's sexual transgressions but calling a wife's abhorrent. As mentioned earlier, all the parliamentary divorces for adultery in the eighteenth century were awarded to husbands, none to wives. Decorum among the aristocracy required wives to ignore their husbands' extramarital affairs.[41] In Massachusetts, however, Puritan reli-

[40] Reliance Drew, Abigail Hamen, Mary Arthur, H. M. E. Caine, Rachel Wormley, and Mary Bates. One petitioner, Mary Arthur, had already been granted separate bed and board because of her husband's cruelty. Perhaps wives would not have complained of the bigamy if their husbands had not compounded the insult with other grievances.

[41] See Keith Thomas, "The Double Standard," *Journal of the History of Ideas*, XX (1959), 195-216, and, for an example of such advice, [George Savile], *The Lady's New Year's Gift, or, Advice to a Daughter* (London, 1688).

gious values strongly infused the English tradition. Puritan ideology, partially to repudiate aristocratic manners, demanded fidelity of both partners. From the sixteenth century through the eighteenth, Puritan reformers attacked the double standard by advocating chastity before marriage, and fidelity after, for men as well as women.[42]

It is striking that in Massachusetts half of all the men's petitions named adultery as the sole major grievance (C), and that these petitions had a high rate of success: 70 percent resulted in divorce, only 4 percent were dismissed, and the remaining quarter did not result in decrees.[43] To obtain divorce a petitioner had to produce two eye-witnesses to the act of adultery or a confession from the accused spouse, or show record of criminal conviction of the adulterers, or of the failure of the accused to answer the court summons. Alternatively, a male petitioner might show that his wife had become pregnant in his absence. In England prior court conviction of the adulterers was prerequisite to a bill of divorce; but in Massachusetts civil court action only seldom, and randomly, preceded or accompanied divorce suits.[44] Usually the governor and Council themselves determined the justice of the adultery charge. Since a wife's adultery was virtually sure cause for divorce, it was not unknown for a restless husband to "frame" his wife by setting up her seduction or by bribing deponents to testify that they had seen adultery committed. In several cases such plots by the husband were manifest or inferable.[45] The two husbands whose petitions were dismissed brought

[42] Thomas, "Double Standard," *Jour. Hist. Ideas*, XX (1959), 203-205.

[43] At least 17 of the 50 adulteries charged in husbands' petitions occurred while the husband was absent at sea or on a military campaign. In almost all of the cases in which bastard offspring were mentioned, the husband had been absent for a year or more. The wives' partners in adultery were neighbors, hired laborers, boarders, or, in a few cases, casual visitors or traveling companions.

[44] Only six of the male petitioners in category C gave evidence of prior court actions. Three were actions to punish the adulterers: Benjamin Bucklin v. Rebeccah Bucklin (1737), Council Recs., X, 112, 121; Thomas Gelpin v. Abigail Gelpin (1743), Mass. Arch., IX, 263-267, Council Recs., XI, 65-66, 73-74; George Raynord v. Mary Raynord (1752), Suffolk Files #129729, Council Recs., XII, 268. Three were actions for the husband to collect money damages from the wife's lover: Thomas Hammet v. Abigail Hammet (1767), Suffolk Files #129747, "Divorces," 37-40; James Dougherty v. Mary Dougherty (1768), Suffolk Files #129750, "Divorces," 45-48; Joshua Gay v. Sarah Gay (1778), Suffolk Files #129784, "Divorces," 101-103, Council Recs., XXII, 46, 48.

[45] For example, Jacob Brown v. Ruth Brown (1758), Mass. Arch., IX, 420-428, Council Recs., XIII, 350, 354; Russell Knight v. Mary Knight (1766), Suffolk Files #129745, "Divorces," 35-37, Mass. Arch., IX, 446-447; Andrew Shank v. Sarah Shank (or Schenk) (1772), Suffolk Files #129766; James Richardson v. Hannah Richardson (1772), Suffolk Files #129769, "Divorces," 70-72; William Sturgis v. Sarah Sturgis (1778), Suffolk Files #129785, "Divorces," 104-106, Council Recs., XXII, 256, 320; Samuel Hemenway v. Hannah Hemenway (1782), Suffolk Files

witnesses who incriminated the accused wives, but the court suspected bribery and believed the wives' contrary testimony.[46]

Clearly, the governor and Council would grant divorce to a man whose spouse committed adultery. Would they grant it to a woman for the same cause? There was no English precedent for such action. Only one suit from seventeenth-century Massachusetts has been found in which a wife sought and received a divorce for the sole cause of adultery—and this decree was subsequently reversed on the husband's appeal.[47] Women in eighteenth-century Massachusetts could be said to have taken a cue from these negative precedents. In contrast to the weight of men's petitions, not a single wife petitioned for the sole grievance of adultery until 1774, and only six did so between 1774 and 1786. Unless we assume that husbands displayed much more virtue than wives, the difference between the numbers of petitions from men and from women in this category (C) suggests a deeply entrenched double standard of marital fidelity. Whether individual women thought that men's adultery warranted divorce remains uncertain; but we can logically conclude that before 1774 women did not expect to obtain divorce for that reason alone and so did not petition.

We can gain an approximation of the governor and Council's response to petitions grounded on husbands' adultery alone, before 1774, by looking at decrees in the other adultery-inclusive categories (D through H). Husbands' suits in these categories, dependent on their substantiation of the adultery charges, had great success. More than four-fifths of their petitions charging adultery and desertion (D), or adultery, desertion, and cohabitation (E), resulted in divorce. Few husbands petitioned on the other adultery-inclusive grounds, and only the ones who proved adultery won their suits. By contrast, the pre-Revolutionary governor and Council gave a woman very little reason to expect divorce for her spouse's infidelity. Seven out of twelve female petitioners before 1774 obtained divorces by proving their partner's desertion, adultery, and remarriage (F), but these decrees took bigamy, as well as adultery, into account.[48] Fourteen women petitioned the governor and Coun-

---

#129804. The legal process attendant on a divorce petition was meant to insure justice to the accused spouse: he or she was allowed to be present when depositions to support the petitioner were taken, and was able to bring his or her own witnesses.

[46] Andrew Shank v. Sarah Shank (1772), Suffolk Files #129766; Samuel Hemenway v. Hannah Hemenway (1782), *ibid.* #129804.

[47] Howard, *Matrimonial Institutions*, II, 334. But John Demos, *Little Commonwealth*, 97, has found in 17th-century Plymouth Colony records a divorce and favorable settlement granted to one woman who chiefly complained of her husband's "act of uncleanes" with another woman.

[48] "An Act against Adultery and Polygamy," passed June 6, 1794, made polygamy (that is, marrying again while one's first spouse was living) a felony punishable by death. *Acts and Resolves, Mass. Bay*, I, 171-172.

cil on other adultery-inclusive grounds prior to 1773. Eight of these received no decrees; one suit with apparent proof of the adultery was dismissed; and three—two of which charged adultery and cruelty—gained decrees of separate bed and board, the same decree which women's petitions charging cruelty alone could obtain.[49] Only two of the fourteen wives won divorces, and their cases were not conclusive on the question of adultery. Sarah Mitchell of Deerfield, who brought suit in 1718 on grounds of her husband's "fornication" with a black woman, obtained a divorce and the return of her marriage portion as well. The uniqueness of the decree suggests that not the adultery, but its interracial nature, was the crucial factor.[50] Hannah Rolfe of Lancaster made the other successful petition, in 1752. Her grievances included desertion, adultery, and cohabitation; her husband Ezra had been jailed for fornicating with a minor and for failing to provide for his bastard child, and he absconded to avoid answering Hannah's petition.[51]

Seventeen hundred and seventy-three was a turning point. In that year, two women who petitioned on the grounds of adultery and cruelty were granted not separate bed and board, but divorce, for the specified cause of adultery. The original notation on Sarah Gould's petition recorded a unanimous decision for separate bed and board, but the formal decree of March 2, 1773, declared her marriage dissolved. Martha Air's petition a few months later resulted in an unequivocal dissolution of marriage bonds on account of Adam Air's adultery.[52] After that, women began to petition for divorce on the sole ground of adultery. The governor and Council (or the Council alone,

---

[49] Not decided: Ann Hall v. William Hall, category D (1753), Mass. Arch., IX, 370-373; Kezia Downing v. Nathaniel Downing, D (1765), Suffolk Files #129742; Lydia Sharp v. Boston (a black), D (1773), *ibid.* #129775; Marcy Robinson v. Leonard Robinson, E (1770), *ibid.* #129755; Sarah Wheeler v. Valentine Wheeler, E (1772), *ibid.* #129792; Hannah Medberry v. Ebenezer Medberry, G (1767), *ibid.* #129746; Eunice Mountfort v. Benjamin Mountfort, G (1771), *ibid.* #129760; Lucy Foster v. Benjamin Foster, H (1755), Mass. Arch., IX, 393-395. Dismissed: Elizabeth Shaw v. John Shaw, D (1748), *ibid.*, 324, Council Recs., XII, 57. Separate bed and board: Mary Clapham v. William Clapham, E (1754), Suffolk Files #129733, Council Recs., XII, 349; Eleanor Gray v. Samuel Gray, G (1747), Mass. Arch., IX, 296-311, Council Recs., XII, 12; Mary Fairservice v. John Fairservice, G (1767), Suffolk Files #129749, "Divorces," 40-44.
[50] Sarah Mitchell v. Michael Mitchell, Council Recs., VI, 305, 621. The older definition of adultery, incorporating the double standard, hinged on the involvement of a married *woman*. Thus a married man's sexual transgression could still be called fornication, if his partner was single.
[51] Hannah Rolfe v. Ezra Rolfe, Mass. Arch., IX, 357-358, Council Recs., XII, 218, 239.
[52] Sarah Gould v. William Gould, Suffolk Files #129772, notation on petition, 56; also "Divorces," 78-80. Martha Air v. Adam Air, Suffolk Files #129779, "Divorces," 81-82.

TABLE IV

ADULTERY-INCLUSIVE CHARGES

NUMBER OF PETITIONS/NUMBER OF FAVORABLE DECREES

		1692–1704	1705–1714	1715–1724	1725–1734	1735–1744	1745–1754	1755–1764	1765–1774	1775–1786	Total
C	men	2/1	1/1		2/1	6/6	4/2	9/5*	12/8	14/11	50/35*
	women								1/1	5/4	6/5
D	men				2/2		1/1	1/1	4/2	8/6	16/12
	women						2/0	2/2*	2/0	6/5	12/7*
E	men	1/1						2/2*	1/0	6/6	10/9*
	women					1/1	2/2*		2/0	11/8	16/11
F	men		1/1				2/0				3/1
	women	1/1		3/0	2/1	1/1	1/1	1/1	3/2	7/6	19/13
G	men							1/0		1/0	2/0
	women						1/1**		6/3**	12/7	19/11**
H	men				1/1	1/1	2/2				4/4
	women			1/1				1/0		1/1	3/2

Note: * Includes legislative divorce.   ** Includes separate bed and board.

between 1776 and 1780) granted five out of the six such petitions during the next twelve years. The increasing number of wives who brought other adultery-inclusive charges also obtained divorces, and almost all of these decrees went on to the record as owing specifically to the adultery charge.[53] (See Table IV.)

These decrees were not quite as unprecedented as they may seem at first glance. In the 1750s, during the interval when the governor and Council declined to dissolve marriages, three women obtained bills of divorce from the General Court on adultery-inclusive grounds. The first was Mary Clapham, wife of a gentleman. After obtaining a decree of separate bed and board from the governor and Council because of her husband's desertion and adulterous cohabitation with a woman in Nova Scotia, she petitioned the General Court, "in whom she apprehend[ed] the Power to be vested," to

[53] Between 1774 and 1786, 5 of the 6 women who charged adultery and desertion. 8 of the 11 who brought suits on account of adultery, desertion and cohabitation, 7 of the 8 who alleged adultery, desertion and remarriage, 7 of the 13 whose grievances were adultery and cruelty, and one whose husband committed interracial adultery all obtained decrees of divorce from the governor and Council. These figures differ slightly from the 1775-1786 column of Table IV because they include the cases of 1774.

dissolve her marriage and assign her alimony. The court obliged her first request, citing as William Clapham's "Violation of his Marriage Contract" his "leaving the said Mary, cohabiting and committing adultery with Another Woman."[54] The two other women who appealed successfully to the General Court both charged their husbands with adultery and desertion. Mary Parker, also a gentleman's wife, obtained her divorce because, the bill said, "Phineas Parker has for sundry Years pass'd left the said Mary, and stands convict[ed] of committing Adultery with another woman." The act granted at the plea of Lydia Kellogg, wife of a laborer of Sunderland, declared only that "it appears to this court that the said Ephraim [Kellogg] has been guilty of the crime of adultery."[55]

The General Court seems to have been more liberal in granting divorces to women before 1773 than were the governor and Council. In enacting bills of divorce for three wives during the 1750s the court presaged actions which the Council would take during, but not before, the Revolutionary period.[56] The legislative divorces, viewed together with the Council's decrees after 1773, suggest that the more whiggish and the more representative the authority, the more likely it was to treat male and female adultery equally as cause for divorce. The transformation of the Council's attitude toward male adultery would be simpler to explain if it had occurred in 1776, when the composition of the Council changed radically. Though some new members replaced old ones in 1773, specific changes in membership do not clearly account for the new pattern of decrees beginning in that year.[57]

Divorce actions in Massachusetts may have paralleled larger political

[54] Court Recs., Dec. 4, 1754, XX, 337-338; Mass. Arch., IX, 381-382; "An Act to dissolve the Marriage of Mary Clapham with William Clapham and to allow her to marry again," Acts and Resolves, Mass. Arch., VI, 165. The Council later awarded Mary her household furniture, worth £100. Council Recs., XII, 386.

[55] Mary Parker v. Phineas Parker, Mass. Arch., IX, 374-380, Council Recs., XII, 337, Acts and Resolves, Mass. Bay, VI, 169; Lydia Kellogg v. Ephraim Kellogg, Mass. Arch., IX, 403-413, Acts and Resolves, Mass. Bay, VI, 173. The Parker and Kellogg divorce acts, and two of the three legislative divorces obtained by male petitioners, were passed without prior decrees of separate bed and board from the governor and Council. Only in the Parker case was prior court conviction of the adulterer mentioned. The men's cases were John Farnum, Jr., v. Elizabeth Farnum, Mass. Arch., IX, 396-398, Acts and Resolves, Mass. Bay, VI, 170; Jonah Galusha v. Sarah Galusha, Mass. Arch, IX, 414, Acts and Resolves, Mass. Bay, VI, 174, Court Recs., XX, 329; and Daniel McCarthy v. Mary McCarthy, Suffolk Files, #129734, Mass. Arch., IX, 418, Council Recs., XIII, 259, 262, Acts and Resolves, Mass. Bay, VI, 177. The three cases reviewed by the Board of Trade in 1758 were Clapham's, Parker's, and Farnum's.

[56] Between 1760 and 1773 seven women filed adultery-inclusive petitions and none obtained divorce, although Mary Fairservice, with a plea of adultery and cruelty, obtained separate bed and board. See n. 49.

[57] "Divorces" list names of Council members present at each decision.

TABLE V

PROPORTION OF ALL PETITIONS CONTAINING ADULTERY CHARGE

	1692-1764	1765-1774	1775-1786
male petitioners	78%	94%	91%
female petitioners	40%	50%	79%

struggles, but did changes in divorce policy also move against the double standard and advance equality between the sexes? In several ways the record of petitions and decrees implies an improvement in women's status. The great increase in the number of women's petitions after 1764 suggests that women were becoming less resigned to their circumstances and were taking more initiative to end unsatisfactory marriages. Women's petitions were more concentrated in the period after 1764 than were men's.[58] The proportion of petitions including adultery charges rose for both sexes, but more emphatically for wives. (See Table V.) The higher the proportion of adultery-inclusive petitions, the greater success petitioners were likely to have. In fact, both male and female petitioners fared better between 1765 and 1786, but only on account of decrees made after independence. From 1765 through 1774 an unusually high proportion of suits remained unresolved, reducing petitioners' chances of favorable action. The proportion of unresolved petitions jumped from 23 percent for the years 1692-1764 to 41 percent for 1765-1774, and then dropped to 13 percent for 1775-1786. This noteworthy improvement in efficiency, along with the rise in the proportion of adultery-inclusive petitions, increased petitioners' likelihood of gaining favorable decrees. Because of the added factor of the new treatment of male adultery, wives' rate of success improved dramatically from 49 percent between 1692 and 1774 to 70 percent between 1775 and 1786; husbands' rate of success rose only from 66 percent to 73 percent. Wives' rate of success almost equalled that of husbands' during the decade after independence.

It is tempting to propose from this evidence that the Revolutionary era ushered in a "new deal" that recognized the injustice of the double standard, evened obligations of marital fidelity, and made redress within marriage more accessible to women. To an extent, however small, acceptance of male adultery as grounds for divorce moved in these directions. Motives for the change in the treatment of male adultery probably originated, however, more in men's political intentions than in their desire for sexual justice. Revolutionary rhetoric, in its repudiation of British "vice," "corruption," "extrava-

[58] See Table I. Half of all men's but 63% of all women's petitions occurred after 1764.

gance," and "decadence," enshrined ideals of republican virtue—of personal and national simplicity, honesty, frugality, and public spirit. In the view of Revolutionary leaders, republicanism required a moral reformation of the American people as well as a political transformation, because a republic's success depended on the virtue of its citizens. As John Adams wrote to his wife Abigail in July 1776, "the new Governments we are assuming . . . will require a Purification from our Vices, and an Augmentation of our Virtues or they will be no Blessings." Samuel Adams stated in 1777, "We shall succeed if we are virtuous. . . . I am infinitely more apprehensive of the Contagion of Vice than the Power of all other Enemies."[59] The dynamism of the words "virtue" and "vice," in Revolutionary usage, derived at least in part from their sexual connotation.[60] Rejection of British "corruption" implied a critique of the traditionally loose sexual standards for men of the British ruling class. The republican ideology of private as well as public virtue also produced an emphasis on marital fidelity, because it focused on the family as the training ground of future citizens. It was wholly consistent that judges in Massachusetts, where patriotic rhetoric evoked Puritan conceptions of righteousness (and thus Puritan standards of fidelity), no longer saw male adultery as venial but called it sufficient grounds for divorce. Such a change in standards for male conduct may well have produced a divorce policy that had the appearance of improving women's marital status.

Petitioners also brought suits on account of important marital breaches other than adultery—namely, desertion (I) and cruelty (J). Desertion suits were the least successful among all the categories. Of ten wives who charged desertion—all but one abandoned for more than three years—only two achieved any favorable result. Five of the petitions were not resolved. Three more were dismissed, suggesting that the governor and Council regarded a husband's willful desertion in itself as insufficient cause to dissolve a marriage.[61] One wife who asked only for her conjugal right to restoration of

[59] John Adams to Abigail Adams, July 3, 1776, and Samuel Adams to John Langdon, Aug. 7, 1777, in Gordon S. Wood, *The Creation of the American Republic, 1776-1787* (Chapel Hill, N.C., 1972), 123-124.
[60] Ian Watt, "The New Woman: Samuel Richardson's *Pamela*," in Rose Laub Coser, ed., *The Family: Its Structure and Functions* (New York, 1964), 281-282, points out that "the eighteenth century [in England] witnessed a tremendous narrowing of the ethical scale, a redefinition of virtue in primarily sexual terms. . . . The same tendency can be seen at work on the ethical vocabulary itself: words such as virtue, propriety, decency, modesty, delicacy, purity, came to have the almost exclusively sexual connotation which they have since very largely retained."
[61] Howard, *Matrimonial Institutions*, II, 333, lists two late 17th-century cases in which women petitioned on account of their husbands' desertion and failure to provide, and the assistants declared the marriages dissolved, but no comparable 18th-

maintenance, since her husband had deserted long before, obtained her object. The court formalized the couple's agreement for yearly maintenance payments by the husband.[62] In the other successful suit Abigail Bradstreet, whose complaints included cruelty as well as desertion, won a decree of separate bed and board with maintenance payments.[63]

Among the eight men who sued because of their wives' desertion, the earlier petitioners fared better than the later. The court declared John Emery of Newbury separated from his wife in 1710 on his complaint that she slandered him and refused to live with him. Two other men obtained divorces on desertion pleas. John Ferre, a husbandman of Springfield, petitioned in 1718 and was ordered by the governor and Council to post notification that if his wife did not return within six months she would be divorced. Ferre obeyed, his wife did not return, and in 1719 the divorce was granted. Jonathan Fletcher's petition of 1734 stated that his wife had departed sixteen years earlier, after two months of marriage. In this case the governor and Council took the unusual step of declaring both parties single and free to marry, the marriage portion to be returned.[64] After 1734, however, men's desertion pleas all failed. The court gave John Williston's petition in 1737 only a first reading, apparently, and dismissed other petitions in 1739, 1740, 1743, and 1786.[65] These dismissals contradicted the implication

century women's suits had that result. The presumption of the law was that seven years' absence by one spouse allowed the other to remarry. The "Act against Adultery and Polygamy" of 1694 (*Acts and Resolves, Mass. Bay*, I. 171-172) exempted from its punishments any person whose spouse had been overseas for seven years or absent more than seven years, so perhaps the Council assumed that decrees of divorce were unnecessary. Two suits dismissed, however, involved absences of five and six years.

[62] That is, this was a separate bed and board arrangement by mutual consent. Ann Vansise v. Cornelius Vansise, "Divorces," 44-45.

[63] Abigail Bradstreet v. Joseph Bradstreet, Suffolk Files #129762, "Divorces," 68-70. Her lawyer, John Adams, argued her case according to canon law. See Wroth and Zobel, eds., *Legal Papers of Adams*, I, 280-285.

[64] John Emery v. Abigail Emery, Council Recs., V, 180. (Abigail also petitioned unsuccessfully for divorce from John for cruelty. Mass. Arch., IX, 162-163.) John Ferre v. Elizabeth Ferre, Council Recs., VII, 165; Jonathan Fletcher v. wife, *ibid.*, IX, 552, 565.

[65] The duration of the wife's absence is not apparent in these cases, except in the last, John Chapin v. Margaret Chapin, Suffolk Files #129856, in which it was three years. One probable reason why John's suit failed was that Margaret was willing to be divorced. Divorce was an adversary process in Massachusetts; separate bed and board, but never divorce, was decreed on the basis of a couple's mutual agreement. Any apparent collusion on the part of the couple to gain divorce invalidated the suit, so that, ironically, one way for a husband or wife to stop a divorce proceeding was to agree to it. See, for example, Sarah Rust v. Francis Rust (Jan. 1784), Suffolk Files #129833, "Divorces," 199-200; and Sarah Rust v. Francis Rust (June 1784), Suffolk Files #129836, "Divorces," 204-205. Cf. n. 80.

of the Ferre and Fletcher cases, and they force the general conclusion that desertion alone, whether by wife or husband, was not considered sufficient cause for divorce. Why not? Certainly desertion violated the marriage contract. In Puritan theory desertion warranted divorce. Under canon law, on the contrary, desertion was not even grounds for separate bed and board unless it was combined with cruelty.[66] Excepting the Ferre and Fletcher cases, the governor and Council acted as though canon law controlled their decisions on desertion.[67] Perhaps the New World offered too great opportunities for desertion for the court to wish to establish desertion as reason for divorce.

Canon law rather than Puritan precept appears to have guided the decisions in cruelty cases as well. Puritan divorce theory allowed divorce for incorrigible enmity between spouses or for dangerous abuse, but canon law prescribed only separate bed and board. Of the twenty-three Massachusetts petitions entered on grounds of cruelty, nine obtained decrees of separate bed and board, three more were settled by separations based on mutual consent, six were dismissed for insufficient evidence, and five were left unresolved. Not a single one gained divorce. However, not all of these petitions asked for divorce. All of the petitioners in this category were women, and almost two-thirds of them requested only separate bed and board with maintenance. It is difficult to tell whether this reflected their pragmatism or their personal preference. Divorce was virtually impossible to obtain for this cause, but separate bed and board was possible. To gain a separation, with alimony, may have seemed a satisfactory solution to the grievance, especially for older women who did not foresee marrying again. Yet even separate bed and board was not easy to obtain, as the six dismissals attested. In all but one of these six cases the wives asked only for separation and maintenance, but the governor and council would not grant the plea.[68]

[66] Wroth and Zobel, eds., *Legal Papers of Adams*, I, 284; Howard, *Matrimonial Institutions*, II, 52-54.

[67] Possibly the change from granting of divorces for wives' desertions before 1735 to dismissing such pleas later represented an "anglicization" of divorce policy. The appearance of separate bed and board decrees during the 18th century, when none, according to Howard, was made during the previous century, supports such a theory; but the change in treatment of male adultery in 1773 opposes it. Cf. John Murrin, "Anglicizing an American Colony: The Transformation of Puritan Massachusetts" (Ph.D. diss., Yale University, 1966); Kenneth A. Lockridge, "Land, Population, and the Evolution of New England Society, 1630-1790," *Past and Present*, XXXIX (1968), 62-80; and Kenneth A. Lockridge, *A New England Town, The First Hundred Years: Dedham, Massachusetts, 1636-1736* (New York, 1970), 167-180.

[68] The records remaining for five of the six cases are not extensive enough to allow evaluation of the "sufficiency" of the cruelty alleged. One woman whose petition was dismissed sued a second time, however, bringing additional evidence, and then won separate bed and board. Mary Lobb v. George Lobb, Suffolk Files

Women who petitioned on grounds of cruelty were significantly more urban—and thus perhaps more sophisticated—than petitioners in general. Fourteen of the twenty-two[69] lived in Boston, three in towns immediately outside Boston, two in other large port towns, and only three in smaller, more remote locations. Perhaps urban women had higher standards for kind treatment in marriage than did rural women, or more readily took official steps to combat physical abuse. Urban women also predominated, though not as strongly, among wives petitioning on grounds of adultery and cruelty (G): ten of the nineteen lived in Boston and three in towns nearby.

The governor and Council usually judged requests for maintenance in cases in which they decreed separate bed and board, although a provincial statute of 1695 located jurisdiction over alimony in the Superior Court of Judicature. Alimony ordinarily took the form of regular cash payments, the amount varying with the husband's wealth.[70] Gentlemen's wives, who married with considerable portions, might ask only for the return or use of their own former property to support themselves. Mary Arthur of Boston did so in 1754 when she sought separation from her husband because of his nine years of abuse. After she obtained the separation, a second petition was required before the Council awarded her her household goods and the income from her Boston real estate.[71] The governor and Council assigned to another Bostonian, in lieu of the alimony she requested, the rent and profit of her

---

#129800. "Divorces," 145-148. In the sixth case, the wife gave evidence of enormous cruelty, but the governor and Council accepted her husband's promise henceforth to treat her kindly as reason to dismiss her petition. Apparently their judgment was mistaken, for the wife petitioned again less than a year later, indicating that her plight had not improved. Margaret Knodle v. Frederick Knodle (1764), Suffolk Files #129743. "Divorces," 32.

[69] There were 23 suits but only 22 petitioners, since Mary Lobb petitioned twice (n. 68).

[70] *Acts and Resolves, Mass. Bay*, I, 209. Some of the alimony awards made by the governor and Council in separate bed and board decrees were as follows: Anne Leonard v. Henry Leonard (a turner, of Boston), in 1743, 5s. per week (Mass. Arch., IX, 268-294, Council Recs., XI, 69, 113-114); Eleanor Gray v. Samuel Gray (a yeoman, of Pelham, Hampshire County), 1747, £6 per year (Mass. Arch., IX, 296-311, Council Recs., XII, 12); Mary Fairservice v. John Fairservice (a trader of Boston), 1767, £12 yearly (Suffolk Files #129749, "Divorces," 40-44); Lucy Purnam v. Scipio Purnam (a truckman, of Newburyport), 1768, 6s. per month (Suffolk Files #129751, "Divorces" 48-51). This last was the most bizarre suit on grounds of cruelty. The couple were black; Lucy accused Scipio not only of treating her cruelly but also of attempting to sell her as a slave. Scipio denied the charges and brought witnesses who impugned Lucy's character. Eventually he agreed to the official separation but objected strongly to paying alimony, claiming "she is at least as well able to support herself as he is himself and Family." See Suffolk Files #129751, 124.

[71] Mary Arthur v. George Arthur, Suffolk Files #129733b, Council Recs., XII, 371, 385.

own real property, removing it from her husband's control. Yet she was not permitted to sell the lands, which were uncultivated and produced no profit, without petitioning again for that privilege. Upon her plea, the General Court enacted a bill allowing her to sell and convey the lands as though she were single, but the Privy Council disallowed it.[72] These alimony arrangements revealed starkly how the marriage bond circumscribed the legal and economic individuality of women.[73]

In three separate bed and board decrees after 1780 the governor and Council failed to mention alimony, although the Massachusetts constitution of 1780 put the matter under their jurisdiction. They granted *divorce* with alimony to two women petitioners, however—the only two such decrees between 1692 and 1786—although no extraordinary characteristics of the cases explain why.[74] It may be that divorced women had earlier sought alimony from the superior courts. Sarah Griffin (Sarah Gould before her divorce) filed a petition for this purpose with the Superior Court of Judicature of Suffolk County on August 31, 1773, but the court appears to have taken no action.[75]

It is doubtful how well the assignment of alimony worked to provide for separated or divorced wives. In those four cases in which the couple mutually

[72] Mary Hunt v. Richard Hunt, "Divorces," 6-11, Council Recs., XIV, 268, 270, 277; "An Act for enabling Mary Hunt to dispose and Convey her lands and interest in Holden," passed Apr. 24, 1762, disallowed by Privy Council Mar. 16, 1763, *Acts and Resolves, Mass. Bay*, VI, 187-188.

Alexander Keyssar, "Widowhood in Eighteenth-Century Massachusetts: A Problem in the History of the Family," *Perspectives in American History*, VIII (1974), esp. 100-103, 114-118, points out that widows commonly faced similar problems: as dower they received the use and profit of one-third of their husbands' real property but not the right to dispose of it. "Dozens" of widows in 18th-century Massachusetts petitioned the General Court to be enabled to dispose of real property because it was not profitable to them. Keyssar's conclusion that "the legal structure aimed at the sustenance, rather than the economic freedom, of widows" (p. 103) could apply to the position of wives separated from their husbands.

[73] Under common law all of a woman's personal property and earnings became her husband's upon marriage, and while she retained title to any real estate she owned, her husband gained the right to its use and income. A husband could not liquidate his wife's real property without her consent—this was the root of the quarrel in Bradstreet v. Bradstreet (n. 63)—but neither could she sell it of her own accord.

[74] Sarah Wheeler v. Valentine Wheeler, Suffolk Files #129792, "Divorces," 128-131, 144-145, Council Recs., XXV, 181, 400, XXVI, 118; Sarah Sawyer v. Abel Sawyer, Suffolk Files #129827, "Divorces," 188-191. Cf. Sarah Vernon v. William Vernon, Suffolk Files #129849, "Divorces," 216-217, 222-224, for an explicit refusal of alimony after a divorce decree.

[75] See Suffolk Files #91716. Her petition is in John Adams's handwriting, according to Worth and Zobel, eds., *Legal Papers of Adams*, I, 285n.

agreed to separation and maintenance no complaints followed.[76] But six of the nine decrees of separate bed and board with alimony were succeeded by further petitions from the wives, because their husbands had not made the required payments.[77] Petitioners who won separate bed and board thus had an ambiguous success, not being allowed to remarry, nor released from the economic constraints of the marriage contract, nor guaranteed current support. The husband's provision of alimony, like his support during marriage, was required by law and enforceable by compulsory process, but his performance actually depended on his own conscientiousness and goodwill.

The records of divorce in Massachusetts are most interesting for what they reveal about men's and women's respective power and advantages within marriage. The alimony petitions emphasize something the divorce suits as a whole suggest, that while marriage was a contract—a covenant, in contemporary language—it was a contract between unequals with disparate obligations. Sexual fidelity and good conduct were expected of both partners, but fidelity was not regularly enforced upon husbands by the threat of divorce until the mid-1770s, and a husband's abusive conduct never warranted divorce. The husband's characteristic obligation was provision of support; the wife's, obedient service. In this, marriage resembled an indenture between master and servant; and, indeed, the marriage relation was only one of a number of dependency relations—such as parent-child and master-servant—in traditional society. The husband's obligation—enhanced by his control over his wife's property and labor—was unequivocal. In a case, for example, in which an aggrieved wife returned to her parents' household, her father sued her husband for the cost of maintaining her during that time, and his view of the husband's responsibility was upheld in court.[78] The wife performed her part in her subjection. Like a servant in relation to a master,

[76] Ann McAlpine v. William McAlpine (1763), Suffolk Files #129737—no information on amount of settlement. Ann Vansise v. Cornelius Vansise (1768), "Divorces," 44-45—alimony of £10 yearly. Ann Lovell v. John Lovell (1773), Suffolk Files #129778—wife received her own estate and earnings. Ann Gardner v. David Gardner (1783), *ibid.*, #129813, "Divorces," 168-170—settlement of £40 plus wife's retention of dower rights.
[77] See the Bradstreet, Gray, and Purnam cases cited in nn. 63 and 70, and Elizabeth Keith v. Mark Keith, Suffolk Files #129738, "Divorces," 24-27, Mass. Arch., IX, 441-442; Mary Fairservice v. John Fairservice (1770), Suffolk Files #129756, "Divorces," 56-57; Mary Hamilton alias Arthur v. George Arthur (1756), Mass. Arch., IX, 399-492, Council Recs., XIII, 140. Those that did not produce subsequent complaints were Thankfull Winehall's case of 1710, which is very sparsely documented (Council Recs., V, 238); Ann Leonard's settlement of 5s. per week; and Mary Hunt's award of her own property (see nn. 70 and 72).
[78] William Sturgis v. Sarah Sturgis, Suffolk Files #129785, "Divorces," 104-106, Council Recs., XXII, 256, 320. See also Burditch v. Sturgis, Suffolk Files #102540.

she contributed continual service and received support. Besides working in the household (many deponents in divorce cases mentioned the industry of wives), she was expected to use frugally what her husband provided. Amos Bliss of Rehoboth felt he had a valid complaint against his wife Phebe because she "behaved herself unfriendly and unsubjectedly toward him; and . . . had linked herself in friendship with her father's Family against him; who . . . had ocationed a great Deal of Trouble, as well as Loss, to his Interest: and he Represented her to be Very Disloyal towards his person: and wastefull and Careless of his provisions and goods''; but Amos was willing to invite Phebe home again if she would act the good and obedient wife and "be in subjection to him."[79] The indenture-like nature of marriage appeared in the practice of a husband's "advertising" his runaway wife, warning others not to harbor or trust her, and refusing responsibility for her debts. A husband would not be bound to provide for his wife if he could not command her services, and he could compel her services by preventing her from obtaining support elsewhere.

Since marriage resembled an indenture contract, divorce should have been more readily available for varieties of nonperformance such as desertion or cruelty. That it was not suggests, first, that the sexual definition of marriage was its essence, and, second, that English divorce policy had more influence on eighteenth-century Massachusetts than might appear at first glance. Although marriage was regarded as a civil contract, and Massachusetts had no ecclesiastical courts, decisions in desertion and cruelty suits were almost entirely consistent with English application of canon law. On the whole, however, Massachusetts divorce practice diverged significantly from that of England. A much wider range of individuals—a laborer, a poor woman, a black servant—were able to obtain divorce with freedom to remarry, while in England only very rich men had that opportunity. In addition, the procedure was simpler than the parliamentary process. No prior ecclesiastical decree or criminal conviction of the adulterers was necessary in adultery cases, although the latter sufficed to warrant divorce. What was more innovative, women were able to obtain divorce with freedom to remarry and after 1773 did so on approximately the same terms as men. When in 1786 Massachusetts enacted a divorce law to codify the practice that had evolved, it allowed divorce for consanguinity, bigamy, impotency, or adultery *in either partner*, and separate bed and board for extreme cruelty.[80]

Throughout the period 1692-1786 husbands found it easier than wives to

[79] Amos Bliss v. Phebe Bliss, Suffolk Files #129799, depositions of Silvanus Martin and Eleazar Bliss, 49, 43.
[80] This law, passed Mar. 16, 1786 (*Acts and Resolves, 1784-1785*, 564-567), also stated that no divorce would be granted if the adultery or cruelty were occasioned by collusion in order to obtain divorce, or if both spouses committed adultery.

obtain divorce—not a surprising circumstance, since men also had the legal and economic independence which married women lacked, occupied all political and religious offices, were more literate than women, exercised greater control over geographic moves and choice of spouse, and by the terms of the marriage covenant could command their wives' obedience. It is more remarkable that the number of women's petitions and their rate of success accelerated during the century, so that in the decade after independence more than half again as many women as men pursued divorce, and their rate of success was almost the same. Divorce pleas by both sexes increased during the Revolutionary period, and efficiency in treating them improved, reflecting modernization of both personal values and bureaucratic procedure. The disproportionate growth in women's petitions suggests that they, even more than men, had rising expectations in marriage; and the changing treatment of their petitions implies that wives' objections were being regarded more seriously—that their status within the family had risen in the eyes of authorities.

The equalization of the consequences of adultery by either spouse, which was unmistakably the reason for the increasing success of women petitioners, may have signified a retreat from hierarchical models and an advance toward ideals of complementarity in the prevailing conception of the marriage relationship. In Hingham, Massachusetts, Daniel Scott Smith has found a consonant change in marriage patterns—a move away from parental control in the direction of individual autonomy in marriage choice—beginning markedly in the Revolutionary years. Smith sees the departure from the stable, parent-run system of selecting spouses as evidence of the "erosion and collapse of traditional family patterns in the middle to late eighteenth century."[81] Furthermore, on the basis of her analysis of New England funeral sermons Lonna Malmsheimer affirms that views of women altered significantly during these years. No longer stressing the rigid subordination of wife to husband as they had done earlier, although still insisting on the importance of the wife's domestic service, the sermons began to focus on friendship, complementarity, and emotional bonds between spouses. The seventeenth-century linkage of woman with moral evil, Eve's legacy, gave way to a new image of woman as a being ruled by conscience and religion.[82] Additionally, writers in contemporary Boston magazines seem to have been preoccupied with the reciprocal obligations and advantages of the sexes. They, too, idealized the complementary nature of men's and women's marital roles: an essayist in the Boston *Gentleman's and Lady's Town and Country*

[81] Smith, "Parental Power and Marriage Patterns," *Jour. Marriage and Family*, XXXV (1973), 426.
[82] Lonna Myers Malmsheimer, "New England Funeral Sermons and Changing Attitudes toward Women, 1672-1792" (Ph.D. diss., University of Minnesota, 1973).

Magazine, for example, of September 1784, described "matrimonial felicity" as the uniting of two congenial souls, "the man all truth, the woman all tenderness; he possessed of cheerful solidity, she of rational gaiety; acknowledging his superior judgment she complies with all his reasonable desires, whilst he, charmed with such repeated instances of superior love, endeavors to suit his requests to her inclinations."[83]

By the last quarter of the eighteenth century both parties were evidently restating the terms of the "indenture" of marriage. The divorce court's reprobation of male adultery newly defined one limit to the marital contract. This indicated an improvement in the position of wives, although it did not change their economic status, the essence of their dependency. By making men culpable for adultery, the court may also have heralded a new ideology of sexual roles—one that would encourage families in the young Republic to produce upright citizens. Stricter standards for men's marital fidelity helped enforce ideals of republican character and counteract British social models. The assumption that men could resist the temptation of adultery also implied a nontraditional view of woman[84]—not the devil-as-woman Eve, whose seductiveness absolved men of their sexual transgressions, but the angel-as-woman Pamela, who upheld and typified sexual virtue.

[83] *Gentleman's and Lady's Town and Country Magazine* (Sept. 1784), 194. See also Herman R. Lantz *et al.,* "Pre-Industrial Patterns in the Colonial Family in America: A Content Analysis of Colonial Magazines," *American Sociological Review,* XXXIII (1968), 413-426.
[84] Malmsheimer, "New England Funeral Sermons," finds this kind of shift in ideology in funeral sermons.

5

Honor, Sexuality, and Illegitimacy in Colonial Spanish America

Ann Twinam

In 1754, doña Margarita Martines Orejón of Tasco, Mexico, discovered that she was pregnant. She was eighteen, she was single, she belonged to one of the town's most distinguished families. Her brothers were priests, her ancestors had been conquistadores.[1] Although her lover, Tasco miner don Antonio Villanueva, never married her, he did plot with doña Margarita and her family to hide her pregnancy and to protect her from public scandal. Decades later, don Antonio remembered their affair and

the union from which she became pregnant. In order to guard this fact, which was totally hidden and so without discredit for him or for her, it was not made public knowledge, but their indiscretion remained totally hidden, for the contacts they had in her house were not suspicious nor scandalous, given the high standing of both of them and the luster and reputation of her family.

After doña Margarita had given birth secretly, don Antonio took their son to be baptized. He eventually introduced him as an "orphan" into his own bachelor establishment, which he shared with *alcalde mayor* Miguel de Rivera, his mining partner. For the next two decades these men carefully and lovingly supervised the upbringing and education of the young Josef Antonio.[2]

Doña Margarita remained a spinster in her family home. Another eighteen years would pass before she would publicly come forth and acknowledge her illegitimate son. It was only then that her testimony revealed the high price exacted by her youthful love affair. Remembering those days doña Margarita confessed that "she never had anything to do with any other man, neither before nor after she conceived the said Josef Antonio, nor even after this incident has she ever had relations with don Antonio, but she has lived with honor and sense, and with no loss of her good reputation."

Why would a woman who had paid such a high personal price, who had forfeited her child for her reputation, and who had lived for eighteen years of honorable spinsterhood now publicly admit that she was an unwed mother? Doña Margarita herself supplies the answer: "I do not want to take away the good that could come to him if he knew who his parents were." And so, with the passage of years, the future welfare of her son began to outweigh any detriment to her own reputation.

The particular reason why doña Margarita emerged to confess her motherhood was that her son, Josef Antonio, had made formal application to the Council of the Indies to purchase his legitimation through a *gracias a sacar*. This royal dispensation literally gave petitioners "permission to take" themselves from the legal category of illegitimacy, to move to that of "legitimated" offspring. Such applicants belonged to an exclusive group, as there were few in the Spanish colonies who combined the necessary racial and social background with the resources to pay for such bureaucratic approval. In this case, the social position of Josef Antonio's parents proved more than sufficient, for, like the fathers and mothers of other successful petitioners, doña Margarita and don Antonio were members of their local élites. Fathers of cédula petitioners were typically men of power and wealth in their communities. Some held high rank in the army or the navy or served in prestigious positions in city councils or the imperial bureaucracy. They were judges, landowners, merchants, miners, and clerics who belonged to the peak of a self-consciously defined social pyramid. The mothers of these illegitimates were the daughters, sisters, nieces, cousins, and sometimes even the wives of males of similar preeminence. It is no accident that don Antonio stressed the "luster and reputation" of doña Margarita's family and emphasized his own "high standing."

To win approval from the Council of the Indies it was not sufficient that Josef Antonio confirm the identity of his parents and prove their social rank. He also had to document their marital state at the time of his own conception and birth. Applicants who could show that they were *hijos naturales*, the illegitimate children of single parents, were much more likely to be successful than those who were *adulterinos* (illegitimates with a married parent) or *espurios* (offspring of priests).[3] Given this demand for details, petitioners commonly sought depositions not only from surviving parents but also from relatives, neighbors, friends, or servants who might detail the extenuating circumstances surrounding their births. Decree requests such as Josef Antonio's thus provide rare, intimate, and frank accounts of the sexual and personal relationships between élite women and men and of the emotional ties that linked them with their illegitimate children, surrounding kin groups, and colonial society at large. In this case, since Josef Antonio's mother and father had been single at the time of his birth, and officially acknowledged their parentage, the Council of the Indies readily granted the desired decree in 1780.

Josef Antonio's plea for legitimation was but one of 244 such cases that arrived for consideration by the Council of the Indies during the seventeenth and eighteenth centuries (see graph).[4] Such requests originated from every jurisdiction of Spanish America. The empire-wide distribution of such petitions makes it possible to reconstruct shared colonial attitudes and practices relating to sexuality and illegitimacy[5] (see table 1). The number, chronological, and geographical scope of these detailed requests make them powerful tools with which to uncover some of the lost topics of Spanish America's colonial past.

The history of female sexuality emerges as one such theme. Lacking much research on the subject, we might begin with the assumption that the Roman Catholic cult of virginity importantly shaped popular attitudes concerning female sexual activity. The post-Trent church presented the Blessed Virgin as a role model as it enthusiastically sponsored the reform of feminine orders, founded nunneries in Spanish America, and elevated Therese of Avila and Rose of Lima to sainthood. Although the secular cult of virginity recognized that most women were not saints, it still emphasized the importance of sexual abstinence. A woman was to refrain permanently from intercourse if she remained single or was to maintain her virginity until she became a wife. Presumably, a woman was either "in" sexual control, or "out of" such control, and society did not recognize anything "in between." For that reason, single women who lost their virginity, or wives who strayed, lost any claim to respectability. They were "out of control" and approximated the moral, if not the actual, state of the prostitute.

Clearly this exclusive dichotomy, with its foreshadowing of more contemporary stereotypes of machismo and *marianismo*, omits critical analytical elements such as class, race, and epoch. It is here that the collected biographies of élite women who engaged in premarital or extramarital sexual relations and who bore illegitimate

Graph 1. Frequency of Petitions by Decade, 1730–1820

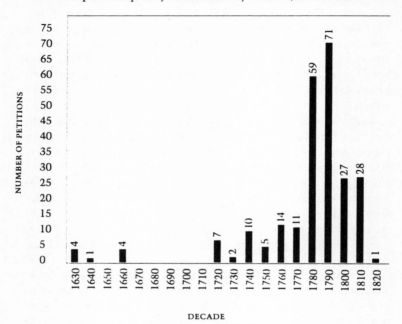

Source: AGI, Audiencias, "Cartas y Expedientes"; Indiferente General, exp. 16, 1535. Before 1720 the Spanish government had no widely publicized or established mechanism through which subjects might submit legitimation petitions. This makes petitions before 1720 difficult to locate. After 1720 the Council of the Indies and the Council of Castille established procedures for such requests. The peak decades of application (1780–90) may well coincide with increased publicity concerning the legitimation options. Probably more important was the movement of illegitimates into established élite ranks in regions such as Cuba, where economic prosperity produced social mobility. A broader issue is still unclear: increase in petitions might reflect a loosening of eighteen-century sexual mores, leading to a corresponding increase in out-of-wedlock liaisons and illegitimate births. Statistics may also reflect a contrary trend of tightening of élite attitudes toward illegitimacy which accelerated the purchase of cédulas to erase birth "stains." At the moment the former appears more plausible than the latter, although individual case histories suggest that both patterns were working simultaneously.

Table 1. Frequency of Petitions by Audiencia and Decade (N 244)

Audiencia	1630	1640	1650	1660	1670	1680	1690	1700	1710	1720	1730	1740	1750	1760	1770	1780	1790	1800	1810	1820
Buenos Aires														1	3	3	9	2		
Caracas											1			1	5	1	1			
Charcas														1		6	4			
Chile																1	4			
Guadalajara													2	1	2					
Guatemala City	1													1	5	5	5	1		
Lima		1												1	10	9	6	2		
Mexico City	3									1	1	4	4	3	1	9	5	3	2	1
Panama														1		1	2			
Quito			2														3	3		
Santo Domingo										6	1	5	1	5	3	20	23	4	21	
Santa Fe				2								1			3	4	3	2		
Total	4	1	0	4	0	0	0	0	0	7	2	10	5	14	11	59	71	27	28	1

Source: AGI, Audiencias. "Cartas y Expedientes"; Indiferente General, exp. 16. 1535. The relative preponderance of petitions from the Audiencia of Santo Domingo (Cuba) is noteworthy. A possible explanation for this situation may be that the geographical and psychological proximity of Cuba to the Spanish mainland, given the frequent sailing between Havana and the mother country, generated widespread publicity and familiarity concerning the legitimation options. The increased economic and social mobility brought by the Cuban sugar boom and slave trade profits seemed to have created upwardly mobile people anxious to erase any legal obstacles hindering that ascent.

children can provide rare glimpses of the fate of those who crossed such forbidden boundaries.

Doña Margarita gives us her idea of the proper sexual conduct expected of the unmarried colonial female. She tells us that she has shown "sense" since the birth of her son, for she has abstained from sexual relations. This control of her sexuality has brought its own reward, for she has now "lived with honor . . . and with no loss of her good reputation."[6] She was not alone in linking the prescribed ideals of feminine behavior with the Latin American concept of honor, as other mothers of illegitimates—possibly because they had violated such standards—seem veritably obsessed with the topic. Their testimony makes clear that honor served as an overarching complex of ideas, attitudes, and values that set the ideal standards for élite behavior, including sexual behavior. We must meet Spanish American élites on their own ground and use their own concept of honor as the lens through which to view colonial sexual standards and practices. Since there were often significant gaps between the ideal and the real, let us first consider the linkage between theoretical norms of feminine sexuality and honor, before we can explore its expression in real life.

Honor

Although members of colonial Spanish society from the most exalted to the most lowly might feel that they possessed honor, it was only members of the colonial élite who defined it in exclusive terms. For them, honor was the ethos which rationalized the existence of the colonial hierarchy.¯ It included those self-conscious differences of birth and conduct that distinguished people who had it (*gente decente*) from those who did not (*gente baja*). Honor molded intra-élite relationships, as those who had honor recognized it in others and treated these peers with an attention and respect that they denied the rest of colonial society.[8]

Honor placed élite families not only in social space, but in family time. Part of honor was inherited, including the concept of *limpieza de sangre* (purity of blood), as those of the upper strata had to prove their ancestors had not been Moors, Jews, or heretics or, in the colonies, Indians or blacks.[9] Honor was not only a heritage of racial and religious purity, but a family history of proper action, as signified by generations of sanctified marriages and of legitimate births. The three most important documents in a colonist's life—the birth certificate, the marriage certificate, and the will—recorded the personal histories of preceding generations by noting whether a person was or was not legitimate. As such, they also provided the basis for elaborate family genealogies that colonial élites maintained and treasured as proof that a chain of religiously confirmed, racially pure marriages and legitimate births bound them to past generations. If there was a break in such continuity, they acted to close it, and a few families even purchased legitimation degrees for dead relatives.[10]

All family members had an immediate responsibility to maintain their own personal honor and thus pass on the collective chain of honor to future generations.

When the chain was broken by illegitimacy, it produced family members who were blood kin but lacked the perquisites of honor. Illegitimate males who did not possess honor could be excluded from public offices and from higher positions in the church, the military, and the civil service. Illegitimate women not only found their pool of potential marriage partners restricted, but their illegitimacy could adversely affect the occupational choices of their sons and the marriage potential of their daughters.[11] Absence of honor could thus limit the social mobility of both sexes, as well as the future of succeeding generations.

Questions of honor, female sexuality, and illegitimacy thus become inextricably linked. Women who engaged in premarital or extramarital sexual relations not only lost personal reputation and honor, but could beget additional family members whose illegitimacy excluded them from family honor. The double standard characteristic of a patriarchal colonial society meant that similar sexual activity did not as certainly threaten the personal honor of the élite male as that of the female. Nonetheless, men who engaged in sexual encounters with females of equal rank did have to consider that public knowledge of a sexual affair could bring certain dishonor to their female lover.

The colonial code of honor thus attempted to control female sexuality through either virginity or marital chastity. There were, however, gaps between how the honor code functioned in theory and how it operated in practice. Those who violated sexual norms need not always pay. The out-of-wedlock pregnancy of doña Margarita shows, for example, that it was possible to manipulate the system for years and avoid loss of honor. Colonial élites employed diverse strategies to achieve such ends. These included "immediate or post hoc matrimony" as well as forms of "private" and "public" (extended engagements, concubinage) pregnancies. The frequency with which élites throughout the colonies resorted to such tactics reveals that there were intermediate positions between the honorable states of unmarried virgin or chaste wife, on the one hand, and the dishonorable positions of single mother or promiscuous spouse on the other.

Immediate Marriage: The Post Hoc Option

The different strategies of élite women facing an illegitimate birth had the same ultimate personal goal: to minimize or to avoid public loss of their honor. The simplest and probably the most frequent solution, if it were possible, was for the pregnant woman and her lover to marry immediately and to have a "premature" but legitimate first child, thereby avoiding all scandal.[12] What may not be well known is that a pregnant woman need not marry before the birth of her child to legitimate it. A long European tradition, with roots in Roman and Canon law and codified in the Spanish medieval code, the *Fuero Real*, provided a fall-back position. If both lovers were single when they had a sexual relationship and were not related by prohibitive degrees of kinship, any subsequent marriage between them, even years after the birth of their illegitimate offspring, would automatically legitimate their children (*hijos naturales*).[13] This legal tradition still found popular expression in Latin America in the seventeenth and eighteenth centuries, and the presumption that such post hoc legitimation could occur significantly affected the immediate and long-term plans of pregnant spinsters.[14] The strategies of "private pregnancy" and "extended engagement" could not have totally or partially protected the honor of pregnant single women without the eventual potential of the legitimating effects of matrimony.[15]

Private Pregnancy

In societies where premarital chastity is the ideal, one simple expedient to mitigate consequences of violating it is to hide the resulting pregnancy so that it apparently never happened. In colonial Spanish America, such "private pregnancies" took a subtle form, for a single woman might be nine months pregnant (privately) but still maintain her public reputation as a virgin and woman of honor. This might be so, even though her condition was known to relatives, selected outsiders, or even a wider social circle, for all would conspire to maintain the distance between her private, pregnant reality and her public, virtuous reputation. Even the Catholic Church cooperated to protect her honor, as the mother's name would not be listed on her child's birth certificate. If a mother was to maintain her public reputation as a virgin, however, she could not openly acknowl-

126   Ann Twinam

Table 2: Classification of Pregnancies in Legitimation Petitions

Type of Pregnancy	Number of Cases	Percentage
Private	67	35.8
Public		
With *palabra de casamiento*	11	
Concubinage	13	
Other[1]	20	
Subtotal	44	23.5
Unknown status of pregnancy[2]	76	40.7
TOTALS	187	100.0

Source: AGI, Audiencias, "Cartas y Expedientes"; Indiferente General, exp. 16, 35.

1. These are cases in which the mother can be clearly identified as having had a public pregnancy, but her status (single, engaged, or married) cannot be determined.

2. These cases do not provide data permitting classification of the mother's status as to private or public pregnancy.

edge or raise her child. Of the 187 mothers of illegitimates who appear in cédula petitions, 67, or 35.8 percent, had identifiable private pregnancies. Their identity was protected on birth certificate, and the mother did not take the child (see table 2).

Private pregnancy could occur because colonial society was flexible and often permitted disparities between a person's private reality and his or her public reputation. Although it may be novel to discuss this dichotomy in terms of sexuality, it has long been customary for historians to recognize this phenomenon in Latin American race relations. A wealthy colonist of mulatto ancestry could be accorded the respectful honorific of "don"—which was not a traditional form of address for those of mixed blood—and could enjoy a public reputation as a "white" man. There could be gaps between a person's private reality—a mulatto mother that most of the town knew had existed—and a person's publicly acknowledged persona—in this case as a rich "white" man of honor. In such circumstances an acquired characteristic such as wealth could blur private reality and provide upward racial and social mobility in the public sphere.[16]

This potential for disparity between private reality and public reputation also benefited pregnant Latin American spinsters. They and their kin could use the ascriptive advantages of birth to prevent loss of élite status even when customary mores had been breached. In the case of élite white women, the public presumption—at least at the start—was toward female innocence and virtue. Just as wealthy mulattos could be white, so pregnant, élite spinsters could still be virgins.

The private pregnancy of doña Maria del Carmen López Nieto demonstrates the lengths to which an unwed mother might go to hide her pregnancy, and the degree to which family members would support her. Doña María and her family belonged to the highest levels of Spanish colonial bureaucracy: her father, don José López Lisperguer, was a judge on the Bolivian high court, or *audiencia*. Nor was doña María's fiancé and lover, don Ramón de Rivera, unequal to her in rank, as he too sat on the high bench. Doña María and don Ramón could not marry, as Spanish law forbade the marriage of high bureaucrats, such as judges, to colonists who lived in the jurisdictions where they served.[17] Technically, doña María and don Ramón had to receive dispensation from Madrid before they could consecrate their union. For this reason don José, doña María's father, prohibited an early marriage. He felt particularly vulnerable, he later admitted, because one of his relatives in Chile who had married without the necessary royal permission had found his later career at a standstill. "Fearful of losing my own post," don José later remembered, "I resisted the marriage, even though I could not stop the union of wills."

Doña María and don Ramón were not disposed to wait either to marry or, as time passed, to have a sexual relationship. Don Ramón finally engineered a transfer and a promotion to Lima, where, since he was no longer in the jurisdiction of his fiancée, he theoretically should have been able to marry without delay. By then, however, it was too late. Doña María discovered that she was pregnant while don Ramón was far away in Lima and unable to help her. Ashamed, and possibly afraid of confessing to her authoritarian father, doña María sought help from her sisters and brothers. They helped her fake an accident, and she received permission from her parents to visit her brother, Dr. José Ignacio, a priest with a parish in Puna. It was there that she gave birth to a baby girl, Gregoria. and there that she died of complications after the birth.

The secrecy surrounding doña María's pregnancy did not end with her death, for her brothers and sisters rallied to protect her reputation beyond the grave. In this case, it may have been as much to spare their father, and to protect family honor, as it was to guard the reputation of a sister presumably beyond such concerns. One of the sisters, doña Nicolasa. a member of the nouveau riche Bolivian silver aristocracy and countess of la Casa Real de Moneda, traveled to Puna to collect her illegitimate baby niece. She took the child back with her to La Plata and raised her in secret. While doña María's mother and father mourned the death of their daughter from complications of an "accident," her brothers and sisters maintained a conspiracy of silence concerning the true cause of her death.

It was only when her father, don José, was about to die that the countess confessed that Gregoria, who was now approaching nine years old, was his illegitimate grandchild. The remorse of don José for condemning his daughter to die away from home and family was enormous, but he died knowing that Gregoria was generously provided for, as he left her the portion of his estate that would have gone to her mother. His children, Gregoria's aunts and uncles, then pressed for her official legitimation, which was readily granted when Gregoria was twenty-two, in 1795, due both to her parents' single status when she was conceived and to her high social rank.

The elaborate obfuscations of doña María's case were not atypical, as confirmation of similar family concealment strategies comes from other parts of the empire. In Mexico City, for example, doña Magdalena de la Vega engaged in sexual relations with *regidor* (city councilman) don Vicente de Borboya. This couple, like their Bolivian counterparts, needed official permission to marry, since don Vicente was a major officeholder. Years later, doña Justa, the natural daughter of this couple. described how her parents' desire to save public face led to a private pregnancy.

Seeing that doña Magdalena was pregnant and recognizing that marriage could not then take place . . . in order to ward off and guard against the danger to her honor and good reputation . . . and the blushes and the emotions to which she would be exposed. they adopted the expedient of moving her to the city of Puebla, under the excuse that she was sick, to the house of her sister, doña Teresa, where she remained hidden until she gave birth.[18]

Like doña María. doña Magdalena died soon after childbirth. A friend of the Mexican couple later remembered, "and this result was so hidden that [doña Magdalena] died with the reputation of a virgin." Death in childbirth claimed doña María and doña Magdalena, as it did 4.8 percent of those pregnant women who appeared in legitimation petitions.[19] In both these cases collusion with brothers and sisters and geographical removal from the scene had temporarily saved their reputations. But what would have happened if doña María and doña Magdalena—as did the majority of their counterparts—had survived this ordeal?

Personal correspondence and oral testimony make clear that both women would have married their fiancés and lovers. Don Ramón, in a letter written to the countess (doña María's sister) two decades after the event, affirmed that "I recognize [Gregoria] as my natural daughter born of your sister doña María del Carmen, who is in heaven and with whom I would have married, as you know, if the royal permission had arrived to do it, but as God chose to carry her away, I was not able to put into practice my desires after I obtained the necessary license and my transfer to Lima."[20]

Father Joaquín del Moral, a confidant of don Vicente de Borboya, confirmed the similar circumstances of the Mexican couple: "Because of the close friendship and confidence [I had] with the subject [don Vicente] he told me various times that when he was trying to contract marriage with doña Magdalena de la Vega, he had a daughter named doña Justa Rufina by her . . . and that he was not able to verify [the marriage] due to the death of doña Magdalena."[21]

The testimony of these witnesses provides evidence about some customary norms that governed sexual relations between colonial couples. Both doña María and doña Magdalena had lost their virginity. However, both women had done so only after they had presumably exchanged the *palabra de casamiento* or "promise to marry" with their fiancés. Their surrender of virginity under such circumstances was not unusual, as local society apparently tolerated (even if it did not condone) premarital intercourse between engaged couples. Nor did these women "lose the respect" of their fiancés because they had engaged in intercourse. Although an élite Latin male customarily demanded virginity of his intended wife, he apparently expected her to prove this aspect of her honor at the time of first intercourse, which might take place significantly before the marriage ceremony.

We see a conscious delineation of such sexual mores in an intimate and revealing letter written by Querétaro regidor don Joseph Martín de la Rocha to his spinster sister, doña Elvira, who lived in Veracruz. The subject was most delicate, as don Joseph confessed that he had fathered an illegitimate child, and he begged his sister to assume responsibility for her baby niece. Don Joseph confessed: "I tell you in all confidence, and confident in the love you have for me, that this baby is my daughter, and I recognize her as such, that her mother was a lady, that nothing takes away from my circumstances that I knew her as a virgin, and that she died in childbirth, and for that reason all my plans have been frustrated."[22]

The manner in which this eighteenth-century élite Mexican male chose to describe this affair to his spinster sister tells us much about customary élite attitudes toward honor and premarital intercourse. Don Joseph is clearly taking pains to inform his sister that he had conducted this affair in an "honorable" manner. What, then, does he consider to be the telling variables in his favor? He informs doña Elvira that his lover was a social peer, as she was a "lady." She was a woman of honor as she was a "virgin" at the time of first intercourse. Nor had don Joseph seduced her with underhanded motives ("nothing takes away from my circumstances that I knew her as a virgin") as the couple had exchanged the palabra de casamiento ("all my plans have been frustrated").

If a couple were social equals and were engaged, the man did not lose honor by claiming the virginity of his intended. Furthermore, even though don Joseph succeeded in shifting the child-care burden to his spinster sister, he acknowledged his responsibility to his daughter and promised to pay all expenses. It is notable that don Joseph insisted that his honor had not been diminished by his conduct of this affair. Perhaps one reason that he could boast of the probity of his actions was that he had rigorously guarded the honor of his fiancé as well, as he had protected her reputation with a private pregnancy. Even after her death, he omitted her name in the crucial letter to his sister, nor is she identified two decades later in the legitimation petition of her daughter, doña Josepha. If don Joseph's unknown fiancé had survived childbirth, she presumably would have suffered no public loss of her honor, and the couple would have married.

What would have been the next step for unwed mothers if, unlike doña María, doña Magdalena, and don Joseph's intended, they had survived childbirth and married their prospective husbands? As long as both lovers were single and not related by prohibitive degrees of kinship, a post hoc marriage ceremony would have automatically legitimated their children. These offspring would have inherited equally with any additional children the couples might have had, and would, in the eyes of the law, have been equal to future siblings in every way.

Immediately after their marriage, in order to save face, such couples might have hidden their indiscretion by introducing these recently legitimated children into their homes as "orphans" or as "adopted" children. As time passed, the couples might eventually allow the true circumstances surrounding their first child's birth to become public knowledge. Even if they did not, they could write "private wills." which were kept from public domain but which fully explained past circumstances and protected the legal rights of their firstborn.

There must have been many unwed mothers who, in conjunction with their lover-fiancés and close kin, engineered private pregnancies, survived childbirth, married, and automatically legitimated their children. Such a successful outcome would mean that these families need never have applied for gracias a sacar. Such records cannot tell us. therefore, about the frequency with which the colonial élites protected female honor by keeping pregnancies private as a preface to matrimony. What the cédulas reveal is the how such pregnancies were organized and the customary roles and responsibilities of the unwed mothers, fathers. and families who engineered them.

Colonists also used private pregnancy to protect a woman's reputation when marriage was not a chosen or a possible conclusion. Such cases occurred either when men refused to wed their pregnant lovers or were unable to do so because they were already married or were priests. Private pregnancies could also protect married women who bore children that were not their husbands'. In these instances the involved parties had to take extraordinary precautions to save the honor of the mother, as well as to care for her newborn.

Such secrecy was not maintained without personal sacrifice. The history of doña X illustrates such costs, as she had to endure not only rejection by her lover but loss of her baby as well.[23] Witnesses agree that doña X belonged to one of the most honored families in Buenos Aires society. It is unclear whether she had a firm promise of marriage from don Manuel Domecq, a merchant who had an extensive commerce in the Argentine interior, but her subsequent actions suggest that she hoped that a marriage would take place. Their relationship resulted in a pregnancy, and in early 1753 doña X gave birth to a baby boy. Apparently she had the child at home, which suggests that her family conspired to protect her and their good name. Immediately after the birth, don Manuel arrived to collect the boy and deposited him at the house of María Josepha de Abalos, a "respectable" married woman whom he paid to care for his natural son. As was common in such circumstances, don Manuel openly acknowledged the child as his—the double standard applied here, as paternity did not negatively affect the reputation of the élite male. He protected the name of the mother, for the birth certificate, issued in February 1753, listed baby Pedro simply as "the natural son of don Manuel Domecq, a Spaniard, and of a lady who is also Spanish."

Consistent with the goal of maintaining the privacy of doña X's pregnancy, don Pedro did not reveal her identity to baby Pedro's foster mother. However, doña X could not tolerate such a separation from her son. She arranged to be introduced to María Josepha, cultivated her friendship, and began to frequent her house. The marked attention she paid to baby Pedro, the many presents she brought him, and the kisses she lavished upon him soon aroused María Josepha's suspicion. Finally, doña X confessed that she was the mother. In testimony that still remains pitiful centuries after the event, María Josepha's daughter, recalled how doña X had begged that "when she would not be able to come and see him, in order not to arouse suspicion, that they send a servant with the baby to her house under some pretext." Doña X's obsession with secrecy—to hide from society her identity as an unwed mother—dictated that she deny her relationship with her child.

Doña X not only continued to visit her child, but she apparently still hoped that her private pregnancy was a temporary expedient until don Manuel would legitimize their union and their son. Don Manuel, however, announced his engagement to another woman. María Josepha's daughter, Juliana, explained doña X's response to this betrayal: "Doña X continued to visit as long as don Manuel Domecq remained single, but when she found out that he was engaged, she became furious, and *never returned to see her son again*" (italics mine).

With don Manuel now openly engaged, doña X had no alternative but to abandon her child if she wished to maintain her public honor.

This wrenching decision on her part illustrates the hard choices faced by unwed mothers whose identity had been protected. The story of doña X, unlike that of most of her peers, ends on a somewhat happy note. Although she relinquished her child, she eventually married, had other children, and held an honored place in Buenos Aires society.[24]

Although an unwed mother might have a public reputation as a virgin while she carried or even after she bore her child, any subsequent recognition of her offspring would stain her honor. Such was the fate of doña Gabriela Márquez, whose early profile—a youthful romance, first promise of marriage, a secret birth—repeats the private pregnancy pattern.[25] Even though her lover, don Antonio de Aguilar, was under twenty himself, he came from a prominent family of Chilean landowners. He recognized his illegitimate daughter, María, at her birth and insisted that he be named as the natural father on her baptismal certificate—which did not name the mother—and he arranged for his sister, doña Mercedes, to take and to raise the baby secretly. For two years doña Gabriela maintained her identity as a private unwed mother and waited for don Antonio to make good his promise to marry her and to legitimate their child. Like doña X, doña Gabriela was betrayed, for don Antonio announced his engagement to another woman. Unlike doña X, doña Gabriela chose her child over her honor. She arrived at doña Mercedes' house, took her two-year-old baby back with her, and spent the remainder of her life as a single mother.

Private pregnancies not only guarded the honor of spinsters who did not marry their lovers, such as doña X or doña Gabriela, but also that of already-married women who lacked this alternative. Married women engaged in extramarital affairs at great personal risk to themselves and to their lovers. Therefore, such cases are rare, and in all such instances it is not surprising to note that the husbands of these women had been long absent. After doña Y from Havana was abandoned by her husband, for example, she eventually had two daughters by don Juan Antonio Moreión. He protected her name during and after their affair, effectively "adopted" their two daughters, and, with great difficulty, given that their daughters were adulterine in the eyes of the law, eventually achieved their legitimation.[26] In Cumaná, Venezuela, don Josef Antonio Betancourt arranged such a private pregnancy for married doña Z. Witnesses expressed much sympathy for her sufferings under her husband, don Esteban Lizcano, who had abandoned her long before he ran off to the Llanos. They remembered "the horrible life (*mala vida*) that Lizcano gave her by his troublesome and ridiculous character, for he even refused to support her, and it was these events that no doubt led her to fall into her present situation."[27] In these two cases private pregnancy saved the honor of these élite women as their married state foreclosed any other options.

Public Pregnancy and Extended Engagements

Although private pregnancies could save honor, they entailed extraordinary precautions on the part of the woman, her lover, and their families. At least 44, or 23.5 percent, of legitimation petitions reflect an alternative strategy of "public pregnancy" where élite women carried, bore, and raised their illegitimate children under the full scrutiny of their social peers. Included in this category are "extended engagements" as well as certain forms of "concubinage." One-fourth of public pregnancies can be clearly identified as "extended engagements" (see table 3). In such cases unmarried women who had exchanged a promise of marriage lived openly for years and even decades in public, monogamous relationships with prospective husbands. Although the documents show that these women felt shame and experienced loss of reputation and honor, their situation was not totally irreparable. Subsequent marriage with their lover could, at any time, transform these unwed mothers into wives, and their hijos naturales into legitimate heirs. The situation of such unwed mothers challenges any stereotypical view of colonial sexuality that characterizes single women as either virgins who were "in control" or nonvirgins who were "out of control," and presumably beyond the pale. Instead, colonial reality was far more complex. "Inbetween" circumstances such as a palabra de casamiento could provide marginal legitimacy to the status of nonvirgin spinster or even to that of unwed mother. Even though a public pregnancy deprived an unmarried mother of honor, public knowledge that there had been a palabra de casamiento provided a mitigating circumstance.

We see such circumstances in the case of doña Juana Díaz de Estrada, the daughter of a former governor of Veracruz, who in the 1690s began a relationship with don Diego de Alarcón Ocaña, a naval ship's captain from Havana. The captain promised to marry her, and as his courtship proceeded, and their sexual intimacies as well, doña

Juana put more and more pressure on him to fulfill this pledge. The captain's secretary. don Agustín Henríquez, remembered those days with great clarity: "I was there on occasions in which the lady rightfully pleaded with him to fulfill his word, reminding him of the damage to her reputation and the discredit of her family."[28]

The captain "swore not to defer it." However he did not fulfill his promise, and the secretary noted that doña Juana's pleas became even "more forceful when she found out that she was pregnant." Finally a daughter, doña María Cathalina, was born. Don Diego still balked at tying the knot. Mother and father treated the birth of their baby in quite different ways. Don Diego showed great joy at her birth. His secretary remembered that "he took her in his arms . . . he recognized her as his natural daughter, and he publicly celebrated her as such in view of all the city."

Doña Juana. far from showing any elation, retreated and was reluctant to face public scrutiny. The secretary recalled that "doña Juana withdrew into great privacy." Her guilt and shame impressed others as well. One witness recalled that she had "visited her house often, and her modesty was such that before the dawn [she had dressed herself so that] not even her fingers could be seen." Now publicly marked as an unwed mother, doña Juana literally went into mourning for an honor that could only be restored by marriage. Unfortunately, she suffered an accident, and although don Diego sped to her side, she was unconscious and died before the couple could be wed. The captain knew he had not satisfied the requirements of honor, as he considered his later "reverses" as a "punishment of God" for "having delayed the fulfillment of his obligation."

The case of doña María Josepha Pérez de Balmaceda, from Havana. shows how a marriage promise could provide a "fallen" woman a measure of public honor, although the protagonist of this case may well have carried her obsession to neurotic extremes. During her courtship, doña María had taken the rare step of demanding, and receiving, a written promise of marriage from her fiancé before she agreed to have intercourse with him. The couple then lived together for years and produced three illegitimate children. Finally, witnesses agree, the marriage was imminent: "after the birth of Pedro Antonio. the said [don Pedro Diez de Florencia] tried very earnestly to fulfill the word that he had given to doña María Josepha, and [the couple] prepared clothes and finery, and fixed up the house."[29]

Just before the ceremony, don Pedro may have had second

thoughts, for he broke off the preparations, took off to Spain to look for a better job, and sailed to Mexico to assume his new position. For years he sent pleading letters, envoys, and money to doña María, begging her to join him and be wed. Doña María may well have had enough of his delays and broken promises, for she claimed fear of the sea and refused to follow him.

Nonetheless, she never let her relatives or local peers forget that she was an engaged woman. She kept her lover's written promise to marry her knotted in a ball that she tied to the rosary that she wore around her neck, and she constantly opened his note and read it aloud to relatives and town officials. As one witness somewhat wearily recounted,

many times [doña María] read that paper in the presence of this witness and of all of her house and family, and many other persons. . . . and even many years after the absence and death of [her fiancé] doña María carried [the paper] hanging from the rosary she wore around her neck which proved her good faith and her well-founded hope that she would have married.

A palabra de casamiento, then, provided a certain legitimacy in that it separated unwed mothers who had surrendered their virginity with a firm promise of marriage from women who engaged in sexual intercourse with no guarantee or possibility of eventual matrimony. Since the gracias a sacar chronicled only those instances where marriage never occurred, it is impossible to calculate the frequency with which colonial élite couples became engaged, produced illegitimate offspring, and then eventually married. It is indicative, however, that colonists throughout the Indies familiarly spoke of this practice, and it was commonplace enough to produce its own patterns.

Couples who had exchanged palabra de casamiento customarily recorded the names of both mother and father on the baptismal certificates of their illegitimate children. Such a public acknowledgment not only indirectly informed society of the couple's marriage promise, but it presumably put pressure on the parties to execute it. This openness could later benefit their illegitimate offspring, who, by presenting their birth certificates identifying them as the natural children of X and Y, could more easily prove their legitimated status.

The baptismal certificate of the illegitimate daughter of doña Thoribia María Guerra Mier and her fiancé, military officer don Lorenzo de Parga, from Valledupar, New Granada, reflects this custom. Sometime before 1779 don Lorenzo arrived in Valledupar, where he met doña Thoribia, the daughter of don Juan Guerra, who belonged to one of the "first families" of the city. Years later don Lorenzo remembered how he had "proposed matrimony with . . . doña Thoribia . . . and under this belief and word had a daughter named doña María Josepha."[30] The couple was waiting for official permission from the military authorities to wed when war broke out, and don Lorenzo was transferred to Cartagena.

Doña Thoribia may well have postponed the baptism of her illegitimate daughter, born in 1779, in the hope that she might first be married and that her child might then be baptized as a legitimated offspring. By 1782, she and her family could apparently wait no longer, but they made sure that the circumstances of doña María's birth were public knowledge. Perhaps it was the family's exalted position that led the local cleric to take the rare option of omitting any reference to the circumstances of the birth of the three-year-old child in her certificate. He simply noted that she was "the baby, María Josefa," rather than that she was an illegitimate child.[31] Such delicacy did not, however, extend to her parents, who were clearly identified as "don Lorenzo de Parga, Lieutenant of Granaderos of the Fixed Regiment of the Plaza of Cartagena and . . . of doña Thoribia de la Guerra, legitimate daughter of don Juan de la Guerra of the Kingdom of Spain and of doña Ana Mestre." To clinch the case, doña Thoribia's family apparently routed out the town notables (who included her mother's kin) to swear on the baptismal certificate to the extenuating circumstances surrounding the birth: "also present in this act the Captain don Diego Facundo Mestre and the Señor Alcalde Ordinario don José Francisco Mestre to witness that this aforementioned baby was conceived under the promise of matrimony."

If doña Thoribia hoped that this certificate might spur the lieutenant to return for a wedding, she proved mistaken. He later cited the demands of war as a rationale for his continued postponements. Doña Thoribia died in 1787 before they could wed, and years later the guilt-stricken father, now a lieutenant colonel, petitioned for his daughter's legitimation.

It is noteworthy that one of the clearest statements concerning such extended "engagements" comes from a Spanish official who customarily reviewed colonist applications for the gracias a sacar. His official commentary appears in the legitimation petition of doña Antonia del Rey Blanco, of Havana, who was born under murky cir-

138   Ann Twinam

cumstances. Her unwed mother, doña Beatris Blanco de la Poza, had spent her young adult years in a Havana convent but was finally forced to leave due to ill health. Even while living at home she did not participate in local society, but remained a recluse in the family house.[32]

Perhaps this inexperience explains why she was particularly vulnerable to the advances of don Lázaro del Rey Bravo, a business associate of her brother. Although don Lázaro had been married in Spain, he had word that his wife had died in his absence, and so he proposed matrimony to doña Beatris, and the couple began a sexual relationship. It was only after the birth of her child that doña Beatris and her family learned, to their horror, that don Lázaro's first wife had been alive when the couple conceived their baby, although she had since passed away. Her family then refused to permit doña Beatris to marry don Lázaro, even though he remained willing to do so. Decades later, when the legitimation petition of doña Beatris' daughter, doña Antonia, appeared before the Council of the Indies, did the legal question surrounding her birth find an answer. Was she an hija natural—the much more acceptable product of a sexual union between single parents—or was she an adulterina, the despised result of an adulterous alliance? As was customary in Spanish law and culture, the royal official did not rule solely on the actual facts of the case, that is, when had doña Beatris and don Lázaro begun a sexual relationship, or when did don Lázaro's wife die. Instead. the official also took into account the couple's intent, that is, how their actions reflected their perception—even if it was an erroneous perception—of reality. The official gave the couple the benefit of the doubt as he ruled that

doña Antonia is an hija natural for all the favorable civil benefits without any legal difficulty, given that it is fully proved by witnesses and by documents that she not only was conceived under this belief and the good faith of doña Beatris her mother, but that even don Lázaro her father thought he was a bachelor and able to carry out the promise of matrimony he seems to have given.

One of the deciding factors in this case was doña Antonia's birth certificate, which the official saw as compelling proof that the couple assumed that they were single and able to wed. The official concluded.

and instead of putting on the baptismal certificate the expression that is customary of their class. that of "daughter of unknown parents," the couple used
the much less common "hija natural of the aforementioned," which goes to
corroborate the mutual understanding of all [concerned], for it is not customary to declare it this way except when the parents are commonly conceived
to be single and with the disposition or the desire to legitimate their offspring
by a subsequent marriage.

These remarks demonstrate that although the tendency of engaged couples to have illegitimate offspring first and to marry later
may have been uncommon, it was apparently common enough to
develop a body of generally understood practice.

What was life like for these unwed mothers who lived for years or
even decades in the expectation of future matrimony? Their case
histories show that their social position might remain, at best, ambiguous. As in the case of private pregnancy, élite women might customarily benefit from an initial presumption that they were innocent. Even when relatives and neighbors knew that a questionable
liaison was occurring, they did not always choose to acknowledge it
openly. As time passed, however, and particularly as extended engagements seemed less and less likely to end in matrimony, the situation of such unwed mothers became more and more difficult.

Public awareness that a single woman was having an affair with
her fiancé, that the couple were living together, or that she had borne
a child was not always immediate. Colonial architecture could co-
operate to hide incriminating evidence, as the homes of the prosperous tended to be large, with many rooms for family, servants, and
servants' children. In the beginning courting couples might find private spaces for amorous activities, and later even the addition of an
extra baby might not make much a spatial impact.[33] Since a traditional charity of Latin American élite families was to care for orphans and homeless children, the presence of minors with vague antecedents was not that uncommon. The few cases I have detailed
here of relatives or nurses who sheltered babies born out of wedlock
illustrate the frequency of infant adoption. Since not all women who
took in children were guilty of sexual transgressions, they provided
the pattern through which unwed mothers might try to assimilate
their sons and daughters into their own homes without scandalous
notice.

The case of Chilean doña María Rosa de la Torre provides some details as to the variety of social interactions that took place as friends and neighbors discovered that a spinster was now an unwed mother.[34] Although doña María Rosa and her fiancé, don Felipe Briceño, belonged to the Santiago élite, their economic resources were not substantial. Doña María Rosa did not have the backing of powerful kin, as she lived alone with her mother—her father had died in Peru. Don Felipe's father had held the prestigious position of alcalde, but he was not himself prosperous.

Lacking the presence of a father, doña María Rosa's home must have provided a convenient locale for don Felipe's courtship and promise of matrimony. In 1775 a baby boy named José Félix was born. A next-door friend, who was also the baby's godfather, later testified that don Felipe had ordered that both his and doña María Rosa's names appear on the baptismal certificate because "he wanted to legitimate him." Although the promised marriage did not occur, there was no immediate public recognition that doña María Rosa had given birth to an illegitimate child. Fray Agustin, a brother of don Felipe and a priest, remembered that when Jóse Félix petitioned to be legitimated he had discovered that

With the entry and communication that I had in the house of doña María Rosa de la Torre, I saw there a little boy whom she loved very much, but I was unclear who his parents were for some time until my brother don Felipe told me that he was his son and also the child of doña Maria Rosa, although they were hiding this, no doubt to protect her honor. But once I was knowledgeable of this, she no longer hesitated in my presence to kiss her son.

Another witness recalled that he had heard a rumor that the infant that doña María was raising was hers but that "because of her honor there was secrecy about this, even though the boy was raised at her side and in her own house." As time passed, doña María Rosa and don Felipe no longer hid their affair. In the meantime doña María Rosa's mother may have died, for, possibly still promising marriage, don Felipe moved into her house. Even then, some neighbors thought they might be married. The precariousness of doña María Rosa's situation became manifest when don Felipe, aiming to make his fortune, left her and their son and took off to the Andean mining districts. Unfortunately, he experienced "total ruin." Even though the signs were not propitious, doña María Rosa did not abandon hope that he would return and carry out his promise to marry her. A friend spoke of the "tears and pleas" that she directed to her erring lover. He never returned to Santiago, and when he died he left the little money he had, not to doña María Rosa, but to his mother.

Doña María Rosa's case illustrates the long-term ambiguities that might surround the lives of unwed mothers as society gradually discovered and acknowledged their situations. Even don Felipe's brother did not immediately know that doña María Rosa's child was his illegitimate nephew, nor did neighbors seem eager to clarify the marital status of the couple. The initial social assumption, perhaps because don Felipe and doña María Rosa belonged to the class that possessed honor, was toward innocence. Even after the passage of years, when the pretense could no longer be maintained, her neighbors seemed more inclined to sympathize, rather than to criticize her situation.

Women such as doña María Rosa might spend years in limbo waiting for their fiancés to marry them and only discover in middle or old age that their hopes would never be fulfilled. The legal securities of matrimony, such as inheritance from a spouse or reliable maintenance for children, could be denied them. As time passed, many such "engaged" women found that their positions moved beyond ambiguity as the men they had lived with for decades abandoned them to marry, or to take up affairs with, other women. Such abandonment naturally produced bitterness between the unwed mother and her lover, and often soured the relationship between the father and his illegitimate offspring.

Such sentiments clearly emerge in the case of widow doña Antonia Hernández of Havana.[35] She had lived for years with don Nicolás Joseph Rapun, who rose successfully in the bureaucracy and eventually attained the important post of intendent of the Royal Treasury in Havana. Doña Antonia had three children by her first husband and, almost annually, from 1747 to 1752 she presented don Nicolás with an illegitimate child, four of whom survived childbirth. Although don Nicolás did not share her home, all the town knew of their affair and of his daily visits. Don Nicolás promised to marry her, but "His not having married the mother of the petitioners is explained because he put her off with flattering hopes that he was going to do it when he reached the heights that were destined by fortune, and after he succeeded, he continued delaying from day to day. And now that he is the intendent it is impossible to compel him to satisfy that obligation."

Even though doña Antonia tried to sue and force him to marry her, don Nicolás never gave in. He not only broke off their long-term relationship but had a final illegitimate son with another woman.

Although doña María Rosa and doña Antonia were eventually abandoned by their fiancés, they never appear to have been ostracized by friends and neighbors. Social peers might initially be disposed to show tolerance toward women trapped in such "extended engagements" for several reasons. First of all, at any time, their status might change through subsequent matrimony. Although don Felipe may have failed in the mining districts, there must have been others who succeeded in their endeavors and returned in triumph to marry their fiancées and to legitimate their offspring. Even if society were disposed to criticize the relationship of doña Antonia and don Nicolás, he was a man of power in Havana, and doña Antonia would have shared his status if the couple had ever wed.

Testimony in such cases makes clear that, although the strict dictates of honor might demand that engaged women who bore illegitimate children be rejected by their social peers, in practical day-to-day living such was not the case. Instead, neighbors apparently moved with ease and familiarity in and out of such houses. The illegitimate children of these unions played and were educated with legitimate offspring of equal rank.[36] Here, the pervasive tolerance of a Latin Catholic society where sins could always be forgiven seems to have eased the daily exigencies of social discourse. There were limits to this tolerance, however, for unwed mothers generally remained spinsters all their lives, and their children could be subjected to the civil and social barriers imposed against those who lacked honor.[37]

Public Pregnancy and Concubinage

As time passed, women such as doña María Rosa and doña Antonia must have realized that they would pass the rest of their lives as aging "fiancées" and as mothers of illegitimate offspring. If they had any consolation, it must have been that they were honorable women who had followed local customs, as they had engaged in sexual relationships solely as a prelude to matrimony. The real fault lay with their lovers, who had failed to honor the marriage promise. Such rationalizations could not provide comfort to a last group of women, who had publicly entered into affairs without a promise of matrimony or who had become the acknowledged mistresses of clerics or of married men[35] (see table 3). Such women had openly borne their illegitimate, adulterine, or sacrilegious offspring. Their sexual indiscretions were not only public knowledge, but they were neither mitigated by extenuating circumstances such as a palabra de casamiento nor hidden by a private pregnancy. A world of difference separated the status of those single élite women who had lived as the mistresses of bachelors or widowers from those who had had affairs with priests or married men.

The case history of single mother doña Josepha María Valespino of Havana belongs to the first category, as she lived with a Canarian ship's captain, don Amaro Rodrigues Pargo, without a promise of matrimony and eventually bore an illegitimate son named Manuel. Doña Josepha was a woman of means as she owned two houses, some slaves, and valuable jewelry. The captain lived with her when he traded in Havana. He paid her bills, carried the infant Manuel with him on visits to neighbors and to visit his ship, and was generally acknowledged as his father. Significantly, however, he never promised to marry doña Josepha, and when local neighbors described their affair, they characterized it as "illicit."[39]

Eventually, the captain sailed back to his home port in the Canaries. Although he occasionally sent doña Josepha some wool and other items to sell to support Manuel, he never returned to Cuba. The final break between the couple occurred when the captain wrote and asked that doña Josepha send Manuel to live with him in the Canaries. When she refused, the captain broke off all contact and, at his death, failed to acknowledge his son. As the years passed, doña Josepha exhausted her resources in raising Manuel, and when he petitioned for legitimation at twenty-six, he described her as "blind . . . and in the most extreme poverty." The most telling characteristic of this affair is the absence of the palabra de casamiento. However, other more subtle characteristics—the temporal limitations of the relationship, the lack of much commitment to mother and son, as well as outsiders' description of the affair as "illicit"—may also serve to place it within the realm of public concubinage, rather than that of extended engagement.

Legitimation petitions additionally reveal some rarer cases where women publicly defied the civil and ecclesiastical codes of honor, to engage in sexual affairs with clerics or married men. Significantly, such documents do not provide much information as to how society treated those who trespassed such forbidden boundaries. No

doubt petitioners wanted to make the strongest case possible for legitimation and would omit any information concerning any possible ostracism of their mother or father. Instead, more than others,
such legitimation requests emphasize the discretion of the lovers or
detail the exalted personal connections of the participants or confirm their willingness to pay exorbitant sums to achieve the desired
legitimation. Especially here, only the most powerful and wealthy
made such applications, as the Council of the Indies was less likely
to approve them[40] (see table 3).

It is probably no accident that two of the most extraordinary of
such cases originated in Bolivia, for the silver millionaires of La
Plata and Potosí combined the wealth and connections that were the
prerequisites for such pretensions. The petitions of don Melchor and
don Agustín Varea y Lazcano of La Plata, for example, emphasized
their notable parental backgrounds. Their mother, doña Gertrudis
de Varea y Lazcano, belonged "to one of the principal, distinguished,
and richest families" of Potosí.[41] Her lover, don Domingo Herboso y
Figueroa, was a priest and dean of the cathedral of La Plata. He be-

Table 3. Parents' Marital State and
Success of Legitimation Petitions (N 142)

	Father's Marital Status									
	Single		Priest		Widower		Married		Unknown	
	N	%	N	%	N	%	N	%	N	%
Yes	70	87.5	11	78.6	5	83.3	9	69.2	16	55.2
No	8	10.0	3	21.4	1	16.7	4	30.8	13	44.8
?	2	2.5	—	—	—	—	—	—	—	—
Total	80		14		6		13		29	

	Mother's Marital Status						
	Single		Widow		Married		Unknown	
	N	%	N	%	N	%	N	%
Yes	83	88.3	5	55.6	7	87.5	16	51.6
No	11	11.7	2	22.2	1	12.5	15	48.4
?	—	—	2	22.2	—	—	—	—
Total	94		9		8		31	

Source: AGI, Audiencias, "Cartas y Expedientes"; Indiferente General, Exp.
16.1535.

longed to an extremely powerful political clan, as his father had been president of the Audiencia of Charcas, thus ranking among the top dozen executive officers in the Spanish Empire. Don Domingo's uncle was an archbishop, his brother was a high treasury official in Lima (contador mayor del Tribunal Real de Cuentas), and another brother was governor of the nearby province of Cochabamba.

Family rank and wealth, however, could not obscure the fact that doña Gertrudis was an unwed mother, while the father of her two sons, don Domingo, was a priest. Witnesses who testified in this case emphasized the care the couple had taken to avoid public scandal. Although don Domingo openly visited doña Gertrudis, the lovers maintained separate residences. The couple did not recognize their sons on their baptismal certificates, but listed them as *expósitos*, or "abandoned."[42] One witness, who lived near doña Gertrudis, remembered that don Domingo "in particular used a certain caution and reticence because of the dignity and nature of his position."

After don Domingo's death, his now-adult sons apparently found some acceptance in La Plata society. At least they found witnesses who could testify that they were looked upon "with reputation and honor in all their dealings . . . in the houses of . . . distinguished persons." Their still-surviving mother may well have lost most pretensions to honor. Although the petition contains much information on family pedigree and wealth, the sole comment on her immediate situation is the rather defensive note that her sons "looked on her with respect and veneration."[43] Family wealth and rank notwithstanding, the brothers never fully restored their honor through legitimation.

During those same years that doña Gertrudis and don Domingo carried on their affair in La Plata, a few blocks away, spinster doña Juana Risco y Agoretta lived openly with a married man. Although Dr. Francisco de Moya y Palacios was a regidor and alcalde in the rich silver town of Potosí, where he was married to the daughter of a royal official, his residence was with doña Juana in La Plata. The couple had five illegitimate children, all of whom reached high positions in local society. One daughter married a lawyer, another a high court judge and another a regidor, while one son became a priest and the other a lawyer. The money from silver seemed to smooth all paths, and when one of her widowed daughters, herself a silver magnate, petitioned for legitimation, she not only received it but later used her wealth to purchase a title of nobility.

We know little, however, of the fate of doña Juana. The few com-

146   *Ann Twinam*

ments on her situation bear some resemblance to those made concerning her neighbor, doña Gertrudis. Witnesses noted that her lawyer son, don Agustín, still lived with her, even though he had the means to establish a separate residence, because of "the love and veneration that he feels for her."[44] It is difficult to know what the rest of society thought.

Epilogue

It is important to remember that the large majority of the women whose stories appear here did not benefit from the strategies designed to preserve or restore honor. Once a single woman engaged in premarital sex, the surest method to protect or to restore her honor was through matrimony. The most "successful" private pregnancies, extended engagements, and cases of concubinage were those in which the woman married her lover and automatically legitimated her offspring. The gracias a sacar cédula cases were, by definition, those where eventual marriage did not occur or did not lead to such automatic legitimation, but necessitated an official intervention.

What, then, was the final fate of the mothers? Although a detailed examination of their later lives is beyond the scope of this paper, some general trends can provide a final commentary. The cédula documents fail to provide follow-up stories on more than half (N 104) of them, but it should come as no surprise that nearly two-thirds of those whose fate we do know remained spinsters and widows (see table 4).

Table 4. Fate of Unwed Mothers (*N* 191)

Later Fate	Private Pregnancies		Other Pregnancies	
	N	%	N	%
Spinster, widow	13	19.4	38	30.7
Married lover	2	3.0	12	9.7
Married other	3	4.5	4	3.2
Died in childbirth	4	6.0	5	4.0
Religious	2	3.0	—	—
Unknown	43	64.1	65	52.4
TOTAL	67	100.0	124	100.0

Source: AGI. Audiencias, "Cartas y Expédientes"; Indiferente General, exp. 16, 35.

In this work I have considered the later lives of some of them. Included among them are spinster doña Margarita of Tasco, Mexico, whose story introduced this paper and who, after eighteen years, voluntarily ended the secrecy of her private pregnancy to recognize her son. Doña Gabriela of Chile also gave up the benefits of a private pregnancy, retrieved her daughter, and remained single after her lover became engaged to another. The extended engagement of doña Beatris of Havana ended in spinsterhood when her family forbade her to wed her fiancé. Doña María, of Chile, continued to raise her son alone after she could not pry her lover from the Andean mining districts. Doña Antonia, also of Havana, remained a widow and the mother of four illegitimate children after intendent don Nicolás Rapun broke his promise to marry her. The histories of these women, with their traumas of delayed marriage and ultimate betrayal, are typical of those of the rest.

The next most common fate of the women, marriage, has not been considered here. Fourteen, or 7.5 percent, eventually married their lovers. For various reasons, however, these marriages could not automatically legitimate children conceived before the ceremony, and the families made applications for the gracias a sacar. Affairs between first cousins, for example, fell under this classification, and such couples needed official church permission to wed. Any children conceived before such marriages were classified as incestuous, and could not be automatically legitimated by a post hoc ceremony. Subsequent marriage also failed to legitimate offspring born when one of the lovers had been married to someone else. Don Cayetano Yudice, of Guatemala, presented such a legal tangle to the Council of the Indies when he fathered four children with doña María Dominga de Astorga. Their first two children were adulterine, as they had been born while his wife was alive. Their third child was conceived when his wife was alive but was born after she died. Their fourth child was born when don Cayetano was a widower, but before he married doña María. After much debate the Council decided that the couple's eventual marriage had automatically legitimated only their fourth child and that their first three offspring could be legitimated only through gracias a sacar.[45]

There were a few instances—among them was doña X of Buenos Aires—where a woman had an illegitimate child and then married another man (N 7; 3.8 percent). The infrequency of this option shows that élite women who lost their virginity closed dramatically most options of marriage to anyone other than their lover. Equally note-

148   *Ann Twinam*

worthy is the cédula mothers' avoidance of the religious life, as only two (1.0 percent) eventually entered convents. It may well be that the existence of other women whose status was equally ambivalent provided sufficient peer support, so that women who had lost honor did not consider their plight so dire as to necessitate rejection of secular society. Convents were not refuges for unwed mothers.

The last group of women (N 9; 4.8 percent) had the worst fate of all, as they died during or soon after the birth of their illegitimate babies. The stories of doña María of La Plata, doña Magdalena of Mexico City, and doña Juana of Veracruz are typical of those whose maneuverings to protect their honor paled in comparison to their ultimate tragedy.[46]

Conclusion

Colonial élites of the late seventeenth and eighteenth centuries structured their actions according to their understanding of the ethos of honor, either as they abided by its norms or as they tried to escape its consequences. The honor code emphasized control of female sexuality through virginity and marital faithfulness. However, Spanish American élite women could be not only "in control" and "out of control," but also somewhere "in between." The large majority of the women who appear in cédula petitions fit somewhere "in between." They were neither single virgins nor faithful wives who possessed honor because they were "in control." Nor were they promiscuous wantons devoid of honor who were "out of control." These élite women used ambiguities inherent in the honor code to maintain an intermediate position and sometimes regain an honorable state in spite of their violation of prevailing sexual codes.

Two distinct and, at times, complementary tactics permitted such flexibility. One was the socially recognized dichotomy between private reality and public reputation. Although not without cost or risk of eventual disclosure, a successful private pregnancy permitted a woman to preserve honor no matter what the severity of her sexual indiscretion. A second, and not mutually exclusive, option for some women was eventual marriage to their lovers. Critical here was the degree to which a sexual relationship had violated honor and the extent to which it approached dishonor. As in the case of race, where Latin society consciously distinguished a complex range of colors, so too in sexual relationships society recognized varying degrees of illicit activity. Just as colonists perceived mulattoes as neither white nor black, women who engaged in premarital or extramarital sex were neither virgins nor whores. Instead, just as society acknowledged indeterminate areas where racial mobility might occur, some sexual relationships permitted the preservation or recovery of honor. The closer the sexual violation was to what was permissible within the honor code, the easier the restoration of honor.

Prevailing canon and civil law, as well as popular custom, provided fine guides as to the measure of dishonor attached to illicit sexual relationships, as well as to the illegitimate products of such unions. Thus, single parents who had exchanged the promise of matrimony—and their resulting hijos naturales—were among the mildest offenders of prevailing codes, requiring only a post hoc ceremony to automatically restore all parties to honor. Although couples engaged in adulterous relationships might also eventually marry and obtain some social acceptance, marriage would not legitimize their offspring, who had to seek restoration of honor through the gracias a sacar. Women who engaged in sexual relationships with priests found themselves too far removed from the honor code. They not only lacked any marriage option, but they found that the Council of the Indies was most reluctant to legitimize their offspring. Even here, however, the council was at least willing to consider a legitimation plea, for the state bureaucracy complemented the creative ambiguity that was inherent in a colonial society with few absolutes. The Council of the Indies thus became a court of last resort when human frailty broke the chain of honor that linked Spanish American élites to their past, bound them to their present, and defined their responsibility to the future.

150   Ann Twinam

Notes

1. The account of doña Margarita is taken from Archivo General de Indias, Seville, Spain (hereafter AGI), Mexico 1770, no. 35, 1780. Two of her brothers were priests. In 1596 one of doña Margarita's ancestors had participated in the "pacification and population of the Californias."

2. Ibid. His father spoke of the "love and affection" that his partner had shown toward Josef Antonio, who was left money in his will. Don Antonio himself mentioned that he "looked on him with the affection of a son." It was not uncommon after private pregnancies for fathers to raise their illegitimate children. Further discussion of such topics can be found in my "Honor, Paternity, and Illegitimacy: Unwed Fathers in Colonial Latin America," paper given at the 45th International Congress of Americanists, Bogotá, 1985.

3. The distinction among such categories can be found in the *Siete Partidas*, 6 vols. (Valencia: Thomas Lucas, 1757), *Quarta Partida*, Tit. 15; Sexta Partida, Tit. 13.

4. The full documentation concerning gracias a sacar derives from the petitions and testimony submitted to the Council of the Indies and the sub-Council of Gracias y Justicia and the resulting cédulas if the request was successful. The petitions can be found in the "Cartas y Expedientes" section of the Archivo General de Indias under each audiencia designation. Another rich source are *legajos* 16 and 1535, in Indiferente General, which contain copies of the actual cédulas issued when a petition was successful. These decrees contain a paragraph or so about the particulars of each case, but not the tens, and sometimes hundreds, of pages common in a petition. The 244 cases that I have collected include 101 cases with a full petition as well as resulting cédula, 41 with full petition (some of these include petitions that were denied), and 69 cases of cédula only; 5 came from other sources (Council testimony). The 28 remaining cases are a special category, as they derive from index references to cases from 1799 to 1820 that appear in nineteenth-century handwritten indexes to each section but that, with the exception of Santo Domingo, cannot be located in the archive. To make the coverage as complete as possible, these cases were included in the 244 totals when calculating factors such as total number of cases, time of petition, and geographic distribution of cédula requests. The 28 index cases were not used in calculations concerning other variables, which are based on data bases that vary according to the topic. For example, when calculating relative success rate of petitions, the data base used only those cases where there are petitions and either refusals or issuance of cédulas. When data concerning the mothers of illegitimates were examined, the computer data base considered each mother only

once, rather than counting her two or three times if she had more than one illegitimate child.

5. It also permits us to analyze regional variations, although such a detailed analysis is beyond the scope of this paper. It is notable, however, that the Caribbean is overrepresented in cédula requests, as 36.5 percent (N 89) of petitions originated from Santo Domingo, primarily Cuba. The South American audiencias accounted for 39 percent (N 95) of the remainder, with petitions from Panama north equaling 24.5 percent of the total (N 60). See table 2.

6. AGI, Mexico 1770, no. 35, 1780.

7. Given the importance of honor in understanding Spanish and Spanish American value systems, the topic needs further investigation. Relevant works include: Julian Pitt-Rivers, *People of the Sierra*, 2d ed. (Chicago: University of Chicago Press, 1971). By the same author, see *Mediterranean Countrymen: Essays in the Social Anthropology of the Mediterranean* (Paris: Mouton, 1963), and "Honor," *International Encyclopedia of the Social Sciences*, ed. David L. Sills, 2d ed. (New York: Macmillan and The Free Press, 1968), pp.503–11; J. G. Peristiany, *Honor and Shame: The Values of the Mediterranean* (Chicago: University of Chicago Press, 1966); Jane Schneider, "Of Vigilance and Virgins: Honor and Shame and Access to Resources in Mediterranean Societies," *Ethnology* 10, no. 1 (January 1971): 1–23; Ramón Gutiérrez, "Marriage, Sex, and the Family: Social Change in Colonial New Mexico, 1690–1846" (Ph.D. dissertation, University of Wisconsin, Madison, 1980). By the same author, see "From Honor to Love: Transformation in the Meaning of Sexuality in Colonial New Mexico," in *Interpreting Kinship Ideology and Practice in Latin America*, ed. Raymond T. Smith (Chapel Hill: University of North Carolina Press, 1984), and "Honor Ideology, Marriage Negotiation, and Class-Gender Domination in New Mexico, 1690–1846," *Latin American Perspectives* 12 (Winter 1985): 81–104.

8. AGI, Guadalajara 368, no. 6, 1761. The petition of Pedro Minjares de Salazar contains just one of many classic testimonies as to the self-conscious way that élites distinguished who was "in" and who was "out." Witnesses noted that Minjares (who thought he was legitimate and found out in adulthood that he was not) had been treated as a man of honor, "for all have cooperated to honor him and to attend him publicly and privately, frequenting his house, dealing with him with particular confidence and intimacy, inviting him to their functions, being with him, and finally treating him with the same courtesy that is given to any other noble and distinguished person." Also notice here the conscious distinction made between private and public spheres.

9. AGI, Santo Domingo, 1474, no. 11, 1789. For that reason petitioners com-

152   *Ann Twinam*

monly included witnesses who could attest that they "have always been known, held, and commonly reputed to be white persons, Old Christians of the nobility, clean of all bad blood and without any mixture of commoner, Jew, Moor, mulatto, or *converso* (a Jew converted to Roman Catholicism) in any degree, no matter how remote."

10. AGI, Indiferente General 16, 10 October 1789. Havana widow doña Gabriela Rizo legitimated her dead husband and deceased father-in-law.

11. Not only illegitimates, but also those related to illegitimates might experience limited upward mobility in the Spanish colonial bureaucracy or in local officeholding. Doña Petronila Peralta, for example, asked to be legitimated because her son-in-law had applied for a public post in Buenos Aires. One of the ostensible reasons that he had been rejected was the unacceptable illegitimacy of his wife's mother (AGI, Buenos Aires 161, no. 2, 1762). The husband of doña María Rosa Aguilar y Márquez requested her legitimation as he feared it might otherwise damage the officeholding potential of their children (AGI, Chile 290, no. 9, 1792). The occupation of public notary, which often dealt with sensitive matters such as "closed wills," demanded that holders be not only discreet but also of legitimate birth (AGI, Charcas 562, no. 30, 1796). Illegitimacy could also hinder marital alliances. Doña Juana de Figueroa filed a petition of legitimation because the relatives of her fiancé opposed the match due to her birth (AGI, Caracas 299, no. 20, 1788). Doña Gregoria de Rivera y López was legitimated so that she might contract a marriage equal to her state (AGI, Charcas 560, no. 15, 1795). A number of petitions originated from parents who left only illegitimate children and wanted to provide legally for their inheritance. See the case of don Manuel de Escalada in AGI, Buenos Aires 183, no. 14, 1771. Others, such as don Josef Cañete de Antequera of Paraguay, applied for petitions because they felt illegitimacy deprived them of honor (AGI, Buenos Aires 228, no. 27, 1770). The data base breakdown of general reasons given by petitioners for legitimation requests shows that 45.4 percent (N 98) wanted it for "honor and inheritance"; 27.3 percent (N 59) for "honor"; 6.0 percent (N 13) for "inheritance"; 10.6 percent (N 23) for "occupational" reasons; and 10.6 percent (N 23) for "other" reasons.

12. For that reason the only sure method to measure the frequency with which Latin American élites customarily engaged in premarital sex would be to use parish records to compare marriage dates with baptismal records of firstborns. On the subject of premarital sex and illegitimacy, see essays by Lavrin in this volume.

13. See Barry Nichols, *An Introduction to Roman Law*, rev. ed. (Oxford: Oxford University Press, 1979), pp.84–85. Also, Domingo Cavalario, in *Insti-*

tuciones del derecho canónico, 3 vols. (Paris: Librería de don Vicente Salvat, 1846), 2:178–96, discusses the marriage prohibitions. I thank Professor Asunción Lavrin for this reference. The original Spanish civil law is cited in the "Fuero Real", book 3, title 6, law 2. "Si one sotero con muger soltera ficiera fijos e despues casar con ella, estos fijos sean herederos." (If any single man has children with a single woman and later marries her, then these children are heirs.) "Fuero Real ", in *Opúsculos legales del Rey don Alfonso el Sabio*, 2 vols. (Madrid: Imprenta Real, 1836), 2:79. Most of the Spanish ordinances concerning illegitimacy, however, appear in the fourteenth-century *Siete Partidas*.

14. Numerous references in the cédula cases make it clear that post hoc legitimation was a popular option. Knowledge of such automatic legitimation figured in the strategy of the parents of doña Rafaela Espinosa de los Monteros, who was eighteen months old when they married. Her parents assumed that their marriage, per custom, automatically legitimated her, but they later found out that since they were first cousins, and thus related by prohibitive degrees of kinship, the post hoc legitimation did not apply. They, therefore, purchased a cédula for her, so that she might inherit equally with her siblings (AGI. Caracas 259, no. 4, 1779).

15. For an example of such a case see Ann Twinam, *Miners, Merchants and Farmers in Colonial Colombia* (Austin: University of Texas Press, 1982), pp.118–23.

16. C. H. Haring, *The Spanish Empire in America* (New York: Harcourt Brace, 1963), p.126.

17. The account of doña María del Carmen López Nieto is taken from AGI, Charcas 560, no. 15, 1795.

18. The account of doña Magdalena de la Vega is taken from AGI, Mexico 1771, no. 6, 1785.

19. See table 5.

20. AGI, Charcas 560, no. 15, 1795.

21. AGI, Mexico 1771, no. 6, 1785.

22. The account of don Joseph Martín de la Rocha is taken from AGI, Mexico 1778, no. 6, 1793.

23. The account of doña X is taken from AGI, Buenos Aires 250, no. 14, 1785.

24. It was rare for an unwed mother to wed another man. Although witnesses refused to identify her, they did testify to her situation.

25. AGI, Chile 290. no. 9, 1792.

26. AGI, Santo Domingo 1484, no. 14, 1793.

154 *Ann Twinam*

27. AGI, Caracas 200, no. 22, 1788

28. The account of doña Juana Díaz de Estrada is taken from AGI, Santo Domingo 421, no. 1, 1723.

29. The account of doña María Josepha Pérez de Balmaceda is taken from AGI, Santo Domingo 425, no. 2, 1741.

30. The account of doña Thoribia María Guerra Mier is taken from AGI, Santa Fe 720, no. 26, 1796.

31. In only four of the 216 cases are children referred to without any notice of illegitimacy, but simply called *"niño"* or *"niña."*

32. The account of the legitimation of doña Antonia del Rey is taken from AGI, Santo Domingo 1483, no. 38, 1792.

33. For example, note the opening quote by don Antonio Villanuena in which he refers to the "contacts . . . in her house."

34. The account of doña María Rosa de la Torre is taken from AGI, Chile 297, no. 21, 1796.

35. The account of doña Antonia Hernández is taken from AGI, Santo Domingo 1467, no. 1. 1782.

36. It was not uncommon for prominent members of local society to testify in favor of an illegitimate's petition and to note that they had played together and gone to the same schools.

37. See table 5 and note 11.

38. There is a final group of 20 women (45.5 percent) who can be classified as having had public pregnancies, but the exact circumstances (i.e., extended engagement, concubinage) are unknown.

39. The account of doña Josepha María Valespino is taken from AGI, Santo Domingo 1456, no. 5, 1761.

40. The question of success or failure of the petition is a very complicated one, as the guidelines of the Council of the Indies changed according to circumstances such as time period, sex of petitioner, and amount they were willing to pay. See table 5. Cases were most likely to be turned down if the petitioners had not supplied data on the marital state of the mother and father. Presumably such petitioners were either ignorant of the details demanded by the Council, or they deliberately omitted facts that might prejudice their cases. The most successful petitions involved single parents. The Council discriminated less against the illegitimate children of married women than against those of married men. Perhaps because most of these women had been abandoned by their husbands, the Council was more sympathetic to their difficulties.

41. The account of the Varea y Lazcano is taken from AGI. Charcas 554, no. 25, 1791.

42. A knowledgeable observer, however. would have noted an additional comment on the certificates that the babies had been "exposed" at the house of doña Gertrudis. although she was not identified as their mother.

43. AGI, Charcas 554, no. 25, 1791. The Council of Gracia y Justicia of the Council of the Indies originally approved this petition if the brothers were willing to pay the extraordinary sum of 8,000 pesos apiece. When this decision went to the king, however, the council was overruled. This is the only case that I have discovered in two centuries' records where higher officers rejected a Council decision on legitimation.

44. AGI, Charcas 562, no. 22, 1796.

45. AGI, Guatemala 411, no. missing, 1784.

46. The fate of a woman was not much different if her honor had been protected by a private. as compared with a public pregnancy. Women with private pregnancies still tended to remain single. They were much less likely to marry their lovers than women with public pregnancies. This makes sense, however. when we consider that couples who went to the extreme of organizing a private pregnancy must have been either much more likely to marry when they could (and thereby avoid cedula applications) or much more likely to hide the pregnancy because they knew that they would not marry. because of personal aversion, current marriage of one party, or involvement of a cleric. The two women who went into convent had had private pregnancies.

6

Les naissances illégitimes sur les rives du Saint-Laurent avant 1730

Lynne Paquette and Réal Bates

INTRODUCTION

Les caractéristiques démographiques de la population canadienne sous le Régime français sont de mieux en mieux connues. La fécondité des premiers colons, notamment, a été remarquablement analysée par Jacques Henripin[2], puis par Hubert Charbonneau[3]. Cependant, un secteur limité de ce phénomène reste relativement dans l'ombre: les naissances illégitimes.

Les études sur le sujet ont été peu nombreuses jusqu'à maintenant, faute de données adéquates. Le généalogiste Cyprien Tanguay fournit une liste des naissances illégitimes par décennie, mais seulement à partir du début du 18e siècle. Dans le volume IV de son *Dictionnaire généalogique*, il mentionne seulement 171 naissances illégitimes pour la période 1701-1730, pour les paroisses catholiques de la Nouvelle-France[4]; or nous en avons relevé 565 pour la période 1700-1729. Il ne fait aucun doute que son décompte est incomplet, pour plusieurs raisons. Il n'a dû vraisemblablement considérer comme illégitimes que les enfants déclarés comme tels dans les registres alors que notre définition en englobe davantage. D'autre part, comme Mgr Tanguay s'intéressait avant tout aux familles, il a probablement fait moins d'efforts dans la collecte des naissances illégitimes. Le phénomène lui paraissant moralement condamnable, il a pu omettre plusieurs de ces naissances. Il ne fait aucun doute que le scrupuleux prélat voulait protéger nos ancêtres et leur donner un certificat de bonne moralité, qu'ils n'ont d'ailleurs

---

[1] Ce texte est un condensé des principaux résultats (revus) du mémoire de maîtrise de Lyne Paquette, *Les naissances illégitimes sur les rives du Saint-Laurent avant 1730*. Université de Montréal (démographie), 1983. 202 p. Réal Bates est présentement agent de recherche au Programme de recherche en démographie historique de l'Université de Montréal.
[2] Jacques Henripin, *La population canadienne au début du XVIIIe siècle* (Paris, Presses universitaires de France, 1954). 129 p.
[3] Hubert Charbonneau, *Vie et mort de nos ancêtres* (Montréal, Presses de l'Université de Montréal, 1975), 267 p.
[4] Cyprien Tanguay, *Dictionnaire généalogique des familles canadiennes* (Québec, Eusèbe Sénécal). IV: 607-608.

pas toujours mérité. Il ne faut pas trop l'en blâmer, car il ne faisait que refléter la pensée de l'Église et la mentalité de son époque.

De même l'abbé Ferland[5], pour démontrer la pureté de nos origines, écrivait jadis ce qui suit:

> A l'appui du tribut rendu à la pureté des moeurs de nos ancêtres nous citerons une autorité qui ne peut être soupçonnée de flatterie: ce sont les registres de Notre-Dame de Québec, où furent inscrits presque tous les baptêmes qui se firent dans le gouvernement de Québec, jusque vers l'année 1672. Sur six cent soixante-quatorze enfants qui furent baptisés depuis l'année 1621 inclusivement, jusqu'à l'année 1661 exclusivement, on ne compte qu'un seul enfant illégitime.

Il continuait de plus belle: «Depuis 1661 jusqu'à 1690, on rencontre le nom d'un seul autre enfant né de parents inconnus. En sorte que dans l'espace de 69 ans, deux enfants seulement sont nés hors du légitime mariage des parents.» Or, on en dénombre 32 d'après nos calculs.

Dans la paroisse de Notre-Dame de Montréal, E.-Z. Massicotte[6] ne relève pour sa part aucun baptême d'enfant né hors mariage de 1642 à 1685. De 1686 à 1730, il mentionne 92 naissances illégitimes alors que nous en relevons 206 pour la même période.

S'il faut en croire ces auteurs, ainsi que certains contemporains, le libertinage est restreint dans la colonie et les problèmes de moeurs n'existent pratiquement pas. La lecture de l'ouvrage de Robert-Lionel Séguin, *La vie libertine en Nouvelle-France au XVIIe siècle* (1972), livre un portrait tout autre, beaucoup plus révélateur de la sexualité de nos ancêtres. Notre étude s'inscrit dans cette perspective plus large. Elle veut éclairer un point particulier de la fécondité: les naissances illégitimes du début de la colonie jusqu'à 1729.

Les relations sexuelles hors mariage sont à l'origine du phénomène des naissances illégitimes. Bien qu'il s'agisse d'un phénomène marginal, l'étude de toute population ne saurait être complète sans l'analyse de l'illégitimité.

1 - Définition des termes

Il semble nécessaire de lever certaines ambiguïtés sur le terme de l'illégitimité et l'assimilation trop rapide que l'on a tendance à faire entre conceptions prénuptiales, enfants abandonnés, enfants trouvés et enfants illégitimes.

---

[5] J.-Baptiste-Antoine Ferland, *Cours d'histoire du Canada* (Québec, N. S. Hardy, 1882), 14.

[6] E.-Z. Massicotte, «Comment on disposait des enfants du roi», *Bulletin des recherches historiques*, 37 (1931): 49-54.

L'enfant illégitime est celui qui a été conçu et est né hors d'un mariage légitime. La notion de conception prénuptiale se réfère plutôt à l'enfant qui, né à l'intérieur du mariage, a cependant été conçu avant[7]. Dans un milieu fortement soumis à l'emprise de la morale chrétienne et aux pressions sociales, les mères abandonnaient parfois leur enfant. Ceci explique qu'en Nouvelle-France la presque totalité des enfants abandonnés ou trouvés étaient illégitimes. Cependant, tous les enfants illégitimes n'étaient pas abandonnés et parmi ceux qui l'ont été, se trouvaient des enfants légitimes. On retrouve peu de traces d'enfants abandonnés ou trouvés au 17e siècle. Le problème s'est plutôt manifesté au 18e siècle et surtout à partir de 1750[8].

Il ne fait aucun doute que le problème de l'illégitimité est relié à un contexte religieux, social et culturel particulier, et que selon le lieu et l'époque, le problème ne se pose pas de la même façon. La société de la Nouvelle-France étant fortement marquée par l'idéologie chrétienne, la distinction entre légitimité et illégitimité est bien nette et mérite que l'on s'y arrête.

2 - Sources

Pour cette recherche, nous avons utilisé les données fournies par le Programme de recherche en démographie historique (PRDH) de l'Université de Montréal et le *Dictionnaire* de René Jetté[9]. Après avoir dépouillé les registres paroissiaux et les recensements du Québec ancien, les chercheurs du PRDH ont entrepris, à l'aide de l'ordinateur, la reconstitution de l'ensemble de la population québécoise depuis l'origine du pays[10]. Comme, pour l'instant, les familles n'ont pas été reconstituées au-delà de l'année 1729, notre étude se limitera à cette date.

Les renseignements complémentaires ont été recueillis dans le *Dictionnaire* de René Jetté qui termine ses observations en 1730. Pour obtenir des informations sur les événements survenus après 1730, concernant le destin des illégitimes et celui de leurs parents, nous avons consulté le *Dictionnaire généalogique* de Cyprien Tanguay. Certes ce dernier ouvrage est lacunaire — et d'autant plus pour les illégitimes dont le destin est souvent difficile à suivre — mais les informations qu'on y trouve ne sont pas négligeables.

---

[7] Pour connaître ce phénomène en Nouvelle-France, voir Réal Bates, *Les conceptions prénuptiales dans la vallée du Saint-Laurent avant 1725*. Mémoire de maîtrise, Université de Montréal (démographie), 1985, 178 p., et la deuxième partie de cette note de recherche.

[8] De la Broquerie Fortier, «Les «enfants trouvés» sous les régimes français et anglais au Canada français - 1608-1850», *Laval Médical*, 33,7: 533.

[9] René Jetté, avec la collaboration du Programme de recherche en démographique historique de l'Université de Montréal, *Dictionnaire généalogique des familles du Québec des origines à 1730* (Montréal, Presses de l'Université de Montréal, 1983), 1 176 p.

[10] Voir Yves Landry, «Le registre de la Nouvelle-France: un outil pratique au service de la démographie historique et de l'histoire sociale», *Revue d'histoire de l'Amérique française*, 38,3 (hiver 1985): 423-426.

La collecte de données a permis de relever 749 enfants illégitimes nés avant 1730 dont 697 ont pu être repérés par leur acte de baptême, 39 autres ont été trouvés par un acte de décès et 12 par un acte de mariage. Un seul a été retrouvé à l'aide du recensement. Nous ne possédons toutefois pas la même quantité d'informations sur tous les enfants illégitimes.

L'information relative aux parents de ces enfants n'est pas complète dans tous les cas. Au total nous connaissons les mères de 500 enfants illégitimes (soit 385 femmes différentes) et les pères de 364 de ces enfants (soit 323 hommes différents). Le tableau 1 expose ces variations.

TABLEAU 1

Répartition des enfants illégitimes et de leurs parents selon certaines caractéristiques
- Canada avant 1730 -

	Nb absolu	Nb relatif (%)
Enfants illégitimes:		
Nombre d'enfants décédés	290	38,7
Nombre d'enfants mariés	115	15,4
Nombre d'enfants de destin inconnu	344	45,9
Parents d'enfants illégitimes:		
Parents inconnus	201	26,8
Mères inconnues - pères connus	48	6,5
Pères inconnus - mères connues	184	24,6
Parents connus	316	42,1
Total	749	100,0

3 - L'intensité du phénomène

Notre première observation concerne la rareté des naissances illégitimes. Plus nombreuses entre 1700 et 1729 (1,49%) qu'avant 1700 (0,83%), elles ne forment que 1,25% des naissances de l'ensemble de la période (voir tableau 2). La France de l'époque connaissait une réalité semblable: environ 1% de naissances illégitimes dans la France rurale, plus dans la France urbaine[11]. Nous constatons également que ces naissances sont deux fois plus nombreuses dans les paroisses de Québec, de Montréal et de Trois-Rivières, que nous assimilons à des villes (1,93%), que dans les autres paroisses, essentiellement rurales (0,87%).

---

[11] Jacques Dupâquier, *La population française aux XVIIe et XVIIIe siècles* (Paris, Presses universitaires de France, 1979), 59.

TABLEAU 2

Proportion (en %) de naissances illégitimes par période et selon l'habitat
- Canada avant 1730 -

Habitat	Nombre de naissances	Avant 1680	1680-89	1690-99	1700-09	1710-19	1720-29	ind.	Avant 1700	1700-29	Total
Rural	illégitimes	17	20	40	90	83	102	-	77	275	352
	totales*	4 004	4 109	4 636	6 818	8 472	12 268	-	12 749	27 558	40 307
	proportion de naissances illégitimes	0,42	0,49	0,86	1,32	0,98	0,83	-	0,60	1,00	0,87
Urbain	illégitimes	22	18	57	73	78	127	-	97	278	375
	totales*	5 002	1 396	2 540	2 932	3 338	4 004	-	9 138	10 274	19 412
	proportion de naissances illégitimes	0,44	1,29	2,24	2,49	2,34	3,17	-	1,06	2,70	1,93
Indéterminé	illégitimes	1	3	4	7	1	4	2	8	12	22
Total	illégitimes	40	41	101	170	162	233	2	182	565	749
	totales*	9 207	5 508	7 180	9 757	11 811	16 276	2	21 895	37 844	59 741
	proportion de naissances illégitimes	0,43	0,74	1,41	1,74	1,37	1,43	-	0,83	1,49	1,25

* «totales» signifie le nombre de naissances légitimes et illégitimes

REVUE D'HISTOIRE DE L'AMÉRIQUE FRANÇAISE

Le taux global de fécondité illégitime (nombre de naissances illégitimes pour 1 000 femmes non mariées en âge de procréer)[12] calculé
pour l'année 1681 révèle le même phénomène, c'est-à-dire un taux plus
élevé en milieu urbain, où il est de 11,2 pour mille, comparativement
à 7,4 pour mille à la campagne (voir tableau 3).

TABLEAU 3

Taux global de fécondité illégitime en Nouvelle-France selon le type d'habitat en 1681

Lieu	Nombre de naissances illégitimes en 1680-1682 (1)	Nombre annuel moyen de naissances illégitimes (2)	Population féminine non mariée de 15-49 ans (3)	Taux % (2)/(3)
Rural	5	1,7	226	7,4
Urbain	6	2	179	11,2
TOTAL	11	3,7	405	9,1

1. Nombre de naissances illégitimes pour 3 années.
2. Moyenne annuelle des naissances (colonne (1)/(3)).
3. Population féminine célibataire et veuve de 15 à 49 ans tirée du recensement de 1681.
   n.b. Sont ici considérées comme urbaines les paroisses de Québec, de Montréal et de Trois-
   Rivières, et comme rurales toutes les autres.

Qu'est-ce qui explique cette plus forte proportion de naissances
illégitimes en milieu urbain? La ville abrite sans doute temporairement
les filles de la campagne qui portent un fruit illégitime et fuient la
réprobation de leurs voisins ou espèrent accoucher subrepticement et
anonymement. Mais on peut penser également que les villes, par leurs
fonctions diversifiées (maritimes, commerciales, administratives et
militaires) et le brassage de population qu'elles permettent, favorisent
une plus grande promiscuité et un contrôle social plus difficile à exercer
et donc une intensité plus grande des comportements menant à des
naissances illégitimes.

Soulignons aussi l'évolution du phénomène dans le temps. Le 17e
siècle ne représente que le quart de toutes les naissances illégitimes
antérieures à 1730. La fréquence des naissances illégitimes augmente
tout au long du 17e siècle et se maintient à un niveau encore plus élevé
au 18e siècle. Cette croissance résulte en grande partie des modifica-

---

[12] Le taux global de fécondité illégitime est un indice nettement préférable à la proportion
de naissances illégitimes comme indicateur de l'illégitimité relative. En effet, il rapporte les
naissances illégitimes à la population susceptible de vivre cet événement, cependant que la proportion de naissances illégitimes est dépendante du nombre de naissances légitimes. Si, par exem-
ple, le nombre de naissances légitimes pour une période baisse, la proportion de naissances illégitimes montrera une croissance si le nombre de ces naissances se maintient. Malheureusement le
calcul de ce taux exige des recensements distribuant la population selon le sexe, l'âge et l'état
matrimonial, ce qui est rare pour une population ancienne.

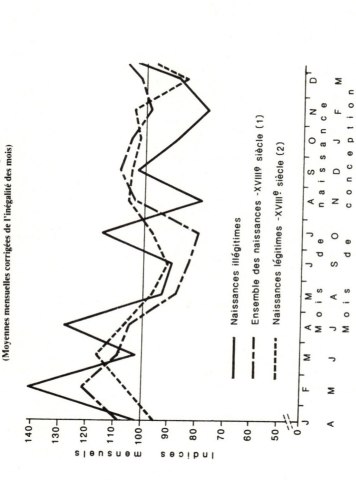

FIGURE 1

Mouvement saisonnier des naissances légitimes et illégitimes
(Moyennes mensuelles corrigées de l'inégalité des mois)

Sources: 1 R. Roy et al. «Quelques comportements des Canadiens au XVIIe siècle d'après les registres paroissiaux», *Revue d'histoire de l'Amérique française*, 31.1 (juin 1977): 61.
2 J. Henripin, *La population canadienne au début du XVIIIe siècle* (Paris, Presses universitaires de France, 1954): 42-45.

tions survenues dans le marché matrimonial qui a été particulièrement déséquilibré au 17e siècle. Le manque de femmes dans la colonie durant ce siècle a favorisé la précocité et l'intensité des mariages et par conséquent a réduit la natalité illégitime.

4 - Le mouvement saisonnier

L'analyse du mouvement saisonnier des naissances illégitimes met en relief le lien existant entre les conceptions (naissances moins neuf mois) et le renouveau printanier ou les travaux des champs (figure 1). Le cycle saisonnier des conceptions se caractérise par une valeur maximale au printemps avec un indice de 140 en mai. Un niveau relativement élevé se maintient durant la saison estivale. Après une baisse en août et septembre, octobre accuse une reprise. Puis l'hiver annonce une chute où les indices se retrouvent à un niveau relativement bas. Les enfants illégitimes sont donc des enfants du plein air, d'aucuns seraient tentés de dire des enfants des haies.

Le mouvement saisonnier des naissances légitimes présente certes des similitudes, mais aussi quelques différences notables. Alors que les conceptions illégitimes sont rares en janvier, les conceptions globales demeurent au-dessus de la moyenne annuelle durant ce mois. Ici également le printemps se traduit par une vigoureuse poussée de conceptions qui se poursuit jusqu'en juin. On peut comprendre la forte intensité du phénomène durant ces mois témoins du retour de la belle saison et des premiers sourires printaniers.

5 - Le destin des enfants illégitimes: évaluation de la mortalité infantile

Nous connaissons pour 362 enfants l'âge au décès (ou leur survie après 15 ans). Pour 43 autres l'âge est indéterminé (plus de trois ans, moins de 20 ans, etc.) et pour 344 le destin est inconnu. Après avoir distribué les indéterminés comme les cas connus[13], nous obtenons la répartition suivante des enfants illégitimes selon leur âge au décès:

morts avant un an	220	(29,4%)
morts entre un et 15 ans	66	(8,8%)
morts après 15 ans	119	(15,9%)
destin inconnu	344	(45,9%)
TOTAL	749	(100,0%)

En supposant que tous les enfants de destin inconnu ont survécu à leur premier anniversaire nous obtiendrions un taux de mortalité infantile (minimum) de 294 pour mille. Cette hypothèse est trop optimiste pour être vraisemblable. Elle permet cependant de constater que la mor-

---

[13] A l'exception de deux individus morts après 15 ans, les renseignements concernant ces indéterminés permettent de les répartir selon l'âge au décès des cas connus morts avant 15 ans.

talité infantile des bâtards était des plus élevée. Dans une table de mortalité non corrigée, analogue à celle de H. Charbonneau[14], le quotient de mortalité avant un an serait de 381 pour mille, près de trois fois plus considérable que celui obtenu (135 pour mille) pour les ancêtres canadiens du 17e siècle.

Mais pour cerner de plus près la réalité il nous faut élaborer une table de mortalité corrigée. Celle-ci tient compte du sous-enregistrement des naissances et des actes de baptême perdus non retrouvés. Ceci ajoute 66 enfants dont 49 seraient morts avant un an[15]. Il s'agit ensuite de répartir les 344 enfants de destin inconnu[16]. Les hypothèses retenues conduisent à une mortalité infantile de 605 pour mille. Pour le 17e siècle, H. Charbonneau[17] a trouvé un taux corrigé de 211 pour mille et J. Henripin[18], pour le 18e siècle, de 246 pour mille. Il resterait à voir le pourquoi de cette forte surmortalité des bâtards; mais la situation de rejet dans laquelle se trouvaient les mères, conduisant parfois à l'abandon des enfants et à la pratique de la mise en nourrice, n'y est certainement pas étrangère. A l'âge de 15 ans, seulement 22% de ces enfants auraient survécu, soit trois fois moins que les enfants légitimes.

6 - Les parents des enfants illégitimes

Après cette vue d'ensemble sur les naissances illégitimes et le destin des enfants qui en sont issus, nous examinerons maintenant la situation des parents de ces enfants, dans la mesure tout au moins où l'information recueillie le permet: il convient en effet d'interpréter les informations qui suivent avec certaines réserves puisque nous ne connaissons pas l'identité des mères de 33% des enfants illégitimes et des pères de 57% d'entre eux.

6.1 - L'état matrimonial et l'âge des mères à l'accouchement

Qu'en est-il de l'état matrimonial et de l'âge des mères à la naissance de ces enfants? On constate que les deux tiers d'entre elles sont célibataires alors que les veuves en représentent le quart et que pour 8% il s'agit de femmes mariées ayant commis l'adultère (voir tableau 4).

---

[14] Hubert Charbonneau, *op. cit.*, 121.

[15] En nous appuyant sur les procédés statistiques de H. Charbonneau, *op. cit.*, chapitre 3, nous avons obtenu 21 ondoyés décédés à moins de trois jours, 16 naissances sélectivement omises et 29 naissances perdues non retrouvées. Les deux premiers groupes correspondent à des décès très tôt après la naissance. Des 29 autres enfants, 12, soit 40%, seraient décédés avant 1 an. Hubert Charbonneau, *op. cit.*, 122.

[16] Des 344 enfants au destin inconnu, 118 sont nés de parents inconnus et 54 ont une mère connue mais sont nés avant 1700. Comme nous n'avons pas retrouvé de mariage pour ces 172 enfants, ils sont probablement tous morts avant 15 ans: nous les avons donc distribués selon l'âge au décès des enfants morts avant 15 ans. Les 172 autres dont la mère est connue et qui sont nés après 1700 ont été considérés comme décédés au même âge que les cas connus. Cela donne 223 enfants morts avant 1 an, 66 entre 1 et 15 ans et 55 après 15 ans.

[17] Hubert Charbonneau, *op. cit.*, 125.

[18] Jacques Henripin, *op. cit.*, 106.

248   REVUE D'HISTOIRE DE L'AMÉRIQUE FRANÇAISE

TABLEAU 4

Répartition des naissances d'enfants illégitimes selon l'état matrimonial de la mère à l'accouchement
- Canada avant 1730 -

État matrimonial de la mère à l'accouchement	Nombre absolu	Nombre relatif (en %)	
		Mères connues (n = 500)	Ensemble des mères (n = 749)
Célibataire	331	66,2	44,2
Veuve	129	25,8	17,2
Mariée	38	7,6	5,1
État indéterminé	2	0,4	0,3
Mère inconnue	249	-	33,2
Total	749	100,0	100,0

Pour mieux juger de cette répartition, il faudrait connaître les proportions, selon l'état matrimonial, des femmes en âge de procréation (15-44 ans) dans l'ensemble de la population. En 1681 seulement 1,5% de ces femmes sont veuves. Même si cette proportion de veuves a pu augmenter dans les décennies suivantes, il n'en reste pas moins que, proportionnellement à leur nombre, les veuves auraient plus d'enfants illégitimes que les deux autres groupes et que les femmes mariées en ont très peu (de déclarés tout au moins...).

Les mères d'enfants illégitimes ne sont pas des fillettes victimes de leur naïveté. En effet, l'âge moyen des mères à l'accouchement (tous états matrimoniaux confondus) est de 25 ans pour l'ensemble de la période. Cet âge concerne tous les accouchements d'illégitimes, peu importe le rang de ceux-ci (66 mères sur 385 auront en effet plus d'un enfant illégitime). Si on ne tient compte que de l'âge au premier accouchement, la moyenne passe à 23,3 ans.

La répartition des mères célibataires selon l'âge au premier accouchement, présentée au tableau 5, est très révélatrice. La grande majorité ont leur enfant avant 25 ans et seulement moins de 5% d'entre elles sont âgées de 30 ans et plus. Cela se comprend fort bien puisque plus on avance en âge, moins il y a de filles célibataires. L'âge moyen est ici de 21,6 ans. Or notons qu'entre 1621 et 1725 l'âge moyen au premier accouchement légitime pour les femmes célibataires qui se marient est également de 21,6 ans[19]: on peut penser que les filles-mères ont été victimes de fausses promesses de mariage, ou, dans quelques cas, vivaient en concubinage puisqu'elles ont accouché de leur premier enfant illégitime au même âge que celles qui se sont mariées.

La situation matrimoniale particulière du 17e siècle tend probablement à expliquer les différences d'âge entre les périodes. L'âge au

---

[19]   Réal Bates, *op. cit.*, 134.

TABLEAU 5

Répartition des mères (célibataires) suivant l'âge à la naissance de leur premier enfant illégitime
- Canada avant 1730 -

Âge	Avant 1700		1700-1729		Total	
	nb	%	nb	%	nb	%
Avant 20 ans	38	52,1	64	32,0	102	37,4
20-24 ans	26	35,6	78	39,0	104	38,1
25-29 ans	5	6,8	38	19,0	43	15,7
30 ans et plus	1	1,4	11	5,5	12	4,4
Âge indéterminé	3	4,1	9	4,5	12	4,4
Total	73	100,0	200	100,0	273	100,0
Âge moyen	20,0		22,2		21,6	

mariage étant en effet plus précoce au 17e siècle, les femmes ont accouché d'un enfant illégitime à un âge moins avancé.

6.2 - Le destin matrimonial des mères

Il importe de connaître ce que deviennent les mères des enfants illégitimes après leur accouchement. Nous avons pu suivre leur destin. La plupart des filles-mères (77%) se marient et, par cette union, près du tiers légitiment leur progéniture en épousant le père de l'enfant. Près de la moitié se marient avec un autre homme alors que 23% demeurent célibataires. Une seule se destine à la vie religieuse (voir tableau 6).

TABLEAU 6

Destin matrimonial des mères célibataires après la naissance de leurs enfants illégitimes
- Canada avant 1730 -

Destin	Nombre absolu	Nombre relatif (%)
-épousent le père	80	29,3
-épousent un autre homme	131	48,0
-demeurent célibataires	62	22,7
Total	273	100,0

Que 23% de filles ayant accouché d'un enfant illégitime restent célibataires, c'est beaucoup, compte tenu de la nuptialité à cette époque. Selon Charbonneau[20] «il serait étonnant que le célibat définitif féminin ait dépassé l'ordre de 10%». Faudrait-il en conclure que la venue d'un enfant hors mariage a nui à certaines filles dans leurs chances de se marier? Pas nécessairement. Il faut prendre en compte que a) nombre

---

[20] Hubert Charbonneau, *op. cit.*, 158.

de ces filles peuvent avoir connu une union après 1729 (ou hors Canada) qui a échappé à Tanguay; b) que les mères célibataires forment une population sélectionnée: par définition, seules sont soumises au risque celles qui sont célibataires; celles qui ne se marieront jamais sont donc plus susceptibles de devenir mères célibataires.

6.3 - Les pères des enfants illégitimes

Seulement 323 pères sont connus. Mais pour certains nous ne connaissons guère plus que le nom et, parfois, la profession (soldat, commis, etc.). A toutes fins pratiques, il n'y a que 268 pères (pour 305 enfants) dont nous connaissons suffisamment de caractéristiques pour permettre l'étude statistique qui suit. C'est peu.

La plupart des pères sont célibataires (84%). Un sur dix est marié alors que la proportion de veufs s'élève à 6%. L'âge moyen de ces hommes à la naissance de l'enfant est de 29,3 ans. Quant à l'origine géographique, 99 (soit 46%) des 215 pères dont nous connaissons l'origine sont natifs de France.

Parmi les 226 pères célibataires, 190 (84%) se marieront: 100 (44%) avec la mère de l'enfant, 90 (40%) avec une autre femme. 16% resteront célibataires. Les mêmes réserves qu'en ce qui concerne le destin matrimonial des mères (voir point 6.2) doivent être émises ici, d'autant plus qu'on peut facilement imaginer que la proportion des pères n'épousant pas la mère de l'enfant augmenterait considérablement si nous pouvions connaître l'identité de tous ces pères inconnus.

Les pères se retrouvent surtout chez les militaires et les domestiques (61% des 184 pères dont nous connaissons la profession). Il faut mentionner que les militaires ne manquent pas dans la colonie. A plusieurs reprises l'Église reprochera à ces hommes leur genre de vie instable et leur mauvaise conduite avec les filles:

> Ayant remarqué que plusieurs jeunes gens, et particulièrement les gens de guerre, sous prétexte de rechercher des filles en mariage, se comportent de manière fort licencieuse avec les dites filles, qui se laissent abuser, sous l'espérance de les épouser, dans la persuasion qu'elles ont que les fautes et les accidents qui leur peuvent arriver en ce sujet, seront autant de motifs à leurs parents de poursuivre leurs dits mariage...[21]

L'augmentation du nombre d'enfants illégitimes issus de soldats, signalée par l'évêque de Saint-Vallier, força, au 18e siècle, les autorités à permettre les mariages des soldats alors qu'ils avaient été interdits pendant un certain temps[22].

---

[21]   Jean de la Croix de Saint-Vallier, *Rituel du diocèse de Québec* (Paris, Simon Langlois, 1703), 604 p.
[22]   Émile Salone, *La colonisation de la Nouvelle-France: étude sur les origines de la nation canadienne-française* (Paris, Guilmoto, 1906), 467 p.

6.4 - *Les récidivistes*

Nous avons tenté de mesurer quelle était la proportion de récidivistes parmi les mères et les pères d'enfants illégitimes. Il ressort clairement que la majorité de ceux-ci n'en ont eu qu'un (voir tableau 7). Il n'en reste pas moins que 17% des mères ont accouché illégitimement plus d'une fois, dont 7% au moins trois fois. Pour quelques-unes de ces femmes, les grossesses sont nombreuses. On signale ainsi pour une femme huit enfants illégitimes alors que deux autres en auront six. Il s'agit dans le premier cas du couple Thérèse Ménard et Jean Desnoyers. Mariés à la gaumine en 1709, ce couple aura huit enfants. Le mariage ne sera réhabilité, et ne deviendra donc légitime qu'en 1724. On retrouve également 11 femmes ayant accouché de quatre enfants et plus. Ainsi, au moins 11%[23] des enfants illégitimes ne peuvent être le fruit d'«accidents». On peut sans doute évoquer l'hypothèse de la prostitution. Dans certains cas, les jugements du Conseil souverain le confirment, mais dans le cas où tous les enfants d'une récidiviste proviennent du même père, il s'agit le plus souvent de concubinage pour des couples qui se sont peut-être vu refuser le mariage par l'Église ou les parents.

TABLEAU 7

Répartition des mères et des pères selon le nombre d'enfants illégitimes qu'ils ont eus
- Canada avant 1730 -

Nombre d'enfants	mères		pères	
	Nombre absolu	Nombre relatif (%)	Nombre absolu	Nombre relatif (%)
1	319	82,9	297	91,9
2	39	10,1	18	5,6
3	16	4,2	6	1,9
4	5	1,3	-	-
5	3	0,8	1	0,3
6	2	0,5	-	-
8	1	0,2	1	0,3
Total	385	100,0	323	100,0

Chez les pères, il existe quelques cas de récidive, mais en beaucoup moins grand nombre que chez les mères. Il faut toutefois se rappeler qu'on ignore l'identité de la plupart des pères.

---

[23] Onze pour cent égalent le nombre d'enfants illégitimes de mères ayant accouché quatre fois et plus (55) divisé par le nombre total d'enfants (500).

CONCLUSION

En somme, il ressort de notre étude que la natalité illégitime en Nouvelle-France a été faible au 17e siècle bien qu'elle ait augmenté progressivement au début du siècle suivant. Les proportions de naissances illégitimes sont de l'ordre de 0,8% au 17e siècle et de 1,5% dans la période 1700-1729. Pour expliquer cette augmentation, il reste à déterminer quelle part il faut accorder aux transformations économiques, à l'amélioration des conditions de vie, aux facteurs sociologiques et à l'évolution des mentalités. Le relèvement de l'âge au mariage demeure sans doute le facteur déterminant. Pour sa part, l'importance des naissances illégitimes dans les villes, même s'il s'agit de petites villes nullement comparables aux villes européennes de la même époque, n'est-elle pas liée au milieu urbain lui-même, à la nature des relations qu'il engendre, aux types de rapports sociaux qui y existent?

La variation des naissances illégitimes durant l'année est peut-être due aux conditions de l'environnement, telles que le climat ou les réjouissances populaires. Il semble que ces deux facteurs impriment leur marque au cycle saisonnier qui ne correspond pas à celui des naissances légitimes.

La forte surmortalité infantile des enfants illégitimes confirme leurs conditions de survie difficile.

On peut tracer une sorte de «portrait-robot» de la fille-mère canadienne aux 17e et 18e siècles. Celle-ci est canadienne de naissance et native du milieu rural. La plupart des mères d'enfants illégitimes sont célibataires et plus de 70% sont âgées de 15 à 30 ans, dont le tiers entre 20 et 24 ans. La grande majorité de ces filles se marient, et par cette union le tiers légitimeront leur progéniture en épousant le père de l'enfant.

A cette fiche descriptive de la fille-mère, on peut joindre une esquisse du portrait du père. Le plus fréquemment celui-ci est un célibataire âgé d'environ 30 ans qui exerce un métier instable.

Ces quelques éléments d'information n'épuisent certes pas le sujet de l'illégitimité en Nouvelle-France. Trop de renseignements nous manquent sur les parents des bâtards et sur le destin de ceux-ci. Il reste de plus à voir l'évolution du phénomène dans les dernières décennies du Régime français, ce que permettra bientôt la banque de données du PRDH.

7

Women and the Family in Eighteenth-Century Mexico: Law and Practice

Edith Couturier

Abstract: During the eighteenth century, Mexican family law remained almost unchanged while the ways in which families chose to use the inheritance law altered significantly. At the beginning of the century, women of most economic classes—from artisan families to the nobility—usually received legally binding dowries that protected them at the death of their husbands and provided their children with inheritances. By the end of the century, however, the practice of awarding dowries had almost completely ceased. This essay explores possible explanations for this change through a discussion of the various ways in which women held power and property, depending upon their position in the family.

European and United States historians, during the last two decades, have suggested that the eighteenth century marks the transition in elite families from marriages arranged for their economic and social benefits to marriages conceived for more affectionate and emotional ties. Based on reading and analysis of sources as diverse as letters, diaries, censuses, and wills, as well as a growing body of secondary materials, Phillippe Ariès, Daniel Scott Smith, Randolph Trumbach, Lawrence Stone, and many others have traced changes in marriage and family institutions in England and the United States (Ariès, 1962; Smith, 1974:119–36; Stone, 1977; Trumbach, 1978; Wheaton, 1980: 3–26).

In the field of colonial Hispanic-American history researchers are beginning to explore similar documents as well as other

primary materials in tracing family changes from the late seventeenth to the beginning of the nineteenth century. Such quantitative collections as parish registers and censuses are beginning to yield rewards through the efforts of skilled investigators (McCaa, 1984:477–501). These records and the behavioral patterns they yield can sometimes be supplemented by letters, often dictated to scribes and placed in the records of legal proceedings (Lavrin and Couturier, 1981:278–313).

An examination of a selection of legal sources, especially the notarial archives, where most legal documents were registered, reveals at least one significant change in the position of women in the family during the last half of the eighteenth century and the early nineteenth century. The formal *carta dotal* or dowry, which was a legal statement of the value of the commodities that the bride would receive upon her marriage, begins to decline before 1750 and virtually disappears by the fourth decade of the nineteenth century. The disappearance of the dowry cannot be explained through the

*Edith Couturier, Administrator, Division of Fellowships and Seminars, National Endowment for the Humanities, received the Ph.D. from Columbia University. Her principal research interest is in eighteenth- and nineteenth-century family history and women's history.

usual historical sources. We can only speculate about the causes that made the family stop awarding dowries, and individuals cease supporting the charities which had been established to give dowries to poor young women. It is possible that the decline of the dowry, which was almost always a statement of the bride's family's resources, may have reflected a decline in the importance of the maternal lineage. A new emphasis in the nineteenth century on the nuclear household, and the growth of the idea of romantic marriages (Mitterauer and Sieder 1982:128–32), or perhaps the adoption of different methods of assuring family continuity, are possible explanations for the decline of the dowry.

Legal documents have been used by Latin American historians, working on the colonial period, to analyze a great variety of topics in economic and social history. These legal sources include various codifications of statutes, voluminous records of law cases, printed pleas by attorneys in disputes, and, finally, the rich archives of the notaries. The notaries were the licensed private individuals who maintained the official records of such legal transactions as wills, contracts, mortgages, loans, dowries, charitable foundations, and chaplaincies.

With but one exception (discussed below) no significant change occurred in the statutes on family law during the eighteenth century; it is only through the study of the notarial archives that we can find data that inform us as to how families used the rigid laws on inheritance in flexible ways to provide for family members and to perpetuate and memorialize the family name. Viewing the family through the notarial archives provides us with a window into the lives of particular households and reveals changes over time in the position of women in the family.

The law established the framework for the rights and privileges, as well as the limitations, accorded women as family members—first as daughters and heirs, then as wives and partners in the enterprises of marriage, and finally as mothers and future guardians of children. The law, various kinds of materials explicating the law, and the ways in which families used the law, reveal, sometimes in rich detail, the fabric of portions of their lives.

The basic family law code, the Laws of Toro, a brief early sixteenth-century codification of Spanish law, governed inheritance, transfer of property, and guardianship in New Spain throughout the colonial period and for the first few decades after independence. An examination of the guidebooks common to a notarial practice, the notarial documents themselves, and the published pleas, all reveal a striking adherence to these laws and well as to the older codes, the *Partidas,* upon which the Laws of Toro were based. Notaries who failed to uphold the law risked losing their licenses.[1]

[1] Both ecclesiastics and notaries advised families on the disposition of their property. A survey of notarial materials and guides can be found in Agustín G. Amenuza y Mayo, La Vida privada española en el protocolo notarial (Madrid: Ilustre Colegio Notarial de Madrid, 1950: xxi–xxiv). A typical example of advice given to priests can be found in Pedro de la Fuerte, Breve compendio para ayudar a bien morir (Seville, 1640), which includes examples of considerations for making a will even when the strictness of the inheritance laws is considered. See also Suma moral para examen de curas, y confesores, que a la luz del sol de las escuelas Santo Thomas dio al publico, written by Friars Vicente Ferrer and Luis Vicente of the University of Valencia and printed in Mexico City in 1778. The most extensive treatment of the rights of women written specifically for notaries, can be found in Pedro de Sizguenza, Tratado de cláusulas necesarias para juezes, abogodos, escribanos. . . . first published in Madrid, 1720, and reprinted at least three times. Materials about the place of the wife in the family make up a substantial portion of the book. It details such matters as the prior contracts of the woman before marriage, the claims of the dowry, and

Two provisions in the Laws of Toro governed the special position of propertied women during the colonial period: the dowry and partible inheritance. The law suggested and custom confirmed that parents should furnish their daughters with an advance share of their inheritance at the time of their marriage.[2] Families would request that the notary issue a *carta dotal* to the future son-in-law. These legal documents contained an inventory and evaluation of the jewelry, slaves, household effects, paintings, clothing, and some cash, elements which formed the content of the bulk of colonial dowries. The husband usually contributed a sum of money to this *carta dotal,* which was called an *arras* and could not exceed 10 percent of his goods. The value of the woman's contribution plus the *arras* represented the first claim on a husband's estate, and was included in the maternal line of succession (Lavrin and Couturier, 1979:286; Ferrer, 1778:391–92).[3]

A second major provision in the Laws of Toro, which governed the fate of daughters in the colonial family, stipulated strict partible inheritance. All legitimate offspring inherited equally. While the law also provided that a testator might set aside one-fifth or one-third of the value of an estate to assign to a favored heir or group of heirs, most colonial testators seem to have chosen an equal division of the estate. Even when provision was made for the most common kind of *mejora* (enlargement of inheritance) of 20 percent of the estate, the law or custom often mandated that the expenses of funeral and settlement costs be subtracted from the portion that favored one heir.[4] From a preliminary survey of the notarial records in four provincial cities (Puebla, Guadalajara, Querétaro, and Monterey), it would appear that provincial families used the *mejora* far less frequently than those in the capital.[5] In a kind of symbiotic relationship between the family and the law, testators made a remarkable effort to treat each offspring equally. Even in the cases where there had been an entail established, parents often enjoined the favored heir to care for his or her siblings. In more than 600 wills which

---

underlines her importance by explaining her rights as guardian of the family property. Other notarial guides include Pedro Murillo Velarde, *Práctica de testamentos en que se resuelven los casos mas frequentes que se ofrecen en la disposición de las ultimas voluntades* (Manila, 1755) and Juan Alvárez Posadilla, *Commentarios a las Leyes de Toro* (Madrid: 1796).

[2]At least as early as the seventeenth century and continuing through the early years of the eighteenth century, upper-class families often embedded the legal provisions of the *carta dotal* in a formal marriage contract. Both partners, or their families, contributed at the time of the marriage. The latest contract that I have found is 1720 (AGN, José Manuel de Paz, 27 January 1720). In the eighteenth century the marriage contract disappears; the dowry determined the marriage settlement until its disappearance.

[3]The Hispanic institution of the dowry was a cross between the Germanic custom in which the woman retained her property, and the Roman dowry in which the maternal property passed into the hands of her husband. In Hispanic law, the husband had the right to the administration of the dowry, but he

could not alienate it without his wife's permission, and the law obliged him to return the value in his will (Cossio y Corral, 1949:501–54).

[4]In the notaries between 1640 and 1780, which Asunción Lavrin and I explored in Puebla and Guadalajara, the use of the *mejora* was relatively infrequent. For principles of selection of cases see Lavrin and Couturier (1979:281–82). In a subsequent survey of 10 percent of the active notaries in Mexico City between 1655 and 1775, sampling every twenty years, we found that the *mejora* was much more frequent in the capital.

[5]Spanish law also permitted families to entail their estates, but it appears to have been a costly and difficult procedure. In the 300 years between 1521 and 1821, only about 100 families chose to create these *mayorazgos.*

Fall, 1985   JOURNAL OF FAMILY HISTORY   297

Asunción Lavrin and I examined in the notarial archives of five Mexican cities, we found no examples of efforts to disinherit children. (Since the law permitted disinheritance, a full examination of the law court records might reveal such cases.) In reading wills from the middle of the seventeenth century through 1790, the consistency with which families obeyed the strict rules on inheritance and divided their family property equally was impressive (Lavrin and Couturier, 1979:283–84).[6]

The equality of all legitimate offspring before the testamentary law, while a principal reason for the instability of elite families with large numbers of children, did provide women with an equal place in one aspect of family life. In fact, as daughters and heirs, women might have been favored since it was more common for women than for men to receive property at the time of their marriage. This gave daughters and their husbands a possible economic advantage over the sons. Dowries, representing a payment of the inheritance in advance, emphasized the importance of the maternal line of descent and ascent. If the woman died without issue, the value of the dowry had to be returned to her own family.

If we follow both the woman and her dowry into the marriage, the significance of the dowry as the eventual property of her lineage emerges. Even though the husband had the right to the administration of her dowry as well as any additional inheritance the wife might receive from her parents or others, he had no claim to that property since it must be inherited by her children. The dowry, as well as other property of the wife, received the special protection of the law, since the first claim

on the estate of a husband was the return of the value of the dowry to the widow. The woman had the right to decide if she wished the objects returned to her, or the sum of money which had been specified in her original dowry document (Colange; 1965:5–57).

The typical dowry consisted principally of movable goods and only rarely might it include a house. Productive property, such as haciendas or mines, tended to be willed to the male offspring. Nonetheless the dowry could be used as security for loans. Frequently, in the latter part of the eighteenth century, when a man or woman did mention the dowry as collateral for a loan, the woman was asked to resign her right to the special protection of the Laws of Toro and the *Partidas*. Despite this clause in many contracts, so far we have not found cases in which a creditor received his or her money before the claims of the dowry.

Although the husband had the power to administer the dowry, the special rights of women permitted them to separate it from the goods of their husbands. As early as 1693 Phelipa Tello de Guzmán sued to reclaim the value of her dowry, and to remove her property from the control of her spendthrift husband (Archivo Histórico del Arzobispado de Michoacán: 1693).[7] In cases between 1781 and 1809, John Kicza found five examples of successful efforts to maintain either familial or woman's control over the dowry, as well as her inherited property (Kicza, 1981).

The dowry was not the only way in which the inheritance law gave the woman and her heirs leverage in the eventual control of marital property. The form of

---

[6]An example of fears that younger siblings might be deprived can be found in Archives of Washington State University, Papeles de del Condes de Regla, Testament of the Count of Jala, 1772.

[7]I am indebted to Ascunción Lavrin for calling this case to my attention. She also lent her notes from the Guadalajara archives and her notes from the microfilm copies of the Michoacán Archives which I have used in the preparation of this paper.

community property later called the *sociedad de gananciales* dictated that the woman (or man) and their heirs should receive half the increase in the estimated value of all the property of the couple at the dissolution of the marriage by the death of one of the pair. Again the evidence from the notaries indicates that the law was applied and that widows received the *gananciales* from the marriage (Cossío y Corral, 1949:501–54).[8]

Despite the legal disabilities under which married women lived, they sometimes did contribute as independent entrepreneurs in economic life, even though they may have had to ask their husbands' permission to sign contracts, borrow money officially, and carry on other activities necessary for the conduct of business. Most women did appear to be submerged in the conjugal family, but the Guadalajara, Puebla, and Mexico City archives contain examples of a small number of married women whose activities left traces in contemporary documents. Kicza (1981:39–59) reports that of the 49 female owners of retail tobacco outlets in Mexico City in the middle of the eighteenth century, only 6 were married, 17 were single, and 26 were widows. These figures reflect the relative independence of women in each of these three legal positions.

It was only as a widow that a woman emerged as an independent person in her own right. While a widow might and often did continue her husband's business and was usually named the guardian of her minor children, she could never possess the *patria potestad,* the fundamental legal power that only a male enjoyed. Moreover, if a widow remarried, she automatically lost the right to the guardianship of the persons and estates of her children (Otero, 1956:209–41).

It was only in the absence of an adult male with the legal power and life experience and expectations of power and control that a woman would emerge as a controlling force in governing both the fate of her family and her own life. In both law and practice widows possessed more influence than unmarried single women with property, but there are examples of single women wielding considerable economic power. Tutino's study (1983:359–81) of Josefa de Velasco y Obando demonstrates how a legal vacuum allowed a woman of education and ability to preside over a large and varied series of estates as the administrator of the older sister. When her older sister, the owner of the domain of the Counts of Santiago died, a younger married sister inherited them, and the brother-in-law forced Josefa de Velasco y Obando into a minor economic role, as he assumed the control of his wife's estates.[9]

At another place in the economic spectrum, Juana Roldán, an unmarried daughter of an Indian nobleman-cacique of Cholula in Central Mexico, had amassed a relatively large amount of money as a petty trader. In this case, it was the presence of a stepmother, drawing in part upon the special rights of the

---

writing the will the testator stated the value of his property at the time of marriage, and the amount of the wife's dowry. Following the death of either of the marriage partners, an appraiser evaluated all the couple's assets, and subtracted the amounts they had owned at the time of the marriage, including the dowry. The remainder was the sum called *gananciales.* The remaining spouse received half of this sum, and the heirs of the deceased spouse received the other half. The marriage was viewed as a joint economic effort, and the widow was entitled to half the assets accumulated during the years of the matrimonial partnership.

[9]Other examples of single women exercising power can be found in Archivo General de la Nación Mexicana (Ramo Tierras, 650 exp. 2) and Gallagher (1978:171). This is discussed also in Couturier (1981b); also see Couturier, 1978:135–40.

---

[8]The amount of the *gananciales* was determined in the course of the settlement of the estate. In

Fall, 1985   JOURNAL OF FAMILY HISTORY   299

widow, who deprived the offspring of part of their patrimony, including property amassed by their deceased sister, Juana Roldán (Gallagher, 1978:171; Couturier, 1981b:7-12).

The special position of the widow derived from her legal right to inherit the dowry which she had brought into the marriage, the additional property which she might have inherited, her right to half of the *gananciales* of the marriage, as well as her customary position as a guardian of her children (Ots Capdequí, 1918:162-82). In addition to these special legal advantages, the widow (with children) had probably accumulated a group of male *compadres*, who had served as baptismal sponsors to her children, and hence had a special, quasi-familial role in the protection of her family. Marriages of her daughters also supplied her with additional *compadres*, as the grandparent was the favored ritual parent (i.e., baptismal sponsor) for the next generation, and hence enjoyed bonds of special kinship with her sons-in-law as a co-parent. This extended her circle of influence and power far beyond the confines of her immediate family.

While law and custom allowed widows substantial scope in the conduct of family affairs, our knowledge about widows is still too limited to know how many of them possessed the training, confidence, and resources to conduct family business. The cases of seven widows of varied background and ethnic groups demonstrate a variety of strategies by women at all social levels for maintaining the family estate and controlling individual family members. This evidence is drawn from Mexico City and Puebla during the eighteenth and early part of the nineteenth centuries.

The wealthiest and poorest of these women possessed the greatest independence, although even these women de-

pended upon male family members and *compadres*. The third Countess of Miravalle (1701-1763), groomed from childhood to inherit her family's extensive properties, struggled to maintain her family's place within the upper levels of the Mexico City elite, despite the loss of their most important source of income in one of the eighteenth-century Bourbon reforms. She was partly successful in this; one of her tactics consisted of limiting or delaying the marriages of her children. She married one of her daughters extremely well, kept two other daughters unmarried, and delayed or forbade the marriages of her sons, so that they could enjoy the income from chaplaincies (Couturier, 1981c:9-12). The second Countess of Regla (1768-1819) conserved a somewhat larger patrimony when widowed in 1809, and prevented her incompetent son from administering the family estates (Couturier, 1978:141-43). A third widow, Juana Petra Larrasquito from the city of Puebla, possessing a large dowry and inheritance herself, governed her family, provided for a crippled daughter, expanded the family circle of businesses, and arranged the marriage of only one of her nine children—a daughter, who received a substantial dowry (Couturier; 1981b:21-25; ANP, Protócolos de Joseph Saldaña; 1768, fols. 4-78).[10]

Two widows with more modest properties at their disposal, but still to be counted among the elite of Puebla since they possessed substantial houses, a coach, and at least one hacienda, fared less well. María Isabel Echegaray (the

---

[10]By persuading her sons to remain single, one daughter to enter a convent, and by keeping her other daughters at home, the widow prevented the division of the family property. Only one of the offspring had legitimate heirs; the others could be expected to leave their money and property so as to benefit their nieces and nephews.

mother of the famous Jesuit historian Francisco Antonio Clavijero) and her widowed mother proved unable to prevent a drastic reduction in the estate following her husband's death. Despite her own inherited contribution to her conjugal families' social and economic position, and her husband's ability to accumulate money, the combination of an excessive number of male children (for whom marriages could not be arranged), lack of powerful Spanish merchant sons-in-law, and a relatively rapacious brother-in-law, caused her financial situation to deteriorate rapidly. Her death only a year after that of her husband was believed to be a reaction to the financial difficulties of the family (Couturier; 1981b:15–20; Ronan, 1977:1–4; ANP, Antonio Bermúdez de Castro, 1742; Joseph Saldaña, 1752.

Another widow in similar circumstances, María Catharina Uriarte, married one of her daughters to a merchant, and apparently followed the pattern established by her husband in the marriages of two other daughters by not granting her a dowry. The widow continued some of the businesses of her husband, but sold the hacienda as she was unable to meet mortgage payments (Couturier, 1981b:10–14; ANP, Joaquín González de Santa Cruz; 1739).

The Indian towns of Cholula and Amozoque, on the periphery of the city of Puebla, were the homes of two women of strength and determination who used the special position of widows to accumulate property and power. María de la Presentación married an Indian Cacique, and obtained control of properties of her stepchildren by clever utilization of her widow's rights. Both her dowry and loans to her husband were repaid to her from the earnings of an adult stepdaughter who had died at the same time as her husband. She succeeded in frustrating the intent of

the laws, which was to preserve property for the next generation. In another case, Micaela Carrillo, a *mestiza* widow with a small inheritance expanded her wealth and provided houses and trades for her two legitimate sons. In the years of her widowhood she had three illegitimate daughters for whom she also provided. Largely through her participation in the pulque trade of late colonial Mexico, both as a producer and then as a seller, Macaéla Carrillo became a relatively wealthy person in her community. She is a special example of the possibilities open to a widow in the society of an Indian town in the late eighteenth-century Mexico (Couturier, 1981a:362–75; 1981b:6–10).

Colonial families could use the law flexibly in order to protect themselves against the operation of the law of partible inheritance. The requirement or custom that all property be sold at the death of the testator, so that the proceeds could be distributed to the heirs, could threaten a substantial loss in values because these auctions were akin to forced sales. Families evaded this rule by leaving specific items to individual family members, and disposed of immovable properties to their offspring during their lifetimes. Other measures included the establishment of chaplaincies which could provide income for family members or collateral kin, and preserve wealth within the lineage by establishing a kind of annuity administered by the church. For nuclear family deferring or prohibiting marriage prevented the eventual dispersion of family property since their heirs almost always left their estates to a nephew, a niece, or other collateral kin. While all propertied families delayed the effects of partible inheritance at the level of each generation, the wealthier units could care for the eventual needs of the lineage through their control over marriage and marital property, and through the assumption that offspring would obey the family leader in these decisions.

Even though a change in the customs of marriage in the eighteenth century did take place and increasing numbers of unions were made in defiance of parental wishes, we still have only slight evidence of this alteration. Our information on illegitimacy in upper-class families and growing numbers of unequal marriages, is still too fragmentary to draw firm conclusions, although some sources do seem to indicate slow alterations in marriage patterns (Nazzari, 1984; Chowning, 1984).

In Mexico as in other parts of Latin America the practice of awarding daughters legally certified dowries declined throughout the eighteenth century.[11] Out of a total of approximately 300 marriages in the cities of Guadalajara and Puebla between 1648 and 1725, 78 percent of the marriages were dowered, while in the period between 1726 and 1793, only 57 percent of the marriages recorded in the archives mentioned dowries (Lavrin and Couturier, 1979:294). In 500 marriages in Mexico City recorded in the period between 1655 and 1715, 75 percent of the women received dowries, while in the years between 1735 and 1793, 62 percent of the marriages reported these dower gifts.[12] If we look only at the period between 1755 and 1775, the decline is more

telling. In this period only 59 percent of the women were dowered.[13]

Silvia Bravo Sandoval and I read the complete notarial files for six notaries who had active practices in Mexico City in the years between 1775 and 1811, and we found few actual dowries in these files. The dowries rarely contained the *arras*, the common promised financial contribution of the groom in earlier centuries. The few dowries found were all large, as the practice of endowing women from less affluent families disappeared.

For the earlier part of the nineteenth century an index of notarial documents indicates that for 1829, out of a total of 2,732 separate cases in the files of 38 notaries practicing in Mexico City, only 28 dowry documents were listed (Potash, et al., 1982).[14] In the 1847 index. the dowry seems to have almost disappeared (Potash, et al., 1983). The practice of formally granting a dowry to a bride at the time of her marriage declined during the course of the eighteenth century. There was no new legislation which could help to account for this change and published sources are silent on the reasons that made families decide to stop issuing these documents.

Two economic reasons might be adduced for this change. Since a large part of the value of dowries tended to be movable property, such as jewelry, clothing, household effects, and cash, the relative

---

[11]In a study of dowries and wills, which Asunción Lavrin and I carried out in the records of the notaries in five Mexican cities, we counted those dowries that appeared as legally notarized documents, and those dowries that were noted in the wills. Since we counted dowries that had been awarded many years earlier, our figures err on the high side. The legally awarded dowry declined much more rapidly than our figures would suggest.

---

[12]These data derive from searching 10 percent of the active notaries in Mexico City in the years between 1655 and 1775, sampling every 20 years.

---

[13]This figure exaggerates the real number of dowries awarded or mentioned in the documents, as one of the 1775 notaries kept the records for the charitable lotteries charged with awarding dowries to needy women.

---

[14]We do not know if these were issued at the time of the marriage, or if they resulted from families attempting to take advantage of the special protections of the dowry in order to prevent their property from possible seizure for debt.

loss of value of these commodities might help to account for one aspect of this decline. As textiles, silver, and gems became more available during the eighteenth century, the importance of counting the value of these commodities and putting this value into a legal document might have diminished.

A second economic impetus for the decline and disappearance of the dowry has been suggested by Muriel Nazzari (1984) in a summary of a massive research project on the dowry in the city of São Paulo, Brazil. In Brazil the dowry was intended to provide for the establishment of a young couple in a society where alternative means for the support of a new household were lacking. At roughly the same time as the practice of dowry granting declined in the Mexican cities studied by Asunción Lavrin and myself, Nazzari observes that the amount of money families wished to place in dowries declined as a percentage of their total estate. Observing the economic changes in the city of São Paulo, Nazzari suggests that the new positions open to young men in the bureaucracy and the professions diminished their need for a father-in-law to provide the means to support them.

Mexican materials fail to support the hypothesis that an expanding bureaucracy and the growth of professions brought about a change in family patterns. Moreover, the data from Mexico also indicate that often very well-to-do men received dowries, and that these frequently played little role in the establishment of a family livelihood. For a possible explanation of the change in Mexico, it is necessary to look at some other motivations for the decline of the dowry.

It is possible that in Mexico, as well as in the United States and Europe, an increasing number of young men and women below the age of 25 were selecting their own partners in defiance of the

wishes of their parents (Smith: 1978; Twinam, 1984; Seed, 1980; also see Arrom in this volume). The rise of individualism in marriage choice and the concomitant decline in the corporate concept of the family was reflected in Mexico through the introduction of a new law— the Pragmatic Sanction on Marriage of 1779. In this law the authorities decried the increased independence of minor offspring in their choice of marital partners and made the state responsible for preventing marriages without parental permission.

The only study of the issue of matrimonial choice in New Spain includes data to 1779, so we do not know how strictly the state carried out its dicta after that date. We do not know if it upheld the rights of the parents to decide on their offspring's matrimonial choices, or how often the courts ruled in favor of the children (Seed, 1980). A further investigation of these records might enlighten us on the question of matrimonial choices. Sources such as plays and novels, newspapers, and additional work in the notarial records tracing marriages and economic movements might help to explain the changes in matrimonial ties.

With the decline and disappearance of the formal custom of granting dowries the right of a married woman to receive property in advance of the death of her parents, and hence her special advantage over her brothers and other sisters, terminated. The protection that she had received as the owner of a dowry, after the death of her husband, may also have disappeared.

These changes in the position of women within the family do not portend a worsening of her position. It is possible that women became property owners in far larger numbers in the nineteenth century; it is certain that they had greater educational opportunities, and slowly

Fall, 1985   JOURNAL OF FAMILY HISTORY   303

began to enter public life through their roles in philanthropies.[15] New conditions in nineteenth-century life for middle-class urban women may have lessened dependence upon male family members, upon whom even the wealthiest and most self-reliant colonial widow had leaned. The protection of the dowry still enclosed a woman within the confines of a traditional and authoritarian family. Her loss of a special economic position signified a loosening of the propertied bonds that tied her to her family of origin or lineage. It also signified a strengthening of the nuclear family household or family of procreation, a trend that mirrored the general patterns traced in similar periods of modernization in Europe and the United States.

---

[15]"My impression that women became property owners in far greater numbers in the nineteenth century is based on scanning the notarial archives in the cities of Puebla and Mexico for the eighteenth century; and continuing this search with two notaries in varied years between 1800 and 1878. These impressions seem to be confirmed by the large numbers of women who appear in the indices collected by Robert Potash, et al. (1982, 1983) for the years 1829 and 1847. Approximately one-fifth of the transactions involved women. This hypothesis for Mexico agrees with the conclusions of Norton (1984) and Lebsock (1984) who reviewed a much more varied body of material in summarizing changing conditions for women in the transition from the colonial world to the nineteenth century in the United States.

BIBLIOGRAPHY

Archivo General de la Nación Mexicana. Cited as AGN.
    Ramo de Tierras, 650, exp. 2
Archivo Histórico del Arzobispado de Michoacán in Genealogical Society of Utah.
  1693 Section 2, Legajo 90, reel 166504
Archivo de Instrumentos Públicos de Guadalajara
Archivo de Notarías de Puebla. Cited as ANP.
Archives of Washington State University, Pullman Papeles del Conde de Regla
Aries, Phillippe
  1965 Centuries of Childhood: A Social History of Family Life. Translated by Robert Baldick. New York: Vintage Books.
Arrom, Silvia M.
  1978 "Marriage Patterns in Mexico City, 1811." Journal of Family History 3:376-91.
Chowning, Margaret
  1984 "Combining Business and Kinship: Patterns of Inheritance and Formation of Family Empires in Nineteenth-Century Michoacán." Paper presented at the American Historical Association, San Francisco.
Colange, Alfredo
  1965 "Aestimatio dotis." Anuario Histórico del Derecho Espanol 35:5-57.
Cossío y Corral, Alfonso de
  1949 "El regimen económico del matrimonio en las legislaciones Americanas." Anuario de Estudios americanos 6:501-54.
  1963 La sociedad de gananciales. Madrid: Instituto Nacional de Estudios Jurídicos.
Couturier, Edith
  1978 "Women in a Noble Family: The Mexican Counts of Regla, 1750-1830." In Asunción Lavrín, ed., Latin American Women: Historical Perspectives, pp. 129-49. Westport, Conn.: Greenwood Press.
  1981a "Michaela Angela Carrillo: Widow and Pulque Dealer." In David Sweet and Gary Nash, eds., Struggle and Survival in Colonial America, pp. 362-75. Berkeley: University of California Press.
  1981b "Family Economy and Inheritance in Eighteenth Century Puebla: A Study of Five Families." Paper presented at the Middle Atlantic Conference on Latin American Studies, Philadelphia.
  1981c "Family, Politics and Business in Eighteenth Century Mexico City: The Case of the Countess of Miravalle." Paper presented at the fifth Berkshire Conference on Women's History, Vassar College.

Ferrer, Vicente y Luis Vicente
1778   Suma moral para examén de curas, y con-
       fesores, que á la luz del de las escuelas San-
       to Tomas dió al público. Mexico City: Im-
       prenta Nueva Madrilena de d. Felipe de
       Zúñiga y Ontiveros.

Gallagher, Ann Miriam
1978   "The Indian Nuns of Mexico City's Mon-
       asterio of Corpus Christ, 1724–1821." In
       Asunción Lavrin, ed., Latin American
       Women: Historical Perspectives, pp. 150–
       72. Westport, Conn.: Greenwood Press.

Kicza, John E.
1981   "La mujer y la vida comercial en la ciudad
       de México a finales de la colonia." Revista
       de Ciencias Sociales y Humanidades. Uni-
       versidad Autónoma Metropolitana, Atzca-
       potzalco 2:39–59.

Lavrin, Asunción and Edith Courtürier
1979   "Dowries and Wills: A View of Women's
       Socio-economic Role in Colonial Guadala-
       jara and Puebla, 1640–1790." Hispanic
       American Historical Review 59:280–304.
1981   "Las mujeres tienen la palabra: Otras
       voces en la historia colonial de México."
       Historia Mexicana 31:278–313.

Lebsock, Suzanne
1984   Free Women of Petersburg: Status and
       Culture in a Southern Town, 1784–1860.
       New York: Norton.

McCaa, Robert
1984   "Calidad, Clase, and Marriage in Colonial
       Mexico: The Case of Parral, 1788–90."
       Hispanic American Historical Review 64:
       477–501.

Mitterauer, Michael and Reinhard Sieder
1982   The European Family. Translated by Karla
       Oosterveen and Manfred Hörzinger, Chi-
       cago: University of Chicago Press.

Nazzari, Muriel
1984   "Women and Property in the Transition to
       Capitalism: Decline of the Dowry in São
       Paulo, Brazil (1640–1870)." Paper pre-
       sented at the American Historical Associa-
       tion, Chicago.

Norton, Mary Beth
1984   "The Evolution of White Women's Ex-
       perience in Early America." American
       Historical Review 89:593–617.

Otero, Alfonso
1956   "Patria potestad." Anuario de Historia de
       Derecho Espanol 26:209–41.

Ots Capdequí, José María
1918   Bosquejo histórico de los derechos de la
       mujer casada en la legislación de Indias."
       Revista General de Legislación y Jurispru-
       dencia 132:162–82.

Potash, Robert A., et al.
1982   Guide to the Notarial Records of the Ar-
       chivo General de Notarias, Mexico City,
       for the Year 1829. Amherst, Mass.: Uni-
       versity Computing Center.
1983   Guide to the Notarial Records of the Ar-
       chivo General de Notarias for the Year
       1847. Amherst, Mass.: University Com-
       puting Center.

Ronan, Charles
1977   Francisco Javier Clavijero, S. J. (1731–
       1787): Figure of the Mexican Enlighten-
       ment. Rome and Chicago: Institutum His-
       toricum S.I. and Loyola University Press.

Seed, Patricia
1980   "Parents versus Children: Marriage Oppo-
       sitions in Colonial Mexico, 1610–1779."
       Ph.D. diss., University of Wisconsin.

Smith, Daniel Scott
1974   "Family Limitation, Sexual Control, and
       Domestic Feminism in Victorian
       America." In Mary Hartman and Lois
       Banner, eds., Clio's Consciousness Raised,
       pp. 119–36. New York: Harper Torch-
       books.
1978   "Parental Power and Marriage Patterns:
       An Analysis of Historical Trends in Hing-
       ham, Massachusetts." In Michael Gordon,
       ed., The American Family in Socio-His-
       torical perspective, 2d ed., pp. 87–100.
       New York: St. Martin's Press.

Stone, Lawrence
1977   The Family, Sex and Marriage in England,
       1500–1800. London: Routledge and
       Kegan.

Trumbach, Randolph
1978   The Rise of the Egalitarian Family. New
       York: Academic Press.

Tutino, John
1983   "Power, Class, and Family: Men and
       Women in the Mexican Elite, 1750–1810."
       Americas 39:359–81.

Twinam, Ann
1984   "Unwed Mothers in a Spanish Colonial
       Elite." Paper presented at the Sixth Berk-
       shire Conference on Women's History,
       Smith College.

Wheaton, Robert
1980   "Introduction: Recent Trends in the His-
       torical Study of the French Family." In
       Robert Wheaton and Tamara K. Hareven,
       eds., Family and Sexuality in French His-
       tory, pp. 3–26. Philadelphia: University of
       Pennsylvania Press.

8

Women and Means: Women and Family Property in Colonial Brazil

Alida C. Metcalf

How women owned property in the past is a fascinating question for historians to explore. Control over property, in most cultures, translates into power. Those who own resources, be they of a family or a community, have the means to exercise power over others. Paradoxically, in Latin cultures, women have traditionally held many rights to property spelled out in custom and law,[1] yet Latin cultures have strong patriarchal overtones in family and community life. Why, then, if women hold rights to property, is family and community life not more egalitarian? Or, put another way, why do women have any rights at all to property in patriarchal cultures?

Mediterranean societies inherited this tension between women's rights to property and patriarchal values from Roman society. Roman law recognized the rights of women to property, yet in public affairs, women had a limited voice.[2] After the disintegration of the Roman Empire, the Roman cultural inheritance combined with the values of the Germanic tribes to create distinct legal traditions and unique family patterns throughout Europe.[3] In the Mediterranean region it is impossible to point to one common family type,[4] but it is fair to say that among the Mediterranean peoples of Italy, Spain, Portugal, and Greece women retained their rights to family property. Yet, throughout the Mediterranean can be found a belief in patriarchy expressed through the male values of honor and shame.[5] Thus, within these Mediterranean cultures, a tension remained between the accepted patriarchal values of the culture and the fact that women did own property.

The new world inherited this contradiction from Spain and Portugal. According to Spanish and Portuguese law, women held clearly defined rights to family property as heirs and as wives. In spite of these rights and responsibilities for family property, Latin American historians characterize Spanish and Portuguese America as patriarchal and paternalistic. No historian yet has argued that based on their equal rights to family property, men and women were equal in the family or in the community.[6] Women's rights to family property, it would seem, did not translate into power for women in the family or in the community. Why?

To answer such a question, historians must examine the lives of women not as a class apart from society, but in their proper context – that is, in their families and in their communities. Latin American scholars have successfully restored women to history by illustrating the many roles of women in Latin American societies.[7] There was no such thing as "a woman's experience," for a woman's life differed depending on her family's social class, her race and ethnicity, where and when she lived, if she married, her religious beliefs, and the work she did. Similarly, studies of family life in the Latin American past have shown how very important families were to the economic and political development of Latin America.[8] But as yet the role of women within their families and especially how women viewed property still remains shrouded.[9] This article reconstructs the lives of women in such a context in colonial Brazil. Its goal is to see if women exercised their rights to property in their families, if they held power within their families, and if and how their decisions affected the communities in which they lived.

The "women of means" or the women of the propertied class of the colonial town of Santana de Parnaíba, are the focus of this study. These women came from families that owned land and slaves, dominated the local community institutions, and bequeathed their property through careful inheritance strategies to their heirs. These women had legal rights to the family property. Their attitudes and decisions could therefore have a tremendous impact not only on the family, but on the family's dependents (such as slaves and retainers) and on the community as well.

Santana de Parnaíba, a rural large town in the province of São Paulo, lies on the Piratininga plateau on the Tietê River, just upstream from the city of São Paulo. In 1775, it had a population of 4,714 souls. Fields of sugar cane, pastures for horses and cattle, and small plots of corn and beans dotted the still forested hillsides in the late eighteenth century. The majority of households in the town (509 or 73 percent) did not possess slaves in 1775. These were peasant families who worked the land themselves and primarily produced crops for their own subsistence. The households that did own slaves in 1775 (186 or 27 percent) owned over 1,000 slaves, the majority of whom worked on the larger farms. Still, the vast majority of the slaveholders (80 percent) owned less than ten slaves and only two families in 1775 owned more than fifty.[10]

The women of means came from the propertied class of Santana de Parnaíba, a modestly affluent group of families by the standards of colonial Brazil. While the richest families of Parnaíba did belong to the provincial elite of São Paulo, they were considerably less moneyed than the elite of all of Brazil. The women of means of Parnaíba, therefore, are not representative of the wealthiest strata of Brazilian society. But their lives probably are typical of those women from the local elites of the towns of colonial Brazil.

Women in Portugal and Brazil had specific legal rights to family property set out in the Portuguese legal code. The code recognized that women owned half of the community property held in a marriage.[11] At inheritance, regardless of any will, daughters were entitled to an equal share of their parents' property.[12] Thus, in principle, women had basically the same rights as men to the family property.[13]

The Portuguese laws of marriage clearly stipulated that wives owned half of the property accumulated by the couple during their years of matrimony. The law refers to the "charter of halves" (carta de ametade) that underlay marriage. This made the husbands and wives the co-owners (meeiros) of the community property.[14] Before the law, then, husbands and wives equally owned whatever property they acquired during their marriage. While married, a husband had to consult his wife before selling, lending, or obligating her share of the community property.[15]

The majority of the men and women who married in Portugal and its dominions married by a charter of halves and became the co-owners of the community property. The law did recognize a second kind of marriage, a marriage by contract, in which men and women did not equally own the community property. In these marriages, property was owned according to the details set forth in the contract signed by the bride and groom.[16] Marriage by contract, however, rarely appeared in colonial Brazil; no evidence of it has surfaced in Parnaíba.

The community property that a man and a woman possessed during their years of marriage legally belonged to their children after their deaths. All children inherited equally, daughters and sons alike. Primogeniture only governed the inheritance of the entailed estates (*morgados*) of the nobility.[17] Few entailed estates were ever formed in Brazil; therefore, in virtually all families in Brazil, children inherited equally from the estates of their parents. When a husband or a wife died, a local judge supervised the evaluation of the community property and its division. The surviving spouse kept his or her half of the community property, while the half of the deceased passed on to the heirs. Each heir received an equal share (*legitima*). Therefore, inheritance took place twice, after the death of each spouse. Children could expect to receive property twice during their lives: after the death of their father and again after the death of their mother.[18]

Yet Portuguese law did differentiate between men and women. Title LXI of the code begins with the statement, "By law it is decreed, that with respect to the fraility of women's reason, that they may not make themselves financially liable for another."[19] This law pertains to the role of surety (*fiador*), someone who with his property guaranteed the actions of another. The law excluded women from this role as a "favor" and to "protect" them, to use the language of the law. This provision, which dated from a Roman Senate law passed in the first century A.D., reflected the fact that in Roman society, to provide liability was a civil act limited to men.[20] In the Portuguese codification, the principle, known by its vulgarized Latin "Senatus Consulto Valleano," remained. Exceptions were made for women who obligated themselves and their property to free a slave or to provide a dowry for a young woman. In such cases, women were expected to carry out their intentions, as was the woman who attempted to skirt the aspect of the law by donning the attire of a man.[21]

Surety, or liability, was an important business transaction placed primarily in the hands of men. Men were favored too with the powerful role of guardian of orphaned children. The law designated minor children with inheritances as "orphans,"[22] and judges granted to each a guardian (*tutor*).[23] These guardians not only cared for them, but administered their inheritances until they came of age. Women were not permitted, as a general rule, to serve as guardians and to administer the inheritances of minors. The exception were mothers and grandmothers of children who did not otherwise have guardians. If these women "lived honestly," had not remarried, and wished to become guardians of the children, they could become guardians. These women, would, however, have to pledge their own property as surety (and renounce their "right" to the Valleano Law) or produce a guarantor (*fiador*) who would guarantee their actions.[24] Once a woman was granted the right to serve as a guardian, she gave up her right to remarry. If she did remarry, she lost the guardianship and even if she again became a widow, she might not regain her position as guardian. No such provision against remarrying applied to men.

The law code especially distrusted widows. It provided a means to take from them their own rightful property. Title CVII begins with the statement, "wishing to overcome the frailty of reason of widows, who after the death of their husbands squander what they own." The title empowers local judges to take property away from widows who "maliciously" or "without reason" had given away or lost their property.[25] The rationale behind this law is clear: it protected the rights of heirs whose inheritances might be diminished by the actions of incompetent widows. The law extended no such protection, however, to heirs whose future inheritances were in the hands of incompetent widowers.

Portuguese Law gave women clearly defined rights to property as daughters, as wives, and as widows. Yet the law also limited the independent actions of women because of their "frailty of reason." The law sought to protect family property which women might squander by "protecting" them, i.e. depriving them of rights granted to men. Laws alone, however, do not shape the contours of human lives. Family customs, local conditions, and attitudes towards women all played important roles in molding the lives of women.[26]

Not only did communities in colonial Latin America inherit the customs of their European colonizers, but over time conditions there created new customs which affected the actual practice of inheritance. Specific characteristics of the region of São Paulo during the colonial period, for example, set a precedent for extensive female involvement in family affairs. In the seventeenth century, São Paulo was on the edge of a vast *sertão*, or frontier to the north, south, and west. Women in towns like Parnaíba wielded tremendous influence over family property when men left the community to explore and exploit the riches of the interior.

Soon after Parnaíba was founded in the 1590s, men left the small settlement in search of Indians – who would become their servants, laborers, and *de facto* slaves – and for gold. Men were gone for months at a time, leaving women behind to run the farms. In the seventeenth century, families in São Paulo favored their daughters with large dowries that far eclipsed the inheritances of their sons.[27] Wills and inventories from seventeenth-century Parnaíba likewise reflect the fact that sons often gave up their own inheritances to provide dowries for their sisters. Whether this practice indicated the power of women in seventeenth century São Paulo or whether it was a marriage strategy to maximize family resources, is still not yet known. But for whatever reason, in the first one hundred years of Parnaíba's history, women not only held right to property according to law, but custom gave them the greater share.[28]

In eighteenth-century São Paulo men continued to spend long periods of time away from towns like Parnaíba in the gold fields of Minas Gerais, Mato Grosso, and Goiás. In their absence, women again remained in Parnaíba and oversaw the family farms. It was only at the end of the eighteenth century when the region began to produce sugar for export that men were less likely to absent themselves from home. In Parnaíba, families continued to favor a daughter and a son-in-law over their own sons, even if the dowries were smaller than they had been the century before. Daughters and sons-in-law tended to remain in Parnaíba while sons migrated to the west.[29]

The location of Parnaíba on the edge of a vast frontier gave women roles to play in the management of the family business. Another important factor which determined when a woman controlled family property was the demographic history of her own family and class. Since most of the business activity in the colony, be it farming, commerce, mining, or credit transactions, was accomplished through the family, families regulated everyone's access to property. The history of her own individual family determined if, when, and how a woman would manage property. Since the families of the propertied class of Parnaíba shared many common patterns of family life, it is possible to outline a characteristic family cycle for this social group.

A family cycle consists of the different kinds of households that exist over the lifetime of a family.[30] During certain stages of the cycle, women are more or less likely to exercise control over family property. To understand how women owned property, then, it is first necessary to reconstruct the family cycle. Using the manuscript censuses from the late eighteenth century, it is possible to do this for the elite families of Parnaíba.

In the late eighteenth century, the family cycle began when couples married, formed their own households, and created nuclear families. The construction of a nuclear family began a long, stable, and prosperous period. The community property grew as couples inherited property from both sets of parents and invested in their farms, slave laborers, and business ventures. Their families expanded as children were born.

Death interrupted this nuclear stage of family life. When wives died, men tended to remarry almost immediately and reestablished nuclear families, causing little change to the structure of family life. In these reconstructed nuclear families, for example, widowers managed the property that their younger children inherited from their mothers until the children married or came of age (at twenty-five years). When widowers remarried, they received a dowry from the bride's family which became part of the new community property. Thus family stability and prosperity continued. Widowers retained control over much of the community property and, moreover, through the dowry they received from their second wife, they began to create a new community property.

But when husbands died first, their widows were less likely to remarry. These families became single-parent households headed by widows. This matrifocal stage did represent a major change in the structure of the family. While this stage might endure for a long period of time, compared to the nuclear family, it was a time of waning resources. Widows presided over a time when half of the community property, that which had belonged to their deceased husbands, passed to their children, the legal heirs. Thus compared to the nuclear family, the single-parent household was a time when the family contracted. The family property, as well as its members, diminished.

The fact that husbands were usually a good deal older than their wives played a major role in the family cycle, for it virtually assured that single-parent households headed by widows would occur. In 1775, for example, the mean age of husbands was 49.6 years, while that of wives was 38.9. Thus many women became heads of households after their husbands died and the household composed of a widow and her children became a common phase of the family life cycle.

In Figure One, the basic contours of this family cycle are depicted. The majority of all heads of households among the slaveowning population in Parnaíba in 1775 were married men. Yet in the older cohorts of heads of households, households headed by women became more common. The majority of the households headed by women consisted of a widow and her children. The family cycle transferred authority over the family to women in its later stages when many families were headed by women. Coincidentally, widowhood was also the time when Portuguese law sought to limit the legal rights of women.

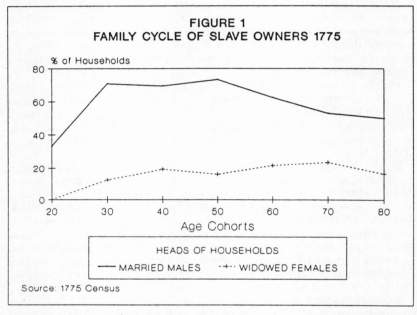

FIGURE 1
FAMILY CYCLE OF SLAVE OWNERS 1775

Source: 1775 Census

This family cycle suggests that three discrete periods characterized the lives of women: as single women, as married women, and as widows. Not all women lived through each of these phases, but those who did found that they had distinctly different rights and responsibilities for family property during these times of their lives.[31]

Women began their lives as daughters. As young and unmarried women, they exercised little control over family property. Until they married or reached their age of majority (25 years), daughters lived with their families and owned no property of their own. Whatever they earned became a part of the community property owned by their parents. In a sense, they were like their brothers who also worked for their fathers until they married or reached the age of twenty-five and were considered "emancipated" from their fathers' authority.[32]

Women who did not marry but who remained single were, unlike their brothers, rarely likely to leave home while their parents were still alive. While sons followed their fathers' footsteps into the wilderness, single women remained at home. The responsibility for caring for the parents as they aged fell to these women.[33] Anna

Caetana de Jesus, for example, never married. Her father acknowledged in his will that she had "served" him for many years. Single women like Anna Caetana sometimes earned income. In his will, her father wrote that "since she was twenty-five she has sewed and spun and from that work has purchased some gold and silver."[34] Concerned that his heirs would take advantage of Anna's income and consider it theirs by inheritance, Anna Caetana's father took pains to reiterate in his will that he had borrowed money from her on more than one occasion and that "everything which she has is hers."[35]

Unmarried daughters might accumulate property by their own initiative, as Anna did, but more commonly they inherited property after their parents died. Then they received their equal share of the community property assembled by their parents. Usually a single daughter's property continued to remain part of the family farm which her surviving parent managed and controlled. For example, after Anna Caetana de Jesus's father died in 1793, she continued to live at home. Her inheritance from her father became a "share" of the family farm which her mother, as the new head of household, managed. In 1798, the household appeared in the census. Anna's mother, eighty-two years old, was listed as the head of household which contained Anna and four slaves. They gave their occupation as "farmers."[36]

The demands of survival in a rural economy were high, which forced unmarried women to live with other family members and to pool their shares of the family property. Twenty-five households in the 1775 census were those formed by co-resident sisters, co-resident sisters and brothers, and nuclear families extended laterally to include sisters and brothers. While these households represent a mere 4 percent of all types of households in 1775, they greatly outnumbered the households of single women living alone. Only one single woman of means lived alone in 1775.

Occasionally, unmarried women did live alone and managed their property by themselves as Anna Caetana de Jesus did after her mother died. But hers was not an easy existence as can be seen in a petition she filed in 1816. In that petition, she complained that her neighbor "violently entered her lands because she is a woman and took the lands by brute force."[37] Precisely at the time when she inherited authority over property from her family, her ability to exercise it was challenged by her neighbor who invaded her lands. Anna successfully used local institutions to plead her case and enlisted the support of three influential men in the community. But as the 1820 census reveals, she was only a small farmer with four slaves, while her coveting neighbor, Antonio José de Miranda, was a sugar planter with seventeen slaves. The latter held the rank of adjutant in the town militia, a position which strengthened his authority, and which would make it difficult for Anna Caetana to stop his incursions into her land.[38]

Women who never married experienced a life course not unlike Anna Caetana de Jesus's. Single women continued to live with their families – with their parents until they died and after that with the families of a brother or a sister. Authority over property, if ever, came late in life. Then, as property owners, single women relied on family and kin for support, because they were perceived as vulnerable in the community. Due to the difficulties of living alone, most single women moved in with their kin. Those who had no kin, moved to the town center where they were served by a slave or lapsed into genteel poverty.

The second stage of a woman's life began with marriage. When women of propertied families married, their families provided a dowry which became part of the community property a wife shared with her husband. For modest families, dowries usually contained the essential items needed to set up a new household. Paschoal Fernandes Sampayo and his wife produced four relatively similar dowries as they married each of their daughters. The largest dowry included a pair of sheets, a tablecloth, three hand towels, four table napkins, two pillowcases, a coverlet, a tin basin, an oil lamp, two silver spoons, a cotton mattress, three eights of gold worked into jewelry, a wooden chest, six tin plates, one slave, and 64,000 *reis* in money.[39] Similarly, Maria Ribeira's three daughters received dowries of table linens and tableware, bedding, chests, and a little gold or silver.[40] What was given in dowries tells much about the world of women and the customs of family life. These families lived without great material wealth. The simple bed with its mattress stuffed with wool and cotton, sheets, and a coverlet served as the new couple's first and most important possession – the conjugal bed. Tablecloths, napkins, plates, forks, spoons allowed the new bride to set her own table which symbolized the creation of a new family unit. A long wooden chest stored clothing and linens. A horse provided a mount for the bride to attend mass and to visit her natal family. A dress, shawl, and silk stockings marked her status and set her apart from other women. If the dowry included land, there the couple would open up their own fields with the aid of the slave(s) given away in the dowry.

The dowries given by wealthy families included productive property such as land, slaves, and money. Anna Ribeira, daughter of Lucrecia Leme de Barros, received eight slaves, 32 eights of gold, and the very large sum of 1,600,000 *reis* as well as the usual household furnishings and trousseau.[41] Maria Buena's dowry included twelve slaves, a farm, a house in Parnaíba's town center, and gold and silver, while José Correa Penteado gave his daughter eight slaves and gold as well as household furnishings and an expensive dress.[42]

Dowries given by wealthy families usually included land which suggests that families intended for their daughters to settle nearby. Land was especially attractive to sons-in-law who were marrying into families in Parnaíba, for they themselves did not yet own land. Some families promised the lands directly to their sons-in-law. Manoel Correa Penteado wrote in his will that he pledged 500 square *braças* (1,100 square meters) to his son-in-law wherever he wished.[43] When Francisco Xavier de Assumpção's daughter married he turned over one fourth of his lands to his new son-in-law.[44] The lands included in the dowries of women like Maria Pires de Barros, who received a farm and a farmhouse, or Catharina de Siqueira Leite, who received two tracts of land, immediately gave the couple a productive base for their new household.[45] Because couples received land in their dowries, they settled near the brides' parents and often inherited the brides' natal homesteads.[46] João Coelho Duarte and his wife, for example, lived on her parent's farm after they married and eventually inherited the farm.[47]

The dowries of women of means involved more than the property, both real and symbolic, that women needed to set up their households. Because whom a daughter married carried important consequences for the whole family, fathers, mothers, and even brothers negotiated with prospective sons-in-law over the contents of the dowry. José Correa Penteado wrote in his will that "I married my daughter to Manoel Ferras de Campos to whom I promised 4,000 *cruzados* (1,600,000 *reis*) and eight slaves of which he is paid and satisfied and for which he has signed a receipt in my book [of accounts]."[48] Miguel Garcia Lumbria wrote in his will that his brother-in-law still owed him money, "money that he promised me for marrying his sister."[49]

Clearly it was the custom for a suitor to discuss not just marriage, but property with the fathers of young women. The comments of one father in his will suggest that it was unusual not to do so. He wrote that he married his daughter to José Mendes dos Santos "who asked for her without a dowry." In spite of this, the father gave him twelve slaves, a house in the town center, and a farm next to his own.[50] This statement implies that the father expected a prospective son-in-law to inquire about the dowry before committing himself to marriage. That this prospective son-in-law did not do so seems to have impressed his father-in-law, for he mentioned it in his will, but it did not alter the custom of granting dowries to daughters.

Dowries, with their symbolic and productive property, not only allowed a new couple to establish themselves, but reverberated through the bride's family. Dowries were intimately linked to inheritance, for although granted when a daughter married, they contained productive property that came from the community property of the parents to which the other brothers and sisters would have rights at the time of inheritance. Large dowries could reduce the prospective shares that siblings would receive; small dowries would increase them. Thus, the size of dowries affected all members of the family.

The custom of granting dowries came to Brazil from Europe where it appeared throughout the Mediterranean world.[51] In Italy the dowry was considered a daughter's share of the family property and took the place of an inheritance which was limited to male heirs.[52] In regions of France, Jean Yver shows how a practice known as *l'option* evolved whereby sons or daughters who had received dowries could opt to keep the dowry and not receive an inheritance or return the dowry and inherit with the other heirs.[53] In Portuguese inheritance law, dowries could not be larger than an equal share of the estate plus the free third (*terça*).[54] At inheritance, daughters and sons-in-law had to report the value of their dowries.[55] If that value was larger than an equal share, they were entitled to property from the free third. If the dowry plus the free third still exceeded an equal share, they returned the excess.[56]

Once married, a woman's dowry became part of the community property owned equally by husband and wife.[57] A wife legally owned half of all property acquired in the marriage and had specific rights to it set out in the law. A husband could not sell or alienate the lands which belonged to the couple without his wife's consent.[58] Similarly, a husband could not become the guarantor (*fiador*) of another's property without his wife's acquiescence.[59] If husbands gave away land or money without their wives' approval, those gifts were deducted from the husbands' share of the community property.[60]

While women legally owned half of the community property in marriage, in practice husbands managed it "with their consent." Judges referred to the husband as the *cabeça de casal* or the "head of the couple" who acted for the two in legal and business transactions.[61] Thus, when a wife's father or mother died, the judges who supervised inheritance often cited the husband as heir of the estate because he was the head of the marriage and thus represented the interests of his wife. For example, Salvador Martins Leme as "head of his wife Thomazia da Rocha Camargo" stated to a judge in 1799 that he received a slave, a horse, and a saddle as a dowry from his wife's parents and that since he was satisfied with the dowry, he did not wish to inherit from their estate.[62] Similarly, his brothers-in-law were considered "heirs" of the same estate as "heads" of their wives. Even though the inheritances involved were those of their wives, the judge paid them to the husbands, who would manage them as part of the community property.

Because husbands were legally responsible for the community property, the role that married women played in determining how to invest or to manage the community property was restricted to consulting, influencing, and approving their husbands' actions. The degree of such influence would obviously depend on individual personalities, but one might expect that during the early years of a marriage, given the young age of wives, women exercised little real influence over how their husbands managed the community property. Instead, the evidence implies that the real business partners were the wife's father and her husband. This relationship began when the prospective son-in-law first discussed the dowry with his father-in-law and developed into a complex business relationship after the celebration of the marriage vows.[63]

The close ties between father and son-in-law, and the consequent influence of the son-in-law within his wife's family, can be seen in the family of Antonio Correa de Lemos Leite, the highest ranking officer of the militia in Parnaíba in the late eighteenth century. According to the census of 1775, Antonio's son-in-law José lived with his young wife in a neighboring household. Two years later, Antonio acquired an appointment in the officer corps of the militia for his son-in-law. When Antonio died in 1782, his son-in-law served as the executor of the estate. Because of the dowry which his wife had received from her parents, they eventually inherited one-third of the original family farm. In 1798, Antonio's son-in-law appeared in the census as a captain in the local militia, a sugar planter, and an owner of ten slaves. In 1802, a notarial document refers to him as the "sergeant major," the highest rank obtainable in the provincial militia, and states that his farm "formerly belonged to [his father-in-law] Antonio Correa de Lemos Leite."[64] Thus José had virtually inherited his father's-in-law position in the community. His favored position within the family was largely due to the patronage, in the form of the dowry and military appointment, which he received from his father-in-law.[65] Similar cases can be reconstructed from family histories, a fact which suggests that the bonds between father and son-in-law were of enormous significance for the future of the family property.[66]

After their fathers died and when husbands absented themselves in the interior, married women became more active and influential in the management of the family property. When husbands left home to do business in the interior, their wives assumed the management of the family property. They became the heads of households and made many decisions concerning the future of the family. For example, Andreza Buena de Camargo lived alone for twenty-five years while her husband was in the interior. In 1775, she lived with her daughter Maria, then in her mid-twenties, and five slaves. They planted on lands belonging to Andreza's aunt, Maria Garcia.[67] When Andreza died in 1788, her husband had still not reappeared. In the inventory of her property, the judge responsible for inheritance matters (known as the *juiz de orfão* or orphans' judge because he monitored the management of the property of minors) wrote that her husband Lourenço was "away in the mines of Goiás, no one knows if he is alive or dead."[68] During those twenty-five years, Andreza was the *de facto* head of household. She managed the property and held full responsibility for the survival of her family.

Just as married women became the heads of their families in the absence of their husbands, so too did widows become responsible for their families after their husbands died.[69] For this reason, widows exercised more authority over, and responsibility for, family property than single or married women. Most of the women who appear in the historical record as buying and selling land, filing petitions, managing ranches and businesses, and serving as heads of households were widows. As widows, they held property in their own right, their share of the community property, which rarely could be taken from them. In addition, many held their children's inheritances until they came of age. Many widows served as executrices of their husbands' estates. Not only did they oversee the process of evaluating and dividing the property, but they had to collect the outstanding debts.

Widows who managed the property of their children had to consult the orphans' judge before selling, loaning, or encumbering this property; thus the judge became the ultimate arbitrator of what they might or might not do. Moreover, their responsibility for their children's inheritances could be taken away if they could not produce a guarantor who would make himself responsible for their actions. Nevertheless, because widows owned property and often supervised the property of their minor children, they had to interact with community institutions.[70]

As Table One makes clear, nearly all of the women of means who headed households in 1775, were widows.[71] These thirty-three widows owned 212 slaves or 18% of all the slaves in the county, they managed sixteen farms, and produced 600 bushels of corn, 60 bushels of beans, 1,560 pounds of cotton, 8 bushels of rice, and 83 quarts of rum. The richest and most powerful women in the community were widows, such as Anna Maria Xavier, who owned forty slaves, a farm, and a gold washing field. In 1786 she petitioned the Crown for a land grant on the site where she had ordered her slaves to destroy a runaway slave camp that had formed in the hills outside of Parnaíba.[72] Thomazia de Almeida, another powerful widow, owned a farm and twenty-two slaves. Her sons Antonio, João and Mathias, all soldiers who lived with her, owned ten more slaves. The family had a large herd of horses and cattle, and their farm produced 83 quarts of rum and 325 pounds of cotton.[73]

288   journal of social history

Table One
Female Heads of Households, 1775

Marital Status	N	%	Mean Age
Single	1	3%	53
Married (Spouse Absent)	3	8%	41
Widowed	33	89%	52
Total households	37	100%	49

Source: 1775 Census of Parnaíba.

Clearly, it was not an uncommon sight for townspeople to see widows, dressed in their traditional black, filing documents with the notary, discussing family inheritance matters with the orphans' judge, or directing the labor of free laborers and slaves on the family farm. But as the division of Antonio Francisco Lima's estate in 1758 makes clear, widows were not automatically granted the right to administer their minor children's property, a usual procedure with widowers.

When her husband died, Maria Dias Ferreira wanted to become the guardian of her children and manage her husband's share of the community property after his death. But her husband died intestate, i.e., without writing a will. Thus, she had not been designated by her husband as her children's guardian. The orphans' judge selected her brother, not her, as the guardian of the children. Maria petitioned the High Court of Rio de Janeiro and the Overseas Ministry in Lisbon to reverse the local orphans' judge's decision. While she waited for an answer, the judge in Parnaíba proceeded to order that all the property belonging to her children be auctioned in the public square and the monies deposited in the Orphans' Fund where it would be loaned out at interest until the children came of age. Maria managed to stall him by requesting that he wait until an answer came from Lisbon. The letter from Lisbon finally arrived, naming her the guardian of her children, provided that she did not remarry. After proposing her father as her guarantor (fiador),[74] Maria became her children's guardian and received their inheritances. Maria managed this property until her father, old and blind, decided he could no longer be responsible for his grandchildren's inheritances. He asked the judge to auction off the property and place it in the Orphans' Fund. Maria only managed to retain the property by producing another bondsman, her son-in-law, and this action again averted the auction. Thus for Maria to be given control over the family property, she had to have the permission of the local judge, which in this case required appealing the case to Lisbon. Moreover, she needed the support of her male kin, who agreed to make themselves liable for her actions.[75]

In Maria Dias Ferreira's tenure as guardian, which lasted almost twenty years, she gradually relinquished control over her children's inheritances. When her two daughters married, for example, their husbands approached the judge and asked for the inheritances due to their wives. Several years later, the judge declared the two oldest boys of age, and Maria, as required, paid them their inheritances. Thus, while Maria managed the community property that she and her late husband had accumulated, she gradually lost control over it as her children married or came of age. Under her tenure, half of the community property was transferred to the children through dowries and inheritances.[76]

The time when widows presided over the household was a time of transition as the family property slowly passed from one generation to the next. It was a time of dwindling resources.[77] Furthermore, boundaries between family and community eroded as outside authorities appeared to appraise, auction, and divide the property according to law. For all of these reasons, this stage in the family cycle was a potentially volatile time for inter-familial relations.

This stage also offers clues to what women thought about their role in the family and what they wanted for their children. Several widows ensured that the family farm would not be sold or divided after their deaths by transferring title to their share of the farm to individuals before they died. For example, when Gertrudes de Jesus sold her share of the farm, which consisted of half of the original farm plus two shares she had purchased from two of her daughters, to her son-in-law, José, she allowed her son-in-law to inherit virtually all of the family farm. Thirty years after Gertrudes' husband died, her son-in-law owned five-sevenths of the original farm. Thus Gertrudes prevented the division of the farm after her death. This kept the farm intact, and she favored her son-in-law's family. From later censuses, we know that his descendants owned more property and had higher social status than her other children.[78]

Izabel da Rocha do Canto also favored an heir by selling her share of the family farm to him. She sold that which she had received as her share of the community property in the division of her husband's estate, which amounted to half of the family farm, to her son Policarpo. She stated in her will that after they registered the sale with the local notary, she agreed that he could pay her less than the amount stated in the legal contract because of the "ruin" and "decay" of the property. Her son thus acquired half of the family farm for less than its assessed value in his father's estate inventory. Such an action ensured that he would eventually own the family farm.[79]

The actions of Gertrudes and Izabel suggest that they saw themselves as transitional figures. Rather than become matriarchs themselves, they chose to reinforce the power of a younger male. The question of who that new male family leader would be was an important one. Usually a father's extensive dealings with one son-in-law elevated that son-in-law to the position of heir apparent. When the position of the son-in-law had been well established before the patriarch's death, there would be little that the other sons and sons-in-law could do about it. But if a patriarch died before establishing a son-in-law, sons might try to position themselves as heirs apparent to their fathers. This was particularly true at the end of the eighteenth century when the lands traditionally given to the sons-in-law became more valuable with the spread of the sugar economy in São Paulo.

Power struggles often erupted during this time of the family cycle. Men in the family might challenge a widow's authority. Izabel da Rocha do Canto, who sold her share of the family farm to her son, may have been manipulated into doing it by her son. After her husband died, she became the guardian of her younger children, one of whom was Policarpo, aged thirteen. Only two years later, Policarpo betrothed himself, apparently without his mother's permission, so that

290   journal of social history

once married, the orphans' judge would declare him emancipated and therefore force his mother to pay him his inheritance from his father's estate. Izabel wrote to the judge: "I do not concur that he should be given his inheritance...because he has done this without informing me and because of his disobedience."[80] One month later, Policarpo married his fiancée. One year later, he received his inheritance. Several years later, his mother sold him her half of the family farm.

If power struggles erupted between men in the family who contended to become the next family leader, widows might become power brokers. Josepha Pais de Camargo presided over a particularly volatile time in the family's life history. When Josepha's husband died in 1793, she became the guardian of her five children and received their inheritances, promising to "manage them well," and to "feed and clothe" her children.[81] She gave as her guarantor Captain Vicente de Morais e Camargo. Three years later, Captain Vicente asked the orphans' judge to remove him from his position as guarantor saying that the property had "deteriorated" and that he did not wish to be made responsible for the losses suffered in the children's inheritances. Two weeks later, Josepha produced a new guarantor, her son-in-law, José Luis Alves. In the new agreement she remained in control of the inheritances of three children, while two were "emancipated"[82] by the orphans' judge and granted their inheritances.[83]

After making her son-in-law her guarantor, all of Josepha's sons but one left Parnaíba and moved into the frontier. Thus it would appear that Josepha had favored her son-in-law, and made him the new family leader. But in 1804, Josepha's son-in-law petitioned the judge asking that the farm be sold so that he could receive his share in cash. When asked of her opinion, Josepha complained that since she owned one-half of the farm, plus the share which she bought from her son Antonio, if it were sold she would be "dispossessed with no place to live."[84] She asked instead that José Luis be adjudicated the monetary value of his share so that the farm would remain intact. Dissatisfied with this turn of events, José Luis wrote to the Crown Magistrate in São Paulo arguing that since the farm had been greatly undervalued in its last appraisal, if he were given only the monetary value of his share, he would be denied his rightful inheritance by his mother-in-law. The Crown Magistrate appeared convinced by José Luis' letter but he did not authorize the sale of the farm.[85]

Eleven years later, when Josepha prepared her will, the conflict within the family comes into better focus. Josepha wrote that soon after José Luis married her daughter, she signed an agreement with him which stated that she would turn over the entire farm to him, including the slaves and sugar mill, on the condition that he would resolve several legal suits for her, and that he would support her and her younger children. But Josepha complained bitterly that his house became "opulent" while hers "deteriorated," that her slaves died while working for him, and that when her son Antonio returned from the frontier and saw how she had suffered, he fought with José Luis and forced him to leave the farm. Then Josepha stated that José Luis compelled her to sign a document which enumerated what she owed him (presumably his share of the farm), but that as far as she was concerned, she owed him nothing since she had "served him like a slave." Finally, Josepha left half of her free third (terça) to her son Antonio, stating that it be adjudicated in shares of the farm "so that he will have the largest share."[86]

Thus, in her will, Josepha tried to undo what she had done many years before. Perhaps she regretted the alienation of her sons, or perhaps she became a pawn of her son, Antonio, who resented his brother-in-law's position. By signing over her farm to her son-in-law many years before, she had favored him and had given him a strong position within the family. That action inadvertently began a long period of family conflict during which time she tried to regain her position of family leader. Her actions proved difficult to undo, however, for despite the statements in her will, four years after she died, her son Antonio appeared in the census living a marginal existence on a small farm with two slaves and a woman, perhaps his common-law wife, and two young children. His occupation was listed as a farmer and the farm produced only corn and beans for household consumption. José Luis and Rita, on the other hand, owned twenty slaves. Their farm produced rum in the sugar mill as well as corn and beans for household consumption. Thus despite his conflict with Josepha and Antonio, José Luis eventually inherited the family farm and became the dominant male of the next generation.[87]

Widowhood began a difficult time in women's lives. Quite apart from the emotional duress of losing their husbands, widows took on the responsibility of managing their own property and, if they were named guardians, that of their children as well. As widows women found themselves in a position of power in their families, but it was not the position once held by their husbands. Men in the community and even men in their own families might openly challenge their authority. A widow who wished to retain her independence had to maneuver skillfully between men who competed with each other and contended for her power. Regardless of how well a widow established herself in her family and community, her tenure came to an end with her death. The family cycle began again and men once more asserted their dominance over it.[88]

This article has explored women's relationships to family property in Santana de Parnaíba by examining women's legal rights to property and placing those rights within the context of the family cycle. This analysis shows that single women had little opportunity to exercise their rights to family property. Only rarely did single women achieve a measure of freedom brought about by the unencumbered inheritance of property. Married women co-owned the family property, but their husbands, unless absent, managed that property as the recognized head of household. Only widows could independently control the property which as women they legally owned. Although widows achieved a measure of autonomy denied to single and married women, law and custom nevertheless prevented them from assuming the rights granted to men. Moreover, widows presided over the transfer of property from one generation of men to the next. Property devolved through the family according to established legal principles and local custom, and women could not fundamentally alter that process. In a sense, widows received only the right to freely benefit from family property until it was inherited by younger men and women. Widows thus served as conduits for the mantle of authority as it passed from their husbands to their sons-in-law or occasionally sons.

The many similarities between Portuguese law and Roman law suggest that when the Portuguese legal code was written, the framers borrowed heavily from the Roman legal tradition. That tradition recognized women's rights to family

292   journal of social history

property. But the Roman legal tradition had an equally strong patriarchal cast which systematically denied women the independence and autonomy granted to adult males. This too is reflected in Portuguese law.

Colonial Brazilian society embodied the same contradiction between a woman's right to family property and a woman's lack of a public voice as in Roman society. Theoretically, given their legal rights to family property, women could have had great power in their families in ancient Rome and in colonial Brazil. Instead, women bowed to patriarchal authority in the family and the community. Although the family cycle in Santana de Parnaíba opened up small spaces for women when they might experience the independence and authority usually held by men, during those times women did not and could not fundamentally alter the patriarchal character of Brazilian colonial life. Why did patriarchal authority prove so durable given the tradition of female property ownership in colonial Brazil? Since women's rights to family property did not translate into private or public power, the ways in which patriarchal values were reinforced in family and community life may explain why women were not able to use their control over family property to assert themselves. Thus, further study of the cultural inheritance of patriarchy may well elucidate this puzzling contradiction between women's legal rights to property and their absence of a public voice in Latin and Latin American societies.

ENDNOTES:

The author wishes to thank Colin Wells and Susan Treggiari for their perceptive comments on an earlier draft of this article.

1.   Caroline Brettell, Men Who Migrate, Women Who Wait: Population and History in a Portuguese Parish (Princeton, 1986); Heath Dillard, Daughters of the Reconquest: Women in Castilian Town Society, 1100-1300 (Cambridge, 1984); Isabel Moll-Blanes, "Women and Property in Spain, from the 18th to the 20th Century," Paper Presented to the Social Science History Association, November 21-24, 1985, Chicago, Illinois; Edith Couturier, "Women in a Noble Family: The Mexican Counts of Regla, 1750-1830," in Latin American Women, pp. 129-149, ed. Asunción Lavrin (London, 1978); Muriel Nazzari, "Women, the Family and Property: The Decline of the Dowry in São Paulo, Brazil (1600-1870)" (Ph.D. dissertation, Yale University, 1986), and Asunción Lavrin and Edith Couturier, "Dowries and Wills: A View of Women's Socioeconomic Role in Colonial Guadalajara and Puebla, 1640-1790," Hispanic American Historical Review 59 (1979): 280-304 all document the extensive rights that women held to family property in Iberian and Latin American societies.

2.   This paradox has been highlighted in the recent studies of women and family life in antiquity. In Fathers and Daughters in Roman Society: Women and the Elite Family (Princeton, 1984), pp. 3-61, Judith Hallett questions why women had so few legal rights and such a limited public voice in Roman society, when they clearly wielded tremendous influence, especially within the family. This paradox is a recurrent theme in the work of other classicists; Suzanne Dixon reinforces the notion that the Roman mother was a powerful socializing force for men in Roman society, see The Roman Mother (London, 1988), while Jane F. Gardner in Women in Roman Law and Society (London, 1986) clearly delineates how Roman law limited the rights of women.

3.   See Harold J. Berman, Law and Revolution: The Formation of the Western Legal Tradition

(Cambridge, 1983) for a very interesting analysis of how Roman law, ecclesiastical canon law, and Germanic tribal customs combined in the eleventh century to create the western legal tradition.

4.   For an excellent review of the new studies of family life and demography which portray the uniqueness of the many regions of the Mediterranean and a critique of the limitations of the old view of the Mediterranean family "model," see David I. Kertzer and Caroline Brettell, "Advances in Italian and Iberian Family History," in *Family History at the Crossroads: A Journal of Family History Reader*, pp. 87-120, ed. Tamara Hareven and Andrejs Plakans (Princeton, 1987).

5.   The traditional view of the Mediterranean family is articulated in the work of John Campbell, *Honour, Family, and Patronage* (Oxford, 1964); John Peristiany, ed., *Honor and Shame: The Values of Mediterranean Society* (London, 1965); and John Peristiany, ed., *Mediterranean Family Structures* (Cambridge, 1976).

6.   Fiona Wilson is also intrigued by this paradox. See her analysis of women and property in nineteenth-century Peru: "Marriage, Property, and the Position of Women in the Peruvian Central Andes," in *Kinship Ideology and Practice in Latin America*, pp. 297-325, ed. Raymond T. Smith (Chapel Hill, 1984).

7.   The studies of women in Latin America by Silvia Arrom, "Marriage Patterns in Mexico City, 1811," *Journal of Family History* 3 (1978): 376-391, and *The Women of Mexico City, 1790-1857* (Stanford, 1985); Inga Clendinnen, "Yucatec Maya Women and the Spanish Conquest: Role and Ritual in Historical Reconstruction," *Journal of Social History* 15 (1982): 427-442; Ann Miriam Gallagher, "The Indian Nuns of Mexico City's Monasterio of Corpus Christi, 1724-1821," in *Latin American Women*, pp. 150-172; Sandra Lauderdale Graham, *House and Street: The Domestic World of Servants and Masters in Nineteenth-Century Rio de Janeiro* (Cambridge, 1988); Asunción Lavrin, "Women in Convents: Their Economic and Social Role in Colonial Mexico," in *Liberating Women's History*, pp. 250-277, ed. Bernice A. Carroll (Chicago, 1979); June Nash, "Aztec Women: The Transition from Status to Class in Empire and Colony," in *Women and Colonization: An Anthropological Perspective*, pp. 134-148, ed. Mona Etienne and Eleanor Leacock (New York, 1980); Susan Socolow, "Women and Crime: Buenos Aires, 1757-97," *Journal of Latin American Studies* 12 (1980): 39-54; Susan Soeiro, "The Social and Economic Role of the Convent: Women and Nuns in Colonial Bahia, 1677-1800," *Hispanic American Historical Review* 54 (1974): 209-232, and Wilson, "Marriage, Property, and the Position of Women," all make an enormous contribution to the history of women in the Latin American past.

8.   Among the many studies of elite family life in Latin America those by the following historians have established the basic contours: David A. Brading, *Miners and Merchants in Bourbon Mexico, 1763-1810* (Cambridge, 1971); Rae Flory and David Grant Smith, "Bahian Merchants and Planters in the Seventeenth and Early Eighteenth Centuries," *Hispanic American Historical Review* 58 (1978): 571-594; Doris Ladd, *The Mexican Nobility at Independence, 1780-1826* (Austin, 1976); Susan M. Socolow, *The Merchants of Buenos Aires: 1778-1820: Family and Commerce* (Cambridge, 1978); Elizabeth Anne Kuznesof, "The Role of the Merchants in the Economic Development of São Paulo, 1765-1850," *Hispanic American Historical Review* 60 (1980): 571-592; Richard Lindley, *Haciendas and Economic Development: Guadalajara, Mexico, at Independence* (Austin, 1983); John Kicza, *Colonial Entrepreneurs: Family and Business in Bourbon Mexico City* (Albuquerque, 1983); Diana Balmori, Stuart F. Voss, and Miles Wortman, *Notable Family Networks in Latin America* (Chicago, 1984); Linda Lewin, *Politics and Parentela in Paraíba: A Case Study of Family-Based Oligarchy in Brazil* (Princeton, 1987), and Darrell E. Levi, *The Prados of São Paulo Brazil: An Elite Family and Social Change, 1840-1930* (Athens, GA., 1987).

9.   Couturier, "Women in a Noble Family," Levi, *The Prados of São Paulo*, Nazzari, "Women, the Family and Property," and Wilson, "Marriage, Property, and the Position of Women," are some of the few studies that explore women in the context of their families in the Latin American past.

10. 1775 census of Santana de Parnaíba, Mapas de População, hereafter MP, Arquivo do Estado de São Paulo, hereafter AESP, 125-125.

294   journal of social history

11. This was not an inheritance from Roman law. In Roman society, women did not own half of the community property, only that which they had brought into the marriage as a dowry. Their husbands administered the dowry as they saw fit during their marriage, but had to return it when the marriage ended by death or divorce. See W.W. Buckland, *A Text-Book of Roman Law from Augustus to Justinian* (Cambridge, 1975), pp. 107-112, and Gardner, *Women in Roman Law and Society*.

12. This was an inheritance from Roman law. Daughters inherited on an equal basis with sons. See J.A. Crook, "Women in Roman Succession," in *The Family in Ancient Rome: New Perspectives*, ed. Beryl Rawson (Ithaca, 1986), p. 59.

13. The laws of property ownership in Portugal followed the principle of partible inheritance of family property and community property in marriage. These principles are clearly spelled out in the *Ordenações Filipinas* codified in 1603. These were the laws transferred to colonial Brazil.

14. *Ordenações Filipinas* (Lisbon, 1985; rpt. Rio de Janeiro: 1870), Liv. IV Tit. XLVI and XLVIII.

15. For an excellent overview of marriage in colonial Brazil, see Maria Beatriz Nizza da Silva, *Sistema de casamento no Brasil colonial* (São Paulo, 1984).

16. *Ordenações* Liv. IV, Tit. XLVII.

17. *Ordenações*, Liv. IV, Tit. C.

18. *Ordenações*, Liv. IV, Tit. XCVI.

19. *Ordenações*, Liv. IV, Tit. LXI.

20. *Ordenações*, Liv. IV, Tit. LXI, note 3 and Buckland, *A Text-Book of Roman Law*, p. 448. J.A. Crook suggests that the law evolved in Rome as a way to prevent husbands from compelling their wives to put up their own property as surety for their husbands' or husbands' colleagues' actions; see "Feminine Inadequacy and the Senatusconsultum Velleianum," in *The Family in Ancient Rome*, pp. 83-92.

21. *Ordenações*, Liv. IV, Tit. LXI. These exceptions are virtually identical to the exceptions in Roman law; see Buckland, *A Text-Book of Roman Law*, p. 449.

22. Thus an "orphan" was any heir who was a minor, not a child who had lost both parents, as in the meaning of orphan in contemporary English.

23. "Tutors" were an inheritance from Roman law. Children in Roman society who were not yet adults had tutors who administered their property, as did women. A father, as the head of the family served in this role, but in the event of his death, tutors were appointed for his children; Buckland, *A Text-Book of Roman Law*, p. 142.

24. *Ordenações*, Liv. IV, Tit. CII. In Roman law, women were not allowed to be tutors until A.D. 390 when mothers were allowed to assume this role, provided that they did not remarry and renounced their right to the Senatusconsultum Velleianum; see Buckland, *A Text-Book of Roman Law*, p. 150-151.

25. *Ordenações*, Liv. IV. Tit. CVII.

26. As family historians and anthropologists have shown, local custom often works against the principles set forth in law. This is well illustrated in John Cole and Eric Wolf's analysis of inheritance in two Italian communities in *The Hidden Frontier: Ecology and Ethnicity in an Alpine Valley* (New York, 1974), pp. 175-205. Dixon makes the same point in *The Roman Mother*, as does Gardner in *Women in Roman Law and Society*.

27. Nazzari, "Women, the Family and Property," pp. 68-123.

28. In Galicia and parts of Portugal, women also inherited the larger share of the family property; see Brettell and Kertzer, p. 97. Possibly the early settlers of São Paulo reproduced an inheritance custom from their homeland.

29. Metcalf, "Fathers and Sons." Muriel Nazzari's research on dowries granted in eighteenth-century São Paulo shows that women's shares of the family property decreased as families gave smaller dowries which did not greatly exceed the value of their sons' inheritances; see "Women, the Family and Property," pp. 171-235; In Portugal, Brettell finds that women were generally favored with bequests from the free third; see *Men who Migrate, Women Who Wait*.

30. The family cycle is a useful way to conceptualize how families change each generation. For a definition of the family cycle see Tamara Hareven, "The Family as Process: The Historical Study of the Family Cycle," *Journal of Social History* 7 (1974): 322-329. According to historical demographers, the changes in the family cycle structure the transfer of authority and property from one generation to the next. See Robert Wheaton, "Family and Kinship in Western Europe: The Problem of the Joint Family Household," *Journal of Interdisciplinary History* 5 (1975): 601-628; Lutz Berkner, "The Stem Family and the Developmental Cycle of the Peasant Household: An Eighteenth-Century Austrian Example," *American Historical Review* 77 (1972): 398-418.

31. Several scholars emphasize that the lives of women differed depending on their civil status. In colonial Mexico, Couturier shows how single women who inherited property and a family title did achieve autonomy and independence, as did widows who administered family property after the deaths of their husbands; see "Women in a Noble Family." A.J.R. Russell Wood distinguishes between single, widowed, and married women in "Female and Family in the Economy and Society of Colonial Brazil," in *Latin American Women*, pp. 60-100. However, his portrayals of these stages in a woman's life are stereotyped and do not bear up in empirical research. Wilson ("Marriage, Property, and the Position of Women") also investigates the different property rights of daughters, sisters, wives, and widows. Her conclusions about the rights of single, married, and widowed women to property are strikingly similar to mine.

32. The dependency of children within their families derived from the principle of *patria potestas* in Roman law. The head of the family (*paterfamilias*) held authority over all in his household until his death; this was known as the *patria potestas*. A son under the authority of his father (*filiusfamilias*) could not acquire income on his own, unless expressly emancipated from the *patria potestas*. See Rawson, *The Family in Ancient Rome*. In Portuguese law the idea of a *filhofamilias* remained; he was a son who had not yet married or reached his age of majority.

33. Brettell argues that in the Portuguese parish of Lanheses women were favored in the allocation of the free third so that they would remain at home and care for their ageing parents. Brettell, *Men Who Migrate, Women Who Wait*, p. 56.

34. Will, Luis Mendes Vieira, 1793, Inventários e Testamentos, hereafter IT, AESP, 565-88.

35. Ibid.

36. 1798 Census of Parnaíba, MP, AESP 127-127.

37. Petition of Anna Caetana de Jesus, 1816, Requerimentos, AESP 342-93A, 3-15.

38. 1820 census of Parnaíba, MP, AESP 133-133.

39. Inv. Paschoal Fernandes Sampayo, 1789, Inventários do Primeiro Oficio, hereafter IPO, 14,757, AESP 709-97. The *real*, plural *reis*, was the currency of colonial Brazil. 64,000 is written 64$000 in the documents; the "$" means thousand, hence 64 thousand *reis*. To simplify matters, I have omitted the "$" in the text. 64,000 *reis* was almost the value of the slave included in the dowry who was evaluated at 76,800 *reis*.

40. Inv. Maria Ribeira, 1755, IPO 13,884, AESP 627-15.

41. Inv. Lucrecia Leme de Barros, 1743, IPO 14,863, AESP 719-707.

42. Will, Francisco Bueno de Camargo, 1736, IT, AESP 514-37; will, José Correa Penteado, 1739, IPO 14,688, AESP 700-88.

43. Will, Manoel Correa Penteado, 1745, IPO 14,406, AESP 676-64.

44. Inv. Francisco Xavier de Assumpção, 1786, IPO 13,996, AESP 639-27.

45. Inv. Maria Pires de Barros, 1753, IPO 14,562, AESP 689-77; Inv. Catharina de Siqueira Leite, 1759, IPO 13,738, AESP 615-3.

46. See Metcalf, "Fathers and Sons."

47. Inv. Benta de Camargo Pais, 1799, IT 590-93.

48. Will, José Correa Penteado, 1739, IPO 14,688, AESP 700-88.

49. Will, Miguel Garcia Lumbria, 1745, IPO 14,499, AESP 683-71.

50. Will, Francisco Bueno Camargo, 1736, IT, AESP 514-37.

51. The custom of granting dowries can be found in Roman law, see Percy Ellwood Corbett, The Roman Law of Marriage (Darmstadt, 1979; rpt. Oxford, 1930), pp. 147-204, and Gardner, Women in Roman Law and Society pp. 97-116. The dowry survived throughout the Mediterranean, see Diane Owen Hughes, "From Brideprice to Dowry in Mediterranean Europe," Journal of Family History 3 (1978): 262-296. Dillard, Daughters of the Reconquest pp. 366-67, discusses of the importance of the dowry in medieval Spain, while Stanley Chojnacki in "Dowries and Kinsmen in Early Renaissance Venice," Journal of Interdisciplinary History 5 (1975): 571-600, studies who granted dowries to whom in Italy. Dowries were an important part of the family property throughout Latin America, see Lavrin and Couturier, "Dowries and Wills" and Nazzari, "Women, the Family and Property."

52. Brettell and Kertzer, pp. 99-101.

53. Jean Yver, Egalité entre héritiers et exclusion des enfants dotés (Paris, 1966).

54. The terça was that portion of an individual's estate that could be allocated freely by writing a will. It usually went towards masses, freedoms for slaves, or dowries for poor kin. The free third could be used to favor one heir over the others. If dowries were larger than an equal share (legitima) then the excess came out of the free third, regardless of any will.

55. Ordenações, Liv. IV, Tit. XCVII. This was known as collatio bonorum in Roman law. Children who had received dowries returned them and all brothers and sisters inherited equal shares. See Buckland, A Text-Book of Roman Law, p. 325.

56. See Metcalf, "Fathers and Sons" for an analysis of how the granting of dowries favored some heirs over others. In "Women, the Family and Property," Nazzari illustrates how the seventeenth-century families of São Paulo ignored the law and allowed daughters to keep their dowries in lieu of inheritances, regardless of how large the dowries were.

57. Since most marriages in Brazil were by a charter of halves and included a dowry, it is unclear what became of the dowry. It appears that in Parnaíba the dowry disappeared into the community property owned by the couple. Nazzari concludes the same in her study of the dowries of São Paulo, see "Women, the Family and Property," pp. 9-10.

58. Ordenações, Liv. IV, Tit. XLVIII.

59. Ordenações, Liv. IV, Tit. LX.

WOMEN AND MEANS   297

60. *Ordenações*, Liv. IV, Tit. LXIV.

61. The *cabeça de casal* was similar to the *paterfamilias* of Roman law, although the power of the *cabeça de casal* was not as great. See above, note 32.

62. Inv. Benta de Camargo Pais, 1799, IT, AESP 570-93.

63. In Roman society, women often remained under the authority (*patria potestas*) of their own fathers rather than passing to the *patria potestas* of their husbands, see Beryl Rawson, "The Roman Family," in *The Family in Ancient Rome*, p. 19 (see also note 32, above). Such a situation would create the basis for a strong relationship between fathers and sons-in-law.

64. Land Sale, 1802, Livros de Parnaíba 85, AESP 6065-17.

65. These events in this family history have been reconstructed from the following sources: census of 1775, MP, AESP 125-125; Inv. Mariana Dias, 1775, IT, AESP 553-76; Inv. Antonio Correa de Lemos Leite, 1782, IT, AESP 556-79; Martim Lopes Lobo de Saldanha to Antonio Correa de Lemos Leite, 28/July/1776, *Documentos interessantes para a história e costumes de São Paulo* (São Paulo, 1895-), 75: 180; Saldanha to Leite 22/June/1778, *Documentos interessantes*, 80: 163-164.

66. For a fuller discussion of this pattern in Parnaíba see Metcalf, "Fathers and Sons." The alliance between fathers and sons-in-law was a common pattern in Latin America. Among the many who have described this pattern are: Brading, *Miners and Merchants*, Socolow, *The Merchants of Buenos Aires*, and Kuznesof, "The Role of the Merchants."

67. 1775 census of Parnaíba, MP, AESP 125-125.

68. Inv. Andreza Buena, 1788, IPO 14,474, AESP 681-69.

69. Marriages could be dissolved by ecclesiastical divorce. Divorce existed throughout the colonial period in Brazil, although it was not very common; for example, only three divorce cases exist for eighteenth-century Parnaíba. Grounds for divorce were established according to canon law, see Nizza da Silva, *Sistema de casamento*, pp. 210-249. In Roman society, divorce was more common and well established rules existed in the law for the separation of property. See Gardner, *Women in Roman Law and Society*.

70. The position of widows in Parnaíba is similar to that in other areas of Latin America and Iberia. See Couturier, "The Mexican Counts of Regla," and Couturier, "Five Widows and their Families in Eighteenth-Century Puebla," Paper Presented to the Social Science History Association, November 21-24, 1985, Chicago, Illinois; and Dillard, *Daughters of the Reconquest*, pp. 96-126.

71. The large numbers of single women who headed households in São Paulo found by Elizabeth Kuznesof and others were not women of means. Rather they were poor women who survived in the towns and cities by working in a cottage textile industry, as domestic servants, and as prostitutes. See Kuznesof, "The Role of the Female-Headed Household in Brazilian Modernization: 1765-1836," *Journal of Social History* 13 (1980): 589-613, Eni de Mesquita, *As mulheres o poder e a família: São Paulo, século XIX* (São Paulo, 1989), and Maria Odila Leite da Silva Dias, *Quotidiano e poder em São Paulo no século XIX* (São Paulo, 1984).

72. Household of Anna Maria Xavier, 1775, MP, AESP 125-125; Land Grant Petition, 1786, Requerimentos para Sesmarias, 82-4-30, AESP 325; Land Grant, 1786, Patentes e Sesmarias, AESP 22:111.

73. Household of Thomazia de Almeida, 1775, MP, AESP 125-125.

74. The *fiador* was liable for any loss; hence if Maria mismanaged the property, her father would be required to make up the difference.

75. Inv. Antonio Francisco Lima, 1758, IT, AESP 535-58.

76. Ibid.

77. Dillard also notes that widowhood was a time of dwindling resources as the community property was divided among the heirs. See *Daughters of the Reconquest*, p. 100.

78. Gertrudes' grandson, son of her son-in-law José, owned twenty four slaves in 1820 and planted sugar, cotton, and rice, while her son Cosme, namesake of her husband, owned no slaves in 1820 and worked as a scribe. Inv. Cosme Ferreira de Mereilles, 1760, IPO 14,789, AESP 711-99; Inv. José Pedrozo de Navarros, 1794, IPO 14,726, AESP 707-95; Land Sale, 1790, Livros de Parnaíba, 56: 45-46, AESP 6061-13; and six households from the 1767, 1775, 1798, and 1820 censuses, MP, AESP 125-125, 127-127, 133-133.

79. Will, Izabel da Rocha do Canto, 1775, IPO 15,204, AESP 536-137.

80. Inv. Balthezar Rodrigues Fam, 1758, IT, AESP 536-59.

81. Inv. Ignacio de Morais e Siqueira, 1793, IT, AESP 563-86.

82. "Emancipated" was the term used to designate an heir who had come of age. In this case, one son had reached the age of majority (25 years) while a daughter had come of legal age because she had married.

83. Inv. Ignacio de Morais e Siqueira, 1793, IT, AESP 563-86.

84. Ibid.

85. Ibid.

86. Will, Josepha Pais de Camargo, 1815, IT, AESP 571-86.

87. Households of Antonio de Morais and José Luis Alves, 1820, MP, AESP 133-133.

88. Wilson makes similar observations on the roles of widows in nineteenth-century Peru, see "Marriage, Property, and the Position of Women."

9

Ownership and Obligation: Inheritance and Patriarchal Households in Connecticut, 1750–1820

Toby L. Ditz

THE lively debate about the texture of community life in the early American North still bears the impress of an older, now-frayed consensus. Louis Hartz's liberals and Frederick Jackson Turner's democratic frontiersmen, the lucky heirs to a seventeenth-century natural rights tradition and America's material riches, created a middle-class society, at once egalitarian and individualist.[1] This image has its counterpart in the domain of family life and property relations. Freed by American abundance to stand alone, farmers confined their loyalties to their immediate families, maintaining only loose ties with kin and neighbors outside their households. "Possessive individualism" in public life was yoked to a conjugal or nuclear family orientation in domestic life. America's open environment also diminished the importance of inheritance. Cheap land and opportunities for emigration severed the close connection between family property and the social standing of new generations.[2]

In reaction to this familiar portrait, scholars have recently provided useful alternatives on at least two fronts. Several have stressed regional

[1] Richard D. Brown, "Modernization and the Modern Personality in Early America, 1600-1865: A Sketch of a Synthesis," *Journal of Interdisciplinary History*. II (1972), 201-228; Charles S. Grant, *Democracy in the Connecticut Frontier Town of Kent* (New York, 1961), 31-54; Louis Hartz, *The Liberal Tradition in America: An Interpretation of American Political Thought since the Revolution* (New York, 1955).

[2] James T. Lemon, "Comment on James A. Henretta's 'Families and Farms: Mentalité in Pre-Industrial America'," *William and Mary Quarterly*. 3d Ser., XXXVII (1980), 689, 693-695; Jackson Turner Main, *The Social Structure of Revolutionary America* (Princeton, N.J., 1965), 219-220; Stephanie Grauman Wolf, *Urban Village: Population. Community. and Family Structure in Germantown. Pennsylvania. 1683-1800* (Princeton, N.J., 1976), 307-310, 315-323.

diversity and uneven development. They have identified regions that had different degrees and kinds of involvement in the Atlantic economy and that promoted distinctive patterns of social life and culture. They reject the image of a homogeneously liberal, individualist, or entrepreneurial culture on the reasonable grounds that such homogeneity is characteristic only of more fully integrated market societies and nation-states. Their works, taken together, suggest a collection of interrelated but distinctive part-societies taking shape within the ambit of an imperial system and developing Atlantic economy.[3]

Second, historians have begun to use the concept "household patriarchy" to describe community organization in the eighteenth century, especially in New England. Household patriarchy refers to both internal and external aspects of domestic organization. It describes authority relations in which heads, and not others within households, have the formal right to make final decisions about internal matters. Patriarchal household heads speak for their dependents in dealings with the larger world. The civic status of household dependents is an indirect or secondary one; the community reaches them primarily through the actions and voices of the heads.[4]

This notion of communities based on patriarchal households provides a coherent picture of the main lines of power and authority in regions where family farms predominated during the colonial period, particularly in New England, where congregational forms of worship and strong townships reinforced an economy based on household labor. Colonial New England's towns drew a bright line between propertied heads of households and everyone else. Above that line, independent proprietorship admitted most white men into a community of persons who, like themselves, were empowered to participate fully in civil affairs. Complex distinctions based on moral standing, age, and density of local kin networks as well as wealth marked off "better sorts" from others, informally defining those eligible for positions of leadership—selectmen, deacons, and other local notables. Nevertheless, independent proprietorship or, in the language of republi-

---

[3] Jack P. Greene and J. R. Pole, "Reconstructing British-American Colonial History: An Introduction," in Greene and Pole, eds., *Colonial British America: Essays in the New History of the Early Modern Era* (Baltimore, 1984), 11-14; James T. Lemon, "Spatial Order: Households in Local Communities and Regions," *ibid.*, 86-122; John J. McCusker and Russell R. Menard, *The Economy of British America, 1607-1789* (Chapel Hill, N.C., 1985).

[4] On household patriarchy in 17th-century England see Lawrence Stone, *The Family, Sex, and Marriage in England, 1500-1800* (New York, 1977), and in America see Nancy R. Folbre, "The Wealth of Patriarchs: Deerfield, Massachusetts, 1760-1840," *JIH*, XVI (1985), 183-197, and Mary P. Ryan, *Cradle of the Middle Class: The Family in Oneida County, New York, 1790-1865* (Cambridge, 1981), 22-25, 31-35. For a general discussion see Jacques Donzelot, *The Policing of Families*, trans. Robert Hurley (New York, 1979), 48-52.

canism, the possession of a "competence" established a rough equality among household heads.[5]

The independence and civic standing of men in family-farm areas also rested on the capacity to marshal the labor of women, children, servants, and occasionally slaves. The status of independent proprietor thus entailed its complement, the status of household dependent: a person who lacked the formal capacity to participate in public life and who was subject to the authority of household heads. Unmarried persons, even as adults, were in principle supposed to remain under the jurisdiction of their fathers or masters,[6] and the system of poor relief also placed poor and "incompetent" persons who had no kin under the jurisdiction of household heads. Such persons were, in theory, servants subject to the authority of a master.[7] The tendency to segregate all persons into two categories—propertied household head or household dependent—partly explains the difficulties created for colonials by the growing numbers of "strolling poor," propertyless adults under no one's jurisdiction. Such persons were frightening anomalies—free, but lacking the property that admitted them as equals into the community of men capable of governing themselves.[8]

The present analysis puts households at the center of community life and highlights the often dense and complex ties among kin and neighbors. Yet its implications for family property relations are not yet fully worked out. Historians who write in an anti-Hartzian spirit, whether or not they avail themselves of the notion of patriarchal families—and many do—usually argue that American yeomen adhered to a patrilineal family ideal: conservation of ancestral homesteads and continuation of their family names on local land were paramount goals.[9] This interpretation stresses

[5] Edward M. Cook, Jr., *The Fathers of the Towns: Leadership and Community Structure in Eighteenth-Century New England* (Baltimore, 1976), 81-94; Bruce C. Daniels, *The Connecticut Town: Growth and Development, 1635-1790* (Middletown, Conn., 1979), 119-139; Christopher M. Jedrey, *The World of John Cleaveland: Family and Community in Eighteenth-Century New England* (New York, 1979), 63-65; Jackson Turner Main, *Society and Economy in Colonial Connecticut* (Princeton, N.J., 1985), 30-31, 34, 52-56, 137-151; Michael Merrill, "Cash Is Good to Eat: Self-Sufficiency and Exchange in the Rural Economy of the United States," *Radical History Review*, No. 3 (1977), 64-65; Michael Zuckerman, *Peaceable Kingdoms: New England Towns in the Eighteenth Century* (New York, 1970), 187-219.

[6] Hence the sometimes outmoded laws forbidding unmarried adults to set up housekeeping without the permission of town fathers (Connecticut General Assembly, *Acts and Laws . . . of the State of Connecticut in America* [Hartford, Conn., 1796], 293).

[7] *Ibid.*, 232-236; David J. Rothman, *The Discovery of the Asylum: Social Order and Disorder in the New Republic* (Boston, 1971), 3-56.

[8] Douglas Lamar Jones, "The Strolling Poor: Transiency in Eighteenth-Century Massachusetts," *Journal of Social History*, VIII (1975), 28-54.

[9] Jedrey, *World of John Cleaveland*, 78-79; James A. Henretta, "Families and Farms: *Mentalité* in Pre-Industrial America," *WMQ*, 3d Ser., XXXV (1978), 22, 24-26; John J. Waters, "Patrimony, Succession, and Social Stability: Guilford, Connecticut in the Eighteenth Century," *Perspectives in American History*, X (1976), 139, 149-150, 159-160, and "Family, Inheritance, and Migration in

the importance of inheritance in family-farm areas, but, as will be argued, the emphasis on the preservation of family estates misconstrues the inheritance strategies of family farmers in several fundamental respects.

The first part of this essay examines inheritance practices in late colonial Connecticut. In line with revisionist thinking and previous studies of inheritance, it contends that Hartzian imagery inadequately describes the colonial inheritance practices outlined in this study. But although the practices found here reinforced patriarchal household organization, they did not display a lineal orientation toward property. The essay then explores the impact of commercialization on inheritance. It shows a dramatically different pattern of inheritance emerging in one highly commercialized river-valley town by the early nineteenth century. Inheritance practices became more egalitarian and displayed an individualist orientation toward the possession and use of property. Their logic was no longer compatible with patriarchal households; the connection between inheritance of family property and life chances had weakened. In this setting, but only in this setting, Hartzian imagery holds true.

The essay draws on data from a larger study that compares inheritance practices in four towns located in the upland and interior of eastern Connecticut with those in Wethersfield, a minor port town on the Connecticut River just below Hartford. By avoiding some of the drawbacks of community studies, the comparative strategy provides a better foundation for generalizing about rural towns. It also allows one to probe for links between commercialization, inheritance, and related aspects of family life.

The towns were chosen because they represent well the commonalities and contrasts between Connecticut's valley and upland areas. The valley and the uplands did have much in common: family farming dominated agriculture in both areas, and their development took place within the common limits established by Connecticut's courts and legislature. But they differed in other important ways. As Darrett B. Rutman has argued, early American communities varied in the extent to which they developed outward linkages, offering "a continuum extending from the near self-contained to the fully integrated."[10] During the late eighteenth and early nineteenth centuries the Connecticut Valley was undergoing more rapid commercialization than the uplands. Generally speaking, valley towns were distinguished from upland communities by their more direct and sustained participation in the Atlantic economy and in provincial politics and culture. On Rutman's continuum, the valley was a more fully integrated area; the upland, closer to the self-contained.

Benefiting from its rich alluvial land, Wethersfield, incorporated in

Colonial New England: The Evidence from Guilford, Connecticut," *WMQ*, 3d Ser., XXXIX (1982), 82-86.

[10] Rutman, "Assessing the Little Communities of Early America," *WMQ*, 3d Ser., XLIII (1986), 177.

1635, was the largest and most densely settled of Connecticut's nonurban towns.[11] The four upland towns of Bolton, Coventry, Union, and Willington (as their boundaries were defined in 1753), located in what is now Tolland County, were incorporated between 1712 and 1734 when Anglo-Americans began leaving the valley and coastal areas to settle the eastern interior.[12] These towns had more rugged terrain and less fertile soil than Wethersfield[13] and sustained thinner, though growing, populations.[14]

Although the agriculture of Wethersfield and the upland rested on diversified family farming, their economies differed in other respects. Wethersfield's agriculture was rapidly becoming commercialized in the period 1750 to 1820. The town's soil, like much valley and coastal land, was well suited to food crops, and Wethersfield's farmers worked their land more intensively than did their upland neighbors. By the late eighteenth century, they concentrated, with increasing emphasis, on market gardening, becoming noted for their onion fields. Wethersfield remained a leading market-gardening town throughout the first half of the nineteenth century.[15]

Wethersfield's economy and occupational structure were more diverse than those of the upland towns. Some families participated in interregional and export trade throughout the eighteenth century, building and owning

[11] Daniels notes that Wethersfield was the largest "secondary center" on the Connecticut River (*Connecticut Town.* 152). He uses the term to distinguish agricultural communities that also served as secondary ports or significant market centers from rural towns without these functions and from urban centers (*ibid.*, 146-152).

[12] Because upland towns were smaller than their valley counterparts, I had to choose several in order to generate enough probated estates to make the comparison. My strategy was to select a cluster of towns that represented a range of conditions typical of the eastern upland.

[13] Classifying Connecticut towns by soil type and topography, Daniels has created a productivity index for each town. Wethersfield rates a highest ranking of "8," while Coventry gets a "3," Bolton, a "2," and Willington and Union each a "1." Daniels, *Connecticut Town.* 186-190.

[14] In 1774 Wethersfield had a population of 3,489 and a density of over 85 persons per square mile. Its density rose to over 106 persons per square mile by 1820. Union, the smallest upland town, had a population of 514 and a density of 17.31 in 1774; Coventry, the largest, had a population of 2,056 and a density of 45.37 in 1774. Although all the upland towns grew faster than Wethersfield after the Revolution, none had a population even half as dense as Wethersfield's in 1820. Evarts B. Greene and Virginia D. Harrington, *American Population before the Federal Census of 1790* (New York, 1932), 58-60; U.S. Bureau of the Census, 4th Census, *Population Schedules for the Year 1820 in the State of Connecticut* (Washington, D.C., 1821), Vol. I (Hartford County), Vol. VIII (Tolland County). Figures on densities are derived from Cook, *Fathers of the Towns.* 199-212, app. 2.

[15] Connecticut, Office of the Secretary of State, *Statistics of the Condition and Products of Certain Branches of Industry in Connecticut. for the Year Ending October 1. 1845 . . .* (Hartford, Conn., 1846); John C. Pease and John M. Niles, *A Gazetteer of the States of Connecticut and Rhode Island* (Hartford, Conn., 1819), 89; Howard S. Russell, *A Long. Deep Furrow: Three Centuries of Farming in New England* (Hanover, N.H., 1976), 374; Henry Reed Stiles and Sherman Wolcott Adams, *The History of Ancient Wethersfield. Connecticut: Comprising the Present Towns of Wethersfield. Rocky Hill. and Newington* (New York, 1904), I, 174, 615.

ships that they loaded with agricultural cargoes bound primarily for the West Indies.[16] Shipping brought in its wake artisanal services devoted to processing agricultural products for export.[17] In Wethersfield's case, as in many others, a comparatively inegalitarian distribution of wealth accompanied its increasingly diverse and commercial economy: it had more landless and near-landless men, who supported themselves as mariners and casual laborers; it also had a larger proportion of wealthy families than did most rural Connecticut towns.[18]

Residents of the four upland towns were much more reliant on farming in the eighteenth century; these communities supported the usual complement of artisans, but artisans were largely part-time farmer-craftsmen who served the needs of the local farm population.[19] Upland farmers practiced the extensive agriculture typical of much of New England. Like their neighbors elsewhere in Tolland County, they devoted more of their land to pasturage than did valley farmers, relying more heavily on dairying and livestock to wrest surpluses from their unyielding soil.[20] Although all the towns sold some goods on extralocal markets, levels of agricultural specialization were low, and none of the towns participated directly in export trade or served as market centers for other towns.[21] To this extent their involvement in the Atlantic world was indirect and attenuated.[22]

[16] Stiles and Adams, *Ancient Wethersfield*, I, 541, 545-556, 555-595.
[17] Daniels, *Connecticut Town*, 194-195; Grace Pierpoint Fuller, "An Introduction to the History of Connecticut as a Manufacturing State," *Smith College Studies in History*, I (1915), 10; Pease and Niles, *Gazetteer*, 89-90, 291-292, 300-301, 303.
[18] Main, *Social Structure*, 34n: in this early work Main classified Wethersfield as a typical commercial agriculture town partly because it had the comparatively high average wealth, concentration of wealth, and degree of occupational specialization that he was then using to distinguish commercial from subsistence-plus agricultural towns. See also Main, *Society in Connecticut*, 132-135.
[19] Daniels, *Connecticut Town*, 194-195, app. 8. Daniels finds that the number of artisans in these towns (as in most other Connecticut communities) was very closely correlated with the towns' population ranking relative to all other towns in the colony.
[20] Percy Wells Bidwell and John I. Falconer, *History of Agriculture in the Northern United States, 1620-1860* (New York, 1941 [orig. publ. Washington, D.C., 1925]), 119-120; Pease and Niles, *Gazetteer*, 291-292, 300-303; Max George Schumacher, *The Northern Farmer and His Markets during the Late Colonial Period* (New York, 1975), 21-25. In Willington and Union substantial effort also went into lumbering.
[21] Daniels, *Connecticut Town*, 145. Cook has created an index of "commercialization" based on each town's share of its colony's taxes (for the year 1774 in Connecticut) divided by the town's total acreage. This is probably more properly an index of productivity than of commercialization. Taken together, population densities and the index indicate that Coventry was a relatively prosperous country town, while the other communities were less productive: Cook's rankings of the upland towns range from Coventry's .724 to Willington's .427. Wethersfield gets a ranking of 1.301. Cook, *Fathers of the Towns*, 79-80, 200-201. See Lemon, "Spatial Order," in Greene and Pole, eds., *Colonial British America*, 108-110.
[22] Depending on the system of classification one uses, the upland towns were typical "country towns" or "subsistence-plus" towns. Daniels, *Connecticut Town*; Main, *Social Structure*; Toby L. Ditz, *Property and Kinship: Inheritance in Early Connecticut, 1750-1820* (Princeton, N.J., 1986), 11-13.

Growing populations and easily exhausted soils in the upland eventually encouraged experimentation with commercially oriented nonagricultural enterprises. By the 1820s, firms manufacturing textiles, glass, paper, and other goods for export and regional trade appeared in all the upland towns except Union. Usually short-lived and small, these businesses had not yet reduced significantly the uplanders' dependence on land. But they were the beginnings of a trend; manufactures would play a steadily increasing role in the economies of the upland communities throughout the antebellum era, accounting for between 43 and 77 percent of the value of all goods produced there by 1845. In contrast, Wethersfield remained much more reliant on agriculture and the processing of agricultural goods: nonagricultural goods amounted to only 27 percent of Wethersfield's total output in 1845.[23]

The study includes all property holders who died in the selected towns and whose estates were probated in the years 1753-1755, 1772-1774, and 1820-1821—186 estates in all. The population includes both testate and intestate property holders, and those with landless as well as landed estates. Unlike local studies that follow a selected set of families through time, the data are not limited to families that persisted over generations.[24] The analysis rests on lifetime transfers, as recorded in deeds or mentioned in wills, as well as on postmortem transfers.[25]

The great majority of property holders whose estates entered probate in the colonial era were married fathers (75 percent, n = 119); most of them were farmers or farmer-craftsmen who had enough land or other produc-

[23] In 1820 Coventry had two paper mills, a glass company, a carding machine shop, and a cotton mill. Bolton/Vernon, which would soon become a leading textile center, already had three textile mills; Willington, a glass company and woolen mill. J. R. Cole, *History of Tolland County. Connecticut* . . . (New York, 1888); Fuller, "Manufacturing State," *Smith Coll. Studies in Hist..* I (1915); Pease and Niles, *Gazetteer.* 89-90, 291-292, 300-301. For the value of nonagricultural goods in the upland towns and Wethersfield see Connecticut, *Condition of Industry in 1845.*

[24] The study does exclude families who distributed their property informally. Others have estimated that unprobated populations had less wealth, fewer debts, and fewer kin than did probates. See Bruce C. Daniels, "Money-Value Definitions of Economic Classes in Colonial Connecticut, 1770-1776," *Histoire Sociale/Social History.* VIII (1974), 347; Alice Hanson Jones, "Wealth Estimates for the New England Colonies about 1770," *Journal of Economic History.* XXXII (1972), 115-118; Main, *Society in Connecticut.* 9-10, 17-18, 45-49, 60-61 (reporting, for Connecticut, less wealth bias than others have found or estimated); and Daniel Scott Smith, "Underregistration and Bias in Probate Records: An Analysis of Data from Eighteenth-Century Hingham, Massachusetts," *WMQ.* 3d Ser., XXXII (1975), 104.

[25] Overall, 48% of the probate population made wills, and 32% passed on property to heirs during their lifetimes. Some intestate property owners had transferred property to heirs during their lifetimes; they should be considered informally testate. Fifty-nine percent of the probate population used wills or made lifetime transfers or did both. These percentages were considerably higher for landowners; see below, n. 40.

tive property during their lifetimes to provide for their household dependents without having to rent land or work for wages.[26] Their inventories suggest that the handful of ministers, merchants, and former sea captains among them, with one exception, combined their calling with farming. In short, although the probate population included a few local notables, men of the "middling sort" dominated. By the early nineteenth century, the population was more diverse. Fathers were now only a bare majority (55 percent, n = 67); both women and single men appeared in increasing numbers.[27]

The owners of probated estates in Wethersfield and the upland were, at any given time, quite similar with respect to sex, marital status, family responsibilities, and rates of testacy. They differed significantly only with respect to wealth, a difference consistent with the contrast between the upland and river-valley economies of these communities: Wethersfield property holders were, on average, wealthier than their upland counterparts and their wealth was distributed more unevenly in each time period. The difference was particularly striking in the 1820s, chiefly because a higher proportion of Wethersfield's probated estate holders were near-propertyless men.[28]

THE COLONIAL ERA

Whenever the social standing of the next generation depended heavily on inheritance, independent proprietors faced a dilemma. The desire to see all children well settled encouraged division and dispersion of parental estates. But a family's present and future well-being also depended on the continued productivity of the working farm or other enterprise. This tension between "unity and provision" generated strategies for preserving family property that broadly resembled those of small and middling

[26] Eighty percent of the colonial married men (n = 89) died owning at least 40 acres or other productive property such as a shop and craftsman's tools (or had given such land or other productive property to heirs during their lifetimes). For estimates of the acreage necessary for subsistence and "comfortable" family farms in late colonial New England see Clarence H. Danhoff, *Change in Agriculture: The Northern United States. 1820-1870* (Cambridge, Mass., 1969), 136-138; Main, *Society in Connecticut.* 125, 140-142, 163, 200-210, 233-234; and Darrett B. Rutman, "People in Process: The New Hampshire Towns of the Eighteenth Century," in Tamara K. Hareven, ed., *Family and Kin in American Urban Communities. 1700-1930* (New York, 1977), 27-28.

[27] Women made up 22% and childless men another 22% of the probate population in 1820 and 1821 (n = 67). In the colonial era, women were only 16% of the probate population; childless men were only 9% (n = 119).

[28] In the 1820s, 33% of all probates in Wethersfield (n = 36) were adult men who had fewer than 20 acres and no other significant productive property to pass on to heirs. Only 13% of the upland probates fell into this category (n = 31). The contrast is muted, although it does not disappear, when one considers only fathers. Ditz, *Property and Kinship.* 34-35, 173-176, 177-189, contains a detailed profile of the probate population.

property holders in Europe.[29] First, household heads used their wills to limit the number of children or siblings who inherited ownership of their main estates. Second, they created shared rights, giving several heirs simultaneous claims in the same property. Heirs who received the bulk of the family estate did not possess exclusive rights to use it or dispose of its revenues, and along with their inheritance came legally binding obligations to others.

The logic of the Hartzian position is that special American conditions diminished, even eliminated, this tension between unity and provision. Comparatively free from material scarcity, and aware that their children's social fates did not depend so heavily on inheritance, American parents could give free rein to the dictates of affection and pursue egalitarian inheritance practices, launching each of their children into the world with the aid of small but equal inheritances or with intangibles such as skills and influence. By the same token, they did not need to saddle their heirs with the duties and obligations that were the signs of mutual dependence on parental property; heirs got property that was exclusively their own. Nor, in the Hartzian perspective, were shared rights compatible with the individualist and entrepreneurial orientations of American families. Property arrangements imposing legally binding obligations on heirs and curtailing their ability to manage and to dispose of property as they chose were in conflict with such values.[30]

In the late colonial era, upland and valley estate holders used similar inheritance strategies that had two main features, neither of which fits Hartzian logic. First, they practiced extensive partitioning but stopped well short of egalitarian share-and-share-alike inheritance practices. They intended to ensure that family property would securely establish at least one heir as an independent proprietor. Second, estate owners created shared rights in property. Their practices established legally enforceable obligations between parents and children (both minors and adults) and among siblings and other kin.

Equality and Inequality. Connecticut's colonial intestacy statute provided that daughters and sons were to receive equal shares of their parents' estates, with the exception of a double portion for eldest sons. If a decedent had no children, sisters and brothers inherited equally. As in other English colonies, Connecticut property owners, unless they were

[29] Excellent general statements of the unity-and-provision problem can be found in William J. Goode, "Family and Mobility," in Reinhard Bendix and Seymour Martin Lipset, eds., *Class. Status. and Power: Social Stratification in Comparative Perspective*, 2d ed. (New York, 1966), 592; Jack Goody, "Introduction," in Goody, Joan Thirsk, and E. P. Thompson, eds., *Family and Inheritance: Rural Society in Western Europe. 1200-1800* (Cambridge, 1976), 1; H. J. Habakkuk, "Family Structure and Economic Change in Nineteenth-Century Europe," *Jour. Econ. Hist.,* XV (1955), 1.

[30] Lemon, "Comment," *WMQ.* 3d Ser., XXXVII (1980), 693-695; Wolf, *Urban Village.* 307-310, 315-323.

married women, could bypass these rules by leaving wills or by disposing of their property before death.[31]

As American Revolutionaries debated the proper social foundations for their new republic, they reformed their inheritance laws. Although limited in practical effect, these reforms resonated with symbolic meaning. Condemning the dynastic inheritance practices of landed aristocracies and wishing to protect the new nation against the corrupting effects of a "monied aristocracy," legislators abolished primogeniture and reduced the effectiveness of entails wherever colonial assemblies had not already done so.[32] Connecticut's intestacy statute had always been comparatively egalitarian, but the new state legislators joined in the spirit of reform mainly by eliminating the double share for eldest sons.[33]

A few men endorsed impartibility and, with it, dynastic inheritance policies. In colonial Connecticut, Ezra Stiles recorded the advice of a resident of Stonington, Thomas Chesebrough, in what amounts to the classic rationale for impartibility: "keep your Estate in one Hand; never divide it or cut off any, especially Lands. . . . And by this Means with Frugality & Industry, the Estate will increase vastly in a few descents. 'Tis not good to be upon a Level, or under the Foot of every Scoundrel."[34] Here Chesebrough yoked impartibility to the goals of accumulation and attainment of family rank and distinction. Although dynastic inheritance practices are usually associated with securely established landed elites, the passage reminds us that they were also sometimes characteristic of people of middling estate who hoped to attain elite status through intergenerational accumulation.[35] "Frugality & Industry," coupled with a judicious, if seemingly harsh, inheritance policy, could lead to the desired social rank in time.[36]

[31] Acts and Laws . . . of His Majesty's English Colony of Connecticut in New England in America (New London, Conn., 1750), 49-54; Conn. General Assembly, Acts and Laws (1796), 163-172. See also Charles M. Andrews, The Connecticut Intestacy Law (New Haven, Conn., 1933), and George L. Haskins, "The Beginnings of Partible Inheritance in the American Colonies," Yale Law Review. LI (1942), 1280-1315. In principle, married men could not override their wives' dower right to a life-estate in one-third of their husbands' land.

[32] Stanley N. Katz, "Republicanism and the Law of Inheritance in the American Revolutionary Era," Michigan Law Review. LXXVI (1977), 1-29.

[33] They also modified the effect of entails and similar transfers. Connecticut General Assembly, The Public Statute Laws of the State of Connecticut. Revised 1821 (Hartford, 1821), 199-213, 301, 310; Zephaniah Swift, A System of the Laws of the State of Connecticut. 2 vols. (Windham, Conn., 1795-1796), I, 247-250, 267.

[34] Thomas Chesebrough, Memoir, in Franklin Bowditch Dexter, ed., Extracts from the Itineraries and Other Miscellanies of Ezra Stiles. D.D.. LL.D.. 1755-1794. with a Selection from His Correspondence (New Haven, Conn., 1916), I.

[35] See, for example, Ralph E. Giesey, "Rules of Inheritance and Strategies of Mobility in Prerevolutionary France," American Historical Review. LXXXII (1977), 271-289.

[36] Perhaps Chesebrough found it easier than most to dispense harsh advice because he was a bachelor who never had to balance the desire for accumulation against the wish to provide for all children. His advice also has a manipulative cast,

TABLE I
INHERITANCE OF REAL PROPERTY BY THE CHILDREN OF LANDHOLDERS

	All Children N	Do Inherit %	Sons N	Do Not Inherit %	Dtrs. N	Do Not Inherit %
1750s						
Wethersfield	131	76	62	15	69	33
Upland	71	75	36	17	35	34
Subtotals	202	75	98	15	104	34
1770s						
Wethersfield	147	71	72	12.5	75	45
Upland	92	75	44	7	48	42
Subtotals	239	72	116	10	123	44
Totals	441	74	214	12	227	39
1820s						
Wethersfield	89	76	43	14	46	33
Upland	84	83	41	10	43	23
Totals	173	80	84	12	89	28

Note: Figures include children who, though dying before their parents, were capable of inheriting through their legal representatives.

Chesebrough was fighting an uphill battle; advocates of partibility were more in tune with the practices of colonial landholders. Only 9 percent of the eighty-six colonial landholders in this study gave all the family land to a single heir, and only 6 percent of the eighty-three who had more than one child or sibling did so.[37] Desire for family distinction and fear of "scoundrels" were not strong enough to persuade these landholders to turn to unigeniture. That inheritance practices were resolutely partible is easiest to see from the perspective of potential heirs. Seventy-seven landed parents had 441 children: 74 percent of these children received land (see Table I). Childless estate holders were virtually unanimous in selecting their heirs from among their brothers and sisters, and they were

"Let not your Scheme be known, but encourage others to divide their Estates: for hereby you will be more likely to buy their Lands . . . and the more their Estates are divided, the more it will add to your Superiority." He may have written this passage partly with tongue in cheek (as well as in recognition of the prevailing custom of partibility), but it, along with the language of "Scoundrel," suggests that his advice is embedded in a sense of the social world as a place of chronic competition and mistrust. In his imagery, the patriarch's deepest loyalties and duties are to a lineal family constantly threatened by the schemes of others: "The Head of the Family should consider himself as the Head and Patron & Father of the rest, always take their Part, and never suffer them to be opprest." Dexter, ed., *Extracts*, 1-2.

[37] These cases of unigeniture were scattered, appearing in both Wethersfield and in the upland, and in the 1750s as well as the 1770s.

only a little less enthusiastic about extensive partitioning. Fifty-four percent of the siblings (n = 39) of the nine landed but childless estate holders inherited land. Overall, almost two-thirds of the landed upland and Wethersfield families split their realty among three or more heirs (65 percent, n = 86).[38] Among these colonial estate owners, then, the effort to establish as many heirs as possible on family land outweighed the attractions of intergenerational accumulation or fears of rendering the family's hold on land precarious.

Studies of European peasants and yeomen emphasize that, other things being equal, population growth led to less partitioning of property so long as continuity on family land was an important goal.[39] From this perspective it is not surprising that Americans were more prone to divide their land than were their comparatively land-short European counterparts. But the rate of partitioning among the landholders in this study was very high—higher, for example, even than Philip J. Greven, Jr.'s well-known study of inheritance in New England might lead one to expect.[40] At first glance, this enthusiasm for partitioning seems to support the view that distinctive American conditions weakened or severed the link between family

[38] Even fewer deliberately singled out one or two heirs. Over three-quarters (77%) of those who had more than two heirs (n = 74) found some land for at least three of them. The practice of reserving land for one or two heirs did not cluster. No more than 27% and no less than 21% of the upland or Wethersfield landowners pursued this tactic in the 1750s or the 1770s.

[39] Lutz K. Berkner and Franklin F. Mendels, "Inheritance Systems, Family Structure, and Demographic Patterns in Western Europe, 1700-1900," in Charles Tilly, ed., *Historical Studies of Changing Fertility* (Princeton, N.J., 1978), 209-225; Habakkuk, "Family Structure and Economic Change," *Jour. Econ. Hist.*, XV (1955), 11-12; Cicely Howell, "Peasant Inheritance Customs in the Midlands, 1200-1700," in Goody *et al.*, eds., *Family and Inheritance in Europe*, 117, 154-155. In some land-scarce contexts, of course, impoverishment was an imminent threat and impartibility had nothing to do with strategies of accumulation. For impartible customs in Europe and England see, for example, Lutz K. Berkner, "The Stem Family and the Developmental Cycle of the Peasant Household: An Eighteenth-Century Austrian Example," *AHR*, LXXVII (1972), 398-418; Emmanuel Le Roy Ladurie, "Family Structures and Inheritance Customs in Sixteenth-Century France," in Goody *et al.*, eds., *Family and Inheritance in Europe*, 61-67; and Margaret Spufford, "Peasant Inheritance Customs and Land Distribution in Cambridgeshire from the Sixteenth to the Eighteenth Centuries," *ibid.*, 156-176. In family-farm areas elsewhere and in the 20th century see John W. Cole and Eric R. Wolf, *The Hidden Frontier: Ecology and Ethnicity in an Alpine Valley* (New York, 1974), 158-159, 206; and Michel Verdon, "The Stem Family: Toward a General Theory," *JIH*, X (1979), 87-105.

[40] Greven, *Four Generations: Population, Land, and Family in Colonial Andover, Massachusetts* (Ithaca, N.Y., 1970), 176-177, 222-228. Waters also shows less partitioning in 18th-century Guilford, Conn., than found here ("Inheritance and Migration," *WMQ*, 3d Ser., XXXIX [1982], 79-83). The fact that these studies do not include intestate estate holders only partly accounts for the difference. Most *landed* estate holders in the upland and Wethersfield did avail themselves of deeds or wills or both when making their inheritance decisions. Rates of "informal testacy" (property holders used deeds or wills or both) for Wethersfield and the upland respectively were 68% and 69% in the 1750s, 79% and 88% in the 1770s, 65% and 75% in the 1820s.

property and life chances. Yet studies of inheritance in colonial New England, whether or not they find persistent, extensive partitioning, show that property holders made fine discriminations among their heirs.[41] New England landholders did not adopt share-and-share-alike methods.[42] Although they divided their property, the inequalities they created indicated that they were responding to the tension between unity and provision as its terms were posed in their time and place.[43]

Straightforward egalitarian practices were not the rule among Wethersfield and upland probates. One starts with sons because most inheritance studies stress that the key decision for farm families concerned the transfer of land from fathers to sons. The colonial fathers in this study were very reluctant to cut off sons from land, with the result that all but 12 percent of sons got some realty (Table I). At the same time, fathers often stinted the inheritances of some sons in order to advantage others. For example, Jeheil Rose of Coventry, who died a prosperous farmer in 1773, willed his youngest son, Timothy, land and personal property worth over £1,100 lawful money. He gave his only other son, Jeheil Junior, an inheritance worth only £450. He was not snubbing Jeheil, who got his father's silver shoe buckles and sixty-eight acres, with buildings; but Timothy, who inherited twice as much land, with all the livestock and farm implements not left to his mother, and who took over as creditor to seventeen neighbors owing his father sums ranging from 7s. to £71, was clearly the heavily favored heir.[44] His inheritance placed him among Coventry's more substantial farmers. A wealthy man who had only two sons, Jeheil Rose

[41] Greven, *Four Generations;* Waters, "Inheritance and Migration," *WMQ.* 3d Ser., XXXIX (1982), 64-86, and "Patrimony," *Perspectives Am. Hist..* X (1976), 129-160. For more extensively partible practices see, for example, Jedrey, *World of John Cleaveland.* 58-94; Barry Levy, "The Birth of the 'Modern Family' in Early America: Quaker and Anglican Families in the Delaware Valley, Pennsylvania, 1681-1750," in Michael Zuckerman, ed., *Friends and Neighbors: Group Life in America's First Plural Society* (Philadelphia, 1982), 35; and Daniel Snydacker, "Kinship and Community in Rural Pennsylvania, 1749-1820," *JIH.* XIII (1982), 41-61.

[42] Present-day families who do not own businesses typically adopt share-and-share-alike distribution schemes, as did smallholders who had come to rely primarily on wages rather than land in areas dominated by putting-out systems. Habakkuk, "Family and Economic Change," *Jour. Econ. Hist..* XV (1955), 10; Hans Medick, "The Proto-Industrial Family Economy: The Structural Function of Household and Family during the Transition from Peasant Society to Industrial Capitalism," *Social History.* No. 3 (1976), 310-313; Marvin B. Sussman, Judith N. Cates, and David T. Smith, *The Family and Inheritance* (New York, 1970), 1-5.

[43] For a lucid summary of the unity and provision problem in colonial New England see Jedrey, *World of John Cleaveland.* 74-84.

[44] Jeheil Rose, Coventry, will, signed Apr. 7, 1773, and inventory, taken June 1773, fol. 3271, Windham Probate District, Estate Papers, Connecticut State Library, Hartford. Judging from the Coventry Land Records, one assumes that neither son had received any land by deed from their parents, nor had Jeheil Junior, who had married two years earlier, received any from his in-laws. Coventry Vital Records, Barbour Collection, Conn. State Lib., 251.

was maximizing the chance that one of them would match and, with industry, surpass his parents' social standing.

Landholders like Rose who had more than one son did not follow a principle of strict parity. In nearly half of such families in the 1750s, one or more sons inherited shares of parental property that were at least double the value of the shares received by their less favored brothers (46 percent, n = 26 estates). More parents cut corners in the 1770s: almost two-thirds gave favored sons double portions or more (65 percent, n = 34).[45] Typically, however, the inequalities were not extreme. Even when parents singled out one or two sons for favored treatment, most who had enough property to do so gave the others at least twenty acres or its equivalent in cash and movables.[46] Middling and better sorts tried to anchor one or two sons securely on family land, while giving a foothold to others.

When partibility is the prevailing norm, the fates of daughters relative to sons become particularly interesting. In the present study, when daughters were heavily disadvantaged, it was not simply because impartible practices favored one heir and excluded all others—male and female alike. The literature on New England family farmers assumes that women rarely owned land, in part because inheritance studies have created an impression that women inherited land only when they had no brothers.[47]

[45] Wethersfield holders were, in this respect, always somewhat more egalitarian than their upland counterparts. In the 1750s one or more sons got at least a double share in 41% of those Wethersfield families in which there was more than one son (n = 17). The comparable figure for the upland was 56% (n = 9). In the 1770s the figures for Wethersfield and the upland, respectively, were 57% (n = 21) and 77% (n = 13).

[46] In the colonial era 37 landowners could have given 20 acres or its equivalent to each son. Only 9 of them deprived any of their sons of a 20-acre inheritance. The less well-situated landholders, those who could not give each son at least 20 acres or its equivalent (n = 23), were more egalitarian than the landed population as a whole. Only 7 (30%) favored any son with a double share. They did not, however, use share-and-share-alike strategies. Two-thirds of them saw to it that one or more sons got at least a 20-acre minimal basis for independent standing in their home communities. Significantly, 19 of the 23 smaller colonial holders came from Wethersfield. Especially in Wethersfield, where farmers worked their land intensively, parents could reasonably hope that a son who inherited 20 acres, could, with effort and luck, create a modest working farm. Thus the smaller holders pressed partibility up to, but not beyond, the point of viability.

[47] Greven, Four Generations. 131 (his data on the increased exclusion of sons from land leave the impression that daughters inherited no land); Jedrey, World of John Cleaveland. 74-81, 201n (no quantitative evidence given); Jackson Turner Main, Connecticut Society in the Era of the American Revolution (Hartford, Conn., 1977), 22-23, 74n (only indirect evidence offered). There is more systematic evidence on inheritance by southern daughters. See, for example, Jean Butenhoff Lee, "Land and Featherbeds: Parents' Bequest Practices in Charles County, Maryland, 1732-1783" (unpublished MS, 1984); Daniel Blake Smith, Inside the Great House: Planter Family Life in Eighteenth-Century Chesapeake Society (Ithaca, N.Y., 1980), 231-238; and Gail S. Terry, "Wives and Widows, Sons and Daughters: Testation Patterns in Baltimore County, Maryland, 1660-1759" (M.A. thesis, University of Maryland, 1983).

It comes as a surprise, then, that fully 61 percent of the daughters in the colonial portion of this study inherited some parental land (see Table I). Although the ideal may have reserved land for sons,[48] estate owners often violated it primarily because most had far too little *personal* property to provide adequate inheritances for daughters. Daughters in colonial Wethersfield and the upland towns did receive personal property worth, on average, one and one-half to two times more than their brothers received. But gross personal estates averaged only about one-third of the value of total estates held at death. Debts reduced the proportion of net personal to total net estate even further, and, if any personalty remained after debts were paid, widows usually took a third or more.

This study includes a few landed parents who did not leave wills; it shows that the daughters of these intestate parents almost always got some land.[49] Men appointed by the courts to distribute intestate estates were charged with seeing to it that daughters received shares equal in value to those of younger sons. They typically distributed to daughters the personal property remaining after the payment of debts, making up the rest of their portions out of fragmentary shares of land. But will makers could also find themselves short of personal property. Those who did not want to burden favored sons with payments of legacies out of future revenues or to leave them without livestock and farm implements often opted to give daughters modest allotments of land. For example, Henry Curtis, of Coventry, willed his eldest son, Henry, one-half of his personal possessions and of his well-stocked sixty-acre farm, but gave the other half of his farmland to his three daughters and to the grandchildren of his predeceased daughter. Thus Ester, Silence, Rhoda, and the heirs of Anna received shares of land one-quarter the value of that inherited by their favored brother. The inequalities become even more extreme when one takes into account Henry Senior's lifetime gifts. In 1760, the year his second son, Bildad, got married, he gave all three of his sons land totaling approximately 270 acres. Thus his daughters' shares of parental land became minute.[50]

As this example suggests, although a majority of daughters inherited some land, formidable gender inequality was still a feature of colonial practices. First, daughters found themselves without any share in parental land more than twice as often as did sons in the 1750s, and by 1770s they were over four times more likely to receive no land (see Table I). This was so because a substantial minority of landholders behaved as conventional wisdom predicts: they simply excluded all their daughters from inheriting land; 31 percent of those who had sons and daughters did so in the 1750s

[48] Main, *Connecticut Society.* 22-23; Waters, "Patrimony," *Perspectives Am. Hist.,* X (1976), 149-150.

[49] Seventy-five percent of the 77 colonial landed parents were informally testate (68% in the 1750s, n = 37; 82% in the 1770s, n = 40).

[50] Henry Curtis, Coventry, will, dated Apr. 6, 1770, fol. 1029, Windham Probate District, Estate Papers; Coventry Land Records, 5: 29, 30, 32, deeds recorded Feb. 1761, Conn. State Lib. (microfilm).

(n = 32), 46 percent in the 1770s (n = 35). The exclusion of daughters
was not due to the direct threat of fragmentation. When families in the
1770s are ranked within each area by the total acreage given to children,
we find that half the landholders who were in the bottom half of these
rankings excluded their daughters in both the upland and Wethersfield.
But so did 30 percent of those in the top half of the upland ranking, and
36 percent of those in the top half of the Wethersfield ranking.

Second, when daughters did get land, as in the Curtis family, they
usually got far less than their brothers. In the 1750s, the large majority of
Wethersfield and upland parents who had sons and daughters either
excluded all their daughters or gave them shares of land no more than half
the value of the land given their sons (66 percent, n = 32). In the 1770s,
the overwhelming majority, 86 percent (n = 35), chose one or the other
of these inegalitarian strategies.[51] Daughters in the 1750s got, in aggregate, far less land than their brothers, and their situation worsened in the
1770s. At the close of the colonial era, daughters in both Wethersfield and
the upland received less than 20 percent of all land distributed to
children.[52]

From mid-century to the Revolution land was becoming scarcer in the
upland towns and in Wethersfield. Wethersfield's population increased by
almost 50 percent between 1756 and 1774, while the four upland towns
grew by over one-third.[53] Only in Wethersfield did changes in agricultural
practice help to offset population increases; uplanders managed by dis-
tributing and using what marginal and undivided land they had left. In light
of these pressures, the continued, even accentuated reluctance to cut sons
off entirely from parental land is interesting. Inheritance practices indicate
that families in both areas adhered resolutely to the vision of establishing
as many sons as they could as local freeholders without jeopardizing the
chances of all.

As the preceding data show, however, holders of probated estates who
died in the 1770s were more likely than those dying two decades earlier
to exclude their daughters from land and to give short shrift to some sons.
This suggests that, although their own farms and businesses were not
immediately threatened, property holders were responding to local land
shortages generally as populations became denser and soil less fertile.[54]

[51] In the 1770s the percentages of inegalitarian families were identical in
Wethersfield (n = 21) and the uplands (n = 14). In the 1750s, they were nearly so
(Wethersfield, 67%, n = 21; the uplands, 64%, n = 11).
[52] In the 1750s daughters took 31% of all such land in Wethersfield, 29% in the
uplands.
[53] Figures from the colonial census of 1756 and of 1774 as found in Greene and
Harrington, *American Population.* 58-60.
[54] Population trends in Windham and Hartford counties, where all the towns in
this study were then located, reinforce the picture of declining opportunity.
Although their populations increased between 1756 and 1774, these counties
grew more slowly and experienced more out-migration than any other Connecticut county (Daniels, *Connecticut Town.* 51-52). After 1750 the general economic
picture in Connecticut was one of slow growth and even decline, as innovations in

The more limited opportunities of the decades just before the Revolution were associated not with a tendency to exclude more children but with sharpened and more widespread inequalities among sons and, especially, between sons and daughters.

In sum, to the extent that such practices were egalitarian, as evidenced by extensive partitioning, the egalitarian goal applied to households or families, not, pace Hartzian logic, to individuals. The colonial solution to the unity-and-provision problem did emphasize providing for heirs more than preserving the integrity of ancestral estates. But these freeholders stretched family resources, forswore the pleasures of intergenerational accumulation, and put their family enterprises at some risk in order to establish as many new households as possible. The sometimes complex and finely wrought inheritance distinctions make sense in light of this orientation toward households. Because the egalitarian impulse applied to families rather than to individuals, there was no contradiction between this impulse and the small inheritances of daughters: they were expected to marry into new households or to remain under their fathers' protection. Also, although landowners were unwilling to dispossess sons entirely for the sake of accumulation, they often rendered the position of some sons precarious in order to establish securely one or two others as independent householders. In inheritance, as in other aspects of life in communities based on household patriarchy, the independence of some was predicated on the dependency of others.

Shared Rights. The second major feature of colonial inheritance practices comprised the reciprocal ties established or reinforced when testators, deed makers, and estate distributors created shared rights among heirs. Property holders could create more or less complex obligations among blood relatives and in-laws, and they could attempt to circumscribe the actions of future generations. By creating legally binding claims (or failing to do so), their decisions had a marked impact on the shape of kin ties.[55]

Colonial testators did not, as a rule, simply devise their property in discrete, individually owned parcels but used their wills to reinforce obligations among family members. The arrangements made by Thomas Fuller, a weaver and farmer in Willington, illustrate one very common

---

agriculture and trade failed to keep pace with population growth and soil depletion (Daniels, "Economic Development in Colonial and Revolutionary Connecticut: An Overview," *WMQ*. 3d Ser., XXXVII [1980], 446-447).

[55] Berkner and Mendels, "Inheritance Systems," in Tilly, ed., *Studies in Changing Fertility*. 213-214; Cole and Wolf, *Hidden Frontier*. 175-205; Colin Creighton, "Family, Property, and Relations of Production in Western Europe," *Economy and Society*. IX (1980), 137-159; Spufford, "Inheritance in Cambridgeshire," in Goody et al.. eds., *Family and Inheritance in Europe*. 156-176. For continental America see good discussions in David P. Gagan, "The Indivisibility of Land: A Microanalysis of the System of Inheritance in Nineteenth-Century Ontario," *Jour. Econ. Hist.*. XXXVI (1976), 128-132; and Snydacker, "Kinship and Community," *JIH*. XIII (1982). 50-51, 55-59.

type of obligation. When David and Solomon, his youngest sons, inherited his farm, they took on the obligation to pay legacies of $46.00 each to their sisters, Mehitabel and Ester. Knowing that this would constitute a burden on the ongoing revenues of the farm, Fuller stated that his sons could pay the legacies in $7.00 annual installments.[56] Many property holders who excluded daughters or sisters from land gave them legacies that would be paid not with cash on hand but out of the future revenues of land inherited by favored heirs.

In a variant on this practice, when a prospective heir who had children predeceased the testator, the latter always gave land or legacies to those children. In the case of legacies, favored heirs then had obligations to the children of their predeceased brother or sister. In some cases, estate owners reinforced the obligation to pay legacies by stating that if their sons or brothers failed to meet their obligations, they would lose all or part of their inheritance.

Use rights putting aside property for retiring parents, minors, and unmarried children were also very common. A near-majority of colonial landholders who had adult heirs gave all or part of their realty to heirs before death (47 percent, n = 83).[57] Parents were especially apt to do so (56 percent, n = 70), with the result that about 61 percent of their married sons (n = 76) got some land during their parents' lifetimes.[58] When landholders made out deeds to sons (and, less frequently, to nephews or sons-in-law), they often reserved use rights for themselves and their wives; less often, they required the recipient to deliver certain goods and services annually. Those who reserved use rights retained managerial powers over the realty. At the same time, as the new owners, their sons would become independent landed men, if not immediately, then in the near future. In the case of the contract for delivery of goods and services, sons also got managerial rights over, and immediate access to, their land along with the formal obligation to provide for parents.

Over and above the dower or equivalent use rights for widows, both will makers and distributors of intestate estates frequently specified that minors or single children were to have the use of certain rooms in the house or of garden plots and the like. When John Pierce, a Wethersfield

[56] A further complication was that Solomon was only 17 when his father died. Until Solomon came of age, his brother had the use of his property, and Mehitabel was not to receive her first payment until Solomon turned 23. Thomas Fuller, Willington, will signed Mar. 4, 1754, fol. 2991, Hartford Probate District, Estate Papers, Conn. State Lib., Willington Land Records, C:72, deed recorded Jan. 1748/49, *ibid.* (microfilm).

[57] The percentages are very similar in Wethersfield and the upland. The figures exclude landowners who had only minor children, but the base population does include probates who died landless or insolvent if they had land during their lives (and as long as they had adult heirs at the time).

[58] Fifty-nine percent of the married sons of colonial landholders got land during their parents' lifetimes in Wethersfield, 63% in the uplands. Far fewer single sons, less than a third, got lifetime gifts of land from parents. Only seven holders in the entire study gave lifetime gifts of land to daughters.

farmer, made his will in 1773, all his children were married except his daughter, Susannah, who was then at least thirty years old. He gave his homelot and several other lots of meadow and pastureland to his youngest son, Samuel. After giving Susannah a small piece of outlying meadowland and confirming that she was to inherit the household furniture already in her possession, Pierce stipulated that while she remained unmarried she was to have "the use and improvement of" the south chamber and adjoining bedroom, a "privilege" in the kitchen and cellar, and that part of the garden she "now has use of." He added in the next clause that if Susannah were still unmarried when his wife died, she was also to have the use of the south lower room and bedroom.[59]

Testators usually did not spell out use rights in such detail, but because Pierce was so careful about allocating formal rights, we have an interesting portrait of a stem family pattern of inheritance—American style. At some point, Pierce had settled his two eldest sons on land in the neighboring towns of (east) Hartford and Farmington—gifts that he confirmed in his will. Samuel remained on his father's farm, and when he married, he and his family lived in the farmhouse with his unmarried sister and parents. During the colonial era eight estate owners established ten sons and a son-in-law on their lands without making out deeds. Such sons got access to much-needed land but lacked formal control over it while their fathers still lived. They could reasonably hope that they would become freeholders eventually, but they had no guarantees.

Although it is impossible to quantify the rich texture of these overlapping rights, one can get a rough sense of the estate holders' proclivities to create shared claims. Fifty-six percent of the colonial deed makers and landed testators did one or more of the following: reserved use rights in their houses or in at least one-third of the land transferred (*not* including the widow's dower) for themselves or some other party; imposed obligations on favored heirs to pay legacies and annuities out of revenues from inherited property; made ownership of inherited property conditional on performing some service; or created entails or entail-like settlements. As Table II shows, landholders were more likely to make use of these devices in the 1770s—about two-thirds of them in that decade in contrast to a simple majority two decades earlier. Wethersfield holders were a little less, but only a little less, inclined to use these devices than were uplanders.

It is important to recognize what these inheritance practices did not do: they did not bind property to a line of male heirs. As mentioned above, social historians who have uncovered complex webs of overlapping rights similar to those just discussed have suggested that the inheritance practices of American family farmers were patrilineal.[60] Indeed, in some

[59] John Pierce, Wethersfield, will signed Feb. 13, 1772, fol. 4255, Hartford Probate Dist., Estate Papers.
[60] Jedrey, *World of John Cleaveland*, 78-79; Waters, "Patrimony," *Perspectives Am. Hist.*, X (1976), 139, 149-150, 159-160, and "Inheritance and Migration," *WMQ*.

TABLE II
SHARED RIGHTS CREATED AMONG THE FAMILIES OF LANDED
ESTATE HOLDERS

	All Landholders			Landed Parents Only		
	Usable Estates N	Shared Rights %	No Shared Rights %	Usable Estates N	Shared Rights %	No Shared Rights %
1750s						
Wethersfield	28	43[a]	57	23	48[a]	52
Upland	16	56	44	14	50	50
Subtotals	44	48	52	37	49	51
1770s						
Wethersfield	26	62[a]	38	24	63[a]	37
Upland	16	69	31	16	69	31
Subtotals	42	64	36	40	65	35
Totals	86	56	44	77	57	43
1820s						
Wethersfield	29	14[b]	86	15	13[b]	87
Upland	21	48	52	15	53	47

Note: Figures do not include widows' life-estates.
[a] In comparing Wethersfield and the upland, chi-square is not significant (based on two-column table, did/did not use shared rights).
[b] In comparing Wethersfield and the upland, chi-square is significant at the .05 level or better.

accounts, devotion to the land and to preserving the family name upon it becomes key evidence that the outlook of American farmers was "traditional, marked by strong patrilineal, English peasant mores."[61]

We have seen already, however, that these landholders rejected one key feature of patrilineal or dynastic inheritance practices: the reservation of the main estate for a single male heir. A second and even more important earmark of patrilineal practices is that the main heirs do not become, in the fullest sense, owners of their inherited land. They have wide managerial powers, but their rights in property are circumscribed by entails, trusts, or other devices that limit current incumbents to life-estates and restrict their power to alienate land or to designate future heirs.

Property owners in colonial Wethersfield and the upland often created a web of shared rights, but they were as uninterested in binding family property to a line of male heirs as they were in impartible inheritance. The unusual practices of one testator illustrate the exception that proves the

---

3d Ser., XXXIX (1982), 82, 86; Henretta, "Families and Farms," *ibid.*, XXXV (1978), 24-26.
[61] Waters, "Patrimony," *Perspectives Am. Hist.*, X (1976), 139.

rule. Deacon John Chapman's will, made in Bolton in 1773, was ordinary in most ways. To his widow he gave a life-estate and to his youngest son, Phineas, half his ninety-eight-acre farm; his four daughters split the other half. He also gave his eldest son, Jeremiah, who was already married, a forty-one-acre farm nearby. But John's treatment of Jeremiah was otherwise very unusual because Jeremiah did not become a freeholder by virtue of his inheritance. John stipulated that his son was to receive only the use and improvement of the land for his natural life, while the fee would go to Jeremiah's children. He also inserted a provision for Jeremiah's wife—that if she should outlive Jeremiah, she should have the use of the entire fifty acres as long as she remained a widow.[62] For reasons that the record does not show, John denied his son the right of alienation and the ability to name his own heirs that were at the core of the independent proprietor's powers over property.

Only four other colonial and early nineteenth-century landholders limited their children or siblings to life-estates while passing ownership to children's or siblings' children (the core feature of entails, strict settlements, and similar lineal arrangements). While landholders may have hoped that their heirs would preserve family property, they did not attempt to enforce such desires by curtailing heirs' legal powers over estates. Indeed, only six property holders altogether tried to regulate in any manner relations between heirs and the heirs' own children or spouses. More generally, a striking feature of these deeds, wills, and estate distributions is their silence about the children of living heirs. In this sense, inheritance practices were shallow in generational depth and thus lacked a key feature of lineal practices. Although grandchildren and nieces and nephews did inherit frequently,[63] the great majority came into their property as representatives of a child or sibling who died before the estate holder. In such cases, they usually appeared as an anonymous group—for example, "the children of my beloved son Charles, predeceased." Only twelve of the estate owners in the entire study mentioned their grandchildren, nieces, or nephews when these children had living parents, and five of them did so in order to leave a token or symbolic inheritance—a valued stopwatch or best dress. In conjunction with divisibility and the willingness to make daughters landed heirs, this is the most telling evidence that inheritance practices of these freeholders were not lineal or dynastic.

In sum, colonial estate holders in Wethersfield and the upland created legally enforceable ties between parents and adult children, and among siblings. When an heir died prematurely, these links could extend to grandchildren and to nieces and nephews. Thus inheritance practices reinforced solidarities among extended kin but without restricting the autonomy of new family heads with respect to the fates of third and future

[62] John Chapman, will, signed Feb. 10, 1773, and inventory, taken Mar. 9, 1774, Bolton, fol. #1171, Hartford Probate Dist., Estate Papers.
[63] Grandchildren and nieces and nephews inherited in 24% of all the families included in this study (n = 186). There was little variation over time or between Wethersfield and the upland.

generations or putting any particular emphasis on (patri)lineages.[64] The urge to retain land within a family line or to accumulate it—the twin goals, we recall, of men like Thomas Chesebrough—was subordinated to two other concerns: to use family property to set up as many households as possible and to pass on the status of independent freeholder to sons.

The colonial pattern of divisibility and shared rights suited communities characterized by rough equality among heads of household and dependency for all others. New England's social structure was founded on a form of independence compatible with—indeed, dependent on—patriarchal household organization. The cornerstone of independence was the standing conferred by possession of a freehold, with all the proprietary powers that went with it. But independence did not refer to the individual standing alone. It was a status implying a complex set of relations with others. Above the bright line, men possessing productive property entered directly and in their own right into the life of the community, trading land, labor, and goods, obtaining credit from one another, and assuming the benefits and burdens of local officeholding. At the same time, the independent man was, almost by definition, a head of household. As landlord implies tenants, or capitalist employer implies wage-laborers, so the independent man existed in a world populated by dependents. As patriarch to his wife and children, and as master to his servants and even slaves, he organized the labor of his household. He was responsible in principle for the material, moral, and spiritual well-being of his dependents; he spoke for them in his political and legal dealings with the larger world. Thus independence did not refer to the abstract autonomy of persons. Rather, it was founded on a clear hierarchy as the privilege of men occupying the status of household head.

Pre-Revolutionary inheritance practices provided a material foundation for patriarchal households. Most sons—husbands and would-be husbands of the next generation—inherited enough property to underwrite their status as household heads, while daughters—wives and would-be wives of the next generation—did not. Moreover, when estate holders gave land in fee-simple to their daughters or, through intestacy, allowed the probate courts to do so, they knew that the law would sharply reduce their married daughters' effective rights in inherited land. Only three estate holders in this study attempted to enlarge their daughters' powers or to provide

---

[64] Elsewhere I call these "extended cognate" inheritance practices to emphasize that they reinforced solidarities within what was, after all, a cognate system of kinship (*Property and Kinship*. 32-34). These practices put a premium on flexible alliances between adult siblings and their families: apart from parents and adult children, they emphasized same-generation solidarities rather than a core group of paternally related men. On inheritance and cognate kinship see also John E. Crowley, "The Importance of Kinship: Testamentary Evidence from South Carolina," *JIH*. XVI (1986), 559-577, and Randolph Trumbach, *The Rise of the Egalitarian Family: Aristocratic Kinship and Domestic Relations in Eighteenth-Century England* (New York, 1978), 13-17, 50-61, 66, 70-71.

additional protection for the powers that married women did retain.[65] Thus daughters who married brought comparatively little real property into their households, and their ability to control it was restricted.[66]

In short, law and practice greatly limited women's possession of and control over land. To be sure, the cultural and economic basis for mutual regard between husbands and wives was very strong in colonial New England. Advice literature and sermons emphasized mutual affection and respect in marriage. The economic vitality of households also depended greatly on women's skilled labor, and, as many have suggested, the importance of women's work may have enhanced the respect accorded them in practice. The cultural emphasis on affection and respect was not, however, at odds with patriarchal household organization. Mutuality in marriage was almost always coupled with another theme—the wife's obligation to obey her husband.[67] And although wives undertook many important economic activities, they did so at their husbands' sufferance and under his authority or risked community censure. Wives deserved respect and could exert influence, but they ordinarily lacked the power to make vital decisions in their own right. The point here is that ability to control the material resources vital to the running of the household economy is an important foundation of the power to make decisions affecting the fates of all household members.[68] It is a foundation that women largely lacked.

The short shrift given to daughters and widows was part of a general pattern designed to ensure that sons attained the status of independent men. Here, two tensions marked inheritance practices. First, estate holders were loath to relegate any sons to the category of permanent dependent, but if they stretched family property too far, they risked that fate for all. Second, as Greven and others have pointed out, the timing of the initiation of sons into the community of freeholders could be a source

[65] Under the common law, husbands became owners of their wives' personal property and gained managerial rights over their wives' realty (but not in principle the power to alienate it permanently). Holders could use equity law to attempt to get around these restrictions, although the status of equitable estates for married women was uncertain in colonial Connecticut. *Acts and Laws* (1750), 119; Richard Morris, *Studies in the History of American Law*. 2d ed. (New York, 1964), 135-138; Marylynn Salmon, *Women and the Law of Property in Early America* (Chapel Hill, N.C., 1986), 101-152, 153-178; Swift, *System of Laws in Connecticut*, I, 300-332, II, 411-423.

[66] If women did not inherit land from parents or siblings, they were very unlikely to get ownership of land through their husbands. Only 8 of the 100 widows in this study inherited ownership of land. Eighty-five of the remaining widows received life-estates or estates during their widowhood.

[67] Edmund S. Morgan, *The Puritan Family: Religion and Domestic Relations in Seventeenth-Century New England* (New York, 1966), 29-64; Stone, *Family. Sex, and Marriage*. 100-102, 123-141; Laurel Thatcher Ulrich, *Good Wives: Image and Reality in the Lives of Women in Northern New England. 1650-1750* (New York, 1982), 35-38.

[68] Mary Beth Norton, "The Myth of the Golden Age," in Carol Ruth Berkin and Mary Beth Norton [eds.], *Women of America: A History* (Boston, 1979), 40-42.

of strain.[69] In order to recreate that community, fathers at some point had to relinquish their control. A few fathers in the present study behaved as the classic image of the patriarch reluctant to give up his power suggests— settling sons on parental land but refusing to give them formal rights in property until the very last moment. But most did not deny title to married sons or to sons who shouldered the responsibility of caring for aged parents.[70] More important, even when fathers delayed, they did not seek to extend their authority over family property to unborn generations. When they did pass on their property, they gave their sons the power inherent in ownership and the independence that went with it.

THE 1820S

Early nineteenth-century estate holders in both Wethersfield and the upland continued to shun unigeniture; extensive partitioning remained the rule. But there the similarities largely ended. In Wethersfield, inheritance practices diverged sharply from the colonial norm, while in the upland the pattern of preferential partibility and shared rights persisted.

On every count, the practices of upland estate holders indicate fidelity to the old way of attempting to solve the unity-and-provision problem. Almost all sons gained a toehold on land (90 percent, n = 41), but one or more sons received an inheritance at least double the value of that going to their less favored brothers in just over half the families in which there was more than one son (six of eleven families, 54.5 percent). Strong gender distinctions also persisted. Although upland property holders were less inclined to exclude daughters from land than their colonial counter- parts had been (Table I), most still gave their daughters merely token shares. Over two-thirds of landholders who had sons and daughters either excluded all their daughters from land or gave them shares worth no more than half the value of the average shares given to their brothers (69 percent, n = 13). As a result, the forty-three upland daughters got only 19 percent of the realty inherited by children or their representatives.

Upland estate owners also used their property to reinforce family obligations. About half of them made arrangements for their own retire- ment, stipulated that favored heirs were to pay legacies from the revenues

[69] Greven, *Four Generations.* 131, 146-150, 229-230; Folbre, "Wealth of Patri- archs," *JIH.* XVI (1985), 183-197.

[70] Some argue that the increased use of lifetime gifts in the 18th century indicates a decline in paternal control over sons. There was a tacit bargain: new opportunities to emigrate or to seek nonlanded employment increased the leverage of sons; fathers who wanted their sons' labor were forced to hand over property earlier than they might have wished. Greven, *Four Generations,* 146-150, 229-30; Richard L. Bushman, "Family Security in the Transition from Farm to City, 1750-1850," *Journal of Family History.* VI (1981), 238-256. Perhaps too much has been made of the increased use of lifetime transfers. The early timing of these transfers is secondary. The use of lifetime gifts indicates more fundamentally that family property was still a very important regulator of the fates of the next generation.

of inherited land, or created other claims that bound inheriting kin to one another (Table II). The majority of landed parents also gave land to heirs during their lifetimes,[71] with the result that two-thirds of married sons received land before their parents died. In short, the transfer of inherited property between the generations remained tied to marriage and retirement, and an inheritance still obligated favored heirs to care for younger or less favored siblings.

In the 1820s, the upland towns remained subsistence-plus communities, but small-scale manufactures were beginning to appear. A large body of research suggests that rural industry may at first encourage partible inheritance practices as families come to rely on supplemental income to augment returns from small parcels of land. The persistence of extensively partible practices in the upland towns is consistent with this literature.[72] Yet upland estate holders did not distribute their property according to a share-and-share-alike principle. Rather, they skimped on the inheritances of daughters and some sons, and they continued to impose obligations on favored heirs, indicating that they were still attempting to resolve the basic tension between unity and provision. New sources of supplemental income and the greater ease of migration after the Revolution altered the context within which holders devised their inheritance strategies but did not remove the basic dilemma.

In Wethersfield, by contrast, inheritance practices changed dramatically, as may be seen in the example of one will maker. Joseph Bulkley, who died in 1821, was one of the wealthiest men in Wethersfield and the father of five grown children. An active farmer and merchant with extensive business dealings in New York, Bulkley owned about three hundred acres, a store on Rocky Hill wharf, a schooner, and an interest in a ship berthed at New York City. He also held shares in five new Connecticut banks and insurance companies as well as personal notes amounting to over $7,000.

Although his holdings were complex, Bulkley's will was short and simple. He gave his wife, Mary, a life-estate in one-third of his property and applied a principle of strict equality to his five sons and two daughters. Each was to receive equal shares of his estate, including monies he had advanced to them for marriage portions or business purposes. He went out of his way to dismiss distinctions between types of property: "for the More Easy Settling of said Estate there Shall be No distinction between Real or personal Estate in said Settlement so that any or Either of My Sons or daughters May Have Real or Moveable Estate as Shall be Most

[71] Fifty-three percent of holders who had adult children (n = 17) did so.
[72] Christopher Clark, "Household Economy, Market Exchange, and the Rise of Capitalism in the Connecticut Valley, 1800-1860," *Jour. Soc. Hist.*, XIII (1979), 178-182; David Levine, *Family Formation in an Age of Nascent Capitalism* (New York, 1977), 13; Franklin Mendels, "Agriculture and Peasant Industry in Eighteenth-Century Flanders," in William N. Parker and Eric L. Jones, eds., *European Peasants and Their Markets* (Princeton, N.J., 1975), 90; E. P. Thompson, "The Grid of Inheritance: A Comment," in Goody *et al.*, *Family and Inheritance in Europe*. 342.

Convenient."[73] As a consequence, sons and daughters alike inherited prime meadowland and personal property, including stocks and debts receivable. Even the basic distinction between real and personal estate, long enshrined in law and custom, was erased. Bulkley's practices were oriented toward the market value of his property, not the qualitative uses to which it could be put.

Bulkley's will was short not only because it omitted the long list of particular properties going to each heir and the calculations creating inegalitarian shares but because it lacked the sometimes ornate clauses that carved out use rights and spelled out the obligations of main heirs. Apart from the widow's dower, Bulkley did not impose indirect claims on property; each heir received an unencumbered inheritance.

Bulkley was typical. In early nineteenth-century Wethersfield the pattern of preferential partibility all but collapsed. As in the upland, most sons inherited land (86 percent, n = 43, Table I), but landholders who had more than one son abandoned the practice of favoring some at the expense of others. Eighty-two percent gave their sons equal or nearly equal inheritance shares (n = 13).[74] In the colonial era, small and large landholders were equally apt to exclude their daughters. Not so in early nineteenth-century Wethersfield. Only four of the thirteen landholders who had sons and daughters reserved their land exclusively for sons; all were among the poorer landed parents.[75] In wealthier families all daughters got land, and in all but one they inherited shares equal or nearly equal in value to the shares inherited by their brothers. In aggregate, Wethersfield daughters inherited a surprising 54 percent of all land going to children. In most families the egalitarian impulse now applied to individual heirs rather than to households.

Equally striking was the disinclination of Wethersfield landowners to use property to reinforce family obligations. Only four of the twenty-nine estate holders who gave land to heirs did so, and parents were no more likely than others to do so (Table II). Thus their practices were individualized in yet another sense: dower rights aside, each heir gained unencumbered ownership of his or her property; heirs were no longer bound to one another by virtue of inheritance. Moreover, marriage and

[73] Joseph modified this principle in only one respect. He said that if there were enough to make up his son Ralph's full share, Ralph was to have his inheritance in the property Joseph owned in New York City, where Ralph and one other son lived. His estate distributors made one further change: they gave two of his sons the stores located on Rocky Hill wharf. Joseph Bulkley, Wethersfield, will, signed Nov. 9, 1818, and estate distribution made in Jan. 1821, Hartford Probate Dist., Estate Papers.

[74] Recall that only 5 of 11 (45%) early 19th-century uplanders gave their sons equal or nearly equal shares. Despite the small number of cases, the difference between Wethersfield and the upland is statistically significant (chi-square significant at the .05 level).

[75] In fact, 20 of the 21 Wethersfield children excluded from land—sons and daughters—were excluded by parents whose total acreage placed them in the bottom half of a ranking of the estates of landed parents (n = 15).

retirement no longer affected the timing of inheritance in most Wethersfield families. Only four (13 percent) of the thirty-one estate holders who had ever owned land deeded realty to heirs during their lifetimes or, on the evidence of wills, settled their kin informally upon their land. Only three of the fifteen parents who had adult children did so.[76] As a result, only 35 percent of the married sons of landed parents (n = 26) got land before their parents died. The timing of inheritance depended on only one important event: the death of the property holder.

All told, the tension between unity and provision all but vanished in Wethersfield as property holders emphasized parity among heirs. The pattern of land division indicates that they were no longer especially interested in setting up new households directly out of family-held property. Taking into account the abandonment of shared rights and the near disappearance of lifetime transfers, these practices suggest that the fates of the next generation were only loosely connected to the inheritance of family property. Young heirs now got a head start in life, and older ones got a windfall, but heads of household no longer used their property directly to ensure that heirs would become independent producers.

These data reflect the collapse of the tension between unity and provision in another way as well. Although the majority of Wethersfield widows still received life-estates in land, rather than ownership of it, their total allotments of land and personal property were more generous than the colonial or contemporary upland norm. In the 1820s, ten of the seventeen Wethersfield widows got more than their statutory share of personal property and land (59 percent). In the colonial era, the majority of holders had settled on the statutory "thirds" as striking the appropriate balance between their wives' maintenance needs and their heirs' need to have access to family property, and only 12 percent of widows (n = 66) got more generous shares.[77] Practices in the upland remained the same in the 1820s: 71 percent of the upland widows (n = 17) got their statutory thirds, and none got more.[78] The pattern is consistent with the literature that suggests that as the fortunes of children cease to depend on family property, the position of spouses improves. The allocation of property becomes oriented to the couple and its needs.[79]

[76] The difference between early 19th-century Wethersfield and the upland in the propensity to use lifetime transfers both among all holders and among parents only is statistically significant at the .05 level or better.

[77] Under Connecticut law throughout the period of this study, widows were entitled to a life-estate in one-third of the lands owned by their husbands at their deaths. They were entitled to ownership of one-third of their husbands' net personal property (one-half if there were no children). *Acts and Laws* (1750), 43-44, 49-51; *Public Statutes 1821*. 180-182.

[78] The difference between the propensities of Wethersfield and upland husbands to provide shares of land more generous than the statute required is statistically significant at better than the .01 level.

[79] Habakkuk, "Family Structure and Economic Change," *Jour. Econ. Hist.*. XV (1955), 10; Talcott Parsons, "The Kinship System of the Contemporary United

In sum, inheritance practices in Wethersfield ceased to reinforce the material foundations for patriarchal households. One starts with the primary fact that sons could no longer count on family property to guarantee their independence. They could not even expect that, if they married, they would receive any portion of their inheritance in advance of their parents' deaths. Nor did the distribution of property reinforce any distinction between household heads and dependents: daughters of parents who died in the 1820s brought as much inherited property into their new households as did their brothers. Finally, because there were no favored heirs and because the passage of property was not bound up with critical life events, no material ties of obligation and dependency bound parents, children, and siblings to one another.

How can such changes be explained? Some historians have argued that the commercialization of agriculture discouraged the creation of the shared rights typical of inheritance practices that were designed to resolve the tension between unity and provision. Such practices created claims on property or its revenues that limited owners' flexibility, but a competitive market environment put a premium on precisely such flexibility, rewarding property owners who were able and willing to alter their mixes of land, labor, and capital in response to market signals. Hence commercialization of agriculture contributed to the collapse of complex, cooperative inheritance practices.[80] In Wethersfield, as farmers turned more and more toward market gardening in the late eighteenth century, the intensification of production probably heightened concern for flexibility and liquidity of assets. This could account for the abandonment of practices that separated the use of land from its ownership or that put a lien on future revenues by using them for marriage portions and legacies.

The maturation of labor markets can encourage landholders to put primary emphasis on the integrity of their business enterprises. Knowing that the life-chances of their children need not depend so heavily on family property, property holders may enhance their enterprises' chances for successful adaptation to market competition by giving all their productive property to the heirs thought most able to manage the enterprises. At the same time, they may limit the other heirs to residual property or small legacies from cash on hand because excluded children could now make their way without owning productive property.[81]

Wethersfield estate holders did not adopt these enterprise-maintenance strategies. They were not concerned to keep land and other productive

States," in Parsons, *Essays in Sociological Theory*. rev. ed. (New York, 1964), 184; Jeffrey P. Rosenfeld, *The Legacy of Aging: Inheritance and Disinheritance in Social Perspective* (Norwood, N.J., 1970), 72, 89, 119-120; Sussman, Cates, and Smith, *Family and Inheritance*. 72, 89, 119-120.

[80] Cole and Wolf, *Hidden Frontier*. 206-221; Creighton, "Family, Property, and Production," *Economy and Society*. IX (1980), 154-159; Howell, "Inheritance in the Midlands," in Goody *et al.*, eds., *Family and Inheritance in Europe*, 149-155.

[81] Verdon, "Stem Family," *JIH*. X (1979), 93-98, 101; Gagan, "Inheritance in Ontario," *Jour. Econ. Hist.*. XXXVI (1976), 126-141.

property together; they were more interested in the interchangeable market value of their various types of property. Heirs were not getting viable productive property but a potential cash fund. This suggests that Wethersfield's comparatively complex occupational structure, perhaps coupled with uncertainties created by rapidly developing and often volatile markets, encouraged property owners to adopt a very foreshortened generational perspective on the use of productive property. Rather than use it directly for maintaining social standing into the next generation, they converted it into a head start or dividend for heirs who had largely made, or would make, their own way.[82] Rather than adopt enterprise-maintenance strategies, they used simple share-and-share-alike practices that more closely resemble those of present-day families than they did the inheritance practices of their upland counterparts.

Cultural factors probably worked in tandem with commercialization to transform inheritance practices in Wethersfield. Several scholars have argued that areas most affected by commercialization became receptive to new cultural ideals about womanhood and family life. Greater occupational specialization, the spread of wage labor, the emergence of centralized workplaces, and the decline of production for local consumption eroded the foundations for household-based labor systems and encouraged the spread of ideals of domesticity. Appearing in the eighteenth century, the new ideals competed with and even displaced patriarchal images in pedagogical treatises, household advice literature, novels, and political discourse.[83] Women and men experiencing the new economic conditions and allied social and political changes forged these principles into a coherent, working ideology in the first three or four decades of the nineteenth century.[84]

Several basic features of the emerging ideology of domesticity were relevant to inheritance. First, in contrast to patriarchal norms, domesticity stressed the equal worth of all children and the importance of their moral autonomy as they entered adulthood.[85] Second, it did not emphasize the mediating function of the male household head. To the contrary, women, especially in their capacity as mothers, became, indirectly, the new

[82] New Jersey testators went even further than Wethersfield estate holders. Many simply asked their executors to sell their estates in order to give heirs cash legacies. Lawrence Friedman, "Patterns of Testation in the Nineteenth Century: A Study of Essex County Wills," *American Journal of Legal History*. VIII (1964), 34-53.

[83] Jay Fliegelman, *Prodigals and Pilgrims: The American Revolution against Patriarchal Authority. 1750-1800* (Cambridge, 1982); Linda K. Kerber, *Women of the Republic: Intellect and Ideology in Revolutionary America* (Chapel Hill, N.C., 1980).

[84] Nancy F. Cott, *The Bonds of Womanhood: "Woman's Sphere" in New England. 1780-1835* (New Haven, Conn., 1977); Carl N. Degler, *At Odds: Women and the Family in America from the Revolution to the Present* (New York, 1980); Ryan, *Cradle of the Middle Class*; Daniel Scott Smith, "Parental Power and Marriage Patterns: An Analysis of Historical Trends in Hingham, Massachusetts," *Journal of Marriage and the Family*. XXXV (1973). 419-428.

[85] Fliegelman, *Prodigals and Pilgrims*. 1-35.

mediators. As the spiritual and moral educators of their children, women were viewed as responsible for raising citizens fit to participate in a republic. Third, and closely related, these ideals provided a more positive evaluation of women's domestic authority. Women's sphere had always been closely associated with the household's interior spaces and immediate surroundings, but the spatial domains of men and women overlapped: fields abutted gardens and orchards; the craftsman's workshed was often within calling distance of the kitchen door. Thus the overarching authority of the head of household expressed itself as a tangible daily presence. By the early nineteenth century, domesticity and an increasingly specialized economy made the kitchen, the nursery, and even the congregation more distinctively feminine places. Domesticity still circumscribed women's scope of action, but it defined for them a comparatively autonomous sphere.[86]

To be sure, by the mid-nineteenth century, domesticity would reinforce women's exclusion from the new, more specialized productive enterprises, but in the century's opening decades women in family-farm areas participated in activities that were becoming increasingly market oriented. In places near cities, such as Wethersfield, women produced and even marketed the garden crops that nourished urbanites and brought cash into their own communities, and young women in more remote rural areas headed for the new textile mills. In these circumstances, the emerging ideology of domesticity and the diminished tension between unity and provision probably had a mutually reinforcing influence on inheritance practices. The foundations for new households were shifting from the terrain of inherited property to that of acquired property and wages; this shift enabled property holders to treat their daughters and sons equally and to be generous to their spouses. The new ideology, to the extent that it was internalized in Wethersfield families, made men want to be more egalitarian. The irony is that the inclination to treat heirs equally developed just as inheritance became less important for the perpetuation of status and class.

The common pattern of inheritance in the late colonial era, followed by diverging practices in the early nineteenth century, has one final implication. Insofar as family property relations shed light on it, an orientation toward property recognizable as possessive individualism developed slowly and unevenly. As others have observed, Anglo-American law, as applied to the freehold, placed a remarkable collection of powers over property in the hands of owners. Under English law, the core attributes of individual ownership—freedom of alienation and testation—were already firmly entrenched by the time the colonists were granted their land in socage tenure. In areas characterized by independent family farms, landholders were also free to make decisions about the use and allocation of their property unhindered by regulations imposed by landlords or

[86] Cott, *Bonds of Womanhood.* 199-200.

others with superior rights in their land. In short, Anglo-American property law and the land tenure system very early provided the legal foundations for an impersonal land market.

Historians have argued that Anglo-American land law combined with land abundance and independent proprietorship to spread an entrepreneurial and individualist ethos widely throughout the countryside.[87] The present study indicates that during the colonial era—and, in the upland, well beyond it—inheritance practices displayed a logic overriding the dictates of possessive individualism. Colonial and early nineteenth-century upland estate holders used their property in ways not necessarily consonant with preserving the unity of their legal powers over land or with market rationality. In their efforts to maintain and reproduce households that were at once patriarchal and independent, they gave the fee to one heir, the rights to use the same property (and sometimes the rights to manage it) to another, and the rights to its revenues to several. Nor did the fact that shared rights reduced new holders' abilities to respond to market-based signals prevent holders from creating them. English law may have established a formal framework that made possessive individualism in the domain of property relations possible. Inheritance practices indicate that the English concept of ownership was also compatible in the American context with property management strategies that supported other social realities.

[87] Hartz, *Liberal Tradition*. 49-53; Lemon, "Spatial Order," in Greene and Pole, eds., *Colonial British America*. 102, 110-112; Alan Dawley, *Class and Community: The Industrial Revolution in Lynn* (Cambridge, Mass., 1976), 30-36; Douglas F. Dowd, *The Twisted Dream: Capitalist Development in the United States since 1776* (Cambridge, Mass., 1974), 45-51, 152-155. The position is summarized in Merrill, "Cash Is Good to Eat," *Radical Hist. Rev*.. No. 3 (1977), 42-49, and in Robert E. Mutch, "The Cutting Edge: Colonial America and the Debate about Transition to Capitalism," *Theory and Society*. IX (1980), 849-850, 856-857, 859-860. On England, see Alan Macfarlane, *The Origins of English Individualism: The Family, Property. and Social Condition* (Cambridge, 1978), 16-21, 80-86. Macfarlane makes English property law the centerpiece for his thesis that the cultural preconditions for capitalist development were established as early as the 13th century.

10

The Spiritual Conquest Re-examined: Baptism and Christian Marriage in Early Sixteenth-Century Mexico

Sarah Cline

S O M E interesting historical research has been conducted on late colonial Nahua views of conversion, based on information in local-level Nahuatl documents; but a similar study of the early colonial era has not been attempted previously.[1] Like so much information from the conquest period, descriptions of the initial evangelization, even from the Spanish point of view, are sketchy. Other than reports from early missionaries—such as Fray Toribio de Benavente Motolinia, who described the Franciscans' mass baptism of natives—little is known about the pace of conversion and the social contours of the baptized population.[2]

A corpus of six Nahuatl-language household censuses from the Morelos region, ca. 1535–40, collectively titled the Libro de Tributos, gives unique insight into aspects of conversion, particularly baptism and Christian marriage, from an indigenous point of view.[3] This body of documents, closely

I acknowledge the Interdisciplinary Humanities Center, University of California, Santa Barbara, for support of this research. My thanks to Patrick Grant and Jeffrey Burton Russell for reading a previous draft of this article, and to J. Benedict Warren and three anonymous referees of the *HAHR*.

1. Stephanie Wood, "The Cosmic Conquest: Late Colonial Views of the Sword and the Cross in Central Mexican Títulos," *Ethnohistory* 38:2 (1991), 176–95; James Lockhart, *The Nahuas After the Conquest: A Social and Cultural History of the Indians of Central Mexico, Sixteenth Through Eighteenth Centuries* (Stanford: Stanford Univ. Press, 1992), 203–60.

2. Fray Toribio de Benavente Motolinia, *Memoriales o libro de cosas de la Nueva España y los naturales de ella* (Mexico City: Universidad Nacional Autónoma de México, 1971), 116–28, 150, 188. My thanks to Monica Orozco for the page references.

3. Libro de Tributos, Museo Nacional de Antropología e Historia, Archivo Histórico, Mexico City (hereafter abbreviated as MNAH-AH), Colección Antigua, vols. 549–51. Volume 549, Huitzillan and Quauhchichinollan, 63 folios; volume 550, Tepoztlan, 97 folios; volume 551, Molotlan, Tepetenchic, and Panchimalco, 122 folios. This article cites archival material that has been published by household number, and still-unpublished material by volume and

examined, can help construct a fuller picture of the conversion process than that presented in Robert Ricard's classic study, *The Spiritual Conquest of Mexico*, which is based on Spanish sources.[4] Ricard did not consider the effectiveness of early conversion and baptism to be a central issue in the course of evangelization; but his dismissal of the question should not end the examination of this moment in colonial history.[5]

The Morelos censuses, moreover, are the earliest and perhaps the only Nahuatl source for such information.[6] Until this study, no empirical analysis of Christian evangelization has been based on local-level, native-language documentation. This type of source has allowed scholars to advance their understanding of Indian culture from the inside. Indians, or at least a select group of Indian males, were taught to write the Nahuatl language in Latin letters as part of colonial policy. Consequently, Indians generated many records in Nahuatl for the colonial administration, but also created many for their own use. These include indigenous histories and other formal texts; but most useful for historians have been the community-centered texts, such as indigenous town council records, wills and testaments, bills of sale, and other mundane documents, such as these censuses.[7]

The process of conversion, or "spiritual conquest," has been studied primarily from the point of view of the Spanish religious. The methods and techniques of the first generation of Franciscans, Dominicans, and Augustinians in Mexico were examined by Robert Ricard in the early part of

---

folio number (see note 16). My thanks to James Lockhart for bringing these censuses to my attention in 1975, and for help in resolving problems of translation.

4. Robert Ricard, *The Spiritual Conquest of Mexico: An Essay on the Apostolate and the Evangelizing Methods of the Mendicant Orders in New Spain, 1523–1572*, trans. Lesley Byrd Simpson (Berkeley: Univ. of California Press, 1966).

5. Ibid., 94.

6. I am unaware of any other existing source with similar information. Newly discovered Nahuatl documentation does come to light from time to time; for example, the Culhuacan wills in Nahuatl resided in a private collection and remained generally unknown to the scholarly community until their publication. They were published as *The Testaments of Culhuacan*, ed. S. L. Cline and Miguel León-Portilla (Los Angeles: UCLA Latin American Center Publications, 1984).

7. The importance of local-level, native-language documentation has been established in recent years. See Frances Karttunen, "Nahua Literacy," in *The Inca and Aztec States, 1400–1800: Anthropology and History*, ed. George A. Collier, Renato I. Rosaldo, and John D. Wirth (New York: Academic Press, 1982), 395–417. On the many types of extant documentation, see James Lockhart, Arthur J. O. Anderson, and Frances Berdan, *The Tlaxcalan Actas: A Compendium of the Records of the Cabildo Tlaxcala, 1545–1627* (Salt Lake City: Univ. of Utah Press, 1986). Full-length studies based on Nahuatl documentation include S. L. Cline, *Colonial Culhuacan, 1580–1600: A Social History of an Aztec Town* (Albuquerque: Univ. of New Mexico Press, 1986); Robert Haskett, *Indigenous Rulers: An Ethnohistory of Town Government in Colonial Cuernavaca* (Albuquerque: Univ. of New Mexico Press, 1991); and Lockhart, *Nahuas After the Conquest*.

this century.[8] In many ways, Ricard's picture resembles what the religious orders themselves painted, and *The Spiritual Conquest* includes a chapter titled "The Virtues of the Founders." Yet Ricard's work is significant for delineating the problems facing the regular clergy in New Spain, as well as their usually practical solutions.

More recently, some scholars have challenged the Ricardian view as incomplete, and have begun exploring indigenous viewpoints using selected texts produced by the friars. A theoretical framework for Indian responses to Christianity has been outlined by J. Jorge Klor de Alva, and the degree to which indigenous thought and beliefs shaped Indians' acceptance and understanding of Christianity has received sophisticated analysis from Louise Burkhart.[9] Burkhart has gone farther than any other scholar in showing how indigenous beliefs shaped the form and content of the Christian message, not just in its reception by the Nahuas but in its original framing by the Spanish religious.

Background of the Spiritual Conquest

The "spiritual conquest," the attempt by Spanish clergy to convert the indigenous peoples of the New World to Christianity, was seen as a necessary companion to the military conquest. For Spaniards of the late fifteenth and early sixteenth centuries, militant Christianity was an integral part of the world view, stemming from their successful struggle to reconquer Spain. It turned their overseas expeditions into missions of discovery, conquest, settlement, and conversion. Conversion was politically important, for it was the legal basis for the Spanish crown's overseas empire.[10] The first phase of religious efforts, in the Caribbean (1492–1519), was not conspicuously successful, since the indigenous population was on the road to extinction. Systematic proselytizing began in Mexico with the mendicant orders—Franciscans, Dominicans, and Augustinians—shortly after the fall of Tenochtitlan.[11]

---

8. Ricard, *Spiritual Conquest*. This work was begun in 1922; it was first published in 1933 in French. See the translator's preface, vii.

9. J. Jorge Klor de Alva, "Spiritual Conflict and Accommodation in New Spain: Toward a Typology of Aztec Responses to Christianity," in Collier et al., *Inca and Aztec States*, 345–66; Louise M. Burkhart, *The Slippery Earth: Nahua-Christian Moral Dialogue in Sixteenth-Century Mexico* (Tucson: Univ. of Arizona Press, 1989).

10. For the political implications of conversion, see Charles Gibson, *Spain in America* (New York: Harper and Row, 1966), 15–19.

11. Cortés requested that Franciscans and Dominicans be sent to New Spain rather than the secular clergy, partly because the regulars were better educated, had experience with evangelization, and were perceived as having higher moral standards. Since administration of the sacraments usually came under the secular clergy's jurisdiction, papal approval of the spe-

The Spaniards' experiences attempting to convert Jews and Muslims on the Iberian peninsula set the precedents for strategies utilized in the New World.[12] On the other hand, the New World populations differed from the Jews and Muslims, who had had contact with Christianity and rejected it. The Indians were to be won to Christianity by preaching and example, not coercion. Moreover, expulsion of those who refused baptism was not an option, as it had been in Iberia. The complex civilization of the Nahuas of Central Mexico put missionary efforts to the test, but dense populations were rapidly converted to the rudiments of Christian belief and practice.

In central Mexico the Spanish administrative structures, both civil and ecclesiastical, were based on the organization of native political structures, particularly the *altepetl*, or province-sized city-state.[13] In the civil sphere, the largest altepetl became the basis for the colonial structure of *cabeceras*, or head towns, with outlying settlements as *sujetos*, or subject communities. In the conquest period, the labor of these native communities was awarded to Spaniards in encomiendas. As for the church, sometime in the early sixteenth century it organized *doctrinas*, with resident clergy in the main settlements, and outlying population clusters designated *visitas*. The visitas were an integral part of the ecclesiastical structure, but their residents saw the clergy only at intervals.[14]

Precisely when these colonial structures were formally established is unclear. The territory was divided among the three main mendicant orders, which assumed the major responsibility for evangelizing the Indians. Because the Franciscans arrived first in 1524, they had first choice; but the Dominicans quickly asserted themselves after their arrival in 1526. The Augustinians, arriving last in 1533, often staked out territories unclaimed by the other two orders.[15]

cial arrangement had to be obtained. Hernán Cortés, *Letters from Mexico*, trans. Anthony R. Pagden (New York: Grossman Publishers, 1971), 332–34; Ricard, *Spiritual Conquest*, 20–21.

12. E. Randolph Daniel, *The Franciscan Concept of Mission in the High Middle Ages* (Lexington: Univ. Press of Kentucky, 1975); R. W. Southern, *Western Views of Islam in the Middle Ages* (Cambridge: Harvard Univ. Press, 1962); R. I. Burns, "Christian-Islamic Confrontation of the West: The Thirteenth-Century Dream of Conversion," *American Historical Review* 76 (1971), 1386–1434; Norman Daniel, *Islam and the West: The Making of an Image* (Edinburgh: Edinburgh Univ. Press, 1962); Joseph F. O'Callaghan, *A History of Medieval Spain* (Ithaca: Cornell Univ. Press, 1975).

13. See Charles Gibson, *The Aztecs Under Spanish Rule* (Stanford: Stanford Univ. Press, 1964); and Lockhart, *Nahuas After the Conquest*.

14. This study uses the term *clergy* to denote all religious personnel involved in the evangelization, though it focuses on the regular clergy. On the visitas, see James Lockhart and Stuart Schwartz, *Early Latin America: A History of Colonial Spanish America and Brazil* (Cambridge: Cambridge Univ. Press, 1983); Ricard, *Spiritual Conquest*; and Gibson, *Aztecs Under Spanish Rule*.

15. Ricard, *Spiritual Conquest*, 20–23, 61–82.

The Morelos Censuses

The set of early sixteenth-century Nahuatl censuses covers six Morelos communities: Huitzillan, Quauhchichinollan, Tepoztlan, Molotlan, Tepetenchic, and Panchimalco. The three volumes of census material are well known to specialists, and portions of them have been published.[16] Although they have been examined carefully for information on social and economic structure, their record of baptisms and Christian marriages has been largely overlooked. Pedro Carrasco points to the large number of unbaptized persons as evidence for the early dating of the censuses, but does not pursue the matter further.[17] The data on individuals' baptismal status and, to a lesser extent, the number of couples joined in Christian marriage, can be analyzed to trace the contours of the spiritual conquest in a central Mexican region approximately 20 years after the fall of Tenochtitlan.

Just as the Ricardian view has its limitations, the Morelos censuses present an incomplete picture, both from the indigenous side and for the entire central Nahua region. To begin with, except for Tepoztlan, the exact location of these towns cannot be pinpointed, although Carrasco has suggested the others may have been near Yautepec.[18] The scholarly literature generally agrees in placing all of these towns in the domain awarded to the conqueror Hernando Cortés, the Marquesado del Valle de Oaxaca. Because it was part of the Marquesado, Morelos had fewer Spaniards, and in some ways the area was relatively isolated from Central Mexico. The censuses are not dated, but all appear to have been composed at the same

16. The censuses for Molotlan and Tepetenchic, both in MNAH-AH, vol. 551, have been published in full by Eike Hinz and his colleagues Claudine Hartau and Marie-Luise Heimann-Koenen, eds., *Zur indianischen Wirtschaft und Gesellschaft im Marquesado um 1540: Aus dem "Libro de Tributos" (Col. Ant. Ms. 551) im Archivo Histórico, México,* 2 vols. (Hanover: Verlag für Ethnologie, 1983). The Huitzillan and Quauhchichinollan censuses (MNAH-AH, vol. 549) will appear in S. L. Cline, *The Book of Tributes: Early Sixteenth-Century Nahuatl Censuses from Morelos* (Los Angeles: UCLA Latin American Center Publications, forthcoming). The Tepoztlan (MNAH-AH, vol. 550; Bibliothèque Nationale, Paris, Manuscrit Mexicain 393) and Panchimalco (MNAH-AH, vol. 551) censuses remain unpublished. Pedro Carrasco has published an excerpt of the Molotlan census, "La casa y la hacienda de un señor tlalhuica," *Estudios de Cultura Náhuatl* 10 (1972), 22–54, as well as a series of descriptions and analyses of the material: "Tres libros de tributos del Museo Nacional de México y su importancia para los estudios demográficos," in *XXXV Congreso Internacional de Americanistas, México 1962, Actas y Memorias,* 1964, 3:373–78; "Family Structure of Sixteenth-Century Tepoztlan," in *Process and Pattern in Culture: Essays in Honor of Julian H. Steward,* ed. Robert A. Manners (Chicago: Aldine, 1964), 185–210; "Estratificación social indígena en Morelos durante el siglo XVI," in *Estratificación social en la Mesoamérica prehispánica,* ed. Pedro Carrasco and Johanna Broda (Mexico City: Centro de Investigaciones Superiores, Instituto Nacional de Antropología e Historia, 1976), 102–17; "The Joint Family in Ancient Mexico: The Case of Molotla," in *Essays on Mexican Kinship,* ed. Hugo Nutini et al. (Pittsburgh: Univ. of Pittsburgh Press, 1976), 45–64.

17. Carrasco, "Family Structure," 186.

18. Carrasco, "Estratificación social," 102–3.

time, probably sometime between 1535 and 1540, to resolve a dispute between Cortés and the crown.[19]

Not knowing the precise location of five of the six towns also raises the question of which religious order evangelized them. All three mendicant orders operated in Cortés' Morelos domain. The Franciscans established themselves in Cuernavaca in 1525, the Dominicans soon after in Oaxtepec (1528), and the Augustinians in Yecapixtla (1535). The Dominicans are known to have established monasteries in Tepoztlan (ca. 1556) and Yautepec (ca. 1550); they were doubtless operating there before the church buildings were constructed.[20] If Carrasco's supposition is correct, it is likely that the Dominicans were responsible for evangelization in all the census towns. The matter is relevant because the Franciscans and the Dominicans had different philosophies of evangelization. The Dominicans emphasized more instruction before baptism than the Franciscans did.[21] The order in charge in a given place could therefore affect the baptismal rates. Despite this and other difficulties in using the censuses, however, these records are extremely valuable for their abundant information on the Nahuas' acceptance of some Christian forms.

The census data were undoubtedly collected for tribute purposes, and they are presented in two forms: house-to-house enumerations and final summaries of specific categories of information. With some variations, the enumerations list the head of household (usually a senior male) and all his dependents, along with their relationship to him. The age of each unmarried child is generally given. A person's baptismal status is noted, and in some cases couples sacramentally married are indicated as such. In the Tepoztlan census (volume 550), the listings for children are not as complete, giving information only on the oldest unmarried child. Married children are listed with their spouses; unmarried younger children have no enumeration for gender, age, or baptismal status. All the censuses specify

19. The analysis of the census data here assumes the dating is contemporaneous. Carrasco, "Estratificación social"; Hinz et al., *Aztekischer Zensus*; and Cline, *Book of Tributes*, all believe that the censuses were completed ca. 1535–1540. See also Cline's detailed discussion of the dating.

Cortés had been awarded in encomienda 23,000 tributaries in 22 named towns. The dispute concerned what constituted the tributary unit. The crown, attempting to curb Cortés' power, wanted a small unit, such as the nuclear family; Cortés sought as large a unit as possible, such as the household, which could be complex. A commission of six was constituted to resolve the dispute, and the census of Cortés' domain was undertaken. Scholars consider the Morelos censuses to be a direct result of this dispute. G. Micheal Riley discusses the dispute in *Fernando Cortés and the Marquesado in Morelos, 1522–1547: A Case Study in the Socioeconomic Development of Sixteenth-Century Mexico* (Albuquerque: Univ. of New Mexico Press, 1973), 28–34.

20. Peter Gerhard, *A Guide to the Historical Geography of New Spain* (Cambridge: Cambridge Univ. Press, 1972), 96; Ricard, *Spiritual Conquest*, chap. 3.

21. Ricard, *Spiritual Conquest*, chap. 4.

the size of the household's fields and the amount and periodicity of tribute deliveries.

Although information on baptism (and sometimes Christian marriage) is given in the individual household listings, it is not found in the final summaries, apparently because it has no economic significance. The summaries indicate only the numbers of people in different civil categories: married couples, with no distinction between Christian marriage and other unions; widows; single persons; and minor children, as well as total tribute goods delivered.[22]

One set of questions for analyzing the census data focuses on the dynamics of baptism: who was baptized first and why; whether baptism affected household structure and economic arrangements; how baptism affected married couples; whether baptismal rates differed between males and females, adults and minors; how Christian names and naming patterns evolved; and how the baptized indigenous perceived the unbaptized. Other questions involve Christian marriage: how extensive it was at this period, who entered such unions, and what were the Indians' attitudes toward and expectations of this institution. The patterns that emerge yield a picture of baptism and marriage in the indigenous context to determine how it affected individual lives, the larger social and economic structure, and the pace of the spiritual conquest.

The censuses reveal significant variations not only in the total number baptized in different places, but also the age and gender of those baptized. In addition, patterns of Christian marriage seem to vary from one community to another. From these data researchers can speculate about the presence and effectiveness of clergy in the region.

Baptismal Patterns

Comparing the tribute levies of households that included baptized persons and those that did not indicates that baptism caused no obvious economic impact, good or bad. Both the baptized and the unbaptized had similar-sized fields and tribute requirements. Since the censuses were apparently compiled for economic reasons, the fact that information on baptism and Christian marriage was collected even in the individual household listings is notable. Such information must have had social significance that warranted recording it, yet apparently it had no economic ramifications.

Spanish sources provide some idea of whom the friars first sought to baptize. Just as the Spaniards used the standard technique of capturing

22. The final summaries are found, respectively, in MNAH-AH 549, fol. 36r, v, fol. 63v; MNAH-AH 550, fol. 1r, v; Hinz et al., *Aztekischer Zensus* 1:139–40 (fol. 44r), 2:117 (fol. 79v); MNAH-AH 551, fol. 113v.

the cacique to hasten military conquest, the friars meant to facilitate large-scale religious conversion by targeting indigenous rulers for baptism. This followed the European practice of converting the monarch so that his subjects would follow suit.[23] Colonial Mexican texts by Nahuas prominently record the conversion of rulers. Even if the purported early baptism of the Indian lords of Tlaxcala is not historically accurate, it is a celebrated episode in that polity's history. In Texcoco, its ruler, Ixtlilxochitl, and some others were said to have been baptized by Fray Martín de Valencia in 1524, perhaps after instruction by Fray Pedro de Gante. Children were also targeted for baptism, particularly rulers' sons.[24]

The Morelos censuses contain evidence that native elites were targeted for baptism, presumably so as to exert pressure on their subjects to convert also. The dynastic rulers (*tlatoque*; singular *tlatoani*) of Huitzillan, Quauhchichinollan, and Tepoztlan, as well as the rulers of Molotlan, Tepetenchic, and Panchimalco were baptized. What is more interesting in these rulers' households, however, is that in a number of cases not all members were baptized. The Huitzillan *tlatoani*'s household comprised 20 people, 11 of whom were baptized. Six of his 8 children were baptized; only the youngest 2 were not. The *tlatoani* had 6 concubines, just 3 of whom were baptized. There were also various unbaptized dependents.[25] The ruler of Quauhchichinollan was baptized, but in his household of 17 only 3 others were, including a concubine, a brother, and a dependent's child.[26] In Tepoztlan, however, the ruler's household of 10 had just one unbaptized person, a slave.[27] Molotlan's ruler's household had 15 people, only 2 of whom were not baptized.[28] Of all the rulers' households, only in those of Tepetenchic and Panchimalco was everyone baptized.[29] Although these are high rates of baptism, unbaptized adults were present even in these elite residences. Therefore the decision to be baptized could have remained an individual one for adults.

The rulers' households in turn are an index to baptismal patterns in the larger communities (see table 1). Quauhchichinollan, followed by Huitzillan, had the fewest baptisms overall, while Molotlan, Tepetenchic, and

23. J. N. Hillgarth, *The Conversion of Western Europe, 350–750* (Englewood Cliffs: Prentice-Hall, 1969).
24. On Tlaxcala, see Diego Muñoz Camargo, *Historia de Tlaxcala* (Mexico City: Editorial Innovación, 1978). On Texcoco, see Fernando Alva Ixtlilxochitl, *Obras históricas*, Mexico (1891–92), 1:399, cited in Ricard, *Spiritual Conquest*, 84. Motolinia also notes the importance of children for indoctrination and the targeting of elites' sons for education. *Memoriales*, 38, 439, 444.
25. Cline, *Book of Tributes*, Huitzillan (H) 1.
26. Ibid., Quauhchichinollan (Q) 1.
27. MNAH-AH 550, fol. 5v.
28. Hinz et al., *Aztekischer Zensus* 1:Hh1.
29. Ibid. 2:Hh1.

TABLE 1: Numbers of Nahua Baptized

	Male	Female	Total baptized	Total in census	Percentage
Huitzillan	77	50	127	1,464	9
Quauhchichinollan	34	5	39	971	4
Tepoztlan[a]	870	828	1,698	3,123	—
Molotlan	382	.425	807	1,057	76
Tepetenchic	337	342	679	813	84
Panchimalco	447	488	935	1,191	79

[a] Incomplete data. Gender and baptismal status unknown for 521 children.

TABLE 2: Baptismal Status by Household

	Baptized[a]								Total households
	All		Some		None		Unknown[b]		
	No.	%	No.	%	No.	%	No.	%	
Huitzillan	2	1	54	30	114	63	10	6	180
Quauhchichinollan	0	0	25	19	104	77	6	4	135
Tepoztlan[c]	218	39	298	54	36	7	0	0	552
Molotlan	48	38	65	50	15	12	0	0	128
Tepetenchic	61	53	52	45	3	2	0	0	116
Panchimalco	69	41	87	51	13	8	0	0	169

[a] These are broad groupings. The category "some baptized" ranges from households with only one baptized to those with only one unbaptized.
[b] Household enumerations are only fragments, due to manuscript damage.
[c] Data incomplete for children. Data in the "all" and "some" categories should be taken as provisional, based on available information.

Panchimalco all had high percentages. Tepoztlan's data are problematic because the information on children is more limited, but the rate of adult baptism is high.

The distribution of the baptized varied from one community to another (table 2). Tepetenchic had the highest percentage of households with everyone baptized—more than half; Panchimalco and Molotlan also had significant numbers in that category, as did Tepoztlan, from available data. Quauhchichinollan had no household at all with everyone baptized, and the two cases in Huitzillan were highly unusual two-person households— baptized couples with no dependents.[30] Households comprising a mixture of baptized and unbaptized were close to half in Tepoztlan, Molotlan, Tepetenchic, and Panchimalco, with Huitzillan and Quauhchichinollan

30. Highly complex households are the norm in most of the Morelos censuses; couples residing alone are very rare.

462 | HAHR | AUGUST | SARAH CLINE

TABLE 3: Numbers of Unbaptized in Mixed Households

Number unbaptized per household	Households					
	H	Q	Tepoz	M	Tepe	P
1	1	0	120	25	20	38
2	4	0	97	21	16	27
3	4	1	34	10	6	10
4	6	1	30	4	3	5
5	5	5	8	1	4	3
6	3	1	4	1	2	2
7	5	2	2	2	1	1
8	2	2	2	0	0	0
9	10	5	0	1	0	1
10	5	3	1	0	0	0
11	1	3	0	0	0	0
12	3	1	0	0	0	0
13	1	1	0	0	0	0
14	4	0	0	0	0	0
Total mixed households	54	25	298	65	52	87

H = Huitzillan, Q = Quauhchichinollan, Tepoz = Tepoztlan, M = Molotlan, Tepe = Tepetenchic, P = Panchimalco

again lagging. The unbaptized constituted the majority in Quauhchichi-nollan, with more than three-quarters of the households showing no one baptized, closely followed by Huitzillan. The number of unbaptized house-holds in Molotlan, Tepoztlan, Panchimalco, and Tepetenchic was negli-gible; especially Tepetenchic, with just 3 cases out of 116.

In the households with a mixture of baptized and unbaptized, the analysis of who was unbaptized gives further insight into the dynamics of conversion. Table 3 compares the numbers of unbaptized in mixed house-holds, showing that generally in Tepetenchic, Molotlan, Panchimalco, and to the extent known, Tepoztlan, only one or two people were unbaptized in a given household, whereas in Huitzillan and Quauhchichinollan the unbaptized generally constituted the majority of household members. The latter two communities show no clustering of baptized members in a few households, and the other four show no clustering of unbaptized. In Hui-tzillan and Quauhchichinollan some of the mixed households could be quite large, with as many as 14 unbaptized members. How isolated the one or two baptized felt in this situation is not known.

In the four communities with high percentages of baptized, the unbap-tized in mixed households provide a means to understand conversion at an advanced but still incomplete stage. Table 4 indicates that in those com-munities the mixed households included more unbaptized adults than children. Children are lumped into a single category, since gender cannot

TABLE 4: Gender and Age of Unbaptized in Mixed Households

	Tepoztlan[a]	Tepetenchic		Molotlan		Panchimalco	
	No.	No.	%	No.	%	No.	%
Men	257	42	37	54	36	91	49
Women	304	47	41	71	47	42	34
Children	65[b]	25	22	26	17	32	17
Total	626	114	100	151	100	185	100

[a] Household enumerations include data for first child only.
[b] Baptismal status of 521 children unknown.

always be determined by the Nahuatl given name. Children in these four communities accounted for less than a quarter of the unbaptized, and a great number of these were newborns.

A much larger number of household heads were unbaptized. Panchimalco had 49, one a woman (29 percent); Molotlan 28 (22 percent); Tepetenchic 22 (19 percent); and Tepoztlan 158 (29 percent). Clearly, heads of households were not dictating the baptismal status of household members, but it is even more interesting that frequently the head was the only one not baptized. Given that the majority of the population in these four communities was baptized, the continuing non-Christian status of household heads in the community at large may indicate either that they were not targeted for baptism or, if they were, they resisted it.

A small but noteworthy group of the unbaptized were slaves. Only a few slaves resided in Tepoztlan, Huitzillan, and Tepetenchic, and many of them were unbaptized. The entire Huitzillan census lists just 1 slave, in the *tlatoani*'s household, where the slave was one of 9 unbaptized residents.[31] The Tepoztlan *tlatoani*'s household, however, contained 6 slaves, just 1 of whom was unbaptized. The community as a whole included 17 unbaptized slaves and 13 baptized; of the baptized, all but one were women. The baptized were concentrated in five households and the unbaptized in 9 households.[32] Tepetenchic had 6 slaves; 3 baptized, 3 unbaptized.[33]

Slaves in early colonial central Mexico generally had held that status since the pre-Hispanic era. Slavery came to an end fairly early in the central region, though it continued in frontier areas, especially targeting natives who fiercely resisted pacification.[34] Slaves in pre-Hispanic society could marry and hold property on their own, but how much their sub-

31. Cline, *Book of Tributes*, H1.
32. MNAH-AH 550, fols. 5r, 6r, 33v, 34v, 37v, 44v, 47v, 48v, 55r.
33. Hinz et al., *Aztekischer Zensus* 2:Hh2, Hh47, Hh48.
34. Gibson, *Aztecs Under Spanish Rule*, 154.

464 | HAHR | AUGUST | SARAH CLINE

ordinate status changed in the colonial period is unclear. Why many of
the slaves in the Morelos censuses are unbaptized is not known. Did the
clergy put less effort into converting them? As the foregoing examples
have shown, rulers and household heads apparently did not coerce adults
in their units to convert; the evidence that unbaptized slaves shared households with baptized residents may enhance the perception that adult baptism was an individual choice. Perhaps continued non-Christian status for
these native slaves was a form of resistance. On the other hand, slave-
owners might have kept their slaves away from the clergy, controlling the
slaves in a manner not possible with kin or other dependents. Or perhaps
slave status brought with it some form of ostracism similar to the treatment
of outside groups in Nahua communities. Here that treatment might have
been applied to exclude slaves from the higher status of the baptized.

Huitzillan and Quauhchichinollan

The two communities where fewer people were baptized present sharply
different patterns from the other four. The contrast suggests that the conversion process was captured at two different points: the initial contact by
the religious in Quauhchichinollan and Huitzillan, and the more advanced
stage in the other four communities. The critical factor is the frequency
of contact with the Spanish religious. This cannot be proven definitively,
since the censuses contain neither explicit testimony of contact with the
religious nor specific evidence for these communities from the religious
themselves. In general, however, in the early sixteenth century, the Nahua
population was dense (although reduced by epidemics) and the number of
Spanish religious was small. These conditions had changed by the end of
the century, with a smaller indigenous population and sufficient clergy to
minister to them.[35]

It is generally accepted that by this later time, everyone in the area
close to Mexico City was baptized or passing as such. The *Códice franciscano* reports that the friars dealt with the delicate matter of Indians
passing themselves off as baptized. When the friars became aware of the
situation, they would secretly baptize those Indians.[36] In the latter sixteenth century, the usual practice was for all central Mexican Indians to
be baptized, and its lack was hidden and cause for further subterfuge.

In the earlier period, however, the data are relatively reliable, and
those for Quauhchichinollan and Huitzillan can be comparatively ana-

35. The sufficient number of secular religious personnel was an argument the secular
clergy used to wrest control of parishes from the mendicant orders.
36. *Códice franciscano, siglo XVI. Nueva colección de documentos para la historia de
México* (Mexico City: Editorial Salvador Chávez Hayho, 1941), 81.

TABLE 5: Gender and Age of Baptized

	Huitzillan				Quauhchichinollan	
	Section 1		Section 2			
	No.	%	No.	%	No.	%
Men	8	14	13	18	6	15
Women	12	22	13	18	3	8
Total adults	20	36	26	36	9	23
Boys	26	47	30	42	28	72
Girls	8	15	16	22	2	5
Total children	34	62	46	64	30	77
Total males	34	62	43	60	34	87
Total females	21[a]	38	29	40	5	13
Total baptized	55	100	72	100	39	100

[a]One female could not be identified as adult or child. She is included only in the total of females.

lyzed. The Huitzillan census is divided into two distinct sections.[37] The first part consists of 41 households closest in the listings to the *tlatoani*'s household. The second part consists of 139 households. The distinction between the first and second sections is quite useful. In both communities, the baptized are a small percentage of the total population (see table 1). Quauhchichinollan had a population of 971, of which only 39, or about 4 percent, were baptized. The total population of Huitzillan was 1,464, with 274 in the first section and 1,190 in the second. The baptized were 20 percent of the population in the first section and just 6 percent of the second section (see table 5). The Quauhchichinollan census and the second section of the Huitzillan census are thus roughly comparable.

In neither Quauhchichinollan nor Huitzillan were adults the majority of the baptized population. Quauhchichinollan and the second section of Huitzillan reported relatively few adult women baptized. The first section of Huitzillan, with its higher percentage of baptized, shows more baptized women than men. Children were the majority of the baptized, and overwhelmingly they were boys. This confirms Motolinia's reports about the targeting of children.[38] Quauhchichinollan shows a great imbalance be-

37. The Quauhchichinollan census is bound between the two sections of the Huitzillan census. At what point the volumes were put together and why an error occurred in the foliation is unclear. The first 41 households in Huitzillan were probably geographically closer to the *tlatoani*'s, but the text provides no confirmation of this.
38. Motolinia estimates that the Franciscans had baptized "more than one hundred thousand persons, most of them children" (*Mis compañeros tienen hasta hoy bautizados más de cada cien mil personas, los más de ellos niños*). Since he uses *niños*, it is unclear whether he means children or just boys. *Memoriales*, 444.

tween baptized males and females. Huitzillan's data show more males than females being baptized, but the percentage difference is not as glaring. In sum, in these two communities, the typical baptized person was a boy.

The age breakdown of the baptized minors also deserves attention. In Huitzillan and Quauhchichinollan, for both boys and girls, the largest number of baptized were between 6 and 10 years old—a very impressionable age. If the Huitzillan and Quauhchichinollan censuses are taken as models of how baptism was introduced, they indicate that infant baptism was not the norm initially. In only one case in either of these censuses is a child baptized at less than a year old: one Tomás was born "half a year ago" (ya tlacoxivitl. yn tlacat).[39]

Judging from the relatively few unbaptized children in the other communities, infant baptism probably became standard as contact with clergy increased. In Panchimalco, for example, census entries indicate a baptized child was "born last year" (ya monamicti yn tlacat). Even more common was the dating of a baptized child's birth to a certain number of days (usually in multiples of 20).[40] According to the Códice franciscano, in the second half of the sixteenth century parents would bring children to be baptized on Sundays at Mass and Thursdays at vespers, but when this custom was established is unclear.[41]

The baptism patterns for households differed slightly between Quauhchichinollan and Huitzillan (table 6). In Quauhchichinollan the most common household situation was that just one person was baptized. This was not the case in Huitzillan, where often several members of a household were baptized. In Quauhchichinollan, 74 percent of the households with baptized had just one baptized person, and it was rarely the household head. In the first section of the Huitzillan census (the one with the closer connection to the tlatoani), only 26 percent of the households with baptized had just one baptized member, while in the second section 47 percent fell into that category. The higher number of Huitzillan baptized in the tlatoani's household (11) and the larger number of households with multiple baptized residents in section one suggest that the tlatoani's baptism did indeed have an influence on his subjects, although it was not decisive. A possible conclusion is that the religious targeted the tlatoani's district first for evangelization.

As to who was baptized in Quauhchichinollan and Huitzillan, it was, as noted earlier, fewer adults than children; but who they were is worth examining. In the first section of Huitzillan it was common—though not the rule—for the householder himself to be baptized. In Quauhchichinollan,

39. Cline, Book of Tributes, H#15. (# indicates the second section of Huitzillan.)
40. MNAH-AH 551, fol. 81r.
41. Códice franciscano, 82.

TABLE 6: Number of Baptized per Household

Number baptized per household	Huitzillan		Quauhchichinollan
	Section 1	Section 2	
1	6	15	16
2	6	12	6
3	3	4	1
4	3	4	2[b]
5	1	1	0
11	1[a]	0	0
Total households with baptized	20	36	25
Total households in census	41	139	135

[a] Tlatoani's household
[b] One is tlatoani's household

TABLE 7: Baptized Person's Relationship to Household Head

	Huitzillan		Quauhchichinollan
	Section 1	Section 2	
Self	7	6	2
Wife	7	3	0
Concubine	3	0	1
Son	12	18	13
Daughter	6	10	1
Brother	4	3	10
Sister	0	0	0
Nephew	3	3	3
Niece	0	5	1
Brother-in-law	3	5	0
Sister-in-law	1	6	1
Other	9	13	7
Total baptized	55	72	39

however, just six men were baptized at all, and of these only two were household heads. The category "other" in table 7 includes a variety of kin, encompassing many complex household situations that are reflected in the size of this category.[42]

For the adults in the community, the baptism of children may not have been initially significant. The baptism of the male household head was clearly important, as seen in collective designations of baptismal status; but whether these notations were judgments by the census taker or by the

42. The complexities of household structure and kinship are the main topics of analysis in the published literature.

TABLE 8: Couples' Baptismal Patterns

	Huitzillan	Quauhchichinollan	Tepoztlan	Molotlan	Tepetenchic	Panchimalco
Husband+/Wife+	7	1	517 (61%)	170 (66%)	137 (78%)	185 (67%)
Husband+/Wife−	9	2	72	14	4	11
Husband−/Wife+	7	0	62 (16%)[a]	22 (14%)[a]	12 (9%)[a]	55 (23%)[a]
Husband−/Wife−	273 (92%)	276 (99%)	198 (23%)	50 (20%)	22 (13%)	46 (15%)
Total	296	279	849	256	175	297

+ Baptized, − Unbaptized
[a]Combined percentage +/− and −/+

household member or members giving the information is unclear. In the Quauhchichinollan census, which has the largest percentage of unbaptized people, scribes wrote the phrase "None of the residents here is baptized" (*y nica chaneque ayac mocuatequia*) as the opening formula for the household.[43] Frequently this blanket statement was incorrect; the households did have baptized members. Examination of the households indicates that in none of the cases of incorrect identification was the household head the baptized person. With the exception of two instances, none of the unacknowledged baptized was an adult.[44] A very interesting case is a household where five members were baptized, including the only couple in the whole census to be married sacramentally, but the enumeration begins, "no one is baptized here."[45] The importance of the baptismal status of the head of household (almost always an adult male) thus emerges; children and non-household heads counted for less.

The overall baptismal patterns for couples indicate that most partners had the same status (table 8). In Molotlan, Tepetenchic, Panchimalco, and Tepoztlan, most people were baptized; and this trend also appears in couples' baptismal patterns (and since the Tepoztlan data are complete for adults, the information on partners' status is comparable to the other censuses). Both partners baptized constituted the clear majority in Tepoztlan, Molotlan, Tepetenchic, and Panchimalco. Unbaptized couples were the majority in Huitzillan and Quauhchichinollan, where virtually no one was baptized. For the four communities that were more mixed, unbaptized couples still constituted a significant minority (see percentages in table 8). Mixed couples were a minority overall in these four communities. In Panchimalco the wife baptized and the husband not was more usual (19 percent) than vice versa (4 percent). There is one example of a Panchimalco household with three couples in which the wives are baptized but the husbands are not.[46] Overall, the differences in the other communities are not as lopsided as in Panchimalco.

In Huitzillan and Quauhchichinollan the baptismal status of parents and minor children often differed. Households included unbaptized parents and baptized children, frequently when there was just one child.[47] A number of unbaptized parents had all their children baptized.[48] More frequently, though, only some minor children were baptized.

Where some children were baptized and others not, no clear pattern

43. Cline, *Book of Tributes*, Q48.
44. Ibid., Q13, Q14, Q17, Q38, Q43, Q47, Q58, Q62, Q65, Q66, Q109.
45. Ibid., Q17.
46. MNAH-AH 551, fol. 108v.
47. Cline, *Book of Tributes*, H2, H20, H22, H39, H#11, H#15, H#22, H#43, H#45, H#59.
48. Ibid., H3, H33, H#10, H#52.

emerges. Sometimes the only one baptized was the oldest, but in other cases, the only minor child not baptized was the oldest.[49] The unbaptized oldest child often appeared where the parents were unbaptized. In one family with five children, the only one not baptized was a 15-year-old son.[50] It might be speculated that it was his own decision not to be baptized. Another unusual situation is a family with three children. The two minors, aged 6 and 3, were baptized, but the married eldest daughter, Teyacapan, was unbaptized and married to a baptized man. Since Teyacapan was surrounded by her baptized husband and siblings, her unbaptized status is noteworthy.[51] If familial pressure was exerted for her to be baptized, she seems to have resisted it.

When only the youngest child was not baptized, perhaps lack of opportunity rather than lack of desire was at work. This was doubtless the case in Molotlan, Tepetenchic, and Panchimalco, with their high baptism rates. Even in Huitzillan, with its lower overall rate, there seems to be some evidence of this. The *tlatoani* and his wife had six of their seven children baptized; only the youngest was not.[52] In Huitzillan and Quauhchichinollan, however, the baptism of the youngest or younger two, but not the oldest, was not unusual.[53] Perhaps the older the child, the more personal the choice.

Christian Names and Naming Patterns

Upon baptism a person took or was given a Christian saint's name. Where the census listing does not explicitly say a person is baptized, the listing of a Christian name is a sure indicator of baptism. In some cases siblings within the same family had the same saint's name, which might suggest that the Christian name was not what the person was usually called. It might also imply that the cleric did not know his parishioners well, for he might have hesitated to baptize siblings with the same name. Individuals clearly knew their Spanish baptismal names, however, because the census reproduces them.

While it was unusual for siblings to bear the same baptismal name, it was common for mothers and fathers to have the same baptismal name as their same-gender children. For men, this was a change from pre-

49. Ibid., H4, H24, H32, H#5, H#10, H#54, H#55, H#61, H#133, Q17, Q31, Q45; and H#61, H#113.
50. Ibid., H#61.
51. Ibid., H#113.
52. Ibid., H1. The *tlatoani* also had another unbaptized child, two years old, probably by another woman.
53. Ibid., H#22, H#36, H#42, H#57, Q14, Q35, Q109.

Hispanic practice, for it was rare for men to have the same Nahuatl name as their sons. Women's Nahuatl names, however, were quite stereotypical, birth-order names (Tiacapan, "oldest"; Tlaco, "middle child"; and Xoco, "youngest"). Duplication of women's Nahuatl and Christian names was frequent within the same nuclear and certainly the same extended family.

Certain phrasing in the censuses may suggest that the Nahuatl name was used as a term of address. One notation says, "She has a child, baptized, named Perico; his local name is Qualchamitl."[54] In the Molotlan census the Nahuatl name is referred to as the *macehualtoca* or "commoner name."[55] There is clearly a perceived difference between the Nahuatl name and the Christian. It is unclear whether one or the other was used by preference, but the distinction was drawn. Another entry reads, "Mexicatl's second younger sibling is named Nicolás; his old-style name is Teuctlamacazqui."[56] Nicolás was a resident of Quauhchichinollan, where few people were baptized, so he may have made a special point of his two names. His Christian commitment was quite strong, for the previous year he had married sacramentally (*teoyotica omonamicti*), the only such union recorded in Quauhchichinollan. By the end of the sixteenth century, the use of Christian given names without Nahuatl ones was quite common. Some Nahuas even took standard Spanish surnames as well.[57]

During the late sixteenth century in the Nahua community of Culhuacan, men's baptismal names showed greater variety than women's; but in nearby Coyoacan, this apparently was not the case.[58] In the Morelos censuses the pattern resembles the one found later in Culhuacan. A closer look at the male baptismal names in the Morelos censuses reveals that they are quite stereotypical. The inventory of all baptismal names comes to a total of 42 men's names and just 20 women's names, but no single community used every name.[59] The dubbing of some Indians with more unusual

54. "*hoca / ypilci / vmoquatequi ytoca pelicco y nican itoca qualchalmitl*," Ibid., H17. The phrase *nican itoca*, translated in this study as "local name," more literally means "here name."

55. Hinz et al., *Aztekischer Zensus* 2:Hh35, Hh50, Hh51, Hh53, Hh57, Hh113.

56. "*ynic umeti ycava / mexicatl - ytoca / niculas yvevetoca / tecuitlamacazqui.*" Cline, *Book of Tributes*, Q17.

57. Cline, *Colonial Culhuacan*, 117; Rebecca Horn, "Indian Women in Mexican Parish Archives: Naming Patterns in Seventeenth-Century Coyoacan" (Paper presented at the Pacific Coast Branch of the American Historical Association, Portland, Ore., 1989).

58. Cline, *Colonial Culhuacan*, 117; Horn, "Indian Women."

59. Men's names are Agustín, Alonso, Ambrosio, Andrés, Antón, Baltasar, Bartolomé, Bernardino, Blas, Calisto, Clemente, Cristóbal, Damián, Diego, Domingo, Esteban, Felipe, Francisco, Gabriel, Gerónimo, Gonzalo, Hernando, José, Juan, Julio, Lucas, Luis, Marcos, Martín, Mateo, Miguel, Nicolás, Oreden, Pablo, Pedro, Perico, Sebastián, Tomás, Toribio, Vicente. Women's names are Agustina, Ana, Ana María, Angelina, Anica, Catalina, Francisca, Juana, Juliana, Inés, Isabel, Lucía, Luisa, Magdalena, María, Marta, Mencia, Mónica, Rocín, Verónica.

baptismal names, such as Damián, Calisto, and Ambrosio, may mean that the cleric had special favorites or that Indians were given saint's names corresponding to the saint's day on which they were born or baptized.[60]

Looking at the data on Christian names for men, it is not surprising that Huitzillan and Quauhchichinollan, with their very small baptized populations, had a very narrow repertoire (Huitzillan 13; Quauhchichinollan 8). The other communities, Tepoztlan, Molotlan, Tepetenchic, and Panchimalco, list between 25 and 31 names. Even so, a few men's names were popular and accounted for the majority. The name Domingo led in all communities, with the all-time high in Quauhchichinollan, where 12 (35 percent) of the 34 baptized males had that name. The Yautepec region was a Dominican stronghold, which may account for the high proportion of Domingos and may lend weight to the supposition that the communities of unknown location were in the Yautepec area. The names Juan, Francisco, and Martín were also popular in all communities. One consideration obviously of no influence in the choice of a baptismal name was the current political ruler of Spain: no one was called Carlos.[61]

Female baptismal names showed little variety; Magdalena was the most popular. In Huitzillan 30 (63 percent) of the 48 baptized females bore that name, while in other communities it represented between 30 and 36 percent of females. It is interesting that the name was not especially common among Spanish women at this time. María was the second most popular name overall, and in Tepoztlan it just beat Magdalena. Ana and Juana were the other two names commonly given. In other parts of central Mexico, María, Magdalena, Ana, and Juana were still popular at the end of the sixteenth century.[62]

Christian Marriage

If data on baptism are copious in the Morelos censuses, evidence of Christian marriage is much less so. Permanent conjugal unions were a standard part of the pre-Hispanic social fabric, but these unions differed from Chris-

---

60. William B. Taylor has found such a pattern for eighteenth- and early nineteenth-century Mexico. See "The Virgin of Guadalupe in New Spain: An Inquiry into the Social History of Marian Devotion," *American Ethnologist* 14:1 (Feb. 1987), 9–23.

61. Carlos was not a common name at the beginning of the sixteenth century in Spain, and when it came into use in the second half of that century it was used among people of high rank. A notable indigenous example in New Spain was don Carlos Ometochtzin, a Texcocan noble, who was tried for apostasy in 1534 by the episcopal inquisition of Fray Juan de Zumárraga and then executed. In general, the Spanish monarch's name was not a usual choice for an Indian's baptismal name, but a number of Indian nobles did take elite Spanish surnames after 1550.

62. Cline, *Colonial Culhuacan*, 117. Magdalena seems not to have been a popular name in late sixteenth-century Culhuacan, however.

tian marriage in some important ways. Divorce was permissible, and so was marriage to more than one wife simultaneously. What's more, concubines had a recognized status. Christian marriage was a lifelong, indissoluble union to one spouse, though remarriage after being widowed was permissible. In practice, concubinage existed in European Christian society, but it was not morally permissible.

The mendicants tried to institute the Christian sacrament of marriage, but they were far less successful, even superficially, than they apparently were with baptism.[63] Fray Alonso de Molina's *confesionario* of 1569 goes into considerable detail about preparing the couple for the sacrament of marriage and about the relationships that prohibited marriage.[64] Molina drew up his confessional manual after the Council of Trent (1545–63), which codified various aspects of Catholic marriage practices, to counter Protestant views of marriage and divorce.[65] Molina's manual makes it explicit that both prospective partners had to be baptized. The Morelos censuses, however, deal with pre-Trent practices, so the parameters of nuptial practice are not clear. Certainly with the few people baptized in Huitzillan and Quauhchichinollan, a minimum requirement for Christian marriage was generally not fulfilled.

Language may be an indicator of shifts in native perceptions of what constituted marriage. The phrase for Christian marriage in early sixteenth-century Nahuatl is *teoyotica omonamicti*, which can be rendered as "took a match through divinity or sacrament." By the later sixteenth century, the modifier *teoyotica*, "through divinity or sacrament," was usually omitted, so the early form found in the Morelos censuses is notable. More commonly, these early censuses refer to marriage with the term *cihuatia*, "acquire a woman"; *oquichtia*, "acquire a man"; or the plural reflexive *ana*, "to take" (for example, *manque*, "they took each other"). Usually the last phrase was followed by a specification of how long a couple without children had been married. A man's wife was called *icihuauh*, "his woman," and a woman's husband *ioquich*, "her man," a variation of the more standard form *ioquichhui*. These usages seem to have been applied to men and women with recognized Christian marriages.

A Nahuatl term for spouse, *-namic*, often found in late sixteenth-century documents, does not appear in this form in any of the Morelos censuses; it may have developed later, when Christian marriage was more

63. Ricard, *Spiritual Conquest*, 110–16.
64. Alonso de Molina, *Confesionario mayor en la lengua mexicana y castellana* (1569; reprint, Mexico City: Universidad Nacional Autónoma de México, 1984), fols. 45r–58r.
65. James A. Brundage, *Law, Sex, and Society in Medieval Europe* (Chicago: Univ. of Chicago Press, 1987), 494–503; W. Van Ommerer, "Tametsi," *New Catholic Encyclopedia*, 18 vols. (New York: McGraw-Hill, 1967–89), 13:929.

firmly established. It is standard by the 1580s, when people would call their partner *nonamic*, "my spouse," and sometimes, with greater affect, *nonamictzin*, "my honorable spouse."[66] In the Morelos censuses the verbal form of -*namic, namictia*, was coming into use with the phrase *teoyotica omonamicti*, "married through divinity or sacrament," meaning Christian marriage; and the negative, *amo monamicti*, "not married." The *tlatoani* of Quauhchichinollan is described as not being married (*amo monamictia*) but having three concubines.[67] In Huitzillan the phrase *ayamo namiqueque*, "they do not yet have spouses," also appears.[68] It may well be that this terminology for marriage is a postconquest development and specifically linked to the Christian concept of sacramental marriage.

Overall, the number of couples whose marriages are explicitly said to be Christian is small. No one at all in Huitzillan apparently had a Christian marriage, and in Quauhchichinollan just one couple did; surprisingly, not the *tlatoani*.[69] For Huitzillan and Quauhchichinollan, the absence of the notation about couples with recognized Christian unions is consistent with the baptismal data. But both Panchimalco and Tepoztlan, which had high rates of baptism, list only two couples whose unions are explicitly noted as sacramental.[70] Tepetenchic had just four such couples.[71] In all these cases, the census taker went out of his way to indicate the difference between Christian marriages and others, but the comparison is not necessarily straightforward.

Only in the Molotlan census do phrases appear suggesting that Christian marriage was the norm. Census entries in other locations might imply that Christian marriage was not standard. Dynastic rulers in Panchimalco, Tepoztlan, and Tepetenchic are among the very few identified as having been married sacramentally.[72] And as noted earlier, the *tlatoani* of Quauhchichinollan is described specifically as not being married, though he has three concubines. Despite its census pattern, however, Molotlan's ruler is not explicitly identified as having a union sanctified by the church.[73] Even more interesting is that five households had varying numbers of couples described as "not married through divinity" (*ha[m]o teoyotica monamictia*).[74] Only five couples are positively described as married sacramentally.[75]

66. Cline, *Colonial Culhuacan*, 60.
67. Cline, *Book of Tributes*, Q1.
68. This is a rare and combined form of -*namic*. Ibid., H#129.
69. Ibid., Q17.
70. MNAH-AH 551, fol. 77v; 550, fols. 5r, 33v.
71. Hinz et al., *Aztekischer Zensus* 2:Hh1, Hh47, Hh114.
72. MNAH-AH 551, fol. 77v; 550, fol. 5r; Hinz et al., *Aztekischer Zensus* 2:Hh1.
73. Hinz et al., *Aztekischer Zensus* 1:Hh1.
74. Ibid., Hh8, Hh11, Hh13, Hh15, Hh28.
75. Ibid., Hh20, Hh33, Hh37, Hh71, Hh73.

For all other Molotlan couples, nothing is said one way or the other about the nature of their marital bond; but it is quite possible that Christian marriage actually was standard here and that only its lack was noteworthy.

The importance of the husband in the Indians' view of marriage (perhaps the male Indians' view) is suggested by the phrasing in a Tepetenchic household enumeration. One Francisco was married to a woman named Juana, and the passage ends, "Francisco was married through divinity" (*deoyotica omonamicti y frcv*).[76] This focus on the husband is consistent with the censuses' use of the male head of household as the point of reference for enumerations.

One highly unusual notation about a Molotlan marriage is in Nahuatlized Spanish. In translation the entry reads: "Domingo Pantli and his wife named Marta Teyacapan do not yet have children; he has been married two years." (*domingo pa[n]tli yn izivauh ytoca maltha teyacapan a[m]o pilhuaque tus anos casato*).[77] The phrase specifying the number of years married, *tus anos casato*, is an entirely standard way for a Nahuatl speaker to render the Spanish phrase *dos años casado*.[78] In these very early Nahuatl texts, which contain virtually no Spanish loanwords, this Spanish phrase indicates a certain level of contact between the Indian scribe and the Spaniards—enough for the Spanish word for "married" (*casado*) to make its way into the scribe's active vocabulary. Because language is embedded in culture, this Nahuatl-speaker's use of a Spanish phrase to indicate married status is especially noteworthy.[79] It is interesting that the couple in question is not specified as being married sacramentally. As explained earlier, in Molotlan the implication of such an omission may be that it was a Christian marriage rather than not. In this case, the Spanish phrasing implies Christian marriage, which was the Spanish norm.

The native practice of having more than one wife or a wife and concubines was something the mendicants had a good deal of difficulty stamping out—and it still has an underground existence today in some parts of central Mexico.[80] Having several wives was an index of status for men and was still standard in some communities in the early postconquest period.

---

76. Ibid., Hh114.

77. Ibid., Hh19.

78. The *t* for *d* substitutions are standard. Nahuatl has no distinction between voiced and voiceless consonants, so substitutions of *b* for *p*, *d* for *t*, and *g* for *k* are typical. For an extended discussion of linguistic questions, see Frances Karttunen and James Lockhart, *Nahuatl in the Middle Years: Language Contact Phenomena in Texts of the Colonial Period* (Berkeley: Univ. of California Press, 1976).

79. For a sophisticated analysis of culture change as measured by language, see Lockhart, *Nahuas After the Conquest*.

80. Ricard, *Spiritual Conquest*, 110–16; Hugo Nutini, "Polygyny in a Tlaxcalan Community," *Ethnology* 4 (1965), 123–47.

In Huitzillan, even though the *tlatoani*, don Tomás, had a wife (*içivahu*), he also had six concubines (*imecava*), three of whom were baptized.[81] In Quauhchichinollan the ruler, don Martín, was said to be not married (*amo monamictia*) but had three concubines (*yeyii imecava*), one of whom was baptized.[82] In Molotlan the ruler had five wives, four of whom were baptized (*yziguagua macuiltin navinti omocuatequia*).[83] The norms of Christian marriage were indeed met by some rulers, for the rulers of Tepoztlan, Tepetenchic, and Panchimalco were married sacramentally, had only one wife, and had no other partners, such as concubines.[84] In those three communities, moreover, the rate of baptism was high.

Baptism did not deter couples from living in polygynous unions. Several census listings show baptized men having two wives, both of whom were also baptized.[85] None of these unions was said to be a Christian marriage, which was expected to be a lifelong union with one partner or, at least, one partner at a time. It might be asked when baptism took place for people in polygynous relationships. Was it before or after the unions were established?

In 1530, the crown attempted to regulate converted Indians' marriage patterns by legislation, setting punishments for a man taking a second wife while the first still lived. Clearly, in the Morelos region between about 1535 and 1540, this decree seems not to have affected practice. Indians were forthcoming in stating their true situations. It is noteworthy that the 1530 royal decree allowed unbaptized Indians to follow their traditional patterns, but by 1551 the rule applied to all Indians regardless of baptismal status.[86] The clergy's concern with stamping out the practice of polygyny reportedly often resulted in the practice of men sacramentally marrying their first or favorite wife.[87]

As for Indian views of Christianity, the question of belief cannot be probed deeply, for the texts generally do not provide the means to do so. There is only a hint about one baptized Indian's attitude toward the unbaptized. A scribe for the Panchimalco census noted that "no one is baptized, they do not know our lord God" (*ayac [mocuat]equia amo quiximaty y totecuio y dios*).[88] The phrasing is entirely standard, and this is the earliest known example of it in local-level texts. in the censuses the more

81. Cline, *Book of Tributes*, H1.
82. Ibid., Q1.
83. Hinz et al., *Aztekischer Zensus* 1:Hh1.
84. MNAH-AH 550, fol. 5r; Hinz et al., *Aztekischer Zensus* 2:Hh1; MNAH-AH 551, fol. 77v.
85. MNAH-AH 551, fols. 8ov, 97v, 98r.
86. Woodrow Borah and Sherburne Cook, "Marriage and Legitimacy in Mexica Culture," *California Law Review* 54:2 (1966), 955.
87. Ricard, *Spiritual Conquest*, 113–15.
88. MNAH-AH 551, fol. 112v.

usual entry simply indicates that someone is not baptized (*amo mocua-tequia*). It is also interesting that the scribe uses the Spanish loanword *dios* for God—indicating again the impact of Spanish Christian ideas and vocabulary. It has been said that the friars used Spanish loanwords in Nahuatl discourse to make the distinction between Christian and indigenous non-Christian concepts; but what actually occurred on either side of the cultural exchange is unclear.[89]

As noted previously, the very fact that the censuses record the baptismal status of individuals, and to a lesser degree the number of Christian marriages, indicates that for the census takers as well as the natives who were enumerated, individuals' Christian status counted for something.

Conclusions

In light of the notion that Nahuas flocked to Christianity in the aftermath of conquest for a variety of political, religious, and psychological reasons, how can the Morelos census material be interpreted? It is likely that the Indians were predisposed to convert, because the pattern in pre-Hispanic central Mexico was that conquered populations took on the gods of the conquering power. James Lockhart has viewed colonial-era Nahuas as needing less to be persuaded than instructed.[90] In the Morelos censuses the baptismal patterns vary, and perhaps the sacramental marriage patterns as well. This leads to the conclusion that the communities stood at two different stages of the conversion process; Quauhchichinollan and Huitzillan essentially at the beginning and Molotlan, Tepetenchic, Panchimalco, and Tepoztlan at a later but not final stage. Although neither Spanish nor Nahua records can confirm the assumption, the variations in patterns seem to be tied directly to differences in the frequency and level of contact with the clergy. This in turn suggests that low rates of baptism and sacramental marriage in some communities can be explained as a function of clerical contact rather than indifference or resistance. Thus the notion of Nahuas readily accepting Christianity is generally supported by the data if communities had increased contact with the religious. Resident or frequently visiting clergy could baptize and catechize the Indians, perform the sacraments, and reinforce the notion of Christian marriage to one wife.

If Quauhchichinollan and Huitzillan are taken as models of communities in the early stages of evangelization, then the Indians cannot be said to have embraced Christianity en masse. In households, baptism was by

89. Certainly Molina's *confesionario*, as well as the works of Sahagún and others, have the highest proportion of Spanish loanwords in the Nahuatl for Christian concepts or practices. For an extended discussion of the problems in translating Christian religious concepts into Nahuatl, see Burkhart, *Slippery Earth.*

90. Lockhart, *Nahuas After the Conquest,* 203–4.

ones and twos, and in the community at large it was scattered, although concentrated somewhat in the *tlatoani*'s district in Huitzillan. The other four communities, Molotlan, Tepetenchic, Panchimalco, and Tepoztlan, show high rates of baptism, with the very old and the very young well represented in the unbaptized population. These communities had a few pockets of unbaptized households, but generally the unbaptized appeared by ones and twos in individual households. Baptism was standard practice, but the pace and the means by which this standard was achieved are not made explicit. The friars themselves noted variations in rates of baptism, with what we might now call quantum leaps in numbers of Christians: the period 1532–1536 was particularly important in central Mexico.[91]

The ideal of Christian conversion was that baptism should be a voluntary decision by each person regardless of class or gender. In Europe, where Christianity was tied to secular politics, conversion of the ruler meant that his subjects became Christians as well; but that European pattern was not replicated in Mexico. This is perhaps the most important conclusion from this study of Morelos baptismal patterns. The mendicant orders, particularly the Franciscans and Dominicans, who had already been involved in missionary efforts in Iberia, seem to have returned to the ideals of the early church, stressing personal religious commitment. Admittedly, in early colonial Mexico some native rulers were targeted for baptism nevertheless, and so particularly were their sons, who in the early period were seen as potential candidates for the Christian priesthood.[92]

The variation in baptismal status even in the highest-ranking Morelos households suggests that the ideal of conversion as an individual decision may have been attained to a considerable extent. The hope of the religious orders was to baptize as many as possible as soon as possible, especially because the demographic disaster was under way in Mexico as it had been in the Caribbean. But in central Mexico, apparently, the mendicants were not converting by coercion. Judging from the Morelos censuses, high-ranking converts and households were not coercing their subjects or dependents. Nor were they obstructing conversion, except possibly among their slaves. Higher rates of baptism for the *tlatoani*'s people in Huitzillan suggest that even if the *tlatoani* did not directly coerce baptism, his own baptism did influence others, if for no other reason than that the friars likely were concentrating on him and his district first.

91. According to Ricard, around 1529 "evangelization made an immense jump, and it is certain the average number of baptisms was much greater between 1532 and 1536 than between 1524 and 1532." Ricard, *Spiritual Conquest*, 91.

92. The failure of the Colegio de Santa Cruz Tlatelolco (founded 1536) was a bitter disappointment to the Franciscans, who had hoped to train caciques' sons for the priesthood. The training of the young men there did produce a core of educated Indians literate in Nahuatl, Spanish, and Latin.

The higher initial rate of baptism for males, like the targeting of rulers, may have brought social pressure to bear on Morelos families; but evidence may show that household heads resisted baptism later, in the more advanced stage of the spiritual conquest. The higher rate for minors, particularly boys, in the communities least touched by Christianity indicates the long-term interests of the clergy. These census data confirm reports by the friars themselves

The baptismal patterns of both adults and children give insight into the dynamics of conversion. The like-baptismal status of couples suggests that the marital bond was strong and that it influenced the decision whether or not to be baptized. With parents and children, the difference in baptismal status can be variously interpreted. It may have been parents' positive response to the opportunity to have their children baptized: their neutrality toward the friars' efforts to baptize the young; or their inability to prevent them. Given all the other indicators. the last possibility seems unlikely. For adults, baptism of children simply may not have seemed particularly important initially, as indicated by the cases in which households were misidentified as containing no baptized members. Actually, the misidentified households generally did not contain baptized adults.

While the decision to be baptized was probably the individual's, particularly for adults, it is unclear how much the baptismal name was an individual choice and whether it was important. It is notable that these names were either freely volunteered by household members or elicited by the census takers. Clearly, as a marker of baptized status, the baptismal name was a more specific way to distinguish one person from another. In Morelos. there was greater choice of male names than female, echoing pre-Hispanic practice; but beyond that. further insight cannot be gained. The endless numbers of Domingos. Franciscos, and Juans; Magdalenas, Marías, and Juanas may have been simply the fashion of the day. The occasional pocket of non-stereotypical names may well indicate a friar with a favorite saint at work, naming his parishioners, showing the effect of individual priests in native communities. But the choice of name may not have mattered much in any case. Certainly in the early sixteenth century, siblings bearing the same Christian name and the wider persistence of Nahuatl names could indicate that Christian names were unimportant.

The paucity of positively identified Christian marriages in the Morelos censuses is difficult to interpret. However, the evidence of multiple wives and concubines even among the baptized indicates the difficulty in changing patterns of a fundamental social institution. The friars themselves reported the difficulty, for they met considerable resistance on this matter. Pre-Hispanic patterns such as polygyny and concubinage were at odds with Christian ideals of marriage. The cases of polygynous unions where all partners were baptized suggest that Christian practice had penetrated only so far, and Spanish legal restrictions hardly at all. On the other hand, a new Nahuatl terminology for marriage seems to have been emerging. Explicit Christian marriage was worthy of mention in some of the censuses, while its lack was noteworthy in others. This is possible evidence that Christian marriage was becoming the norm in some places, while in others it may have been unusual.

Perhaps in those places where Christian marriage is explicitly noted, the friars were preoccupied with the Indians' conversion to Christianity at the most fundamental level; that is, baptism. It may be that they saw continued instruction in the catechism after baptism as the most practical next step, and fulfillment of Christian expectations concerning marriage as something that could wait for a further stage of consolidation.

The outward signs of Christian practice, measured by baptism and Christian marriage, thus show great variation from place to place within a given region a generation after the military conquest of Mexico in 1521. The information on baptism and Christian marriage comes to us as a by-product of more secular concerns—to count the native population and to assess tribute. But the impact of efforts to convert the Nahuas is seen in the very inclusion of that information in a secular census. Baptismal status and sometimes Christian marriage became identifying markers for natives.

Even though historians must generally engage this information on religious commitment in the aggregate rather than on the individual level, it represents, nevertheless, thousands of individual decisions reached through largely unknown means. It can be posited that where the religious had greater contact with the populace, the rate of conversion was higher. But why some people were baptized in places where there was no sustained contact with the friars or any economic or social pressure is unclear. While the task of changing even the outward signs of religious affiliation was a major one, the long-term enterprise of reinforcing and ensuring the Indians' orthodox belief was much more daunting.[93]

93. The reinforcement of Christian belief has been the subject of considerable interest. Some scholars of native culture have pinpointed the confessional as a key mechanism for changing native beliefs and actions. Confessional manuals in Spanish and Nahuatl provide insight as to how this might have operated. See J. Jorge Klor de Alva, "Colonizing Souls: The Failure of the Indian Inquisition and the Rise of Penitential Discipline," in *Cultural Encounters: The Impact of the Inquisition in Spain and the New World*, ed. Mary Elizabeth Perry and Anne J. Cruz (Berkeley: Univ. of California Press, 1991), 3–22. The "primitive" Inquisition and the later exclusion of the Indians from the jurisdiction of the Holy Office (established in 1571) are examined by Richard Greenleaf in two works: "The Inquisition and the Indians of New Spain: A Study in Jurisdictional Confusion," *The Americas* 22 (Oct. 1965), 138–66; and *The Mexican Inquisition of the Sixteenth Century* (Albuquerque: Univ. of New Mexico Press, 1969). The role of the Office of the Protectorate, to which baptized Indians were subject, as a reinforcer of Christian practice has been examined by Roberto Moreno de los Arcos, "New Spain's Inquisition for Indians from the Sixteenth to the Nineteenth Century," in Perry and Cruz, *Cultural Encounters*, 23–36.

11

The Black Family in the Americas

A.J.R. Russell-Wood

"Ah, but a man's reach should exceed his grasp,
Or what's a heaven for?"

(Robert Browning, *Andrea del Sarto*)

THE last decade has witnessed scholarly reappraisal of the African diaspora in the Americas. Studies, based on previously unknown or unused archival sources and employing new analytical skills, have refuted, modified, or accepted only conditionally conclusions advanced for the United States by the sociologist E. Franklin Frazier in *The Negro family in the United States* (1939), and the historians Kenneth M. Stampp in *The Peculiar Institution* (1956) and Stanley M. Elkins in *Slavery: a problem in American institutional and intellectual life* (1959). The French, Dutch, Danish, and Spanish colonies in the New World have not generated a historiographical tradition on the slave trade or slavery comparable with English North America (here referring to the thirteen English colonies and, after 1776, to the United States of America).

The exception is Brazil. From the sermons of António Vieira, S. J. (1608-97), through the ardent abolitionism of Dr. Manuel Ribeiro Rocha (*The Ethiopian ransomed, indentured, sustained, corrected, educated and liberated,* [Lisbon 1758]), to post-independence debate and oratory, Portuguese America has been a fertile breeding ground for the most conflicting views on slavery. Studies by Nina Rodrigues, Manuel Querino, and Arthur Ramos, and the organization of the First Afro-Brazilian Congress at Recife in 1934, attest not only to consuming interest in the institution itself but also in the African contribution to the economic, cultural, and social evolution of Brazil.[1] It comes as no surprise to learn that the classic study of plantation slavery south of the Rio Grande should be from the pen of the Brazilian sociologist Gilberto Freyre. His writings were to provide examples for Frank Tannenbaum's assertions on alleged differences between the two slave systems of Latin America and the United States, best expressed in *Slave and Citizen. The Negro in the Americas* (1947), and whose general thesis was to be accepted by Stanley Elkins. In much the same way as the Tannenbaum-Elkins thesis has been called to account by Arnold Sio, David Brion Davis, and Carl Degler, so too have students of Brazilian history challenged the broader conclusions of Gilberto Freyre.[2]

This process of re-examination reflects changing approaches to the discipline of history, coupled with the development of new analytical skills. Increasing awareness of insights to be gained from comparative history has been matched by enhanced appreciation of scholarly benefits accruing from an interdisciplinary approach to topics viewed previously through the exclusively historical lens. Such changing attitudes have coincided with the application to historical sources of techniques borrowed from the mathematical sciences. On occasion, unbridled enthusiasm has outweighed scholarly caution. The adoption of a comparative approach merely for the sake of being comparative has led to mismatches, superficiality, and the resultingly inadequate study of any single area of those under discussion. Benefits derivable from an interdisciplinary approach have been diminished by the all too common practice of adopting jargon or techniques without adequate preliminary study of the theoretical bases on which these are founded. The pitfall of overreliance on quantitative techniques has been exemplified by the controversy generated by *Time on the cross* once this came under scholarly scrutiny. A valuable gain from such experimentation has been the emphasis placed on nonelitist history and the broadening of the parameters of history as a discipline. The history of the slave trade from the nutritional, epidemiological, demographic, and economic aspects has largely been rewritten thanks to scholars such as Philip Curtin, Roger Anstey, Johannes Postma, Phillip LeVeen, and Pierre Verger.[3] The legal and exploitative aspects of the "peculiar institution" outside the United States have been placed in the broader cultural perspectives by Aguirre Beltrán, Frederick Bowser, Harry Hoetink, Franklin Knight, and Magnus Mörner. In Brazil the historian Emília Viotti da Costa and the sociologists Florestan Fernandes, Fernando Henrique Cardoso, and Octávio Ianni have opened up new avenues of enquiry for study of the Afro-Brazilian.[4]

A third area of scholarly reappraisal concerns the African cultures in the New World. Sociologists, anthropologists, linguists, and historians have run the gamut from denying any African dimension in the evolution of New World societies to seeing any cultural manifestation reminiscent of an African heritage as a survival. Early excesses have given way to more balanced assessments of the African legacy to the Americas and the role of the Afro-American during the colonial and independence periods. For the most part, African traditions, beliefs, and patterns of behavior underwent modifications, adapting to new social, economic, human, and ecological environments. Rather than viewing such modification as indicative of a weakened African legacy, scholars have come to view adaptive capacity as evidence of the strength and con-

A. J. R. Russell-Wood   3

tinuity of African beliefs and life styles in the Americas. *Time on the cross* (1974) by Robert Fogle and Stanley Engerman, and Eugene Genovese's *Roll, Jordan, roll: the world the slaves made* (1974) have, in their very different ways, demonstrated black achievement in a slavo-cratic society. Herbert Gutman's *The black family in slavery and freedom, 1750-1925* represents the fusion of the traditional with the innovative in research techniques, scholarly enquiry, and interpretation. The result is a major contribution in an area of slavery largely ignored by scholars: the slave family in history. Its publication is of importance not only for the historiography of the United States, but of the Americas.

Gutman's thesis and its ramifications reach into the past, present, and future of the United States, but hold lessons for the score or so of repub-lics in the Americas which count populations of African descent. He tilts at Daniel Patrick Moynihan's *The Negro family in America: the case for national action* (1965) and then current scholarship on which it was based. Such conventional views on slavery and the slave family, although not so forcefully and concisely expressed as in *The Negro family,* were shared by scholars of Spanish and Portuguese America. Briefly summarized these views were: slave women had no concept of sexual honor and gave themselves freely to an owner, his sons, or fellow blacks; slaves were licentious and promiscuous; blacks (to quote a Brazilian proverb) "join but do not marry"; the fruits of such fleeting unions were illegitimate offspring; family life and kinship ties had been destroyed by sales, masters' opposition and the internal slave trade in some regions of Spanish and Portuguese America; those few slave households there were, were matrifocal and for the most part children were reared in the absence of the father. Two further commonly held views may be added: that slaves exercised no decision-making capacity and were devoid of established sets of values, beliefs, or modes govern-ing behavior, mimetically following domestic arrangements, life styles, and naming arrangements advocated by owners; secondly, that blacks lacked the capability to adapt to so-called (in the words of Nina Rodrigues) "civilizations of superior races". Students of Latin American history, no less than those of the United States, have been drummed into a state of numbness by such assertions being repeated by one authority after another.

Enter Herbert George Gutman. He asserts that in the United States blacks, be they slaves or freedmen, maintained beliefs and values which governed domestic behavior, patterns of courtship, sexual alliances, and mating. Prenuptial sexual activity was not symptomatic of unbridled sexual licence. Premarital offspring or bridal pregnancy did not imply the absence of sexual standards, nor did they preclude subsequent stable marriages. There were strong social sanctions against promiscuity or marital infidelity. Group pressures among the black community were brought to bear against those lapsing into adultery or fornication. Taboos rooted in exogamous beliefs precluded blacks from following the predominant custom among whites of endogamy and the prevalence of marrying cousins. For blacks exogamy served to maintain, strengthen, and widen kin ties. Slave marriages were stable and permanent. For the most part, children grew up in large families. The typical slave family was doubleheaded, *viz.* with father and mother, and the former played an active role in the life of the family. Gutman challenges the widely held notion that slaves were mimetic. In such matters as completed slave families and early childbirth, there may have been a coincidence between the aspirations of owners and slaves, but slave women were capable of acting in accord with their own beliefs and independent of an owner's demands. By contraception, abortion, or the withholding of sexual information the slave woman made decisions governing her own actions. Such independence and the defining of an Afro-American identity and culture untouched by restraints imposed by owners or overseers were exemplified by the setting up of kinship ties. Familial or consanguineal, infra- and inter-generational, real or fictive, kinship links proved strong and enduring. They were reinforced by naming practices which sought to link different generations of blood kin as well as to reinforce ties among members of enlarged kin groups. Far from adopting a master's name mimetically, Gutman illustrates how slaves exercised a range of options independent of an owner. Offspring were named after blood kin, or were given names linking them to earlier generations of Afro-Americans. Such naming practices strengthened kinship ties and imparted a sense of corporate identity.

Gutman goes further. He maintains that distinctions between the states of single, married, or engaged, patterns of sexual behavior, domestic arrangements, and kinship ties, had been the products of a process of adaptive social and cultural change rooted in a system of values and beliefs shared by Afro-Americans. Transmitted from generation to generation, these came to comprise a cumulative collective experience. Such characteristics were shared by plantation slaves over the entire American south in the 1840's and 1850's despite differences of time, place, and economic context. Gutman has tested the validity of his thesis in two ways: first, by examining slaves from six plantation communities with varying characteristics; secondly, by testing the preservation of beliefs and values and the viability of mechanisms of adaptation when confronted by external circumstances over which the slave could exercise no control.

A. J. R. Russell-Wood   5

Any scholar who has jousted with the history of non-elite groups in the Americas is daunted by two problems: a dearth of information about such groups even in their public activities, let alone in their private domestic lives; secondly, information so fragmentary as to preclude any survey over an extended period of time. All too often such difficulties are reflected in the absence of a sense of development or in the synchronic presentation of a series of disjointed facts. For colonial Spanish and Portuguese America, the problem is compounded by the virtual absence of writings by blacks or mulattos who, in many regions, comprised a demographic majority. Assertions as to the value systems and beliefs of this majority remain largely speculative.[5] Gutman has drawn from sources whose richness and variety can only excite the jealousy of colleagues working on slavery or family history outside the United States. It is to be hoped that his example will stimulate research into archives and plantation records still preserved in private hands. His skillful use of correspondence between slaves and freedmen has breathed life into genealogical evidence, census data, and the records of the Union Army and the Freedmen's Bureau.

The corner-stone of Gutman's account is a birth register for the Good Hope plantation in South Carolina for the period 1760-1857. This register touches every aspect of the Afro-American experience from birth in Africa, through enslavement, plantation slavery in the Americas, emancipation, and rebirth as freedmen. Such evidence has permitted Gutman to adopt what he refers to as "an enlarged time perspective". Conclusions based on Good Hope records as to the development over time of an Afro-American culture have been tested against five other plantation communities. These afford examples of differences of location (Louisiana, Virginia, Alabama, North Carolina), crops (tobacco, cotton, sugar), ownership (resident, absentee), size, age, and varying degrees of economic stability. In all communities, with some minor exceptions, slaves acted uniformly in their domestic arrangements and in their adherence to shared beliefs.

Disruption of slave families resulting from the shift in slave populations from the Upper to the Lower South between 1790 and 1860 provides a further yardstick against which to test the resilience of this Afro-American culture in circumstances over which the slave had no control. Despite forced migration of several hundred thousand men, women, and children, it would appear from marriage registration books kept by the Union Army clergy and records of cotton plantations in Alabama and Mississippi that slave cultures and beliefs not only travelled from the Upper to the Lower South but were preserved intact. Shared beliefs, traditional domestic arrangements, and an Afro-American culture inherited from parents and grandparents provided transplanted slaves with a stable point of reference. Slaves demonstrated their capacity to adapt to the new reality, for example, by the socialization of offspring by parents to prepare them for the trauma of separation, by the establishment of fictive kinsmen, or by resorting to unusual marital arrangements. Such was the strength of this cumulative slave culture that not only did its traditions, mores, and beliefs survive forced sales; emancipation and resulting freedom of choice were to have no impact on traditional domestic arrangements. On the contrary, once restraints had been lifted Afro-American modes of behavior were reaffirmed even more strongly. One example was the refusal by ex-slaves to permit their wives to labor in the fields. This was to contribute to a labor scarcity experienced by white employers in the South after emancipation.

The last four chapters of the first part of *The black family* look at the larger social and cultural significance of the behavioral patterns so far described. Slave-naming patterns reinforce conclusions derived from other evidence as to the concerted efforts among Afro-Americans to strengthen ties between immediate family and enlarged kin groupings. That a child's legal status was determined by the mother led owners only to acknowledge uterine descent among slaves. Scholars, for their part, have tended to belittle the role of the slave father. Gutman has shown that by regularly naming sons after slave fathers parents sought to emphasize the importance of the father. Naming practices illustrated the extent to which slaves acted according to beliefs which were often at variance with those of their owners. Gutman revises current views as to slave surnames. Far from being mimetic or owner-dominated in their choices, after 1720 slaves over the entire South were taking surnames different from those of their masters. In making the selection, slaves consciously sought to preserve ties to their families of origin or to assert an identity independent of the family of their master. Slaves carried these surnames with them into freedom.

Naming practices asserted the "sheer importance of kinship" (p. 197), establishing links across generations from grandparents to grandchildren, while setting up the mechanism for establishing links to enlarged networks of aunts and uncles. These were reinforced by fictive kin ties. "Aunts" and "uncles" represented an extension to the greater society of the obligation to meet responsibilities which would normally have been borne solely by kin connected by blood or marriage. Be they real or quasi, kin obligations often transcended the immediate family, and afforded protection to children pre and post emancipation. In the strength of such ties lies at least a partial explanation of why, after emancipation, ex-slaves chose to remain in a familial and local social setting.

A. J. R. Russell-Wood   7

Viewed against this background of kinship, discussions as to the motives behind slave resistance and flight will have to be rephrased. Maltreatment by owners remained an obvious factor, but potential runaways had to weigh this against the conscious decision to leave kith and kin. Similarly, despite restrictions imposed by slavery, slaves sought to maintain marriage ceremonies or substitute rituals in the preservation of a cohesive slave family. In short, by forging fictive or real kinship ties and in their efforts to preserve the stability and cohesion of the family, slaves were acting independently of owners and in accord with norms of behavior of a cumulative Afro-American culture.

The second part strikes into new territory while serving as a further test of the general conclusions concerning behavioral norms and beliefs among Afro-Americans. Here the focus is on the ex-slaves. The adaptive capacity of the Afro-American and the resilience of slave values were challenged by the Civil War and its aftermath, the voluntary migration in 1880 sometimes referred to as the "Great Exodus", and migrations to the urban North from the rural South in the early twentieth century. Census returns suggest that, despite such disruptive forces, the black family preserved its traditional cohesion. Differences of status and location notwithstanding, the overall conclusion is that familial and kin obligations, beliefs, and domestic arrangements which had been present among plantation slaves in the English North American colonies prior to the American Revolution survived intact and were present in Harlem on the eve of the Great Depression. Such deeply inborn values had enabled first the slave and then the freedman to adapt to changing social, political, and economic realities. At no time in this continuum had white America broken the will of the black by destroying the black family, as Moynihan had maintained; nor was there evidence to support his sweeping assertions about the disorganization of the black family and the resulting tangle of pathology in the black community. According to Gutman, whatever the legacies of slavery may have been, clearly the deterioration of the black family in its broadest sense was not one of the bequests to later generations of Afro-Americans. Despite four major migrations, the domestic arrangements and belief systems of Afro-Americans from the period preceding the American Revolution through to the Great Depression could be described in two words: continuity and conformity.

By his rigorous scholarship, his firm grasp of the broad sweeps and the delicate nuances of his subject, the reassuring melding of quantitative evidence with literary sources, and a directness of language and dynamic style, Gutman will suck all but the most recalcitrant into the vortex of his description, analysis, and thesis. Repetitions and restatements, the sheer mass of supporting evidence, and the bombardment of the reader with facts and examples, compel acquiescence. But doubts there are which remain unallayed and questions there are which go unanswered. On the matter of evidence alone, some will argue that six plantations are not an adequate sample on which to base sweeping generalizations about the black family over a span of 250 years. Nor do federal and state censuses for the rural and urban South in 1880 and 1900 and for New York City in 1905 and 1925 provide adequate data on kinship patterns in the post emancipation era. Although kinship is central to much of the discussion, no assessment is made of differing attitudes on the part of slaves to members of kin groups, real or fictive, who were relatively nearer or more distant from the immediate family. Gutman's enthusiasm over the Good Hope plantation birth register — "this unusually important document" (note 2, p. 556) — is understandable. But the subsequent plantation by plantation approach leaves the reader with a sense of *dejà vu* and apprehensive that further examples, while admittedly selected from different contexts, serve no purpose other than to rubber-stamp conclusions based on this single register.

There is a sameness to the evidence and Gutman has not strayed far from his sources. Enquiry has been stifled on two broader but none the less substantive issues. In his preoccupation with slaves, ex-slaves, and the development of an Afro-American culture, Gutman has paid little attention to the owners, who contributed at the very least to the physical environment of black families. No less important to the black family is health, largely ignored by Gutman because his sources contain little or no bio-medical information. Certainly we now know more about the black family than about the lower class white family at certain periods in the history of the United States.

As with all things bright and beautiful, the absence of counter indications and evidence contrary to the overall thrust of the thesis is disquieting. Some few examples will suffice. The presence of single-parent households over the entire family cycle on the Stirling plantation is so atypical as to deserve more than an explanation based on speculation rather than fact (pp. 104-105, 115-117). We learn that "far more children were born prior to settled unions among the Stirling than among the Good Hope slaves" (p. 115), but that this may merely reflect inadequate information available to those recording births is a less than satisfactory reason. First-generation Good Hope slave families were significantly smaller than those of later generations. Over time this was to distinguish the Good Hope from the Stirling community, but no analysis is made of possible factors which could account for this difference. The Cedar Vale plantation reinforced familial and social aspects present in the Good

A. J. R. Russell-Wood   9

Hope and Stirling communities — with one important exception: fewer children were born before their parents' marriages than in the other two communities (p. 124). Why? Nor is any explanation provided as to why slave women on the Bennehan-Cameron plantation in Orange County, North Carolina, had a first child at a significantly younger age than did the other slaves studied (p. 171).

The hinge on which Gutman's thesis turns is the development among black Americans of a viable slave culture with its own values, domestic practices, and behavioral norms. The shaping of this culture had been in response to initial enslavement, and it was to be susceptible to adaptations as demanded by changes in external circumstances which affected the slave community. It has been estimated that some 170,600 slaves were imported into English North America before 1760.[6] The formative period of Afro-American culture preceded by several decades the War of Independence. And yet it is precisely for this pivotal period that Gutman is weak. That the Bennehan-Cameron community of 1776 *may* have included some African-born slaves and that some were *probably* the children of Africans is more than plausible. Few would disagree with his assertion that "it is among these and other eighteenth-century African and Afro-American slaves that the early Afro-American roots of the common familial and social behavior found among slaves nearly a century later are located" (p. 169). But a caveat is in order. By virtue of the evidence, Gutman's focus is on the few decades preceding emancipation and its immediate aftermath. He has projected backwards from this era a version of Afro-American culture, whose salient features can be well documented for a century. That the cultural roots of the 1860's lay in the 1760's and that there was a cultural continuum over a century is supported by the Good Hope and Bennehan-Cameron plantation registers. But by the 1760's Afro-American culture was already in what might be referred to as the late formative period. Indeed, taking these two slave communities as examples, it could well be argued that Afro-American culture had evolved through to the full manifestation of its major characteristics and by 1760 had reached a stage of development which was no longer formative. The registers of neither community cast light on the responses and adaptive capabilities shown by Africans toward slavery as practiced by British settlers on the North American mainland prior to 1760. On scanty evidence, Gutman attempts a further backward projection from the 1760's, ignoring the fact that by then the process of creolization and the melding of African and Anglo-American beliefs and social mores had already occurred. Initial contacts between the African and the British settler go undescribed and no more than blurred images are gained of the subsequent stages of a dynamic evolution which Afro-

American culture must have undergone in the first five decades of the eighteenth century.

Adherence to certain beliefs and an emphasis on kin networks were central to the formation of Afro-American culture. Random references from the 1720's, 1730's, and 1740's suggest that some West African beliefs and practices were transported to the Americas and manifested themselves on the North American mainland. Less clear are the answers to basic questions. How far may the adaptive capacity of Africans in the New World be regarded as innovative in nature or was it no more than a capability already developed in response to the institution of slavery within Africa? Kinship and the preservation of inherited beliefs and values are of critical importance to migrant groups in general (e.g. Italian and Chinese communities in the United States). What components distinguished the beliefs and standards of the West African in the formation of an Afro-American culture from a general creolization process undergone by migrants? How important was the distinction between forced and voluntary migration in determining the process of adaptation to the New World? How important was the institution of slavery itself and racial factors in making the Afro-American cultural formation a unique experience? Until more is known about the early decades of the eighteenth century, can a meaningful distinction be made between a cumulative slave experience and a set of values and behavioral norms transmitted from generation to generation? A firmer basis for discussion could be established if answers to these questions and information on three aspects alone were forthcoming: West African familial life and the importance of kinship to society and to the administrative hierarchy in Africa[7]; domestic arrangements and beliefs among black slaves on the North American mainland in the years preceding 1750; the extent to which slaves had immediate origins (e.g. the West Indies) other than West Africa. Finally, the Afro-American culture described in *The black family in slavery and freedom* is being examined within the narrow parameters represented by the family. This forms but one aspect of the multifaceted historical reality of the African experience in mainland English America.

The true test of Gutman's thesis and conclusions may well rest beyond the shores of mainland North America. Further studies on slavery (especially within the African continent) across time and space, not merely as an institution but as regards beliefs, values, and patterns of behavior are essential. Only then can the adaptive capacity attributed by Gutman to Afro-Americans be placed in context; and only then will it become evident if this was an uniquely Afro-American phenomenon within the geographical and social context of the English colonies on the

A. J. R. Russell-Wood   11

North American mainland, or an adaptive capability common to enslaved or oppressed groups. More detailed research on the East African slave trade and on African migration to Asia and settlement primarily in India, may provide further points of reference for future discussion of the development of Afro-American culture in North America. Comparisons with Latin America may be revealing, especially for the early period. After the first English landfalls at Jamestown and Plymouth some 12 and 20 years respectively were to lapse before the appearance of black slaves, but in Spanish America blacks were contemporaneous with conquest and in Portuguese America from an early period of plantation agriculture the black was regarded as an indispensable presence. It may well be that Spanish and Portuguese sources may provide evidence on the early formative period of Afro-American culture, while also providing yardsticks against which to test the validity of Gutman's thesis. Moreover, they contain references to a fascinating area not treated by Gutman, *viz.* Afro-Amerindian relations.[8]

Once the historian ventures beyond the English-speaking world of plantation slavery, he is on less sure ground. He must grapple with the problem of semantics on the one hand, and on the other with the difficulties of pinpointing those components and combinations of components which form part of the make up of what is referred to in English as slavery. Acceptance of a Western model (usually based on plantation-slavery in the Caribbean and North America) for slavery has resulted in the establishment of a set of criteria which are, for the most part, wholly inapplicable to non-American societies. Blurred as it is by the racial component, in this regard the American experience represents a variant rather than a norm. The conceptual framework provided by Igor Kopytoff and Suzanne Miers, viewing internal African slavery as (in their words) "an institution of marginality", is of great significance. The concept of "rights-in-persons", emphasis on the relationship of the individual to the kin group, and their enquiries into the varying methods of socialization into servility in Africa have far-reaching implications not only for future studies of internal African slavery, but also for the establishment of the necessary foundations for the study of Afro-American cultures in the New World.[9]

Although all too often considered as representing a so-called Western model, by the very diversity of its manifestations slavery in the Americas defies reduction to a stereotype. Whereas typologies of colonization and settlement have been proposed, based on European experiences in the Caribbean and continental America, scholars have evinced less willingness to set up typologies embracing those components which comprise slavery in different regions and at different periods of European colonization. Only once deviants and norms have been scrutinized under the historical lens (resulting inevitably in fresh points of contrast and comparison) will it be possible to make an evaluation as to the uniqueness or commonplace nature of the development of Afro-American culture in the English North American colonies and in the United States. The 399,000 slaves of West African origin estimated to have been imported into English North America between 1701 and 1870, and their descendants, have been the focus of scholarly attention totally out of proportion to their numerical importance in overall imports of slaves into continental America. In the same period alone, slave imports into Spanish America have been placed at 1,184,600 and into Brazil at 3,036,800. Imports into English North America account for only 4.2 percent of slaves brought to the Caribbean and American mainland during the three and a half centuries of the Atlantic trade.[10] No systematic study of the black family in Spanish or Portuguese America has been made. Gutman's researches for mainland North America prompt consideration in the Latin American context of his views on the development of Afro-American culture. Emphasis will be placed on that period for which Gutman's sources are least satisfactory, *viz.* the colonial era. This enlarged geographical perspective will provide further points of reference for Gutman's generalizations based on English North America, while suggesting new avenues for research on the black family in the Americas.

Slave marriages and slave families were recognized, and in varying degrees protected, under Spanish, French, and Portuguese law. The thirteenth-century codification known as the *Siete Partidas* provided guidelines for slave legislation in the Spanish colonies. These were as follows: slaves could marry each other, and even a free person, provided the latter was informed that the other party was a slave; slaves could marry without an owner's consent, provided they continued to serve the owner; married slaves could not be sold separately, if this would prevent them from living as man and wife; if slave partners had different owners, access for the exercise of conjugal rights could not be denied by an owner and every effort should be made to induce one of the owners to sell his or her slave so that the couple could live together. Neither the *Código Negro Carolino* promulgated in Santo Domingo in 1785 nor the Spanish Slave Code of 1789, while promoting marriage among slaves in the colonies, afforded protection against separation of mother and child. In contrast the *Code Noir* (1685), while sharing some of the provisions of Spanish legislation, was protective of the slave family and imposed penalties against owners who sought to separate husband and wife and sell offspring under the age of puberty. The Louisiana Code of 1806 was equally protective of the slave family, ruling that children under the age

A. J. R. Russell-Wood   13

of ten could not be separated from their mothers. In the Lusitanian world, codifications of 1446, 1521 and 1603 made no references to slave marriages or slave families. The welter of extravagant legislation, decrees, royal orders, and memoranda sent to crown representatives in Brazil rarely dwells on domestic arrangements of slaves. In Portuguese America slave couples and their families could depend less on the word of the law for the protection of family stability and preservation of marital unions than on the attitudes of state and church to provide sanctions against inhumane treatment by masters. Protection under the law for slave families was only legislated in Brazil in 1869.[11]

In general terms the crowns of Spain and Portugal and ecclesiastical policies in their empires in the Americas encouraged slave marriages and the protection of slave families. Royal concern was generated less by altruistic disinterest in the social and moral welfare of slaves than by the realization that slaves settled in permanent unions and with families were likely to be more productive and less prone to threaten the social and economic status quo by flight or rebellion than were unmarried slaves with no family obligations. Churchmen were exhorted to baptize and instruct slaves in Catholic doctrine, provide the church's blessing for unions between slaves, and ensure that they were accorded decent burials. But inter-racial marriages, be they between whites and blacks or between blacks and Amerindians, met with official disapproval. Church encouragement for owners to regularize their illicit unions with slaves met with royal disfavor, based on the following grounds, *inter alia:* official acknowledgment that marriage by a slave to a freed person was one avenue to freedom, not only for a slave mother but for her offspring; increase of the free mulatto population; recognition that a marriage in which one party was white (usually male) and the other black enhanced the prestige of the latter, improving her status and that of her offspring, and that any such social betterment was at variance with slave origins. In 1726 Dom João V attempted to halt interracial concubinage or marriage by ruling that only whites — husbands or widowers of white women — should be eligible to be town councillors in Brazil.[12] Civil and ecclesiastical authorities also opposed sexual unions between blacks and Amerindians. Repeated Spanish royal decrees forbad blacks to live in Amerindian villages. In Brazil a 1755 law declaring the enslavement of Amerindians to be illegal, specifically excluded Amerindian-black offspring born of black slaves. Pombaline legislation promoting marriages between Amerindians and white settlers denied benefits or concessions to Amerindians who married blacks.[13] Despite such official opposition in both empires the numbers of interracial marriages increased during the colonial period.

Policies concerning slave marriages and slave families were tempered in their effective implementation by colonial realities. Enforcement of laws, royal edicts, or rulings of ecclesiastical courts, proved difficult in general and well nigh impossible in regions removed from administrative centers. Whatever restraints may have been imposed by the letter of the law on owners in their treatment of slaves, in reality the owner's will was supreme and his wishes not to be gainsaid. In sixteenth and seventeenth century Spanish Peru, owners disregarded precepts forbidding opposition to slave marriages, division of slave families, or denial of conjugal rights to slave couples. The situation was no better in colonial Mexico. Owners forced slaves to marry against their will, raped wives and daughters, and separated slave families. Examples from Portuguese America illustrate a similar indifference by owners toward domestic arrangements among slaves. In short, evidence from Spanish, Portuguese, and French colonies in the Americas and the Caribbean supports the generally held view that owners abused slave parents and their offspring physically and psychologically and that disruption of slave families was largely owner-inspired.[14] This is but one side of the story of owner-slave relations. Too little recognition has been accorded to the fact that purchase and sale could be vehicles for uniting as well as separating members of slave families. Instances can be cited of owners encouraging slaves to marry, giving gifts and dowries to slave women at marriage, and leaving bequests to slaves and their offspring.[15]

Opposition was often derived from fear and apprehension based on misinformation or figments of the owner's imagination. Masters had to be reassured that admission of a slave into the Catholic church by baptism, and unions sanctified by the church would not automatically result in freedom.[16] A common claim by owners was that marriage placed restraints on the mobility and sale of slaves. This may have been the case in certain economic contexts, e.g. placer gold mining.[17] But research on sales of married slaves in the Lima slave mart in the period 1560-1650 has shown that in this instance at least there was no basis to owners' allegations that marriage lowered the value of slaves. Indeed the reverse may have been true. No less exaggerated were claims that the exercise of conjugal rights by slaves belonging to different masters resulted in affronts to communal decency. If owners opposed marriages for a variety of reasons, sexual intercourse between slaves was not only tolerated but was sometimes encouraged in the hope that resulting offspring would enhance an owner's capital holdings.[18] This explains why fornication often went unpunished whereas adultery among slaves, which could threaten stability and productivity, was punished harshly.

Opportunities for slaves in Spanish and Portuguese America to marry

A. J. R. Russell-Wood   15

were limited by factors other than the degree of cooperation shown by a master. Demography and sexual imbalance were important determinants. In such disparate areas as rural Peru in the early seventeenth century or in the mining regions of Brazil a century later, there was an overwhelming predominance of black males.[19] Environment (rural or urban), occupation (mining, plantation agriculture, small-holding subsistence cultivation, cattle ranching) and skills (mechanical trades, paramedical knowledge) had a bearing on opportunities for mobility and for marriage. The ecclesiastical bureaucracy of both empires posed a formidable hurdle for slaves faced with meeting such prerequisites as furnishing proof that both partners were single, and free of the traditional impediments to marriage. Slaves also had to contend with the rapacity of secular clergy. Complaints that priests charged exorbitant fees for officiating at baptisms, funerals, and marriages were as endemic as they were well founded in both empires. Not without cause did one governor of Minas Gerais refer to the "Doctrine of the Mineral Church" based on avarice, ambition, and self-interest. Finally, in many areas slaves faced difficulties of transportation and lacked the flexibility in determining their own movements which would enable them to gain ready access to a priest. Whites and freedmen of color were no less the victims of these circumstances than were slaves. Civilian administrators and ecclesiastical dignitaries alike commented on the few marriages contracted by white colonists in Spanish and Portuguese America. Exhortations that colonists should sanctify their illicit unions, thereby providing an example, fell on deaf ears.[20]

In Spanish and Portuguese America these factors militated against the solemnization of slave marriages by the church. No systematic study of slave beliefs or domestic arrangements in colonial Latin America has been made, but Gutman's researches suggest guidelines for what at the present state of scholarship can be no more than a tentative survey. Consciousness of their African ethnic heritage was strong among blacks in Latin America. Limited evidence available for colonial Peru suggests that blacks showed a preference for members of their own ethnic group when it came to the choice of a marriage partner. Taboos based on ritual kinship, be this derived from the circumstance of being transported on the same ship to the New World or belonging to the same group of runaway slaves, may have eliminated potential partners from consideration.[21] The evidence is inadequate as to exogamous patterns in the Americas being derived from beliefs prevailing in West Africa. A contemporary study of Cottica Djuka society in Surinam notes that "in former times their society was strictly exogamous", and intralineage marriages would have brought down the wrath of the gods on the two parties. Certainly exogamy could have provided one manner in which the slave could have escaped his or her immediate social environment. If this single example from Surinam were to be confirmed by examples from elsewhere in Spanish and Portuguese America it would support Gutman's views that exogamy provides an instance of the continuation in the Americas of part of a system of beliefs adhered to in West Africa where exogamy was the norm. In Spanish and Portuguese America, no less than in the English colonies, slaves would have been acting in direct contrast to the endogamous marriage pattern predominating among white colonists.[22] Later, when considering the decision-making capacity of slaves, we shall have occasion to note that the choice of marriage partner from a different plantation could be dictated for a variety of reasons.

Little is known about the beliefs of slaves in colonial Latin America concerning courtship and marriage. Even Freyre's *The masters and the slaves* is silent on the subject. In the light of Gutman's insights into courting behavior and prenuptial and bridal pregnancies, the fact that 19 percent of total females sold in the Lima slave mart between 1560 and 1650 were mothers or were pregnant at the time of sale takes on added interest and may be susceptible to new interpretations. Data on subsequent marriages by these pregnant females are not available. Nor is adequate information available on Afro-Amerindian sexual relationships, both within marriage and otherwise, and whether courting styles between blacks were also followed when one of the parties was an Amerindian.[23] Slaves resorted to witchcraft or folk practices to enhance sexuality or further amorous overtures. Charms, amulets, and trinkets imbued with supernatural powers were worn. Special qualities were attributed to mystical herbs, taken in infusions or ground up into fine powder and applied to the body or clothes. Specific objects — a crow's head and feathers, the eyes of a swallow, earth taken from mountains or cemeteries — were used by slaves to induce love in another person. Despite tribal differences, probably such practices had African origins. Doubtless slaves, no less than whites, availed themselves of saints such as Saint Anthony reputed to favor love and marriage.[24]

The Bahian saying that "Negroes do not marry; they just live together" has been accepted at face value as applying not only to modern Brazil but to the colony and empire.[25] But the Brazilian proverb throws no light on forms of marriage, be they Latin American counterparts to jumping over a broomstick, ceremonies performed according to African traditions, or marriages sanctified by Catholic priests. Whether such unions constituted African survivals or creole practices remains moot. Sparse demographic data suggest that comparatively few slaves were

A. J. R. Russell-Wood   17

married by the church in colonial Latin America. The incidence of slave marriages in rural and urban areas of Peru was low in the sixteenth and seventeenth centuries. A sample of slaves of marriageable age sold in Lima in the years 1560-1650 indicates that only 5.5 percent (122) and 9.5 percent (161) of males and females respectively were listed as married. A further 67 slave families were sold as units, but the proportion still remained low. Testamentary evidence bears out these general findings, although in the 26-35 years age group there was an increase with 13 percent of males and 16.6 percent of females being married. Systematic analysis of records for one parish in São Paulo from 1770-1850 shows that slave marriages performed each year averaged between 21 and 25 for the last decades of the eighteenth century, with a progressive decline in the first half of the nineteenth century. Henry Koster, who visited Brazil in the early nineteenth century, observed: "slaves of Brazil are regularly married according to the forms of the Catholic church", but this gives no indication as to the frequency of such marriages.[26] In a very different area of the Americas — the Antilles — in the year 1835 only 28 marriages were recorded among some 240,000 slaves on Martinique, Guadeloupe, and Réunion. Here, as elsewhere, the incidence of slave marriages varied from region to region, and it was alleged that slave marriages had been more frequent on Martinique in the eighteenth century. In the Dutch Caribbean, Catholic clergy were allowed to baptize and indoctrinate slaves, but not to officiate at marriages. The result was widespread clandestine marriages. Although performed by a priest, such marriages were not recognized by the civil authorities, in contrast to Spanish and Portuguese practices.[27]

Be they known as *palenques, quilombos, mocambos, cumbes, mambises, patucos,* or *rochelas,* communities of runaway slaves were established in Spanish and Portuguese America. While many were of a fleeting nature, others — of which the example of Palmares in the northeast of Brazil is an outstanding example — survived for half a century or more despite raids by colonial authorities. Whether African cultural norms predominated, or there was creolization in the development of an Afro-American culture, bore directly on the form of marriage ceremonies performed in such communities free from the restraints of slavery and of official Catholicism. Palmares, described by one scholar as "an African state in Brazil", was the subject of an eye-witness report by Fernão Carrilho who led expeditions against the community in 1676-77, 1683 and 1686. The *capitão-mor* noted: "There is a *capela,* to which they flock whenever time allows, and *imagens* to which they direct their worship. . . . One of the most crafty, whom they venerate as *paroco,* baptizes and marries them. Baptismals are, however, not identical with the form determined by the

18   SOCIETAS—A Review of Social History

church and the marriage is singularly close to laws of nature". Chronic sexual imbalance in such communities prompted raids on neighboring plantations with the specific object of capturing females, and there is evidence to suggest that marital stability was not unknown among runaways. Only when more information becomes available on the internal social organization of such communities will it be possible to ascertain whether marriages performed in the so-called "chapels" followed Catholic or African precepts. The Malinke, known in Brazil as the Malês, practiced marriage ceremonies presided over by their own leader known as *lemane,* and which showed Islamic influence.[28]

Despite the paucity of evidence currently available, scholarly reassessment of familial types and domestic arrangements in the Spanish and Portuguese speaking Americas is long overdue. Recent analysis has challenged the widely held view that the patriarchal extended family was the predominant family type among whites in colonial Brazil and was primarily responsible for the transmission to, and continuation of, Portuguese cultural traditions in the New World.[29] For its part the slave family has largely been ignored by historians of colonial Latin America. Discussion may focus on three aspects: family types; the role of the woman in the slave household; the degree of stability and duration of slave marriages.

Among maroon communities it appears that domestic arrangements ran the gamut from polygamy to monogamy. A historian writing at the end of the eighteenth century about Jamaica noted "Polygamy too, with their other African customs, prevailed among the Maroons universally. Some of their principal men claimed from two to six wives. . . ." In counterdistinction, recent study of a *mocambo* in eighteenth century Bahia, suggests that the close correlation between numbers of adults and numbers of houses may indicate a monogamous marital pattern.[30] Gilberto Freyre has referred to the sexual and family life of the Big House as being characterized by "polygamous patriarchalism", but fails to provide examples from the *senzala,* or slave quarters. Certainly examples may be cited to support the contention that there were double-headed slave families, *viz.* with father and mother present, in the slavocratic societies of Spanish and Portuguese America. But the pressures of slavery militated against integrated family types among slaves.[31]

Discussion of domestic and familial arrangements of slaves must center on the role and status of the mother. The institution of slavery, owners' whims, and prevailing mores in colonial Spanish and Portuguese America exerted on slave women a series of socio-sexual pressures. These militated against an integrated slave family, composed of father, mother, and offspring. The enhancement of the role of the mother and a

A. J. R. Russell-Wood   19

tendency for slave families to be matrifocal resulted. Separation of husband and wife meant that the former became an object of affection, but ceased to be a physical presence in many a slave family. The "law of the womb" prevailed; children inherited the status of the mother. When members of a slave family were sold separately, it was common practice for offspring to be sold with the mother rather than the father. In addition, her very sex placed the slave woman under pressures, while opening to her a range of options denied to male slaves. The status of being married, regardless of whether this had been blessed by the church or was an alternate form of marriage (common law, etc.) did not provide for the slave woman those privileges and recognition of her new-found status accorded to the white woman. She was not protected from overtures to adultery or concubinage made by white owners. Interracial adultery or concubinage resulted in a higher incidence of households headed by slave women. The benefits of such arrangements were tangible, not only for the mother but for her offspring. Concubinage or adultery with a white male could enhance the likelihood of mother and offspring gaining manumission. Furthermore, there was a generally held acknowledgment of the desirability on the part of blacks to whiten. A female slave had more to gain from being a white man's concubine than a black man's wife; her offspring would reap the social benefits of lighter pigmentation. Finally, to be married at all could be a status symbol for whites and blacks alike.[32] If Gutman's views on the emphasis placed on marriage within Afro-American belief patterns are accepted, this social factor would apply no less to slaves than to whites. Marriage — no less than wealth, pigmentation, language ability, place of birth, privilege, and religion — became yet another instrument which divided rather than integrated colonial society in Latin America.

No comprehensive typology of family forms, let alone for slave families, has been established for colonial Spanish and Portuguese America. Donald Ramos' study of colonial Vila Rica is a pioneering, revisionist analysis of the Luso-Brazilian family and his conclusions are relevant to our examination of family forms. He shows that only 5.3 percent of housefuls could be described as comprising patriarchal, extended families: among the heads of these housefuls, non-whites predominated (44.2 percent mulatto, 5.1 percent *cabra*, 37.0 percent black). Two thirds of these heads of housefuls had apparently never married and of these the majority were single women. The matrifocal family (otherwise designated as the *incomplete family* or *partial family*) was the norm rather than the exception, regardless of color or civil status. Partial evidence suggests that 90 percent of female heads of housefuls were non-whites. If this sample is representative, evidently marriage was far from being a cohesive force uniting families in colonial Brazil. Recent studies of family organization in the Caribbean tend to reinforce this view. Normative distinctions between concubinage and marriage evaporate. Incidence of matrifocality becomes determined by prevailing social, economic, and demographic conditions, and is a product of slavocratic societies in particular where mating characteristics gave unusual prominence to interracial liaisons. In this respect Latin America demands a set of evaluative criteria totally distinct from those applicable to English North America. Portuguese and Spanish America afford examples of a different form of adaptive behavior by slaves and free blacks and demonstrate the importance of regional, social, cultural, and economic contexts in determining the type of response by the black population. Indeed, the context rather than the strength of cumulative slave beliefs and values appears to have been all-important.[33]

Formal definition of the type of union becomes of secondary importance to the degree of permanence it afforded to the parties concerned and the stability it provided for their offspring. When dealing with unions between slaves, differentiating aspects such as social, racial, or economic incompatibility, cease to be relevant. Slaves remained beyond the parameters of the social hierarchy prevailing among white societies in Spanish and Portuguese America. Evidence is contradictory. Instances of forced separation of husbands from wives and children from parents can be matched by examples of stability among married couples and their families. Bowser cites examples of stability among slave families in colonial Peru for at least two decades. In the nineteenth century French Caribbean one priest was led to comment on successful and lasting marriages between slaves and noted especially the fidelity of slave husbands, their love of order and cleanliness in their households, and their affection and consideration toward wife and children. Travellers to nineteenth century Brazil were moved to raptures over the apparent benignancy of Brazilian slavery. Richard Burton observed of slavery there that "Nowhere, even in oriental countries, has the 'bitter draught' so little of gall in it" and noted that slaves experienced little fear of the members of their families being separated because "the humane instincts and the religious tenets of the people are strongly opposed to this act of barbarity". This depiction may have been too glowing even for the period of empire in Brazil, contrasting with the picture drawn by Stanley Stein for Vassouras. For the colonial period scattered documentary references suggest that unions between slaves were not permanent and that the slave family was prone to fragmentation and disruption.[34] We shall see that this very instability and impermanency could prompt slaves to flee to maroon communities in the hope of finding familial

A. J. R. Russell-Wood   21

stability otherwise denied to them in a slavocratic society.

The picture which emerges of the slave family in Latin America and the Caribbean is more depressing than that drawn by Gutman for English America. But even here the slave sought to adapt to new realities and came to exercise decision making capacities consciously and independently of an owner. At the present stage of research it is impossible to ascertain whether in the exercise of such options the slave was acting in accordance with traditional African behavior, or was reacting as a creole to New World circumstances. Examples are too spasmodic to permit any categorization of this behavior as comprising part of an evolving Afro-American culture handed down from generation to generation. It may be said that parameters of choice existed for slaves who acted within circumscribed boundaries. The problem confronting the historian is to determine the exact nature of these parameters.

Attitudes of slaves towards marriage exemplify the ability of the slave to act independently of the master. Two illuminating examples are provided by the French West Indies, but may reflect attitudes elsewhere in the Americas. A young slave woman resisted the advice of a local priest that she should marry. Her refusal was based on a conscious decision not to bring into the world a child who would be exposed to the hardships of slavery and whose misery she would be forced to witness. She remained single, although given the less than flattering (for the time and place) nickname of "the virgin of the islands." This decision echoed the words of the Jesuit André João Antonil who wrote that in colonial Brazil slave women sought abortion rather than bring children into a world of suffering. Male slaves also rejected marriage to spare themselves humiliation. In 1842 blacks on Martinique told a local priest that they preferred to remain single rather than marry, only to have an owner force his sexual attentions on the bride the day after her marriage, and have offspring only for these to be abused as playthings of the owner's children or sold according to an owner's whim.[35] Freyre's chronicle of plantation life in Brazil depicts slave women (regardless of age) as having to succumb to the embryonic sexual desires of the young white master. Widely held was the belief that sexual intercourse with a black virgin at the age of puberty cured syphilis and gonorrhea. Slave children of both sexes were the victims of the masochistic tendencies of the owner's children manifested in such games as *manja* and *peia queimada,* or were used in games demanding oxen, horses, or mules to carry heavy burdens or go between the shafts of a cart or buggy.[36]

Slaves sought to undermine their owners' attempts to force them to marry against their will. Writing in 1711, Antonil noted that some owners, rather than forcing legal marriages on slaves, simply designated a male and a female as partners. This practice was based on experience: slaves had been forced to marry and, tiring of their partner, had committed suicide or had resorted to poison or magic to kill an unwanted spouse. Slaves consciously took steps to prevent owners from increasing capital holdings by slave reproduction. To avoid placing a whole family at the whim of a single owner, slaves chose as spouses blacks belonging to another owner. Reports from Guadeloupe in the early 1840's noted that it was rare for slaves to permit themselves to be married to a spouse from the same plantation. Abortion and sexual unions between slave males and Amerindian females similarly represented conscious steps to prevent children being brought into a life of bondage and for the financial benefit of an owner.[37]

In Spanish and Portuguese America legal redress against owners' abuses was available to slaves. This too represented a conscious decision by a slave. By declaring his case openly in the judicial arena, the slave immediately became vulnerable to the vindictive wrath of an owner. It also meant that the slave had to contend with the bureaucratic judicial machinery which was sluggish in both empires unless liberally lubricated, and that the slave or a trusted friend should be literate and able to handle the necessary documentation. Slave litigation focussed on three principal areas, and in each case familial considerations were to be paramount. These were as follows: marriage, either forced on slaves by an owner or opposed by an owner, in some instances leading to the separation of potential partners; separation of families by sale or as the result of an internal slave trade as was the case in Mexico or Brazil; manumission. Appeal could be to ecclesiastical or secular judicial authorities. In seventeenth-century Peru slaves appealed to ecclesiastical courts for assistance in overcoming an owner's opposition to marriage or the *de facto* dissolution of a marriage caused by an owner's intent to separate couples for short or extended periods of time; slaves who had already been separated from partners by an owner's guile or false promises sought reunion with their mates. Blacks, freedmen and slaves, often took the legal initiative themselves. Their petitions received a fair hearing and the ecclesiastical judges made every effort to strike a balance between the interests of slave and owner. Records for Brazil have yet to be systematically studied, but the Portuguese colonial legal bureaucracy afforded fewer opportunities for slaves to seek legal redress than in Spanish America. Petitions were filed with the civil authorities but blacks and mulattos learnt by experience that, while they were not actually denied appellate recourse, unless they could find a protector whose wealth or influence could further the appellant's cause, the obstacles were such as to deter all but the most determined. Owners were known to resort to violence, sometimes culminating in the death of an appellant, to deter allegedly wronged slaves from petitioning crown judges. Even if a case should reach the judge, this in itself was no guarantee of a fair hearing. Despite a system of checks and balances, *ouvidores* were blissfully aware that high-handed or arbitrary sentences would rarely be appealed to the high court in Salvador and, after 1751, in Rio de Janeiro. There may be some truth in the view expressed by Stuart Schwartz that men and women from the opposite ends of the social and racial scales were the most successful in being released on bail or having their cases dismissed.

In Spanish and Portuguese America existed an extra-legal recourse which circumvented normal legal channels, or was resorted to once normal legal procedures had been exhausted, namely: direct appeal to the crown. Petitions by slaves alleged false arrest on spurious charges, physical abuse by owners, or the denial of individual rights guaranteed by law. Appeals alleged owner opposition to marriages (realized or impending) between slaves and especially between male slaves and free black or Amerindian females. In the latter case it was frequently claimed that Amerindian women and their offspring were reduced to slavery in return for being permitted to remain with slave husbands. Illegal enslavement of Amerindian, black, and mulatto females who failed to furnish proof of manumission, with the resulting forced separation from their children, was also ground for appeal. Slave women filed petitions on behalf of themselves and their offspring claiming that testamentary provisions of a deceased owner guaranteeing them their freedom had been ignored by executors. In general it may be said for both Spanish and Portuguese America that those cases of slave petitions which have survived were filed by slaves who were either more resourceful or more desperate than their fellows in seeking any recourse which might preserve a marriage or an integrated family. It cannot hide the fact that, for the most part, slaves were the victims of oppression largely because they were ignorant of their legal rights, limited although these may have been.[38]

Slaves in Spanish and Portuguese America, no less than in the English colonies and the United States, resorted to kinship as a means of overcoming the disruption of marital and familial arrangements. It is not yet possible to ascertain whether such kinship ties represented the continuation of African patterns into the New World, or a response to social conditions in the Americas. Nor, as yet, is there available the wealth of evidence drawn on by Gutman concerning regular kinship patterns and the establishment of networks to permit an assessment of the importance of such ties for persons of African descent in South America. In his study of Djuka society, based on field research undertaken in 1962, A. J. F. Koebben analyzed this bush negro tribe of Surinam as a kinship system. He is forced to acknowledge that the process by which kinship groups were formed is unknown, nor can information be unearthed as to the degree to which this process represents an African legacy or creolization. A similar dearth of information on the importance attached by slaves to kinship in Spanish and Portuguese America makes the formulation of even a thesis speculative. One source which may prove rewarding are notarial and court records concerning manumission. Methods of obtaining letters of manumission were highly individualistic. But all slaves shared aspirations to freedom. Kinship took on great importance in furthering such aspirations when manumission was to be obtained by purchase. Members of an immediate slave family may have pooled their resources to buy the freedom of a father, mother, or sibling. Ties between the immediate family and an enlarged kin network of slaves may well have been used for the same purpose. Such collective efforts may have been unconditional; others may have carried the tacit understanding that new ex-slaves would further the cause of slave kin and that these, once manumitted, would continue the good work thereby producing a cumulative effect. Should an immediate family or enlarged kin network include freedmen, the possibility of outright gift or loan may have been enhanced.[39] In matters of freedom, beliefs and aspirations cut across civil and legal distinctions of slave and freedman and imposed common social obligations on fictive or real kin.

Slaves in Spanish and Portuguese America sought to decrease the disruptive impact of slavery on the family by a process of socialization. This was achieved by the strengthening of kinship networks, and by the creation of a series of fictive or ritual kin ties. The latter could be based on a shared experience (transportation on the same ship to the Americas, membership of the same *quilombo,* work in the same household or plantation) or might reflect common places of origin in Africa, or at least a shared African heritage, adherence to which had survived enslavement, transportation, and slavery. To be of the same nation could be tantamount to actual kinship and imposed shared responsibilities and obligations.[40] Two processes for the creation of such fictive ties were prominent in Spanish and Portuguese America to the point of being institutions in themselves, and existed regardless of distinctions of race or civil status. They were ritual kinship as expressed either by godparenthood *(padrinazgo)* or co-parenthood *(compadrazgo, compadrio)* and the Catholic lay brotherhoods. Whereas these forms of ritual kinship could be used by blacks to extend the family beyond the bounds of consanguinity and affinity, brotherhoods provided the mechanism for slaves and freedmen to establish or reinforce extra-communal ties and to enlarge a network of relationships beyond immediate families and beyond localized occupational environments. Both fictive kinship and the brotherhoods also provided blacks, both slave and free, with a basis for establishing an organizational network of dominance and subordination within the black community. Leaders and potential leaders could be accorded recognition by blacks, but in terms which, because of their religious context, were acceptable to white colonists. Blacks were enabled to resist the homogenizing forces of slavery and to take decisions independently and without their owners' sanction. Ritual kinship and the brotherhoods may be considered within the context of the slave family in Iberoamerica.

That ritual kinship was prevalent among blacks in colonial Latin America is confirmed by facts presented by the governor of Minas Gerais to justify a series of edicts promulgated in 1719.[41] Prompted by fears of a black revolt, the governor had taken measures to punish severely runaways, curb prostitution as a vehicle for manumission, reduce the number of letters of manumission being granted, prevent freedmen of color from possessing slaves or property, and obviate any situation in which any black could come to exert authority over any other black, slave or freedman. It was within this repressive context that the governor made observations concerning ritual kinship which provide an invaluable insight into the little-documented subject of the black family in the colony. It had been noted that at marriages and baptisms, blacks chose as godfathers *(padrinhos)* other blacks who had attained positions of prominence and respect within the black community in the Americas, were of the same nation, or who had been members of ruling families in Africa and betrayed into slavery as the result of dynastic or familial disputes. Preference would usually be given to those who were not already blood relatives. By godparenthood, slaves and freedmen could reinforce ties crossing time and space, asserting African origins pre-dating the initial enslavement of ancestors. Dynastic or familial loyalties which had been disrupted by enslavement could find expression in the New World in the choice of a godparent. In Brazil it appears that the personal qualities and the descent-line of the honoree were of greater importance than the distinctions of civil status, namely slave or free. So widespread was the practice of godparenthood among blacks that the governor ruled that henceforth no black should be eligible to be a *padrinho*. It was alleged that slaves gave to godparents earnings which should rightfully have been handed to their legal owners. It was also feared that such godparents would abuse their authority and incite ritual kin to flight or revolt. The governor claimed that *quilombos* were headed by blacks who had used godparenthood as a stepping stone to positions of leadership in the black community.

Historical sources from Iberoamerica describing ritual kinship refer to *padrinhos* or *padriños* rather than *compadres, viz.* godparents rather than co-parents. Frequently reference is being made to the series of reciprocal obligations more associated with *compadrazgo* or *compadrio.* This is certainly the case in those instances of fictive kin relations being established outside the context of the ritual of Catholic baptism or marriage. *Compadrazgo* could be invoked for purely secular ends. Black godparents played a valuable role in providing the financial means to manumit slave kin. Here choice of godparent by slave parents may have been governed by the desire to reinforce already existing consanguineal or affinal ties, or prompted by recognition of the potential value of a sponsor in furthering manumission. Vertical choice certainly occurred when slaves and freedmen chose whites as godparents. Choice could also be prompted by the need for protection sought by the black partner in the relationship. This protection could take the form of intervention by the white to prevent physical abuse, forced separation of families, or miscarriages of justice. A classic example of this protective role in a purely secular setting was the reaction by free blacks of the Diamond District *(Distrito Diamantino)* of Brazil to an expulsion order by the governor in 1732. As soon as the *bando* was published, freedmen sought out *padrinhos* from among members of the white mining community to protect them from this draconic edict.[42]

Whatever the technical differences between responsibilities imposed on respective parties by godparenthood or co-parenthood, this fictive kinship demanded of the slave or freedman a series of consciously taken decisions. This decision-making process involved the weighing of factors of a familial, domestic, social, financial, ethnic, and religious nature. Ethnographic data do not answer the question of whether such ritual kinship in the Americas had parallels in Africa, were African survivals, or represented syncretism in the Americas. Portuguese colonists viewed the establishment of such fictive kin ties from a perspective honed by an upbringing in which obligations of ritual kin had been prescribed by the Catholic Church and had been extended and elaborated in the secular realm to provide mutual protection and assistance. However mutual obligations and responsibilities very similar to those imposed by *compadrazgo* and *padrinazgo* were present in West African societies. It is unclear whether or not by the establishment of such fictive kin relations in Spanish and Portuguese America, slaves and freedmen were acting in accordance with beliefs and values wholly African in origin or had adapted to the point of accepting a form of relationship molded by

A. J. R. Russell-Wood   27

religious and secular traditions which were Catholic and Iberian.

At an early date in Spanish and Portuguese settlement in the Americas blacks, slaves and freedmen, had formed Catholic lay brotherhoods (*cofradias, irmandades*), especially in urban areas. Membership reflected the heterogeneity of black and mulatto populations of South America. The only conditions imposed on an applicant were that he be God-fearing, of good character, and pay annual dues. Colored brotherhoods ranged from those with a policy of open admissions in the acceptance of members (including whites) to more exclusive brotherhoods. Membership was entirely voluntary. In selecting a brotherhood, a person of African descent was exercising judgment entirely independently of masters. By applying to one whose membership was drawn exclusively from persons originating in a certain region of Africa or of the same nation, blacks were responding more to inherited beliefs and cultural traditions of an African origin than to those espoused by the European community. The annual elections of a president and governing body enabled blacks to exercise the prerogative of selecting leaders from among their own community. At the present stage of research it is not possible to say how far blacks joining such Catholic brotherhoods had adapted to Spanish and Portuguese beliefs and styles of worship, and hence had been institutionalized to some degree, or whether they had adopted external forms of Catholicism in order to conceal from whites a conscious effort to preserve in the New World African religious beliefs which could be handed down from one generation of members to the next.

Brotherhoods played an important role in black communities. Branches cooperated and members benefited from reciprocity agreements. Not only did this ensure that the transplanted slave or freedman could find in a new place of residence immediate access to the local black community, but it also meant that affiliates gave him a network of contacts. Moreover, brotherhoods actively encouraged family enrollment. Rules governing the admittance of women and offspring (when of age) varied as too did the degree of participation permitted to women. Statutes (1820) of the brotherhood of Our Lady of the Rosary of Salvador encouraged husbands to enroll wives. More importantly, membership of a brotherhood constituted a form of security for all family members, providing alms or limited financial assistance to the needy, dowries should funds permit, and the guarantee of a decent burial and funeral with a sung mass. In the event of the death of one or more parents, members of the brotherhood took steps to ensure that infants or minors were given a home. Brotherhoods thus afforded to their members a degree of protection against the uncertainties of a slavocratic society.[43]

In the final analysis the supreme option open to the slave was flight. A distinction may be made between *petit marronage* and *marronage*. From colonial Peru to the French Antilles there were reports of slaves absenting themselves temporarily for periods of up to a week. Some absences occurred with the tacit acceptance of an owner, and might even be central to the slave-owner relationship. Slaves with a trade or versed in a skill such as panning for gold might come to enjoy relative freedom from supervision on the understanding that earnings would be delivered to owners at the end of the week. In exchange, the master was exempted from responsibilities for providing the slave with food. Such tolerance depended on the skills of an individual slave and the overall economic context, but resulted from a decision taken by an owner with his own financial interests in mind. Another form of *petit marronage* was temporary absence dictated by concern felt by a slave for his family. Slaves temporarily absented themselves to visit families from whom they were separated. By such visits the slave took the risk of running foul of the law, being arrested, and punished as would be a *bona fide* runaway. Nocturnal vagabondage presented fewer risks and was prevalent from the Caribbean to Peru. So common was the practice in Lima of slaves belonging to different masters visiting their wives for sexual purposes at all hours that in 1582-83 it was charged that such visits constituted an affront to public morality. If masters tolerated such absences, this did not blind them to the real danger that *petit marronage* could develop into permanent flight from slavery.

In discussing slave flight in Latin America it is not our purpose to treat the prevalence of, or reasons for, flight but to seek to emphasize the significance of the decision on the part of the slave within the context of kith and kin. Certainly a reappraisal of motivation in terms of slave behavior rather than treatment by an owner appears long overdue, as too is the examination of the familial and psychological ramifications of a conscious decision which was to be of vital importance not only for the protagonist but also for his family. Colonists attributed motivation for flight to no better ground than black perversity. Contemporary scholars have listed factors prompting slaves to flee. Prevailing colonial policies, effectiveness of law enforcement, demographic density, composition of the slave body, the nature of the economy, and even topography, varied from region to region and were susceptible to change. Such factors affected the incidence of slave runaways and the relative success of slaves in evading capture. But an as-yet little studied aspect of *marronage* — beliefs associated with concern for family members and for domestic arrangements — may provide the key to the understanding of a behavioral set of motivations shared by slaves throughout the Americas.[44]

Slaves recently arrived in the Americas and who had yet to become acculturated and establish family ties were more prone to flight. In flight they were less likely to be successful than their counterparts who had been acculturated and had family connections. Not only did new arrivals lack the linguistic skills and savvy to pass themselves off as being engaged in legitimate activities when challenged but, perhaps more importantly, they could not avail themselves of the assistance and safe houses which blacks with a network of real and fictive kin relations could use to further their escape plans. Kin ties played an invaluable role for runaways in even such a well-established *quilombo* as Palmares. Kith and kin outside of the *quilombo* tipped off runaways as to the possibility of attack by bush-whacking captains or militia companies, and assisted runaways in purchasing foodstuffs or powder and shot. The absence of such contacts meant that new arrivals attempting flight were often reduced to remaining in the vicinity of, and scavenging off, their former places of labor, with every likelihood of an early recapture.[45]

The more highly acculturated African-born or creole slave enjoyed better odds of making good his escape and evading capture. The longer that he had been in the Americas, the more was it likely that familial concerns would play a part in his final decision to flee. Such concerns provide a new dimension to motivation and to the medley of factors which, regardless of geographical context, contributed to the irrevocable decision to resort to flight. Whether a slave fled alone, or accompanied by his immediate family, this act represented a conscious and irreversible decision to break emotionally with other members of an immediate or extended family or with real or fictive kin such as existed in any slave community. Sometimes flight united relatives or permitted family cohesion to be preserved. Slaves from communities of runaways actively recruited from among those still in bondage and, naturally enough, started by trying to induce relatives to join them in illegal freedom. Slaves fled in order to preserve domestic arrangements or to act in family matters according to their own principles rather than those imposed by owners, for example to overcome owners' opposition to an intended marriage, or to protect a wife from the sexual overtures of an owner. From sixteenth and early seventeenth century Peru come reports of flight prompted by the desire to avoid separation from family or spouse; indeed, where children and parents (one or both) or husbands and wives had different masters, flight often afforded the only possibility for effecting a reunion. Information on, and announcements of, runaways in Latin America and the Antilles suggest that, such was the cohesive force binding black slave families and kin that group flight was common. Such a group especially consisted of husband and wife accompanied by their offspring, husband and pregnant wife, or fictive relatives brought together because of shared community or ethnic origins.[46]

The destination of such runaways were the many slave communities scattered throughout the Americas where life was beyond the jurisdiction of owners. At present there is not enough evidence to ascertain the degree to which communities of runaways represented African states in Latin America. Certainly in establishing a hierarchy of leaders in such communities blacks acted according to their own beliefs and set up their own criteria of selection. Of greater interest to our purpose is the extent to which slaves sought out such communities in the hope of finding a stability and permanency in familial relations which might otherwise have been impossible in slavery. In short, although slaves may well have been seeking to escape the authority of their masters, motivation to flee was also prompted by the desire consciously to assert their beliefs in the importance of certain forms of domestic behavior and interpersonal relations. The push factor of maltreatment could be of less importance than the pull factors created by a relative who had already joined a community of runaway slaves or resulting from cultural and behavioral influences. Such communities were characterized by chronic sexual imbalance, prompting raids to procure women. But views advanced by historians concerning rampant promiscuity in Cuban and Columbian *palenques* or brutality meted out to their many wives by maroons in Jamaica should be tempered by other evidence from Latin America which suggests that at least in the more enduring runaway communities there were family relationships which were stable and permanent. Kinship ties existed which were both inter- and infra-generational and were not necessarily limited to a single community of runaways. In 1830 a military commander of Mayari cited the testimony of a captured black concerning kinship ties existing between runaways in two Cuban *palenques*. As already noted, such ties could provide an early warning system against impending attack.[47] More research is required on domestic arrangements among communities of runaways before assertions can be made as to whether these represent the continuation of African patterns of behavior in the Americas or constitute another example of adaptive capability on the part of Afro-Americans in response to white supremacist, slavocratic societies in Spanish and Portuguese America.

Ties among the black community in Iberoamerica could be established by forming fictive relationships or, in the case of already existing familial ties, enhanced by consciousness of West African origins. Ethnic considerations were manifested in a variety of ways, such as in the selection of marriage partners or godparents, in the choice of a particular brotherhood, or even in the setting up of a shop or tavern expressly to provide a meeting place for members of the owner's nation. This assertion of an African heritage played an invaluable social and psychological role in the adaptation by slaves to Spanish and Portuguese America. In a predominantly hostile ambience such as existed for blacks, identification with national origins enabled transplanted slaves to establish surrogate roots otherwise denied them in New World slavocratic societies. Ethnic consciousness could also be used as a mechanism to socialize offspring against possible forced separation from immediate family. By asserting such ethnic origins blacks sought to emphasize distinctions within the slave community, the criteria for which were established by blacks independent of white-imposed typologies. Finally, in white supremacist societies in which outright rejection of modes of behavior and prevailing values of the Spanish or Portuguese overlords, or even resistance to creolizing forces, resulted in severe punishment, the assertion by blacks of ethnic African origins represented a subtle but effective resistance mechanism to Americanization. If this emphasis did not necessarily meet with the approval of whites, at least it did not arouse their wrath. Indeed administrators in the colonies sought to exacerbate ethnic differences in the hope of preserving the status quo.[48]

Naming practices among blacks outside English North America have yet to be studied, but random examples from South America and the French Antilles suggest further avenues of enquiry. Freyre expressed a widely held view that blacks commonly took the family names of their white owners as surnames. Such mimetism was attributable to vanity, the influence of patriarchalism, or efforts to climb the social ladder. In describing slaves, masters used occupational labels or designations based on the ethnic origin of the slave, e.g. John Shoemaker or Pedro Congo. Reports from Saint Domingue suggest that some owners went so far as to use the additional African name to be more specific in identifying a slave, e.g. "the Congo Diane, called in her country Ougan-Daga". Such names revealed intervention by owners, but there are indications to reinforce the view that by their own choice of names, blacks in the Americas sought to establish a relationship to a place (be it the port of arrival in the Americas, a plantation, or even a township in West Africa), or within a family lineage, or within an inherited cultural tradition. In his study of the Djuka, Koebben describes matriclans each of which had originated in the first half of the eighteenth century from different groups of runaway slaves. Each group derived their names from the names of the original owners of the plantations from which their predecessors had fled. In Brazil, the family name of an owner might well come to be absorbed in the name of the location and the plantation might carry an indigenous or African name rather than an European name. From the French Antilles come names whose origin lay in the contraband trade, and which had been consciously preserved. By the preservation of such names, transplanted Africans in the Americas provided themselves with an anchorage or point of orientation, be it to a place, to a cultural legacy, to a shared experience, or to previous generations.[49]

Our purpose here has been to suggest a pan-American dimension to the situation of the black family in the Americas described by Herbert Gutman for the English-speaking North American mainland. Only time and further research will confirm the validity of an approach which infers values or belief systems from what is essentially behavioral evidence. Likewise only further information from a wider range of sources will enable future scholars to assess in the proper perspective Gutman's contention that marriage and the structure of the family are the most suitable indicators to measure the retention or loss of cultural integrity among slave populations. At the present state of scholarship there can be no doubt but that *The black family in slavery and freedom* is a major contribution to the history of the black family over a period of some two centuries in one area of the Americas. The task awaiting future scholars in this field is twofold: first, to determine whether or not there are other indicators of equal and possibly of greater importance than the family in reconstructing cultural integrity; secondly, to decide whether or not the picture presented by Gutman, based primarily on the records of six plantations, is representative of black families in English-speaking America and if it provides a firm foundation for further research.

Trends in recent historiography have resulted in renewed interest in freedmen of African descent in the Antilles and Spanish and Portuguese America.[50] It is ironical that a definitive history of slavery, let alone of the black family, has yet to be written for any region of colonial Spanish or Portuguese America, or for the republics of Latin America. Certainly domestic arrangements and adherence to values and practices which bore on the life of the black family in English North America had parallels in the Spanish and Portuguese American empires and in the republics of present-day Latin America. Slaves and free blacks had a real need for mutual aid mechanisms which would provide them with moral and physical strength and even financial resources, which were available only as the result of collective endeavors. Only thus were blacks able to cope with physical hardship and psychological despair in a manner which would have been beyond the capabilities of an individual. But such coincidences do no more than confirm that blacks in different parts of the Americas reacted very similarly to the New World and to the institution of slavery as it was present in the Americas. Still in the realm of hypothesis lie answers to questions concerning unique adaptive capabilities and the development of an Afro-American cultural tradition *sui generis*. The search for explanation of these phenomena lies at the

A. J. R. Russell-Wood 33

origins of the African experience in the Americas, not in a later stage of creolization. Of the historian no less than the slave of bygone ages, it will be imperative that his reach should exceed his grasp.

*The author wishes to thank Ronald Walters and Roger Ekirch for their valuable suggestions based on careful reading of an earlier version of this article.

[1]For a discussion of this literature, see Charles R. Boxer, *Race relations in the Portuguese colonial empire, 1415-1825,* (Oxford, 1963), pp. 103-113, and his translation of an anonymous pamphlet entitled *Nova e curiosa relação* (Lisbon, 1764) in "Negro slavery in Brazil. A Portuguese pamphlet", *Race,* V (January 1964), 38-47. Of the numerous studies by Raymundo Nina Rodrigues (1862-1906), Arthur Ramos (1903-1949), and Manuel Querino (1851-1923), only Ramos has found an English translator in the person of Richard Pattee, *The Negro in Brazil* (Washington, 1939). Papers presented at the congress were published under the title *Estudos Afro-brasileiros* (Rio de Janeiro, 1935).

[2]Arnold A. Sio, "Interpretations of slavery: the slave status in the Americas", *Comparative Studies in Society and History,* VII (April 1965), 289-308; David Brion Davis, *The problem of slavery in western culture* (Ithaca, 1966), pp. 223-288, and esp. p. 224, n.1; Carl N. Degler, *Neither black nor white. Slavery and race relations in Brazil and the United States* (New York, 1971), pp. 19-21, 26-39. General conclusions similar to those espoused by Tannenbaum had earlier been drawn by Herbert B. Alexander, "Brazilian and United States slavery compared", *The Journal of Negro History,* VII (October 1922), 349-364, and Mary Wilhelmine Williams, "The treatment of Negro slaves in the Brazilian empire: a comparison with the United States of America", *idem,* XV (July 1930), 315-336. For revisions of the Freyrian thesis, see Boxer, *Race relations,* pp. 100-123 and by the same author, "The colour question in the Portuguese empire, 1415-1825", *Proceedings of the British Academy,* XLVII (London, 1961), 130-137, and *The Portuguese seaborne empire, 1415-1825* (London, 1969), pp. 259-266, 280-281, 312; A. J. R. Russell-Wood, "Class, creed, and colour in colonial Bahia: a study in prejudice", *Race,* IX (October 1967), 133-157 and "Colonial Brazil" in David W. Cohen and Jack P. Greene (eds.), *Neither slave nor free. The freedmen of African descent in the slave societies of the New World* (Baltimore, 1972), pp. 84-133. For a reappraisal of conditions in Spanish America, see Jaime Jaramillo Uribe, "Esclavos y señores en la sociedad colombiana del siglo XVIII", *Anuario colombiano de historia social y de la cultura,* 1 (1963), 3-62.

[3]Herbert G. Gutman, *Slavery and the numbers game: a critique of Time on the cross* (Urbana, 1975). Philip D. Curtin, *The Atlantic slave trade. A census* (Madison, 1969), and his "Epidemiology and the slave trade", *Political Science Quarterly,* LXXXIII, (June 1968), 190-216; Roger Anstey, *The Atlantic slave trade and British abolition, 1760-1810* (London, 1975); Johannes Postma, "The origin of African slaves: the Dutch activities on the Guinea coast, 1675-1795", in Stanley L. Engerman and Eugene D. Genovese (eds.), *Race and slavery in the western hemisphere: quantitative studies,* (Princeton, 1975), pp. 33-49; Phillip LeVeen, "A quantitative analysis of the impact of British suppression policies on the volume of the nineteenth century Atlantic slave trade", in Engerman and Genovese (eds.), *Race and slavery,* pp. 51-81; Pierre Verger, *Bahia and the west coast trade, 1549-1851* (Ibadan, 1964) and his *Flux et reflux de la traite des nègres entre le golfe de Bénin et Bahia de todos os Santos du dix-septième au dix-neuvième siècle* (Paris and The Hague, 1968).

[4]Gonzalo Aguirre Beltrán, *La población negra de México, 1519-1810* (Mexico, 1946), Frederick P. Bowser, *The African slave in colonial Peru, 1524-1650* (Stanford, 1974), Harry

Hoetink, *Caribbean race relations: a study of two variants* (Oxford, 1967), Franklin W. Knight, *Slave society in Cuba during the nineteenth century* (Madison, 1970), Magnus Moerner, *Race mixture in the history of Latin America* (Boston, 1967). For bibliographic references on Brazil, see Russell-Wood, "Colonial Brazil", pp. 132-133, and for a Spanish-American perspective see Frederick P. Bowser, "The African in colonial Spanish America: reflections on research achievements and priorities", *Latin American Research Review*, VII (Spring 1972), 77-94.

   [5]A. J. R. Russell-Wood, "Black and mulatto brotherhoods in colonial Brazil: a study in collective behavior", *Hispanic American Historical Review*, LIV (November 1974), 574-575, 595-597, and Stuart B. Schwartz, "Resistance and accommodation in eighteenth-century Brazil: the slaves' view of slavery", *idem,* LVII (February 1977), 69-81.

   [6]Curtin, *The Atlantic slave trade,* table 65 facing p. 217.

   [7]For an interdisciplinary perspective see essays in Suzanne Miers and Igor Kopytoff (eds.), *Slavery in Africa. Historical and anthropological perspectives* (Madison, 1977). Studies of behavior and domestic arrangements in contemporary Africa include Arthur Phillips, (ed.), *Survey of African marriage and family life* (London, 1953), reprinted with the addition of new material as *Marriage laws in Africa* (London, 1971) under the co-authorship of Arthur Phillips and Henry F. Morris. Lucy P. Mair's monograph was reprinted as *African marriage and social change* (London, 1969).

   [8]On internal African slavery, see Allan G. B. Fisher and Humphrey J. Fisher, *Slavery and Muslim society in Africa. The institution in Saharan and Sudanic Africa and the trans-Saharan trade* (London, 1971), essays in Claude Meillassoux, (ed.), *L'esclavage en Afrique précoloniale* (Paris, 1975) and Frederick Cooper's study of black and brown Muslim masters in the sultanate of Zanzibar in the nineteenth century, *Plantation slavery on the east coast of Africa* (New Haven, 1977). On the East-African trade, see Edward A. Alpers, *The East African slave trade* (Nairobi, 1967), and James Duffy, *A question of slavery* (Oxford, 1967). A preliminary study of the African diaspora in Asia is by Joseph E. Harris, *The African presence in Asia. Consequences of the East African slave trade* (Evanston, 1971). On Afro-Indian contacts in the Americas, see Roger Bastide, *African civilisations in the New World,* trans. Peter Green (New York, 1971), pp. 72-88 and the detailed study by Emilio Harth-terré, *Negros e indios. Un estamento social ignorado del Perú colonial* (Lima, 1973).

   [9]Igor Kopytoff and Suzanne Miers, "African 'slavery' as an institution of marginality", in Miers and Kopytoff, (eds.), *Slavery in Africa,* pp. 3-81.

   [10]Curtin, *The Atlantic slave trade,* table 77, facing p. 269. Curtin's estimates are revised upwards (Brazil, 38 percent; Spanish America, 17 percent; French Caribbean, 17 percent; British Caribbean, 17 percent; United States, 6 percent; Dutch, Danish and Swedish Caribbean, 6 percent) for slave imports to the New World in the period 1500-1870 by William Fogel and Stanley L. Engerman, *Time on the cross* (2 vols. Boston, 1974), vol. I, figure 1, p. 14. See also Curtin's modifications to his own estimates, "Measuring the Atlantic slave trade", in Engerman and Genovese (eds.), *Race and slavery,* pp. 107-128.

   [11]Frank Tannenbaum, *Slave and citizen. The Negro in the Americas* (New York, 1947), pp. 48-53; Herbert S. Klein, *Slavery in the Americas. A comparative study of Virginia and Cuba* (Chicago, 1967), pp. 57-85; Leslie B. Rout, Jr., *The African experience in Spanish America: 1502 to the present day* (Cambridge, England, 1976), pp. 80-87; Bowser, *The African slave,* pp. 254, 273-74; Gwendolyn Midlo Hall, *Social control in slave plantation societies. A comparison of St. Domingue and Cuba* (Baltimore, 1971), pp. 81-112; Hoetink, *Caribbean race relations,* pp. 3-31; Antoine Gisler, C.S.SP., *L'esclavage aux Antilles françaises (XVIIᵉ - XIXᵉ siècle. Contribution au problème de l'esclavage* (Fribourg, 1965), pp. 19-33; Lucien Peytraud, *L'esclavage aux Antilles françaises avant 1789* (Paris, 1897), pp. 143-166; Marvin Harris, *Patterns of race in the Americas* (New York, 1964), pp. 54-78; David Brion Davis, *The problem of slavery,* pp. 233-235, 252-255; Degler, *Neither black nor white,* pp. 26-39.

   [12]Resolution of Overseas Council of January 26, 1726, cited in Russell-Wood, "Colonial Brazil", p. 112. For attitudes of church and state in Spanish and Portuguese America, see Charles R. Boxer, *Women in Iberian expansion overseas, 1415-1815. Some facts, fancies, and*

A. J. R. Russell-Wood   35

personalities (New York, 1975), pp. 36-38; Ann M. Pescatello, *Power and pawn. The female in Iberian families, societies, and cultures* (Westport, 1976), pp. 138, 148-149; Bowser, *The African slave*, pp. 254-255; David Brion Davis, *The problem of slavery*, pp. 273-277; Rout, *The African experience*, pp. 140-145; David M. Davidson, "Negro slave control and resistance in colonial Mexico, 1519-1650", *Hispanic American Historical Review*, XLVI (August 1966), esp. pp. 239-240; Richard M. Morse, "Toward a theory of Spanish American government", *Journal of the History of Ideas*, XV (January 1954), esp. pp. 72-76; Beltrán, *La población*, pp. 248-254; Emilio Willems, *Latin American culture. An anthropological synthesis* (New York, 1975), pp. 35-42; Moerner, *Race mixture*, pp. 35-39.

[13]On crown policies and Afro-Amerindian contacts, see Bowser, *The African slave*, pp. 283-287; Emilio Hart-terré, *Informe sobre el descubrimiento de documentos que revelan la trata y comercio de esclavos negros por los indios del común durante el gobierno virreinal en el Perú* (Lima, 1961) and by the same author *Presencia del negro en el virreinato del Perú* (Lima, 1971) and *Negros e indios;* Moerner, *Race mixture*, pp. 40-41; Rout, *The African experience*, pp. 117-122; James M. Lockhart, *Spanish Peru, 1532-1560. A colonial society* (Madison, 1968), p. 172; Rolando Mellafe, *Negro slavery in Latin America* (Berkeley, 1975), pp. 102-103, 112-113, 116-118; Edgar F. Love, "Legal restrictions on Afro-Indian relations in colonial Mexico", *Journal of Negro History*, LV (April 1970), 131-139. On Brazil, see Waldemar de Almeida Barbosa, *Negros e quilombos em Minas Gerais* (Belo Horizonte, 1972), pp. 87-94; Clovis Moura, *Rebeliões da senzala. Quilombos. Insurreições. Guerrilhas* (Rio de Janeiro, 1972), pp. 106-108; Stuart B. Schwartz, "The Mocambo: slave resistance in colonial Bahia", *Journal of Social History*, III (Summer 1970), 323-326; Boxer, *The Portuguese seaborne empire*, p. 266.

[14]Bowser, *The African slave*, pp. 254-255; Davidson, "Negro slave control", p. 240 and sources there cited; Fernando Ortiz, *Los negros esclavos* (Havana, 1916), pp. 173, 303-304; Gisler, *L'esclavage*, pp. 61-66, 132-133; Miguel Acosta Saignes, *Vida de los esclavos negros en Venezuela* (Caracas, 1967), pp. 213-228. For Brazil, see Stanley Stein, *Vassouras. A Brazilian coffee county, 1850-1900* (Cambridge, Mass., 1957), pp. 155-156; Degler, *Neither black nor white*, pp. 37-39 and sources cited; André João Antonil, *Cultura e opulência do Brasil por suas drogas e minas* (Lisbon, 1711, of which I have used the edition with critical commentary by Andrée Mansuy, Paris, 1968), p. 124 and n. 14.

[15]Boxer, *Women*, pp. 32-33; A. J. R. Russell-Wood, *Fidalgos and Philanthropists. The Santa Casa da Misericórdia of Bahia, 1550-1755* (London, 1968), pp. 182-183, 314; Bowser, *The African slave*, pp. 269-270. For Amerindian manumissions of black slaves, see Harth-terré, *Negros e indios*, pp. 131-138.

[16]Fernão Cardim, *Tratados da terra e gente do Brasil*. Introduction and notes by Batista Caetano, Capistrano de Abreu, Rodolpho Garcia (Rio de Janeiro, 1925), p. 300. Fears at the liberating force of conversion were equally present in the English North American colonies, see Winthrop D. Jordan, *White over black. American attitudes toward the Negro, 1550-1812* (Chapel Hill, 1968), pp. 92-93 Cf. Gisler, *L'esclavage*, p. 91.

[17]A. J. R. Russell-Wood, "Technology and society: the impact of gold mining on the institution of slavery in Portuguese America", *The Journal of Economic History*, XXXVII (March 1977), 59-83; Lockhart, *Spanish Peru*, p. 185; Peytraud, *L'esclavage*, p. 210.

[18]Bowser, *The African slave*, pp. 255, 257-258; Gisler, *L'esclavage*, pp. 63-65; Lockhart, *Spanish Peru*, pp. 178-179.

[19]Russell-Wood, "Technology and society", 66-68; Bowser, *The African slave*, p. 256.

[20]Donald Ramos, "Marriage and the family in colonial Vila Rica", *Hispanic American Historical Review*, LV (May 1975), 212-215; Russell-Wood, "Black and mulatto brotherhoods", 569-571; Bowser, *The African slave*, pp. 236-243; Gisler, *L'esclavage*, pp. 135-136.

[21]Bowser, *The African slave*, pp. 260-261; Richard Price, (ed.), *Maroon societies: rebel slave communities in the Americas* (New York, 1973), pp. 27-28. Cf. the comment made by William Sells, based on twenty years of medical practice in Jamaica, in response to William Wilberforce's *Appeal:* ". . and it is interesting to know that they [the negroes] do not only object to sexual intercourse between relatives, but commonly disallow of it between those who have been shipmates in the same vessel from Africa; as they form an attachment for each other resembling that of a brother or sister, and which is prohibitory of further in-

timacy", *Remarks on the condition of the slaves in the island of Jamaica* (London, 1823), pp. 28-29.

[22]A. J. F. Koebben, "Unity and disunity: Cottica Djuka society as a kinship system", in Price, (ed.), *Maroon Societies*, p. 331; Bastide, *African civilizations*, pp. 55, 58-60. On endogamy, see Freyre, *The masters*, pp. 356-357.

[23]Bowser, *The African slave*, pp. 255-257; Harth-terre, *Negros e indios*, pp. 139-146; Bastide, *African civilizations*, pp. 56-57. Cf. Thales de Azevedo, *Namoro à antiga. Tradição e mudança* (Salvador, 1975), for a general survey of courting patterns in Brazil.

[24]Bowser, *The African slave*, pp. 251-253; Antonil, *Cultura e opulência*, pp. 124, 128; In his *História da América Portuguesa* (Lisbon, 1730), Sebastião da Rocha Pitta noted the use of herbs for amatory ends by people of African descent, cited by Manuel Querino, *A raça africana e os seus costumes* (Salvador, 1955), pp. 80-82. The most thorough study of this fascinating topic is Colin A. Palmer's "Religion and magic in Mexican slave society, 1570-1650", in Engerman and Genovese (eds.), *Race and slavery*, esp. pp. 320-323.

[25]Cited in Donald Pierson, *Negroes in Brazil. A study of race contact at Bahia* (Chicago, 1942), p. 362.

[26]Bowser, *The African slave*, pp. 256-257; Maria Luiza Marcílio, *La ville de São Paulo. Peuplement et population, 1750-1850* (Rouen, 1972), pp. 162, 219; Henry Koster, *Travels in Brazil* (London, 1816), p. 243; Degler, *Neither black nor white*, pp. 36-39; Luis M. Diaz Soler, *Historia de la esclavitud negra en Puerto Rico; 1493-1890* (Madrid, 1953), pp. 172-173; Klein, *Slavery in the Americas*, pp. 95-97.

[27]Gisler, *L'esclavage*, p. 65 and notes; Peytraud *L'esclavage*, pp. 208-212, 242-247; Gabriel Debien, "Le marronage aux Antilles françaises au XVIIIe siècle", *Caribbean Studies*, VI (October 1966), 40; Cornelis Ch. Goslinga, *The Dutch in the Caribbean and on the Wild Coast, 1580-1680* (Gainesville, 1971), p. 369. Cf. the debate between William Wilberforce, *An appeal to the religion, justice and humanity of the inhabitants of the British empire in behalf of the Negro slaves in the West Indies* (London, 1823), pp. 14-15, and William Sells, *Remarks*, pp. 30-35.

[28]R. K. Kent, "Palmares: an African state in Brazil", *The Journal of African History*, VI (1965), 168; see also Edison Carneiro, *O quilombo dos Palmares* (3rd ed.; Rio de Janeiro, 1966), pp. 27, and 71-91; Bastide, *African civilizations*, pp. 49-51. Querino, *A raça africana*, pp. 107-109.

[29]Ramos, "Marriage and the family", p. 200 *et seq.*

[30]Schwartz, "The Mocambo", 329; citation from Bryan Edwards, *The history.. of the West Indies*, quoted by Price, (ed.), *Maroon societies*, p. 241.

[31]Freyre, *The masters*, preface to the 2nd Eng. lang. ed., (1955), pp. xxxiii, xliii; Bowser, *The African slave*, pp. 256, 269.

[32]Degler, *Neither black nor white*, pp. 171-176; Bowser, *The African slave*, pp. 268-271; Ramos, "Marriage and the family", 208. Verena Martinez-Alier, *Marriage, class and colour in nineteenth century Cuba. A study of racial attitudes and sexual values in a slave society* (Cambridge, England, 1974) only mentions slave marriages in passing, but provides insights into interracial domestic arrangements which are relevant to mainland Spanish and Portuguese America, see especially pp. 115-119. On the role of women in general in colonial Latin America, see Charles R. Boxer, *Women*, pp. 35-62; Pescatello, *Power and pawn*, pp. 132-159; A. J. R. Russell-Wood, "Women and society in colonial Brazil", *Journal of Latin American Studies*, IX, (May 1977), 1-34; Roger Bastide (ed.), *La femme de couleur en Amérique latine* (Paris, 1974).

[33]Ramos, "Marriage and the family", 206-207, 218-220; Martinez-Alier, *Marriage*, pp. 124-130; Bastide, *African civilizations*, pp. 30-41.

[34]Bowser, *The African slave*, p. 269; Gisler, *L'esclavage*, p. 66, n.1, and p. 68; Richard F. Burton, *Exploration of the highlands of the Brazil with a full account of the gold and diamond mines* (2 vols.; London, 1869), I, 270-271; Stein, *Vassouras*, pp. 132-140; C. R. Boxer, *The golden age of Brazil, 1695-1750. Growing pains of a colonial society* (Berkeley, 1969), pp. 7-9, 138-140, 171-177; Williams, "The treatment", 325 *et seq.*

[35]Gisler, *L'esclavage*, pp. 61-62; Peytraud, *L'esclavage*, p. 209; Antonil, *Cultura*, p. 132.

[36]Freyre, *The masters*, pp. 150-151, 324-325, 349-350, 395-397.

A. J. R. Russell-Wood   37

³⁷Antonil, *Cultura,* p. 124; Bowser, *The African slave,* pp. 258, 260-261; Gisler, *L'esclavage,* p. 64, n.2; Davidson, "Negro slave control", 239-240.

³⁸Bowser, *The African slave,* pp. 259, 261-267; Stuart B. Schwartz, *Sovereignty and society in colonial Brazil. The high court of Bahia and its judges, 1609-1751* (Berkeley, 1973), pp. 248-249; Russell-Wood, "Colonial Brazil", pp. 91-92, 110-111. The situation was not quite as hopeless as described by Degler, *Neither black nor white,* pp. 37-39.

³⁹Koebben, "Unity and disunity", esp. p. 324; Bowser, *The African slave,* pp. 281-282. Notarial records have been used by Stuart Schwartz in his researches into manumission in colonial Brazil, "The manumission of slaves in colonial Brazil: Bahia, 1684-1745", *Hispanic American Historical Review,* LIV, (November 1974), 603-635.

⁴⁰See note 21 for sources.

⁴¹Much of the scholarly material on co-parenthood is based on village societies of Mexico and Central America. For general discussions, see Sidney W. Mintz and Eric R. Wolf, "An analysis of ritual co-parenthood (Compadrazgo)", *Southwestern Journal of Anthropology,* VI, (Winter 1950), 341-368; Mário Dávila, "Compadrazgo: fictive kinship in Latin America", in Nelson H. Graburn, (ed.), *Readings in kinship and social structure* (New York, 1971), pp. 396-406; Willems, *Latin American culture,* pp. 62-63; George M. Foster, "Cofradia and Compadrazgo in Spain and Spanish America", *Southwestern Journal of Anthropology,* IX, (Spring 1953), 1-28. For a historical perspective from South America, see scattered examples in Stein, *Vassouras,* pp. 147-149; Price, (ed.), *Maroon societies,* p. 21; Bowser, *The African slave,* p. 280. For the Brazilian example of 1719, see Russell-Wood, "Black and mulatto brotherhoods", 573 and sources there cited.

⁴²Russell-Wood, "Colonial Brazil", p. 100 and sources there cited, especially Lourenco de Almeida's letter of April 3, 1732 to crown judge António Ferreira do Valle de Mello (Arquivo Público Mineiro, Secretaria do Govêrno, vol. 27, fols. 127-130); Bowser, *The African slave,* pp. 228-229, 234, 318-319.

⁴³Russell-Wood, "Black and mulatto brotherhoods" and by the same author "Aspectos da vida social das irmandades leigas da Bahia no século XVIII", *Universitas.* VI-VII, (1970), 189-204; Manoel S. Cardozo, "The lay brotherhoods of colonial Bahia", *The Catholic Historical Review,* XXXIII, (April 1947), 12-30; Luiz Monteiro da Costa, "A devoção de N. S. do Rosário na Cidade do Salvador", *Revista do Instituto Genealógico da Bahia,* X, (1958), 95-117. For colonial Peru, see Bowser, *The African slave,* pp. 247-251, and Harthterre, *Presencia,* pp. 12-14.

⁴⁴For an excellent survey of the literature, see the introduction by Price to *Maroon societies.* Petit marronage is discussed in Debien, "Le marronage", 7-9; Jean Fouchard, *Les marrons de la Liberté* (Paris, 1972), p. 381 *et seq,* and his extensive analysis of motivation, pp. 33-129; José Alipio Goulart, *Da fuga ao suicídio. Aspectos da rebeldia dos escravos no Brasil* (Rio de Janeiro, 1972), pp. 25-33. For specific examples of temporary absences in colonial Latin America, see Bowser, *The African slave,* pp. 193, 257 (Cf., Gisler, *L'esclavage,* p. 64); Lockhart, *Spanish Peru,* pp. 188-189; Russell-Wood, "Technology and society", 76-77.

⁴⁵Kent, "Palmares", 167, Cf. 171; Fouchard, *Les marrons,* p. 387-389; Bowser, *The African slave,* p. 190.

⁴⁶Edison Carneiro, *Ladinos e crioulos. Estudos sôbre o negro no Brasil* (Rio de Janeiro, 1964), pp. 26-36; Bowser, *The African slave,* pp. 187, 193-195, 259; Miguel Acosta Saignes, *Vida de los esclavos,* pp. 264, 277, 290; Maria del Carmen Borrego Pla, *Palenques de negros en Cartagena de Indias a fines del siglo XVII* (Seville, 1973) p. 86; Fouchard, *Les marrons,* p. 55. For the use of journal advertisements as sources of information on group flights, see Gilberto Freyre, *O escravo nos anúncios de jornais brasileiros do século XIX* (Recife, 1963); Stein, *Vassouras,* pp. 143-144; Fouchard, *Les marrons.*

⁴⁷Francisco Perez de la Riva and Bryan Edwards, cited in Price (ed.), *Maroon societies,* pp. 57 and 241 respectively; on kinship relations between *palenques,* see José L. Franco, translated in *idem,* p. 46. See also Inès Reichel-Dolmatoff, "Aspects de la vie de la femme noire dans le passé et de nos jours en Colombie (Côte atlantique)" in Bastide (ed.), *La femme,* p. 250.

⁴⁸On official use of conflict stimulation, see Russell-Wood, "Black and mulatto brotherhoods", 601 and sources quoted; ethnic origins of slaves in colonial Latin America are surveyed in Lockhart, *Spanish Peru*, pp. 172-174; Bowser, *The African slave*, pp. 39-44; Curtin, *The Atlantic slave trade*, pp. 97, 98, 109, 111, 113, 189, 190, 207, 240; Carlos B. Ott, *Formação e evolução étnica da Cidade do Salvador* (2 vols., Salvador, 1955, 1957), I, 53-75 and II, appendix 3.

⁴⁹Fꞁeyre, *The masters*, pp. 456-458; Koebben, "Unity and disunity", p. 323; Lockhart, *Spanish Peru*, p. 176; Fouchard, *Les marrons*, pp. 291-298.

⁵⁰See the essays in Cohen and Greene, *Neither slave nor free*, several of which have subsequently been developed into monographs. A sobering assessment of blacks in São Paulo is Florestan Fernandes, *The Negro in Brasilian society* (Eng. trans.; New York, 1969).

12

Marriage Patterns of Persons of African Descent in a Colonial Mexico City Parish

Edgar F. Love

D URING THE THREE CENTURIES OF colonial rule, more than 200,000 African slaves were brought into Mexico.[1] Historians and social scientists have paid relatively scant attention to the fate of the black man in either the colonial or modern period of Mexican history. And although it is generally known that considerable racial mixing, loosely described as *mestizaje*, took place in Hispanic America, scholars have not attempted a detailed analysis of the extent and direction of this miscegenation in terms of actual marriage patterns of persons of African descent. Despite the voluminous colonial marriage records available in the numerous Mexican church archives, few scholars have attempted to delve into such interesting questions as the following:

1. To what extent did Negro slaves tend to marry other Negro slaves rather than persons of other ethnic groups or legal status?
2. Did free Negroes and others of African descent tend to marry within or outside their racial groups and from which racial groups were mates chosen by those who married outside their own groups?
3. What were the marriage patterns of persons having only a little African blood? Did such persons tend to marry within their group or marry upward into the Spanish group?
4. Were interracial marriages between Spaniards and persons having Negroid blood rare, and if so, how rare?

This pilot study of marriages involving persons of African descent deals with these basic questions.[2] The author, utilizing the colonial

---

1. Gonzalo Aguirre Beltrán, *Cuijla: Esbozo etnográfico de un pueblo negro* (México, 1958), p. 8. Dr. Aguirre Beltrán has calculated that during one period, 1595-1640, 88,383 African slaves were introduced legally into Mexico. *La población negra de México, 1519-1810: Estudio etno-histórico* (México, 1946), p. 220.

2. Other types of studies are being made of parish records. *La Academia de*

records of the parish of Santa Veracruz (Mexico City), analyzed most of marriages in which one or both persons were of African descent.[3] The marriages studied covered the period 1646-1746, or, say, five generations.

The parish church of Santa Veracruz was founded in 1526 by Hernán Cortés. In 1568 it was finally completed and officially dedicated by the Archbishop Alfonso de Montúfar.[4] Prior to 1781 the western boundary of the parish extended to Atzcapozalco, including the pueblo of Tacuba, and the southern area of the parish embraced the pueblos of Tacubaya, Mixcoac, San Angel, Coyoacán, Natívitas, and San Agustín de las Cuevas (Tlalpan). The parish church was located in the heart of Mexico City, opposite the Alameda.

The basic statistical information for this study was taken from the records on *Casamientos de Castas* (marriages of persons of mixed blood). During the colonial period, the Church usually recorded all marriages, births, and baptismals in two separate parochial books—one for Spaniards and the other for the *castas* (persons of mixed blood). In the parish of Santa Veracruz, Spanish marriages were recorded in the *Casamientos de Españoles*, and *casta* marriages, including persons of African descent, in the *Casamientos de Castas*.[5] Marriages listed in the *Casamientos de Españoles* of the parish of Santa Veracruz are not, however, exclusively limited to marriages involving Spaniards or whites. One can find in these volumes numerous examples of Spanish men marrying mestizo and *castizo* women, and a few marriages between Spanish men and mulatto women are similarly to be found there.[6] In a few remarkable instances, marriages involving only Spaniards are recorded in the *Casamientos de Castas* of the parish of Santa Veracruz.[7]

The colonial priest, in recording marriages, was required to list

---

Genealogía e Heráldica of Mexico City, for example, is currently engaged in a study involving the use of parish records.

3. The author is deeply indebted to Rev. Ernesto Santillán Ortiz, pastor of the parish church of Santa Veracruz, for granting permission to use the archival records of his parish.

4. Parroquia de la Santa Veracruz, *Ligeros apuntes históricos de la parroquia de la Santa Veracruz de México* (México, 1926), p. 11.

5. The *Casamientos de Españoles* was established in 1568 and the *Casamientos de Castas* in the year 1646.

6. A typical example is the marriage of Carlos de Vayesteros, *español*, to Anna María de Chávez y Rodríguez, *mulata*, March 21, 1730. (Archivo de la Parroquia de la Santa Veracruz, *Casamientos de Españoles*, vol. 9, fol. 101).

7. See, for example, the marriage of Francisco Xavier de Casabajal, *español*, to María Manuela la Pinto, *española*, April 15, 1721. (Archivo de la Parroquia de la Santa Veracruz, *Casamientos de Castas*, vol. 5, fol. 108).

the ethnic status of the couples. An elaborated racial classification scheme, called *casta*, was established by the Spanish authorities and applied by the priests. In the parish of Santa Veracruz the following racial classifications were used in the marriage documents:

Negro (tended to denote a pure black man)
Mulato (Spanish and Negro)
Mulato blanco (Spanish and Negro, usually called a *mulato*)
Mulato prieto (Negro and *parda*)
Mulato lobo (*Pardo* and Indian, commonly called a *lobo*)
Morisco (Spanish and *mulato*)
Mestizo (Spanish and Indian)
Castizo (Spanish and Mestizo)
Indio (an Indian)
Indio ladino (an Indian who had adopted Spanish customs
                    and spoke the Spanish language)
Lobo (same as *mulato lobo*)
Coyote (usually used to denote a mestizo)
Chino (Negro and Indian, or a person born in the Philip-
            pines)
Pardo (Negro and Indian)
Moreno (euphemistic term for a person of African descent)
Español (white)

There are many difficulties surrounding the exact meaning of these terms. Take, for instance, the elastic term *chino*. Dr. Gonzalo Aguirre Beltrán, the leading authority on the Negro in Mexico, maintains that the term was used to denote the offspring of a Negro-Indian couple and that during the 17th and 18th centuries the terms *mulato* and *chino* were synonymous.[8] But Professor Joaquín Roncal asserts that the word *chino* indicated a child born to an Indian-*lobo* couple.[9] On the other hand, Nicolás León, who made a detailed study of the colonial caste system, defines a *chino* as a person having twenty-five per cent Indian and seventy-five per cent Negro blood.[10] In the parish records of Santa Veracruz, the term *chino* sometimes denoted a person of Asian descent, born in the Philippines. Unfortunately, the church records do not always show the place of birth of the *chino*, and without an extensive genealogical investigation it is frequently impossible

8. Gonzalo Aguirre Beltrán, *La población negra de México*, p. 178.
9. Joaquín Roncal, "The Negro Race in Mexico," HAHR, XXIV:3 (August, 1940), 533.
10. Nicolás León, *Las castas del México colonial o Nueva España* (México, 1924), p. 20. León also indicated that the term can mean as well a person from the Philippines.

to know whether a given *chino* was of African or Asian descent. Because of the confusion in regard to the use of the term *chino* in the parish of Santa Veracruz, I have only included *chinos* in the analysis of marriage patterns when the *chino* married a person of African descent.[11]

The term *español* also requires explanation. In colonial Mexico, the term *español* or *blanco* did not necessarily indicate purity of blood. Angel Rosenblat, in his classical study of *mestizaje,* warns that the term

> . . . at no time in the history of America implied purity of blood. A mestizo crossed with a Spaniard was called *castizo;* the *castizo* with a Spaniard was known as an *español;* that is to say, one was white who had one-eighth Indian blood. In a similar manner, the crossing of the mulatto with white produced a *cuarterón;* the *cuarterón* with white a *quinterón;* the *quinterón* with white produced a white; that is to say that one was white who had one-sixteenth Negro blood.[12]

The student of interracial marriages must also contend with the fact that the priests did not always record the ethnic status of both persons in the marriage records. Frequently the terms *"vecino"* and *"natural"* were the only designations used in the parish records of Santa Veracruz to describe one of the partners of a marriage. Frequently the term *vecino* merely meant a resident of a particular city or town, e.g., 'Francisco Joseph Flores, *mulato libre, vecino de esta ciudad."* On the other hand, a given individual simply might be described as a *"vecino de esta ciudad,"* without indicating the *casta* of the person. The *vecino,* whose racial status was not recorded by the priest, is included in this study only when the other party to the marriage was of African descent.

A further complication arose in those instances where the priest used the term *natural,* but did not specifically indicate the race of the party. Generally speaking, the Spaniards regarded the Indians as *naturales.* Professor Gonzalo Aguirre Beltrán describes the Spanish view of the Indian by pointing out that "The Indians were classified as *naturales,* without reason. Their culture kept them submerged in

11. In view of the fact that there were a small number of marriages involving *chinos* recorded in the *Casamientos de Castas,* the adoption of the cited criterion would have an insignificant effect on the delineation of the marriage patterns of persons of African descent.

12. Angel Rosenblat, *La población indígena y el mestizaje en América* (2 vols., Buenos Aires, 1954), II, 137. Rosenblat was referring to the legal definition for white and Negro. Passing was a common practice in colonial Mexico, and some fair-skinned mestizos were able to pass themselves off as white.

nature."[13] But the term *natural,* as used in the *Casamientos de Castas* of Santa Veracruz, did not necessarily mean an Indian. The priests often described individuals as *"mulato natural," "morisco natural," "indio natural," "lobo natural," "castizo natural,"* etc. In other instances, the term *natural* was simply employed to indicate the place of birth, e.g., "Ana Neña, *española, natural y vecina desta ciudad."* Undoubtedly many of the *naturales* married to persons of African descent were Indians, but on the basis of the marriage records, one can only speculate as to the race of those who were simply described by the term *natural.*

In the parish records of Santa Veracruz, the ethnic status of approximately three per cent of the persons marrying individuals of African descent was not indicated. The term *vecino* was used to describe nine males and eleven females; thirty-one males and twenty-seven females were listed as *naturales;* and the remaining twenty-one were unclassified by the priests of Santa Veracruz. Apparently the priests had difficulty in assigning a *casta* classification to these ninety-nine persons and resorted to vague terminology or simply ignored racial groupings. As all of this group of individuals married persons of African descent, it was logical to record these marriages in the *Casamientos de Castas.*

The focus of this paper is on legitimate unions, recorded and performed by the priests of the church. It must be pointed out, however, that many Negroes and mulattoes, especially slaves, would have had difficulty in securing money for the expense of marriage, unless they had masters willing to assume this cost. As a consequence of this financial difficulty and for other reasons, a large percentage of the persons of African descent did not get married. The increase of the Negro population of colonial Mexico was, to a considerable extent, due to the frequency of extra-legal unions and the resultant birth of many illegitimate children. A spot check of the baptismal records of the *castas* indicated that illegitimate births also were common in the parish of Santa Veracruz.

Marriage records of the *castas* are of special interest since the Spanish rulers of colonial Mexico discouraged Africans from marrying outside their racial group. In 1527 the king of Spain declared:[14]

13. Gonzalo Aguirre Beltrán, *Medicina y magia: El proceso de aculturación en la estructura colonial* (México, 1963), p. 76.

14. *Recopilación de leyes de los reynos de las Indias mandadas imprimir y publicar por la magestad católica del rey don Carlos II* (3 vols., 4th ed., Madrid, 1943), ley 5, libro VII, tít. V.

In so far as possible, Negro men who marry should endeavor to marry Negro women. And we declare that these, and the others who are slaves, do not become free because they have married, even though this be the will of the master.

In view of the fact that the Spanish brought to Mexico three times as many Negro males as females, it would have been difficult to have required that all Negroes marry within their racial group. Numerous efforts, however, were made to keep Negroes from marrying or living with Indian women. Negroes and persons of African descent, with some exceptions, were prohibited from living in Indian villages. An elaborate, but none too successful, scheme was established to separate the Indians from the whites and Negroes. But unlike the case in the British colonies, the Negro in Hispanic America was not specifically forbidden to marry outside his racial group.

During the period 1646-1746, the priests of the parish of Santa Veracruz married 1,662 couples, of whom one or both parties of the marriages were persons of African descent.[15] In terms of the ethnic status of the 3,324 persons involved in these marriages, 2,378 (71.5%) of the individuals were of African ancestry, 847 (25.5%) were of non-African origin, and ninety-nine (3.0%) were not given a *casta* classification by the priests. The overwhelming majority, approximately 98%, of the persons listed in the marriage records as having Negroid blood were classified by the priests as Negroes, mulattoes, or *moriscos*. Specifically, 1,748 persons marrying during the period covered by this study were reported to be mulattoes (996 males and 752 females), 329 were Negroes (207 males and 122 females), and 234 were *moriscos* (118 males and 116 females). The remaining persons of African descent included the following: eight *mulatos prietos;* thirty-two *lobos*, five *pardos*, five *morenos*, and seventeen *chinos*.

One of the remarkable features of the marriage patterns of persons of African descent in the parish of Santa Veracruz was the fact that 847 individuals of non-Negroid ancestry married persons of color. The non-African partners of these marriages included 522 mestizos, 126 *castizos*, 116 Indians, 6 *indios ladinos*, and 77 *españoles*. Among the non-Negroid groups, mestizos displayed a greater tendency to marry persons of African descent than did Indians and Spaniards. It is interesting to note that 126 *castizos*, who in view of the harsh restrictions imposed on persons having African blood normally would have been expected to marry other *castizos* or Spaniards, chose instead to

15. All of the statistics of this study are based on the Archivo de la Parroquia de la Santa Veracruz, *Casamientos de Castas*, vols. 1-7.

marry persons of African descent. In choosing spouses having Negroid blood, these *castizos* lessened the social mobility of the children resulting from such unions. Likewise, the marriage of seventy-seven Spaniards to persons of African ancestry represented a departure from the expected Spanish norm.

The marriage record of the parish reveals that in the case of 52.2% of the marriages involving persons of African descent either the husband or the wife did not have any Negroid blood, and only in 47.8% of the 1,622 marriages were both parties of African descent. It is obvious that the efforts of Spanish officials to encourage persons of African descent to marry within their *casta* group was not a marked success in the parish of Santa Veracruz.

The Negroes of Santa Veracruz exhibited a marked tendency to marry either Negroes or mulattoes. In the case of the 207 male Negroes marrying during the period covered by this study, approximately 46.3% (96) married Negro women and 25.1% (62) selected mulatto mates. The remaining forty-nine Negro males married non-African women. Among the Negro males of the latter group, twenty-three married *mestizas*, fifteen wed Indians, seven chose *moriscas*, one took a Spanish wife, one selected a *loba*, one elected to marry a *castiza,* and one married a woman whose *casta* status was not shown in the marriage records.

The 122 Negro women of the parish who married demonstrated an even greater propensity to select a Negro or mulatto spouse. Nearly 78.6% (96) of the Negro females married Negroes, and 16.4% (20) selected mulattoes. Only six Negro females opted to marry other than mulattoes or Negroes. Among the latter group of female Negroes, two married mestizos, two wed *chinos*, and two selected mates of unlisted *casta*.

The marriage patterns of the male and female mulattoes was more diversified than that of their Negro counterparts. Male mulattoes of the parish were only slightly more prone to choose a woman of African descent than one of non-African ancestry. During the period 1646-1746, 996 male mulattoes married, and of this number 532 chose wives from the African *casta* groups, whereas 464 selected wives outside of the Negroid castes. The male mulatto, in selecting a non-Negroid bride, gave first preference to *mestizas*, some 284 marrying women of this *casta*, and second perference to *castizas*, with eighty-six men marrying women from this group. Approximately 42.3% (421) of the male mulattoes chose mulatto wives. Male mulattoes, however, were not apt to marry Negro women. A mere 2.1% (20) of the male mulattoes of the parish elected to marry Negroes. In terms of the general tendencies of the mulatto males, about 70.8% (705) elected to marry either a *mulata* or a *mestiza*, with 42.2% selecting *mulata* wives and 28.6% choosing *mestiza* wives.

The marriage patterns of the female mulatto were not very different from those of the male mulatto. Of the 752 marriages involving female mulattoes, 73.5% married either a mulatto or a mestizo. The female mulatto showed a slightly greater tendency to marry Negroes, in that 8.3% (62) took their husbands from this *casta* as compared with 2.1% for the male mulattoes. On the other hand, forty-one mulatto women married men whose *casta* status was not indicated in the marriage records. A majority of women of this group married men who were listed as *naturales,* probably Indians.

The 234 male and female *moriscos* of the parish displayed an intertesting pattern of marriage which, to a considerable extent, defied the norm that one could have expected to characterize this group. Because of their fair complexion, the *moriscos* were in a favorable position to pass for white.[16] *Moriscos* had only one-fourth Negro blood, and if they married Spanish or *castiza* women, the children resulting from such unions would be in an even better position to emerge from the *castas* altogether. To be sure, approximately 16.9% (20) of the 118 male *moriscos* of the parish were able to wed Spanish women and 12.7% (15) found *castiza* mates, while none of the male *moriscos* entered into wedlock with Negroes, *mulata prietas, lobas* or *chinas,* and only three chose Indian brides. On the other hand, about 18.6% (22) of the male *moriscos* did select mulatto women as their spouses, and the children of these couples remained among the Afromestizo population of Mexico City. And 46.5% of the male *moriscos,* avoiding this tendency toward *mulataje,* chose either a *mestiza* or a *morisca* wife. Specifically, twenty-three *moriscos* selected *morisca* brides and thirty-two wed *castizas.*

The 116 *morisca* women of the parish exhibited a predisposition to seek a mulatto, mestizo, or *morisco* husband. Approximately 75.0% (87) of the female *moriscas* chose husbands from the above three groups, with 40.2% (35) selecting mulatto mates, 33.3% (29) marrying mestizos, and 26.5% choosing *moriscos.* Only seven *moriscas* of

16. *Moriscos* who were slaves were in an inferior position, "since their master found ways to make their situation evident, branding them with hot irons in places where the insignia of servitude could not for a moment be hidden. The faces of many of them were completely covered with brand legends saying: 'I am the slave of señor Marqués de Valle,' 'I am the slave of doña Francisca Carrillo de Peralta.'" Gonzalo Aguirre Beltrán, "Races in Seventeenth Century Mexico," *Phylon,* VI:3 (1945), 215.

the parish of Santa Veracruz married Negroes, and a mere three were wed to Indians. It is rather surprising to note that female *moriscas* were not as apt as males to attempt to cross the color line by marrying persons with higher percentages of white blood. In the case of the *moriscas,* a mere 8.6% (10) chose *castizo* husbands and only one married a white man. The female *moriscas* in no instance married *mulatos prietos, pardos,* or *morenos,* but two did wed *chinos.*

The *Casamientos de Castas* revealed that during the period 1646-1746, only thrity-two *lobos,* seventeen *chinos,* eight *mulatos prietos,* five *morenos,* and 5 *pardos* were married by the priests of the parish of Santa Veracruz. The persons of these five groups numbered only sixty-seven, consisting of thirty-seven males and thirty females. In view of the small number of marriages involving these five *castas,* no detailed attempt has been made to analyze their marriage patterns. A few interesting facts, however, were observed regarding these groups. Only in three instances did persons in them marry Negroes. Indians also avoided marrying into these groups. A majority of the marriages of *lobos* and *chinos* involved free persons of these two groups who married free individuals of other groups.

The marriage records of the parish of Santa Veracruz also provide the social scientist with an interesting opportunity to study the marriage patterns of slaves and free persons. During the period 1646-1746, a majority, approximately 74.6%, of the 2,378 persons of African descent who married were free individuals, and only 21.2% were slaves. The slaves married by the priests of the parish consisted of the following: 159 male Negroes, 88 female Negroes, 188 male mulattoes, 65 female mulattoes, 2 female *moriscas,* 2 *mulatos prietos,* 3 *chinos,* and a *moreno.* Priests of the parish of Santa Veracruz, however, failed to record the legal status, free or slave, of 4.2% of the individuals of African descent. It would be logical to assume that the ninety-nine individuals of this group were free, or that the priests had valid reasons to doubt the status of such persons.

An analysis of the marriages in terms of the legal status of the couples reveals that in the instance of 1,120 marriages both the husband and wife were free. Mulattoes constituted 54.6% of this marital group. The free male mulatto's first choice for a wife was a free mulatto woman, while his second and third choices were *mestizas* and Indian women respectively. Only two free mulatto men elected to marry free Negro women. In contrast, some thirty-nine free mulatto males increased their social mobility by marrying free Spanish women. A majority of the free mulatto women, 291 out of 516, chose mulatto mates; forty-five married *castizos;* twenty-two wed *moriscos;* and 122 selected mestizos. Surprisingly, only thirteen free mulatto women married free Negro men. The marriage patterns of the free mulatto, especially the men, definitely revealed the tendency of this group to favor interracial marriages.

The number of marriages involving free Negroes was very small. In the cases of the nine free Negro women so identified, all but one married either a free Negro or free mulatto male. The marriage patterns of the thirty-three free Negro males were more varied, in that they selected mates from all of the *casta* groups except *mulatas prietas, lobas, chinas, pardas,* and *morenas.* However, in only two instances did a free Negro man marry an Indian woman.

In view of the fact that almost all of the *moriscos* of the parish of Santa Veracruz were free, one is not surprised to find that the *moriscos* perferred not to lower their social status by marrying slaves. During the period of one hundred years covered by this study, only two marriages were recorded of *moriscos* marrying slaves. One of these marriages involved a free *morisco* choosing a *morisca* slave as his wife, and the other marriage was between a free mulatto male and a slave *morisca.* Free *moriscos,* male and female, studiously avoided marrying persons having dark skins.

Despite the fact that the slaves of colonial Mexico were subjected to numerous discriminatory laws, it was possible for the slave, as a consequence of marriage, to improve the status of his children.[17] In view of the fact that the black slaves were not required by law to marry a slave, it was logical for these individuals to prefer free spouses if they could find them. This was particularly true of the male slave, because by marrying a free woman he would ensure that his children would be born free. The status of the child was dependent on the legal status of the mother. In the parish records of Santa Veracruz, 508 persons of African descent and listed as slaves married during the years 1646-1747.

The 253 mulattoes constituted the largest group of slaves whose marriages were recorded. A majority of the male mulatto slaves, 151 out of 188, sought to improve their lot by marrying free women. However, they avoided marrying free Negro women; only three male mulatto slaves elected to wed such women. On the other hand, sixty-

17. A description of the repressive legislation against the Negro can be found in William H. Dusenberry, "Discriminatory Aspects of Legislation in Colonial Mexico," *The Journal of Negro History,* XXXII:3 (July, 1948), 284-302; and Edgar F. Love, "Negro Resistance to Spanish Rule in Colonial Mexico," *The Journal of Negro History,* LII:4 (April, 1967), 89-103.

eight of the male mulatto slaves married free *mulata* women, forty-three chose *mestiza* wives, seventeen wed Indians, eleven picked *castiza* brides, five selected Spanish spouses, two elected to marry *lobas*, and two decided in favor of *moriscas*. The male mulatto slave clearly tended to favor marrying free *mulatas*, *mestizas*, or Indians.

Mulatto female slaves encountered slightly more difficulty than male mulatto slaves in marrying a free spouse. Approximately 38.5% (25) of the slave mulatto women were able to find free husbands, with sixteen marrying free men of African descent and nine being wed to husbands outside of the Negroid *casta* groups. One of the mulatto women slaves was even able to marry a Spaniard.

The Negro slaves of the parish of Santa Veracruz apparently encountered more difficulty in trying to marry free persons. Slightly more than one-third of the 247 number of male and female Negroes listed by the priests as slave were able to marry free individuals. In the case of female Negro slaves, only ten found free husbands, and, with one exception, their husbands were either free Negroes or mulattoes. The Negro male slaves was slightly more successful than the Negro female slave in being able to marry a free person. Seventy-six male Negro slaves (48.4%) did find free wives. Approximately 78.9% of these Negro male slaves chose to marry free mulattoes, mestizos, or Indian wives. Only 15.7% of the male Negro slaves elected to wed free Negro women.

Relatively few free men of the parish married slaves. Specifically, only thirty-seven men listed as free elected to marry slaves, and a majority of the free persons of this group were mulattoes, twenty-one out of the thirty-seven men of this marital group. A mere ten men of non-Negroid blood (eight mestizos, one *castizo*, and one Spaniard) chose to marry slaves.

Most slaves, of course, married other slaves. Approximately 6.7% (113) of the marriages of persons of African descent in the parish of Santa Veracruz during the period 1646-1746 involved male slaves wedding female slaves. The women of this group, with one exception, were either Negro or mulatto. A majority (67) of these women were Negroes. In the case of the male slaves of this marital group, 112 were Negro or mulatto and one was a *chino*. The eighty Negro male slaves of the above group, however, represented 50.3% of the male slaves marrying during the period of this study. Negro male slaves, therefore, tended to marry other slaves of African descent. The above pattern was even more pronounced for the female Negro slave, in that 84% of this group of slaves married either Negro or mulatto slaves.

The legal status of one of the parties was not indicated in 159 marriages involving persons of African descent. This category of marriages was distributed as follows: in the case of 64 marriages the husband's legal status was not indicated and the wife was free, in 5 marriages the husband's legal status was not shown and the wife was a slave, in 49 marriages the husband was free and the wife of unknown status, in 8 marriages the husband was a slave and the wife's status was not listed, and in 33 marriages neither husband's nor wife's legal status was revealed in the marriage records. The most conspicuous fact to be drawn from the marriage patterns of this group is that only five men and eight women of African descent, whose legal status was not indicated, married slaves.

The priests, in recording marriages, were required to indicate the place of birth of the couples. Negroes in colonial Mexico were classified as either *criollos* (born in America) or *bozales* (African born). In the case of the 207 Negro males marrying in the parish, 59 were born in Africa. The marriage records listed these African-born Negroes either by area of origin (Congo and Angola) or by tribes (Malinke, Malemba, and Mandingo). A majority of the *bozales* (41) were from Angola. This fact is not surprising, since a large percentage of the African slaves in colonial Mexico were brought from this area of Africa.[18] As might be expected, the *bozales*, most of whom were slaves, tended to marry Negro slave women.

Scholars have tended to take the position that few Spaniards in colonial Mexico married persons of African descent. For example, the famous Mexican historian Lucas Alamán claimed that it was rare for a Spaniard to marry a person having African blood.[19] But no one has attempted to ascertain precisely the rarity of such marriages. During the period 1646-1746, 4.6% of the marriages in the parish of Santa Veracruz involving persons of African descent were Afro-Spanish weddings. The seventy-seven Afro-Spanish marriages taking place in the parish of Santa Veracrus were as follows:

Negro-*Española*	1
Mulato-*Española*	44
Mulato prieto-*Española*	2

18. Gonzalo Aguirre Beltrán maintains that in seventeenth century colonial Mexico, a majority of the African-born slaves were from the Congo and Angola. *La población negra de México*, p. 245.

19. Lucas Alamán, *Historia de Méjico* (4 vols, 2nd ed., México, 1968), I, 25.

Mulato lobo-Española	3
Morisco-Española	20
Pardo-Española	2
Español-Mulata	4
Español-Morisca	1

As indicated above, the greater number of Afro-Spanish marriages involved free mulatto males marrying Spanish women. In all but five of the Afro-Spanish marriages, the Spanish partner was a woman. One would have expected more *moriscos* than mulattoes to have married Spanish women, but this was not the case.

Five mulatto slaves wed Spanish women, and one Spaniard married a female mulatto slave. One can only imagine what reasons and circumstances would have led Spanish women to elect to marry slaves. In any event, the marriage records do not suggest that the mates chosen by these Spanish women were not their personally owned slaves.

As noted earlier, the Afro-Spanish marriages listed in this study, however, do not represent the total number of such marriages in the parish during the one hundred year period. All marriages studied by the author were taken from the *Casamientos de Castas* of the parish of Santa Veracruz. A spot check of the *Casamientos de Españoles* of the parish revealed that some marriages of Spaniards to persons of African ancestry were recorded in the registry of Spanish marriages. The total number of Afro-Spanish marriages, therefore, probably was slightly greater than indicated in the *Casamientos de Castas*.

This analysis of marriages of persons of African descent represents a pilot study. Theoretically, it would be possible, based on available records in the other parishes of Mexico City, to ascertain the marriage patterns of almost all persons of Negroid blood marrying in the colonial bishopric of Mexico. It must be realized, however, that this type of study sheds light on only one aspect of interracial contacts. In view of extensive concubinage and other types of illicit sexual intercourse among the three races of Mexico, it is obvious that marriage was not the sole or even major basis for the process of *mestizaje* and *mulataje*.

13

The Anatomy of a Colonial Settler Population: Cape Colony, 1657–1750

Leonard Guelke

The subject of this study is the white settler population of the Cape Colony, South Africa, in the first century of its existence.[1] The study seeks to locate settler demography in its regional and economic settings with a view to gaining a stronger understanding of the nature of colonial settlement and expansion. The abundance of primary documents and much genealogical research make it possible for the characteristics of the early white population to be reconstituted in some detail. Slaves, former slaves, and their descendants were excluded from the investigation, because their history, as forced immigrants, was very different from that of the whites. It is also clear that the white settlers, notwithstanding some mingling with other races, which will be examined, comprised a distinct social community defined on the basis of race, religion, and legal status. The results of this study are substantially different from the only other detailed demographic investigation of this period.[2]

The annual census or *opgaaf* of all free people provided the starting point for the study.[3] The demographic life histories, property holdings, and locations of all individual adults recorded in the census years of 1682, 1705, and 1731 were investigated, individual by individual, using a variety of primary and secondary

*The data on which this study rests are taken from an on-going collaborative research project based on the annual *opgaaf*, or census of the Cape Colonial population. I am greatly indebted to Robert Shell for his invaluable contribution to the initial research establishing the data bases and to research assistants Toni Frisby and Doug Marshall, who worked with enthusiasm and dedication, completing and extending the work on these data bases. The SSHRC of Canada supported this research with a generous grant. I am grateful to Robert Ross, Gerrit Schutte, and the participants of the Southern Africa Research Program, Yale University, for many valuable suggestions for improving on the original version of this paper.

[1]The white settlers were predominantly of European descent, but some Cape-born settlers of part-European ancestry were absorbed by the white community. See J. A. Heese, *Die Herkoms van die Afrikaner 1657-1867* (Cape Town, 1971).

[2]R. Ross, "The 'White' Population of South Africa in the Eighteenth Century," *Population Studies* 29, 2 (1975), 217-230. In this study, Ross includes the free blacks as part of the "white" population.

[3]The use of the annual census (or *opgaaf*) as a basis on which individuals were selected for detailed research ensured that the settler population investigated in detail was, in fact, a representative cross-section of the settler population at a moment in time. Although doubts have been cast on the reliability and completeness of the *opgaafs* by some contemporary observers and modern historians, our research experience with them has not lent support to this view. In general the *opgaafs* were found to be remarkably complete when individuals were traced by name over their lifetimes in the actual *opgaaf* entries and checked against other primary documents (see footnote 4).

sources.[4] This strategy permitted the census data to be used in ways hitherto not possible. First, the geographical information available for each individual meant that these data could be aggregated on the basis of geographically meaningful districts. For example, the inhabitants of the Cape District, which included Cape Town and the surrounding rural areas, were reconstituted into Cape Town and rural districts. enabling an analysis to be made on an urban/rural basis. Second, the research procedure enabled a clear separation to be made between "white" settlers and manumitted slaves and their descendants, classified by the Dutch as free blacks.[5] The free blacks were sometimes listed in the census together with whites, but more often they were listed as a separate group at the end of the census.

The research strategy involved classifying the settler population at the time of each census, according to marital status (Table I). The individual cross sections captured the demographic reality at a moment in time and allowed detailed comparisons between the census years to be made. These comparisons were based on the three historical geographical regions: Cape Town, Rural, and Frontier districts. The geographical extent of Frontier District was redefined in each census, to correspond with the area of most recent settlement, and the "old" frontier areas were incorporated into Rural districts. This strategy was adopted with a view to capturing the dynamics of Colonial expansion and settlement, on the assumption that the period of settlement was the critical element defining the regional character of a frontier society and economy.

Although the research design anchored individuals to a particular census year, the demographic information on individual men and women stretched backwards to their births and forwards to their deaths, and a demographic picture for each census covered, on average, a period from twenty-five to thirty

---

[4]The research strategy involved gathering geographical and demographic information for each individual in the census using the following principal printed sources: C. C. de Villiers, *Geslagregisters van die Ou Kaapse Families*, 2nd ed., edited by C. Pama, 3 vols. (Cape Town, 1965); J. Hoge, "Personalia of Germans at the Cape, 1652-1806," *Archives Yearbook of South African History*, 4 (Cape Town, 1946); C. G. Botha, *The French Refugees at the Cape* (Cape Town, 1970); G. C. de Wet, *Die Vryliede en Vryswartes in Die Kaapse Nedersetting 1657-1707* (Cape Town, 1981); and Böeseken et al., *Resolusies van die Politieke Raad 1651-1739*, Vols. I-IX (Cape Town, 1657-1981). These printed sources were used in conjunction with information from: the annual manuscript censuses (Algemene Rijksarchief, VOC Series, The Hague) for the years 1682, 1688, 1691, 1701, 1705/06, 1709, 1711, 1716, 1719, 1721, 1726, 1731, 1736, 1741, 1746, 1751, 1760, and 1770, which were all alphabetized so that an individual could be traced through several years; property records (Deeds Office, Cape Town) including *Old Cape Freeholds* (Vols. I-III) and *Old Stellenbosch Freeholds* (Vols. I and II), which have information on the original grantees of town and country land, the transfer books for these properties, known as *Transporten und Schepenenkennisse*, for the period 1680 to 1790, and, finally, the Receiver of Land Revenue books (Vols. 1-32) which have information on hunting and grazing permits (loan farms); and estate records of the MOOC, C.J. and St. Series (South African Archives, Cape Town) which include inventories for hundreds of deceased estates containing geographical, economic, and demographic information. Wherever possible information was checked against more than one source. This time-consuming process ensured the data on each individual was as accurate as all the sources permitted it to be. In the process errors in the generally reliable *Geslagsregister* were detected and corrected.

[5]The free blacks never enjoyed equal rights with the white population and formed an "under class" of free people, who were almost always designated as "free blacks" rather than simply free persons, the designation for free people of predominantly European origin.

Table I
WHITE CENSUS POPULATION BY MARITAL STATUS

Males	1682		1705		1731	
	No.	%	No.	%	No.	%
Divorced or Separated	–	–	1	0.2	2	0.3
Single, Never Married	27	30.3	182	34.7	137	19.3
Single, Will Marry	11	12.4	77	14.7	138	19.4
Widowed Once	3	3.4	8	1.5	26	3.7
Widowed Twice	–	–	2	0.4	9	1.3
Widowed Thrice	–	–	3	0.6	6	0.8
Married, 1st Time	45	50.6	231	44.1	341	48.0
Married, 2nd Time	3	3.4	19	3.6	51	7.2
Married, 3rd Time	–	–	3	0.6	6	0.8
Totals	89	100.0	525	100.0	711	100.0

Females	1682		1705		1731	
	No.	%	No.	%	No.	%
Divorced or Separated	–	–	–	–	3	0.7
Single, Never Married	–	–	–	–	1	0.2
Single, Will Marry	6	11.3	5	1.9	3	0.7
Widowed Once	1	1.9	19	7.1	45	10.1
Widowed Twice	1	1.9	2	0.8	16	3.6
Widowed Thrice	3	5.7	2	0.8	11	2.5
Married, 1st Time	37	69.8	203	75.7	296	66.4
Married, 2nd Time	5	9.4	37	13.9	70	15.8
Married, 3rd Time	3	5.7	2	0.8	11	2.5
Totals	53	100.0	268	100.0	445	100.0

years on either side of the census. This meant that a minority of individuals appeared in more than one census, but generally in a different marital classification (for example, widowed rather than married). The accuracy and level of detail of individual data improved from the seventeenth to the eighteenth centuries and this is reflected in much fuller pictures for 1705 and 1731 than for 1682.

Historical and Geographical Context

In 1652, the Dutch East India Company (VOC) founded a small settlement on the shores of Table Bay to provide fresh produce and logistical support for its fleets sailing between Europe and Asia.[6] After a slow start in which Company agriculture and livestock trade with the native Khoikhoi pastoralists failed to meet Company expectations, the VOC created, in 1657, a class of freeburghers, provided them with land and slaves and encouraged them to settle. This policy did not improve the situation very much. The first European settlers had difficulty farming on small land grants, which had been given out on the assumption that they would use intensive farming methods, integrating arable and livestock husbandry. An inability to control their slaves and a lack of adequate capital reserves contributed to much of this difficulty.[7] Nevertheless, a tiny settler population managed to fashion a livelihood for itself. Some settlers persevered on the land and developed a farming system based on the extensive cultivation of cereals and the vine and the raising of livestock on the pasture of the open veld. Other settlers established themselves in Cape Town where many of them made a living from calling ships.

In 1679, a period of population growth and territorial expansion was initiated with the founding of Stellenbosch (see Map 1). During the next twenty-five years, the Company encouraged immigration and opened large areas of new lands for settlement. Settlers were granted lands in freehold and had access to large tracts of unallocated pasture land. The pattern of landholding in which freehold grants were only a fraction of the surface area scattered the growing population of settlers and slaves over a considerable area, and fostered a form of life in which rural inhabitants, both free and slave, lived in relative isolation from their neighbors.

Notwithstanding the large areas of available pasture, a growing settler and livestock population pushed ever further into the interior in search of pasture. In 1703 the VOC introduced a new land policy, which made it possible for settlers to rent tracts of land for grazing their livestock. Individuals could now acquire frontier lands for their own exclusive use. As the population grew, increasing numbers of colonists settled permanently on the frontier, where they evolved a

---

[6]M. F. Katzen, "White Settlers and the Origin of a New Society, 1652-1778," in M. Wilson and L. M. Thompson, eds., *Oxford History of South Africa* (Oxford, 1969), I, 187-232.

[7]L. Guelke, "The White Settlers, 1652-1780," in R. Elphick and H. Giliomee, eds., *The Shaping of South African Society 1652-1820* (Cape Town, 1979), 41-67.

SETTLER POPULATION   457

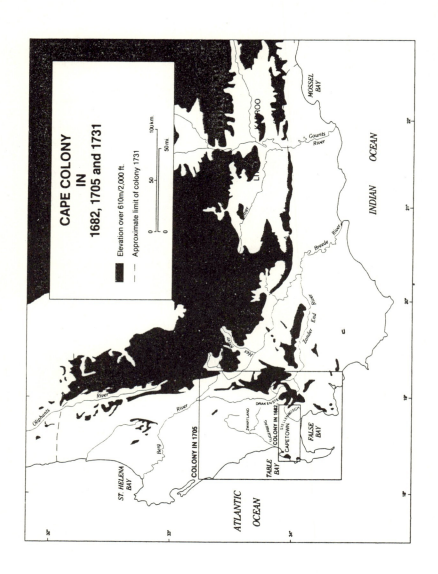

CAPE COLONY
IN
1682, 1705 and 1731

■ Elevation over 610m/2,000 ft.
-- Approximate limit of colony 1731

0   50
0   50 mi.
0   100 km.

new form of life based on extensive pastoralism supplemented by subsistence cultivation and hunting.[8]

The success of arable farming and the lack of markets for colonial wheat and wine prompted the VOC to stop encouraging immigration and to curtail the granting of freehold land. The white population continued to increase, but largely by natural increase. In 1713, a smallpox epidemic ravaged the Colony, and wiped out large numbers of Khoikhoi, many of whom had provided cheap labor for white farmers. As a consequence white farmers became more dependent on slaves. In the years after 1713 there was a rapid increase in the number of slaves in the Colony, considerably altering the population mix of the early years of the century.

The settler population at the Cape comprised a minority of the population (Table II). If in the earlier period of settlement settlers outnumbered their own slaves, they never outnumbered the Khoikhoi, Company slaves, and free blacks combined. The settler population was not homogeneous in terms of ethnicity, wealth, or form of life. There were French Huguenots (from 1688), Germans, Dutch, and Cape-raised settlers. There were townspeople with many occupations, rural cultivators, farmhands, hunters, and frontier pastoralists. There were rich people, poor landless people, and a struggling "middle class" burdened by debt.[9] There were veld-hardy Cape-raised colonists and newly arrived immigrants. There were big planters with dozens of slaves, small planters with few, and many other settlers with none at all.[10] There were literate and illiterate people. There were married people and remarried people, bachelor men of all ages and middle aged widows. There were huge families, small families, and a few childless families. In short, the settler population was about as demographically and socially diverse as any small community could be.

Colonial Outpost – 1682

The census of 1682 captures the situation at the end of the first period of European-directed colonization of the Cape. The Colony was still largely confined to the northern Cape Peninsula, although the small settlement at Stellenbosch foreshadowed a period of territorial expansion.[11] The settler population, 25 years after its inception, numbered fewer than 300 persons, men, women, and children (Table II). The slave population was even smaller, but the unenumerated Khoikhoi were still quite numerous and must have outnumbered all other population groups combined in the region if not in the colony itself. There was also a small number of free blacks in the population, who were listed

---

[8]The classic study of the trekboer is by Van der Merwe, *Die Trekboer in die Geskiedenis van die Kaap Kolonie, 1657-1842* (Cape Town, 1938).

[9]O. F. Mentzel, *A Geographical-Topographical Description of the Cape of Good Hope* (Cape Town, 1944), 98-121.

[10]L. Guelke and R. Shell, "An Early Colonial Landed Gentry: Land and Wealth in the Cape Colony 1682-1731," *Journal of Historical Geography*, IX (1983), 265-286.

[11]The 1682 Colony was tentatively dived into three districts: Cape Town = the hamlet; Rural = the rest of the Cape Peninsula; Frontier = Stellenbosch. The smallness of the population and lack of data on individuals prevented a proper regional analysis from being undertaken.

Table II
CENSUS POPULATION: WHITE SETTLERS, AFRICAN
AND ASIAN SLAVES, FREE BLACKS AND KNEGTS
SUMMARY OF TOTALS

	1682		1705		1731	
	No.	%	No.	%	No.	%
African/Asian slaves	192	33.4	1057	37.8	4303	58.9
"Free Blacks"	49	8.5	111	4.0	295	4.0
White Knegts	45	7.8	66	2.4	83	1.1
White settlers	288	50.2	1559	55.8	2627	35.9
Total	574	100.0	2793	100.0	7308	100.0

Note: Census population excludes Company personnel,
Company slaves and Khoikhoi and San.

among the white settlers in the census. The setter population was distributed among the hamlet of Cape Town, the rural Cape Peninsula, and the newly settled Stellenbosch. The smallness of the population and the paucity of data make a full regional analysis of this population impossible in this period but some general observations about the population can be made.

The settler population comprised 89 men, 53 women and 146 children (84 boys and 62 girls). The adult male settlers outnumbered the adult females by almost two to one (Table III). In this situation it is not surprising that one-third of the male settlers never married in the Colony. The young women of the Colony must have been under intense pressure to marry. The mean age of the first marriage for women was 17.0 years. If marriage was the only option for women, it seems that some care was taken to see that potential husbands were in a position to support them. To acquire some wealth often took time and men were almost 13 years older than women on first marriage. Two white settlers married free black women.

The average number of children parented by men and women settlers was 6.2 and 6.0 respectively. The differences in these figures are accounted for by men and women who remarry and have children by more than one partner. Although men had slightly larger families, women were more likely to remarry than men. At the time of the census 3 men were remarried compared with 8 women. In terms of size of families, men, by marrying younger women, were in a position to have more children than women whose own ages were more important than those of their spouses. Nevertheless, women who remarried had larger families than those who did not. These figures for 1682 however need to be treated cautiously, because of the difficulty in obtaining data on a largely immigrant population.

Immigrant Colony — 1705

In 1705, the Cape Colony was a going economic concern. The settler population numbered just over 1,5000 which represented a 441 percent increase from 1682 (Table I). Immigrants, who came mainly from the Netherlands, France (Huguenots), and German-speaking states, far outnumbered the colonial-born settlers. The new population expanded the area and economic activity of the Colony. In Cape Town a settler population of traders, innkeepers, and artisans made a living catering to calling ships and an expanding rural hinterland. This hinterland included the areas of established settlement near Cape Town, which have been designated the "Rural" district and the newly settled and expanding "Frontier" district of Drakenstein.[12]

Notwithstanding the VOC's interest in encouraging the growth of a stable family-based settler population, male settlers outnumbered female ones by an even greater margin than in 1682. The greatest imbalance of the sexes was found in the Frontier District, where there were 227 men for every 100 women (Table III). The situation in Cape Town and the Rural District was less extreme, but not by much. In Cape Town there were 174 settler men for every 100 settler women and in the Rural District the corresponding figure was 193 (Table III). These

---

[12]Rural District included the Cape Peninsula (excluding Cape Town), Tijgerberg-Swartland and Stellenbosch. The Frontier District corresponded exactly to official Drakenstein.

Table III
WHITE CENSUS POPULATION
ADULT SEX RATIOS BY DISTRICTS

I. 1682 Census

	Males	Females	M:F*
Cape Town	26	12	216
Rural	38	24	158
Frontier	25	17	147
Total	89	53	168

II. 1705 Census

	Males	Females	M:F*
Cape Town	141	81	174
Rural	232	120	193
Frontier	152	67	227
Total	525	268	196

III. 1731 Census

	Males	Females	M:F*
Cape Town	209	143	146
Rural	363	231	157
Frontier	139	71	196
Total	711	445	160

Note: Male to female ratio: 'n' males to 100 females.

Table IV
FUTURE MARITAL STATUS OF SINGLE
MALE SETTLERS, 1705 AND 1731

1705	Cape Town No.	Cape Town %	Rural No.	Rural %	Frontier No.	Frontier %
Single men never married	51	85	70	62	62	71
Single men who will marry	9	15	43	38	25	29
Total	60	100	113	100	87	100

1731	Cape Town No.	Cape Town %	Rural No.	Rural %	Frontier No.	Frontier %
Single men never married	44	59	69	51	24	37
Single men who will marry	31	41	66	49	41	63
Total	75	100	135	100	65	100

figures do not include the nonsettler white population of white farm servants (*knegts*) and Company personnel. The addition of these groups would substantially increase the overall imbalance of the sexes of the white population.

In this period of economic growth, the Colony attracted a good number of single men, many of whom had been Company employees. Men had great difficulty finding marriage partners. About one-third of all adult males in the 1705 census never married in the Colony. The single men who did succeed in finding marriage partners were far more likely to be in the rural or frontier districts (Table IV). The settler men who were married at the census for the first time had married late, on average 30 years old, or thirteen years later than the women.[13] The regional variation was moderate, with Cape Town men the oldest at 32.7 years old (Table V).

Table V
AGE AT MARRIAGE OF
FIRST-TIME MARRIED SETTLERS

	Males				Females			
	1705		1731		1705		1731	
District	Age	N	Age	N	Age	N	Age	N
Cape Town	32.7	14	28.1	36	18.0	21	19.3	63
Rural	28.8	25	27.4	124	16.8	34	18.8	122
Frontier	30.3	24	25.4	47	17.0	25	18.6	57
Colony	30.2	63	27.1	207	17.2	80	18.5	242

Note: Table is based on all adults who were married at the time of the census for the first time.

The pressure on women to marry early was intense, and females were married at extraordinarily young ages. Marriages of girls of twelve, thirteen, and fourteen were by no means uncommon, and fifteen was the mode for the first marriage of all white women recorded in the 1705 census for whom data were available. The regional variations were not as marked as might have been expected. The mean age of first marriage for females married for the first time at the census was 18 in Cape Town, 16.8 in the Rural District, and 17.0 in the Frontier District (Table V).

At the time of the census nine white settlers or 3.6 percent of all married men had free black wives. The regional breakdown is interesting in that it

---

[13]Many of these men were immigrants who comprised 70 percent of the male adult population of 1705. These figures differ substantially from those arrived at by Ross, in "The 'White' Population of South Africa."

Table VI
WHITE MALES WITH "FREE BLACK" WIVES
1705 AND 1731

1705

District	All Married White Males	White Males with Free Black Wives	%
Cape Town	78	3	3.8
Rural	113	5	4.4
Frontier	62	1	1.6
Total	253	9	3.6

1731

District	All Married White Males	White Males with Free Black Wives	%
Cape Town	119	6	5.0
Rural	209	3	1.4
Frontier	70	0	0.0
Total	398	9	2.3

Note: Only men with free black wives at the
time of the census are included.

reveals no major concentration of such marriages in any particular district, although the Rural District was overrepresented and the Frontier District was slightly underrepresented. These marriages are important because they show that the society was prepared to legitimize relationships between whites and free blacks, and that there were individual men who wanted to have free black women as their legitimate wives. There were, undoubtably, far more illicit liaisons between white men and women of other races including free blacks, Khoikhoi and slave women, but such liaisons did not involve the important symbolic stamp of approval accorded to legitimate marriages (Table VI).

The matching of men and women would not typically have involved a man of 30 and a woman of 18. The picture is more complicated than this. A proportion of men, ranging from 10 to 30 percent, married widows, who were considerably older than 18. In fact, widows frequently married men who had not been married before and were approximately the same age or younger than themselves. On the other hand, widowers were more likely to marry women marrying for the first time than they were to marry widows. In these cases the age difference between husband and wife was typically twenty years or more.

Marriages appear to have been quite stable (Table VII). For settler men who were married for the first time at the time of the census the mean length of a first marriage was 23.3 years. There was little difference between Cape Town and the Rural District, but the male inhabitants of frontier Drakenstein had longer marriages with a mean of 25 years (Table VII). The figures were much the same whether marriage ended with the death of the husband or wife. For women the mean length of first marriage was almost identical to that of the men, but where differences did occur women's marriages were slightly shorter, the difference varying from a few months to a year (Table VII).

The unbalanced sex ratios made it far more likely that women would remarry than men. At the time of the 1705 census, 22 men were married for the second or third time as opposed to 41 women (Table I). In terms of the total adult populations of each sex, second and third time marriages accounted for 4.2 percent of adult males, but 14.7 percent of adult females. These figures suggest that the intense pressure to marry was also felt by young widows, most of whom remarried within two years of losing their husbands. For men the corresponding period ranged from two to three years, with Cape Town men remarrying the fastest. There were also a number of older widows who did not remarry.

The remarriage patterns of men and women were evidently more affected by sex ratios than life expectancy differences between them, although there were some major regional differences in this statistic in 1705. The life expectancy of those men and women who were recorded in the census ranged from 45 for women in the Rural District to 58 for men in Cape Town. On the whole frontier men and women lived longest: 56 years for men and 57 for women. The gap in life expectancy was much greater in Cape Town with men living eight years longer than women. The Rural District had the shortest life expectancies – 49 years for men, 45 for women – probably as a result of the severe impact of the smallpox epidemic of 1713 (Table VIII).

The early age of first marriage for women and the relatively disease-free environment were conducive to the raising of large families. There were, however, significant regional and gender differences. Cape Town was the only district in which the average number of all children for first-time married males,

Table VII
LENGTH OF MARRIAGE OF
FIRST-TIME MARRIED SETTLERS

District	Males				Females			
	1705		1731		1705		1731	
	No	N	No	N	No	N	No	N
Cape Town	23.1	15	21.4	53	21.3	11	27.3	17
Rural	22.2	43	27.0	89	21.7	25	25.3	43
Frontier	25.0	31	25.3	35	23.9	10	21.1	12
Colony	23.3	89	25.0	177	22.1	46	25.1	72

Table VIII
LIFESPANS OF ADULT SETTLERS

District	Males				Females			
	1705		1731		1705		1731	
	Age	N	Age	N	Age	N	Age	N
Cape Town	58.6	17	53.9	62	49.8	18	54.9	64
Rural	48.9	59	57.0	194	45.1	38	59.2	130
Frontier	55.8	49	52.7	72	57.0	27	54.2	41
Colony	52.9	125	55.5	328	52.4	83	57.2	235

Note: Lifespans are calculated on all adult settlers
who were alive at the time of the census and
recorded as such.

Settler lifespan in 1705 = 52.7
Settler lifespan in 1731 = 56.2
Change from 1705 to 1731 = +3.5 years

at 5.4, was greater than that of females at 5.3 (Table IX). Theoretically males
would be in a position to have larger families than females if they were able to
have more than one wife of prime child-bearing age. This situation evidently
prevailed to a slight degree in Cape Town, where there was a better balance
between the sexes. First-time married rural district women had larger families
than Cape Town women (5.9 to 5.3) and men smaller ones (4.9 to 5.4) (Table IX).
This reversal of the situation prevailing in Cape Town seems to be explained
partly by the smaller number of males who married more than once. The greatest
family sizes were recorded in the Frontier District, where men on their first
marriage at the census had a mean 6.7 children and women 8.0 children
(Table IX).

Table IX
AVERAGE NUMBER OF CHILDREN
OF ADULT SETTLERS

District	Males				Females			
	1705		1731		1705		1731	
	ANC	N	ANC	N	ANC	N	ANC	N
Cape Town	5.4	36	5.5	88	5.3	32	6.2	73
Rural	4.9	87	7.2	176	5.9	67	7.9	151
Frontier	6.7	45	7.4	58	8.0	43	8.0	58
Colony	5.5	168	6.8	322	6.4	142	7.5	282

Note: ANC = Average number of children an individual
had in a lifetime with all partners.

Women began families within two years of marriage, at a mean of 18.9
years. Thereafter children were produced at regular intervals for a period of 17
years. Women ceased to bear children at a mean age of 35 (Table X). The length
of the childbearing period was longest, at 20.3 years, and the interval between
births was shortest, at 2.0 years, for the Frontier District (Table X). There were
no marked differences between Cape Town and the Rural District. The mean
figures mask considerable variations in childbearing patterns. Just over 10
percent of women had their first child before they were sixteen and 37 percent
were still producing children from 40 to 46. The period of fertility also showed
considerable variation: 28 percent of the women had fertility periods of under 10
years, and in 17 percent of cases the childbearing period was 25 years or more.

Table X
FERTILITY OF FEMALE SETTLERS

District	Number Cases N/Tot[1]	Age at First Child	Age at Final Child	Fertility Period (FP)[2]	ANC[3]	FP/ANC[4]
1705						
Cape Town	18/81	19.1	33.9	14.8	6.3	2.3
Rural	33/120	19.2	33.6	14.3	6.4	2.2
Frontier	19/67	18.3	38.6	20.3	10.1	2.0
Colony	70/268	18.9	34.9	16.0	7.4	2.2
1731						
Cape Town	72/143	20.4	33.8	13.4	6.3	2.1
Rural	152/231	19.9	38.0	18.1	8.3	2.2
Frontier	56/71	19.9	36.2	16.3	8.2	2.0
Colony	280/445	20.0	36.6	16.6	7.8	2.1

Note 1: N = the number of women for whom data were available.
Tot = the total number of settler women in that district at the
time of the census.

Note 2: The number of years between the birth of the first child
and the birth of the final child.

Note 3: ANC = Average number of children of men and women from
all partners.

Note 4: Average number of years between births of children;
calculated by dividing fertility period by total
number of children

Settler Colony — 1731

A decline in immigration and a slow down in economic activity substantially slowed the settler population growth rate. The 1731 settler population of 2,600 was only 68 percent larger than the corresponding figure for 1705 (Table I). This increase paled against the rise of the slave population from just over 1,000 in 1705 to over 4,000 in 1731 (Table II). The slowdown in immigration meant that the settler population was mainly Cape born and raised in 1731. The only significant numbers of immigrants were found in Cape Town where they accounted for almost 50 percent of the total adult settler population. Although the rate of population growth slowed between 1705 and 1731, there was no slowdown in the territorial expansion of the Colony (Map 1). The Frontier District of 1731 encompassed a huge area to the north and east of the cultivated zone, and its inhabitants were almost entirely dependent on livestock raising and hunting. The three-way division of the colony — into Cape Town, Rural District and Frontier District — corresponded to three main areas of livelihood. Cape Town was urban, Rural District included the area of freehold cultivated farms and plantations near Cape Town, and the Frontier District corresponded to the thinly settled livestock frontier.[14] In each of these areas, there were great differences in wealth and social status of individual settlers, but the very richest settlers were exclusively to be found in Cape Town and Rural District.[15]

As a result of the growth of a large colonial-born settler population, there was a marked reduction in the male:female sex ratio from their 1705 levels. Overall men outnumbered females 8:5 with the Frontier District again having the greatest disparity between the sexes with a ratio of two men to every one woman (Table III). The corresponding figures for 1705 had men outnumbering women 2:1 overall with a 7:3 ratio for the Frontier District. Yet the sex ratios were not a good indication of the marriage prospects for single men. Only 24 out of 65 (37 percent) frontier single males at the time of the census never married, compared with 69 out of 135 (51 percent) in the Rural District and 44 out of 75 (59 percent) in Cape Town (Table IV). The paradox of the frontier in which marriage prospects are brightest though males outnumber females by the largest ratios, is resolved if one recognizes that frontier males were "robbing" other areas of their marriageable women. Men on the frontier were evidently succeeding somewhat better in establishing independent livelihoods than single males in the older rural areas and Cape Town.

In 1731 there were 341 adult men (48 percent of the male settler population) in their first marriage. The corresponding figure for females was 295 (comprising 66 percent of the adult female population) (Table I). Men were far more likely to have married partners who had had a previous marriage. In fact, about 20 percent of bachelor grooms married widows. Regionally the figure was highest in Cape Town and lowest on the frontier. About 12 percent of women marrying for the first time married widowers. The regional figure was highest in

---

[14]The Rural District of 1731 included the Cape Peninsula (excluding Cape Town), Stellenbosch to the west of the Hottentots Holland Mountains, Tijgerberg-Swartland, and the Upper Berg River Valley portion of census Drakenstein. The Frontier District included the area to the east of Drakenstein and the Hottentots Holland Mountains, the Lower Berg River Valley and the area north of it.

[15]Guelke and Shell, "Landed Gentry," 277-281.

the Rural District (16 percent) and lowest in Cape Town (10 percent). The mean age of first marriage was lowest for frontier men at 25.4 years compared with 27.4 in the rural district and 28.1 in Cape Town (Table V). The age of first marriage for all men married for the first time at the census was 3.1 years under the figure for 1705.[16] The age of first-time married females at first marriage was 18.5 for the Colony as a whole compared with 17.2 in 1705. Cape Town women were marrying at 19.3; rural women and frontier women at 18.8 and 18.6 respectively (Table V). The mode for all female first marriages which had been 15 in 1705 was 18 in 1731, although the mean age at first marriage had risen by just over a year. Many women were still marrying in their early teens for the first time. The rise in female marriage age almost certainly reflected a somewhat improved male:female sex ratio, and, perhaps, a somewhat less buoyant economy.

In 1731, the number of men married to free black women had decreased from 3.6 percent of married white men to 2.3 percent (Table VI), This decrease is, perhaps, less significant than the regional changes that occurred. The mixed marriages show a marked concentration in Cape Town, where two thirds of the men with free black wives were found. The rest of these marriages were recorded in the Rural District, with none in the Frontier District. If these racially mixed marriages can be interpreted as an indication of the state of race relations, it suggests that racial attitudes were hardening in frontier and rural areas, but easing a little in Cape Town. Although frontier men were most successful in securing white wives, the Rural District men were in almost the same situation as those in Cape Town in terms of marriage prospects (Table IV), yet far fewer of them took free black wives than was the case in Cape Town. There were also long-term liaisons on the frontier between white men and Khoikhoi women, but these unions never gained the approval of orthodox society.[17] In Cape Town a white settler lost social position in marrying a free black woman, but he remained part of settler society. It seems that strong racial ideas were already entrenching themselves in rural and frontier areas long before the closing of the frontier or the advent of industrial capitalism.

In general first marriages for men and women were likely to last on average anything from 21 to 28 years. There were variations by region and in terms of whether the marriage terminated with the death of the man or woman. In cases of men, married for the first time, length of marriage was much the same whether the husband or wife died first. Only frontier men who survived their spouses had considerably longer first marriages than their fellow settlers who died in marriage (25.3 vs 20.6 years). Women in general had longer first marriages than men, ranging from 21 to 28 years, and the longest first marriages of all were recorded for women who survived their husbands in the Rural and Frontier Districts at 27.2 and 27.8 respectively (Table VII). Men were as likely as not to die before their wives, but women, married for the first time, were twice as likely to survive their husbands as the other way around.

Men were far less likely to remarry than women. Approximately 10 percent of the men, married for the first time at the taking of the census, married

---

[16]Interestingly, the age at first marriage was higher for single men who married after the 1731 census: 28.6 for Cape Town, 30.3 for Rural District, and 29.1 for the Frontier.

[17]L. Guelke, "The Making of Town Frontier Communities: Cape Colony in the Eighteenth Century," *Historical Reflections/Reflexions Historiques*, XII (1985), 433-446.

again. The corresponding figure for women was 17 percent. In the case of the males there were no marked regional variations, but, for women, the rate of remarriage was very much higher in Cape Town, with 34 percent of all women registered as married for the first time in 1731 marrying again, than it was for the other districts; the figure was 13 percent for Rural District and 21 percent for Frontier District.

The picture of remarriage can also be analyzed by looking at settlers in second marriages at the time of the census (Table I). A total of 57 men, or 8 percent of the total adult male population, was married for the second or third time. The women who were married for the second or third time numbered 81 persons, or 18 percent of all women. In these figures Cape Town does not stand out as an exception. The vast majority of both men and women marrying for a second time took bachelor spouses. This meant that women, because they tended to survive their husbands, and remarry men not previously married, were often able to partner two or more men in their lifetimes. The problem of the sexual imbalance between male and female settlers was solved to some extent by a system of sequential "polygamy" in which men took turns marrying the women of the Colony.

There was a limit to this system. Women who had passed childbearing age typically did not remarry. In 1731, first-time widows numbered 45 persons or 10 percent of all census women. This group contained 23 persons who would not remarry. They had been widowed for 9 years and their mean age at the census was 50. There were also 17 cases of women who would remarry. Their mean age was 32 and they had been widows for 2.5 years. Whether women ceased to attract men after 40 or decided themselves that, having fulfilled their childbearing function, they no longer needed a marriage partner, or had reached a point at which they wanted to manage their own affairs, is an intriguing question in need of further investigation.

The women settlers of the Cape had proportionally more second marriages than male settlers. This phenomenon is attributable to the early ages at which women married and the imbalance in sex ratios. There was not a marked difference in the lifespans of men and women, although by 1731 women were living 1.7 years longer than men. The general life expectancy of white adults in the census, regardless of gender, increased by 3.5 years from 1705 to 1731. Male settlers lived to a mean age of 55.5 years and women settlers to 57.2 years. The people in the Rural District lived longest with adult males averaging 57 years of life and females 59.2. This was a reversal of the situation in 1705, many Rural District inhabitants recorded in the 1705 census having died in the smallpox epidemic of 1713. The situation in Cape Town and on the Frontier was much the same: the mean age of death for everybody who survived to adulthood was in the early fifties with women living one to two years longer than men (Table VIII). These mean figures do not reveal the great range of lifespans in the settler population. Many settlers died in their thirties and forties, and 50 percent of both men and women had died before they reached 55.

The average number of children for all adult male and female settlers who were recorded with first-time partners at the time of the census confirmed the picture of 1705. In all districts women had larger families than men. Family size was smallest on Cape Town at 6.2, and largest on the frontier at 8.0 (Table IX). The Rural District was close to the frontier figure at 7.9. The family sizes for men were 5.5, 7.2, and 7.4 for Cape Town, Rural District, and Frontier District respectively.[18] The traditional view that rural and frontier people had the largest families seems to be confirmed by these data. Men and women also married at younger ages and began their families at slightly earlier ages than settlers in Cape Town (Table V and Table X).

The women of the 1731 census had their first child at a mean age of exactly 20 years old, which was 1.5 years after marriage and a year later than the women of 1705. The mean fertility period was 16.6 years or an increase of 1.6 years over the corresponding figure for 1705. Regional differences were not marked. Rural District women had their last child a little later than the women of other districts at 38 years old (Table X). Frontier women produced children at a slightly faster rate than those of the other districts, averaging one child every two years. The extremes in 1731 were a little less marked than they had been in 1705. Women having a first child under the age of sixteen comprised 8 percent of all women for whom data were available, down from 12 percent in 1705. At the upper end of the age scale, 26 percent of women in their forties were still bearing children compared with 37 percent in 1705. Although the mean length of the fertility period showed an increase from 1705 to 1731, the proportion of women in low and in high categories declined: 12 percent of women were recorded as having fertility periods of under ten years, compared with 28 percent in 1705 and only 9 percent were still having children after 24 years of childbearing compared with 17 percent in 1705.

Conclusion

The demographic history of the early Cape Colony throws new light on the process of European settlement and the creation of a settler form of colonial life. A key factor in this situation was the problem of colonial isolation and the greater geographical mobility of men. This mobility meant that men were able to move independently and respond to economic opportunity in colonial situations.

At the Cape settler men outnumbered settler women at all times, but the greatest imbalance of the sexes is found in the boom conditions of the early 1700s. The boom created a double problem: it increased the number of men who were in a position to marry and reduced the number of available women per eligible male. This situation pushed male marriage ages up and female marriage ages down, as men competed to secure wives for themselves. A few men married free black women, but for the vast majority it seems that a woman had to be white to be considered an eligible marriage partner. In this period of rapid population growth and economic expansion a distinctive colonial pattern of marriage and family size came into existence almost overnight.[19] The vast majority of young women, whether immigrant or Cape-born, married in their mid

---

[18]In computing data on number of children using Louis Henry's definition of a completed family, namely one in which a marriage survived past the 45th birthday of the wife, the following figures were generated for completed families in 1731: Cape Town 7.6 (N=17); Rural District 8.6 (N=44); Frontier District 8.4 (N=16); Colony 8.3 (N=77).

[19]In Europe both men and women typically married in their early and mid twenties. Men tended to be a few years older than their wives. See L. Gaskin, "Age at First Marriage in Europe Before 1850: A Summary of Family Reconstitution Data," *Journal of Family History*, III (1978), 23-36.

and late teens and shortly thereafter entered a long period of frequent childbearing.

In the years between 1705 and 1731 the colonial economy lost much of its vibrancy, and the rate of immigration declined. By 1731, the settler population was mainly colonial-born and a much better balance existed between the sexes. These factors pushed the age of marriage down for men, who faced less competition for wives, and up for women, who were under less intense pressure to marry. The age of first marriage was lowest for men on the frontier, where they outnumbered women by almost 2:1. Yet, frontier men were not only marrying young, they were also more likely to find marriage partners than men in other districts.

This rather paradoxical situation provides a key to understanding the mechanism of frontier and colonial expansion. Men at the Cape went to the frontier because it was the frontier that offered them the prospect of a livelihood. Like the immigrants of the earlier period, they were using their mobility to go to where opportunities existed. However, unlike earlier immigrants, they had an additional sources of wives next door, in the older settled areas, which was considerably closer than Europe. In taking wives from older areas, the frontier settlers made it more difficult for the single men in them to find marriage partners. In consequence they married later than frontiersmen, or not at all.

Index

Please note: Page numbers which appear in italics are references to tables or illustrations.

DATE DUE

Demco, Inc. 38-293